Left Americana

Left Americana

The Radical Heart
of US History

Paul Le Blanc

Haymarket Books
Chicago, Illinois

Published by
Haymarket Books
P.O. Box 180165
Chicago, IL 60618
773-583-7884
info@haymarketbooks.org
www.haymarketbooks.org

ISBN: 978-1-60846-682-5

Trade distribution:
In the US, Consortium Book Sales and Distribution, www.cbsd.com
In Canada, Publishers Group Canada, www.pgcbooks.ca
In the UK, Turnaround Publisher Services, www.turnaround-uk.com
All other countries, Publishers Group Worldwide, www.pgw.com

This book was published with the generous support of the Wallace Action
Fund and Lannan Foundation.

Printed in Canada by union labor.

Cover and text design by Eric Kerl.

Library of Congress CIP Data is available.

10 9 8 7 6 5 4 3 2 1

To those spirited ones of past generations from whom I learned so much,
and to those of future generations in whom "spirit" may survive
and flourish to bring wondrous things

Letter of Sympathy

Hilda Worthington Smith

One by one they go,
Slipping away while you're not looking,
The older generation.
And now we are the next to grow old—
My generation,
The next to go

One by one.
Where are the dead?
In some green land of hope?
Pacing in quiet meditation
By some celestial river?
Or nowhere—nowhere at all,
Their bodies thrown into earth and flame?
Can this Spirit survive?

Contents

Preface

Engaging with History

This collection of essays, developed over roughly three decades, focuses on aspects of the history of the United States. This history has shaped me, but in some respects the inverse is true: because some of this history has unfolded in my lifetime, I have been able to make my own modest contribution in helping to shape it.[1]

And, of course, the history continues to flow on as I write these words, and as you read them. The very interplay of the writing and the reading—and of our shared thought processes—are an element of the history of our times.

This way of thinking—that we "common people" are part of history, that we all help to make history—is essential to the very meaning of "the Left," which is the topic of the book whose initial paragraphs you have chosen to read. And if you, like me, find yourself in the United States of America, then you are one of a fairly significant number who have engaged in some way (simply by reading this far) with this kind of thinking. Which means that you have become part of the subject matter referred to in this book's title—*Left Americana*.

But we owe it to ourselves, perhaps, to consider a little more seriously the book's title and the subject matter with which the book deals.

What Is the Meaning of This Book's Title?

The term "Americana" is simple enough, so let's get that out of the way first.

My good friend Wikipedia has said: "Americana refers to artifacts, or a collection of artifacts, related to the history, geography, folklore and cultural heritage of the United States." *Merriam-Webster's Collegiate Dictionary* defines "Americana" as "materials concerning or characteristic of America, its civilization, or its culture; *broadly*: things typical of America." Here the word "America" is synonymous with "United States of America." Objections could be made to such an expansive synonym (what about Canada? what about Mexico? what about the rest of the Americas?), but for now, we'll just go with the very common connotation of the term "Americana."

That immediately raises the question—when we refer to "Left" Americana—whether *anything* left-wing is really "characteristic or typical" of the United States. Some of today's spokespeople for US conservatism will indignantly deny that this is possible: to be left-wing is to be quintessentially *un-American*. My belief, documented by various essays in this volume, is that the Left is as American as apple pie. Actually, the author of the original Pledge of Allegiance to the US flag and the man historically credited with inventing the quintessential American game of baseball were left-wing. Christian socialist and Baptist minister Francis Bellamy (younger brother of socialist novelist Edward Bellamy) composed the original Pledge in the 1890s. Civil War hero Abner Doubleday (who it turns out didn't actually invent the game, but apparently did have his Union Army troops play it between battles) was an early member of a network of clubs inspired by the older Bellamy's *Looking Backward*.[2] In fact, American left-wingers played a defining role both in shaping the international Left and in making *this* country what it is today— and what it can become tomorrow. At the heart of the Left are principles of "government of the people, by the people, and for the people," the provision of "liberty and justice for all"—animated by the essential belief that one should "do unto others as you would have them do unto you"—and a society of the free and the equal. I would certainly not claim that all such things have actually been achieved in the United States—but I do believe that there have been many brave and admirable people, and many inspiring struggles, dedicated to making such things a reality.

Helping further to illustrate this point is the publication and popular reception of a best-selling book in 1990, *The American Reader*, edited by President George H. W. Bush's undersecretary of education, Diane Ravitch. The book was neoconservative in tone and perspective, though not entirely so. In Ravitch's description, the book consists of "the classic speeches, poems, arguments, and songs that illuminate . . . significant aspects of American life," and she introduces its penultimate selection, the speech of a conservative president, with the glowing comment: "[Ronald] Reagan described the spread of the global democratic revolution and the power of the idea of freedom." One left-wing critic castigated the volume as presenting "a celebration of the United States, and not an exploration or explanation."[3] The fact remains that a significant number of explicitly left-wing writings and poems and songs are an integral part of that very anthology.

There are plenty of other works that insist more explicitly, and with more documentation and detail, upon the same point—such as Richard Rorty's *Achieving Our Country: Leftist Thought in Twentieth-Century America*, John Nichols's *The "S" Word: A Short History of an American Tradition . . . Socialism*, and Michael Kazin's *American Dreamers: How the Left Changed a Nation*. One need not agree with all that these authors have to say (I certainly don't) in order to acknowledge that—well, yes, they *do* make a strong case for what was implied by Ravitch: a vibrant left-wing tradition is vital in the history of the United States.[4]

A Political Science Detour

As I was preparing this introduction, I could not help but notice that the Internet contains a veritable ocean of infusions from a variety of right-wing libertarian and conservative sources that are dedicated to demonstrating RIGHT-WING IS GOOD, LEFT-WING IS BAD.[5] According to these sources, socialism is defined as "state control of the economy and of our lives"—which is something that I, as a socialist, am absolutely opposed to. Leftists are defined as "those who want to use the government to change human nature"—which, as a leftist, I would fight against to the death, if necessary.

Consistent with these false definitions, there are a number of efforts to construct a left–right political spectrum that are extremely cumbersome and convoluted. This is so, it seems to me, because they are designed to "prove" the Political Correctness of conservatism and capitalism and to make left-wing ideas simply unthinkable for any sane person. Simply the way Left and Right are defined by these twisted pretzels posing as spectrums means that you must ultimately choose to be a "conservative" or a pro-capitalist libertarian— or else show yourself to be demented. The scientific value of these spectrums is largely demonstrated when adherents, applying the spectrums' logic, fail to distinguish between such very different historical and political figures as Karl Marx, Joseph Stalin, Adolf Hitler, and Barack Obama—whose faces, since 2008, I have seen lumped together on a variety of online far-right posters.

None of this is good thinking—it is not even serious conservatism.[6]

In this "political science detour," I want to give more of a sense of what I mean by the term "Left," by defining it—along with other political terms that will be referred to in this book—through the construction of what I think is a more serious political spectrum, one that is consistent with historical realities, and one that people occupying various positions on that political spectrum can acknowledge to be sensible. It is necessary to construct a spectrum that is *objective*, that precludes any value judgment that one position is by definition necessarily superior to another.

I want to start with the historical explanation of the Left and the Right put forward in Crane Brinton's 1950 classic, *Ideas and Men: The Story of Western*

Thought. Brinton (1898–1968) was not a leftist. "His most famous work, *The Anatomy of Revolution* (1938)," Wikipedia accurately notes, "likened the dynamics of revolutionary movements to the progress of fever." The prestigious McLean Professor of Ancient and Modern History at Harvard University, Brinton could count among his most noted protégés Samuel Huntington, an influential American political scientist whose work pushed in decidedly conservative directions.[7] Brinton explained the origins of the terms "Left" and "Right" by referring to developments in the French National Assembly during the early days of the French Revolution, "when the conservatives or monarchists took to sitting in a group to the right of the presiding officer, and the constitutionalists and radical reformers grouped themselves on the left." He elaborated:

> There is a certain symbolic fitness in this, since on the whole the Left wishes to push on to as full a realization as possible of the "principles of 1776 and 1789," the democratic aims of the American and French revolutions, and on the whole the Right wishes a much less democratic society. *Of course, the linear differences suggested by these terms are inadequate to measure the complexities of opinion even in politics.* [Emphasis added.][8]

Democracy (government by the people, rule by the people, power to the people) provides a useful starting point because it is the defining principle for what puts one farther to the left or right on the political spectrum. The farther to the left you are, the more you are in favor of "rule by the people."

If you favor *political* rule by the people, in relation to the government, but stop there, you are a democratic liberal. Favoring an extension of rule by the people over the economy makes you a socialist, positioning you farther to the left. A moderate socialist, or social democrat, willing to compromise on how far to go and at what pace regarding the advance of economic democracy, is not as far to the left as a revolutionary socialist or communist, who is less willing to compromise on when and how rule by the people will be extended (although there is a serious complication here, to be addressed in a moment). Someone who wants the people to rule over themselves directly—without the intervention of any government at all, without voting for *anyone* to rule over them—is farthest to the left, making them an anarchist. Those who are conservatives, inclined to prioritize the conserving of traditional power relations and not inclined to jeopardize those relations by granting increased rule by the people, are naturally farther to the right than liberal democrats. Those who are most opposed to democracy—militantly and on principle—occupy positions at the farthest right end of the political spectrum, and have generally been either absolute monarchists (favoring rule by kings and queens) or fascists of some variety (including Nazis) who favor a permanent dictatorship by super-nationalist (often racist) and militaristic elites. This can be represented visually with the following diagram:

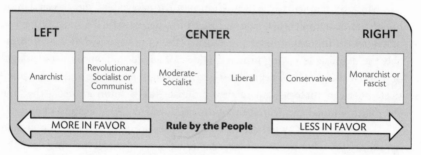

The crucial warning that Brinton offers in the final sentence that I emphasized in the passage above, alerting us that actualities of real-life politics are more complex than this construction indicates, is a fact we need to comprehend and wrestle with. First of all, it is not a foregone conclusion that democracy is possible or desirable in any and all circumstances. Neither is it a foregone conclusion that anarchy will work in modern society (even though it has worked in primitive societies), that socialism is actually possible, or that "rule by the people" is superior to "rule by those who are fit to rule." It is well known that many of the most prominent of the Founding Fathers of the United States, at least partly on the basis of such concerns, emphasized that they sought a republic (rule by elected representatives) but *not* a democracy (which they feared would become a "mob-ocracy"); a typical conservative warning was that democracy would inevitably become corrupt and chaotic, and would in fact pave the way for a tyrannical dictatorship. All of this suggests that the spectrum, in and of itself, does not demonstrate any Political Correctness, however one wishes to define that.

Additional complicating factors abound. There are different varieties of each of these political categories, and there are often different viewpoints on specific issues. Moreover, some of the categories have evolved over time—among early nineteenth-century liberals (and also conservatives), for example, many did not favor allowing a majority of adults the right to vote, and most liberals of the time favored laissez-faire economic policies that opposed social legislation to help workers and the poor and that prevented any regulation of capitalist enterprise, while the positions on those issues were completely reversed by the early twentieth century.

Also, the traditional power relations that most European conservatives wanted to maintain involved monarchies and hereditary aristocracies, while in the United States these power relations had never existed—instead, the most powerful elements had been wealthy and powerful businessmen (first plantation owners and merchants, later bankers and industrialists).

Most dramatically, the way Communism evolved in the Soviet Union under the quarter-century rule of Joseph Stalin—one of the most repressive dictatorships in human history—reflected the opposite of what was presumably the defining left-wing principle (also embedded in Communist ideology) of "rule by the people." Divergences between stated principles and actual practices, between rhetoric and reality, indicate—as Brinton argued—that the left–right political spectrum cannot, by itself, tell us all we need to know.

There is, finally, what seems to me a pseudo-complication that should be addressed. This involves a pro-capitalist way of understanding "rule by the people," advanced by some conservatives who consider themselves free market libertarians. They argue that "we the people" actually do own and control the economy through a system of private ownership combined with a buying-and-selling (or market) economy. Each and every one of us—according to this narrative—has an opportunity (if we work hard enough) to start our own business and to compete freely with other businesses for the patronage of consumers of whatever goods or services we offer. Of course, because each and every one of us is also a consumer, we all "vote with our dollars" for whichever business we want to patronize and for whatever goods and services we would like to consume.

But it is difficult to take this pleasant and democratic-sounding interpretation of capitalism seriously. Many people work *very* hard but do not have the opportunities implied by this happy-face story, and if most people have only thousands of economic "votes" (dollars) per year in the marketplace while a few actually have billions of "votes," it seems ludicrous to present this as a healthy democracy. At least 40 percent of the wealth in the United States is controlled by 1 percent of the nation's families, and an additional 40 percent of the wealth, give or take, is controlled by the next 19 percent of families, leaving the remaining 20 percent or less of the wealth in the possession of 80 percent of US families. This concentration of economic power in a few hands, utilized in good capitalist fashion to maximize private profits (not to enhance freedom or democracy), adds up to an economic dictatorship that—since "money talks"—undermines and distorts and blocks genuine political democracy.[9]

The fact remains that, if utilized critically, the categories of Left and Right can be a useful starting point in making sense of modern history and politics. The same point was emphasized at the close of the twentieth century

by Italian political philosopher Norberto Bobbio (1909–2004) in his internationally acclaimed *Left and Right: The Significance of a Political Distinction*. It
is interesting, however, that rather than making the principle of democracy
a defining criterion, as Brinton does, Bobbio (identifying himself as a lib-
eral-socialist) argues that "the criterion most frequently used to distinguish
between the left and the right is the attitude of real people in society to the
ideal of equality."[10]

"Equality" as a defining principle can be harmonized with that of "democracy," and Bobbio himself goes in this direction: "In relation to the number
of persons, universal male and female suffrage is more egalitarian than only
universal manhood suffrage. Universal manhood suffrage is more egalitarian
than suffrage limited to literate males or by a property qualification." Bobbio
again employs the equality principle (though, as I have suggested, here the
intimately related democracy principle works as well) in his claim that socialism "gives all its citizens social rights as well as libertarian rights, [and there-
fore] is more egalitarian than liberal democracy." He adds: "In relation to the
criterion, the maxim 'To each according to his needs' is, as I have already said,
more egalitarian than 'To each according to his rank,' which characterizes the
hierarchical state to which the liberal state is opposed."[11]

Bobbio also emphasizes that his political spectrum "completely precludes
any value-judgment on the relative merits of equality and inequality."[12] One
can question or challenge the validity or value of any or all forms of equality—a matter not determined by the spectrum—which means that those
favoring greater equality or those favoring less equality, that is, those farther
to the left or to the right, are not automatically defined as "the good guys."

Prejudices and Interests

All of us tend to prejudge certain things, and the reader should be clear on
at least some of my own prejudices. I believe in democracy—genuine democracy: "rule by the people"—as something that is possible and desirable and
necessary, both politically *and economically*, which means I am a socialist. I
believe in equality as well—not in the sense that we are all the same (that is
ridiculous), but in the sense that each person should have an equal right to
life, liberty, and the pursuit of happiness, which means that all should have
decent food and clothing and shelter, along with good health care and access
to a good education, and an equal right to be treated with dignity. And I
believe in freedom—including freedom of expression (speech, press, et cetera), freedom of assembly, freedom of religion, and freedom of thought, and
also the freedom to try to become the kind of person you want to be and to

live your life in the way that you want. I believe we need to have a say in the decisions that affect our lives, and that we must strive for greater knowledge and some degree of intelligent control over those conditions that shape who and what we are. The free development of each should be the condition for the free development of all.

Accordingly, I believe in the right of each person to develop their own creative energies and activities and modes of expression, whether through art and literature and music and theater, or through sports and recreational endeavors and gardening and crafts. I believe that we must also have a sense of community—our relations with each other, our sharing of resources, our mutual assistance, our responsibility for ourselves and each other—and that this "sense" should help to shape the communities of which we are a part and also be a genuine reflection of them. This must be *alive* in the sense of being open, dynamic, and necessarily unfinished and *imperfect*. There are not and cannot be perfect people or groups or communities or societies; attempts to make everything and everyone "perfect" would represent a form of tyranny and inhumanity that must always be resisted.

I identify all of this as essential to being on the left, to being (in my case) a socialist. I am interested in doing what I can to make this a living reality in the life that I lead, the activities and movements and struggles I help to build, and, as much as possible, in the future that I try to bring about.

I am also interested in learning about past experiences of those in the United States who have tried to help move things in these directions. I want to learn about (and from) what they did right and what they did wrong. I want to better understand what has been the interplay of the multifaceted Left with the multifaceted larger realities of which it has been an integral part. And I want to share my understanding of what I have been able to learn with others who may be interested in such things, and who perhaps can make their own contributions to understanding and changing the world. That is the point of the essays in this book.

The Meaning and Shape of US History

In order to explore such things adequately, one must have some sense of the meaning and shape of the overall history of the United States. My particular sense of that history starts with the understanding that it has evolved within a larger global history. Around the world, the activities and relationships people entered into, and the resources they used to get the things that they needed (food, clothing, shelter) and that they wanted—that is, their economic life—shaped the various broad phases of human history within which social and cultural and political life unfolded. Humanity, for most of existence on our planet, existed through hunting and gathering, much later supplemented and finally supplanted by early agriculture. This was necessarily a cooperative and communal form of economy, in which tribes or clans or kin groups shared in the labor and the fruits of their labor required for their survival.

Over the past five thousand years, however, there has been the proliferation of civilizations across the face of the earth, in which powerful minorities have been able—in one way or another, assuming one form of another—to dominate laboring majorities, thereby becoming rich and powerful, as suggested, for example, in Chris Harman's popularization *A People's History of the World* and Eric Wolf's more complex theorization in *Europe and the People without History*. The most dynamic form of economy in human existence has been capitalism, which increasingly came to dominate the economic life of the world, as indicated, for example, in another popularization, Leo Huberman's *Man's Worldly Goods*. This capitalism (in which the economy is privately owned and controlled by a relative few, utilized to maximize profits for the owners, and involving generalized commodity production that draws more and more aspects of human life into a buying-and-selling economy) first blossomed in Europe, then dramatically expanded.[13]

The dynamics of capitalism would finally cause the embryonic development of the United States, by bringing together what Gary Nash calls the "red, white, and black" peoples of early North America. He recounts Native American peoples finding their North American continent being invaded by Europeans, who also invaded Africa and brought to the "New World" enslaved Africans. The colonial embryo developed so dramatically that a new nation was born through the American Revolution, which then unleashed a remarkable process that historian Louis Hacker documents in *The Triumph of American Capitalism*. As it expanded across the continent, the voracious, destructive yet creative and incredibly wealth-producing system increasingly brought together, through conquest, enslavement, and multiple waves of immigration, a variety of peoples which Ronald Takaki describes in rich and eloquent detail in *A Different Mirror: A Multi-Cultural History of the United States*.[14]

Central to the cultural multiplicity of the early American way of life were the perceptions, ideas, and values that took root among the peoples of the United States, the belief systems (various religious and secular ideologies) they utilized to make sense of their reality. What did people think and feel and say? If we can engage with those who went before, we may learn something from their perceptions and insights on the meaning of life, the nature of society and humanity, the possibilities of freedom and human rights, as well as the things they took seriously, the things they thought were funny. Some of what inspired them may inspire us as well. In various ways, the surface has at least been scratched by a variety of compelling works—an amazing feast for the mind, from V. L. Parrington's *Main Currents in American Thought*, Merle Curti's *The Growth of American Thought*, F. O. Matthiessen's *American Renaissance*, Richard Hofstadter's *The American Political Tradition*, Daniel Aaron's *Men of Good Hope*, and C. L. R. James's unfinished classic *American Civilization* down to Pauline Maier's *American Scripture*, Eric Foner's *The Story of American Freedom*, Christopher Lasch's *The Agony of the American Left*, Alan Wald's *The New York Intellectuals*, Michael Denning's *The Cultural Front*, and the essays gathered in *Popular Culture in America*, edited by Paul Buhle.[15]

And there are such anthologies of rich source material as Bernard Smith's *The Democratic Spirit*, Howard Zinn's and Anthony Arnove's *Voices of a People's History of the United States*, Diane Ravitch's already-cited *The American Reader*, and my own *Work and Struggle: Voices from U.S. Labor Radicalism*. This is on top of such collections of documents as the three volumes entitled *Great Issues in American History*, edited by Richard Hofstadter (with Clarence L. Ver Steeg and Beatrice K. Hofstadter), and Herbert Aptheker's seven-volume *A Documentary History of the Negro People of the United States*. Not to mention the unpublished materials in innumerable archives.[16]

Putting all of this together as a coherent and comprehensible whole, something that can be grasped by normal human beings, is an immense challenge, as those who have simply taught undergraduate history courses, even for many years (as I have done) will undoubtedly affirm. A roughly coherent shape of US history could be crafted along such lines as these, to help us organize our perceptions of all that happened:

> Colonial Era (1600s to 1775) → American Revolution (1775–83) → Early Republic (1783–1820) → Antebellum (Prewar) Era (1820–61) → the Civil War (1861–65) → Reconstruction Era (1865–77) and Gilded Age (1870s–1900) → Progressive Era, including and ended by World War I (1900–1920) → the Twenties (1920–29) → the Great Depression (1929–39) → World War II (1939–45) → Cold War Era (1946–90), containing various sub-eras—the Fifties, the Sixties, et cetera → Age of Globalization (1991–?).

Different historians come up with a variety of constructs similar to this, but sometimes with different labels. They may also offer different start times and cutoff points for the various periods they are identifying. They seek to craft a coherent story out of the immense and sometimes bewildering mass of detail that makes up all that happened in the United States.

History can be defined as both a "chaos" and a "discipline." History is *everything that happened* in the past, but it is also *the study of what happened* in the past. It is impossible to study *everything* that happened, because we don't know everything that happened—for so much in the past, there are no historical records. Even if we restrict ourselves to studying what is in the available records, there is too much material to absorb and explain coherently. So historians—with all their biases and prejudgments (prejudices)—narrow things down, deciding what are the important questions to ask, what are the things that need to be explained. And they often approach those questions with some notion of what the answers are or what they should be.[17]

The way particular studies of history are structured, and the way the stories are told, are influenced by the different philosophies, divergent political viewpoints, counterposed values, and dissimilar life experiences (often shaped by different social locations—class, race, gender) of various historians. Nonetheless, even if one disagrees with the way a particular historian interprets past events, it is possible to learn from the information presented, and the insights articulated, by that historian.

Much of my passion for history relates to the belief that it provides a way of understanding ourselves, that it contains the stories of our many families, the stories of people like ourselves (and also people different from ourselves), blending and clashing and flowing onward ultimately to create *us* and our world. And our own experiences, drives, and stories—shaped by what went before—are the stuff of present history and future history.

History from the Top Down and the Bottom Up

This brings to the fore a tangle of controversies that are sometimes associated with the phrases "history from the top down" and "from the bottom up." Three of the outstanding representatives of the "bottom up" viewpoint are Jesse Lemisch, who seems to have coined the term, Staughton Lynd, and Howard Zinn. Lemisch should be considered a primary authority, and his own comments on the position in a 1967 essay deserve attention:

> The American Revolution can best be re-examined from a point of view which assumes that all men [and women] are created equal, and rational, and since they can think and reason they do make their own history. These assumptions are nothing more or less than the democratic credo. All of our history needs re-examination from this perspective. The history of the powerless, the inarticulate, the poor has not yet begun to be written

because they have been treated no more fairly by historians than they have been treated by their contemporaries.[18]

Marcus Rediker, an internationally renowned practitioner of such "history from below," has elaborated that this amounts to "the class perspective 'from the bottom up,' the insistence on the history-making power of those long excluded from the history books, [and] the explicit link between past and present."[19]

It is worth considering the opposite perspective—history from the top down. One such practitioner was historian Francis Parkman, whose eloquently written histories of early colonial America included *The Conspiracy of Pontiac and the Indian War after the Conquest of Canada* and the eight-volume set *France and England in North America*, culminating in a classic work on the French and Indian War, *Montcalm and Wolfe*. Stephen Tonsor argues, quite persuasively, "that Parkman's history of the French and English in North America and Parkman's personality were totally informed by his conservatism; that there was system in Parkman's thought and writing, that indeed Parkman was the very model of the conservative as historian and that had there been no conservatism there would have been no history."[20] Indeed Parkman, the quintessential "Boston Brahmin" from a very wealthy Massachusetts family, had a clearly identifiable attitude toward the "rule by the people" principle, distinguishing left from right. He explained his views in an 1878 essay:

> The present danger . . . is organized ignorance, led by unscrupulous craft, and marching, amid the applause of fools, under the flag of equal rights. . . . The transfer of sovereignty to the people, the whole people, is proclaimed the panacea of political and social ills, and we are rarely reminded that popular sovereignty has evils of its own. . . . Crowded cities, where the irresponsible and ignorant were numerically equal, or more than equal, to the rest, and where the weakest and most worthless was a match, by his vote, for the wisest and the best; bloated wealth and envious poverty; a tinseled civilization above, and a discontented proletariat beneath.[21]

As more than one latter-day historian has noted, Parkman was explicit and consistent in his deep-held beliefs in human inequality rooted in race, nationality, class, and gender—all of which certainly informed the way he told his stories. In a devastating critique, Francis Jennings has been able to document that Parkman made his conservative interpretations more coherent and persuasive by distorting his sources and sometimes even making up "facts."[22]

Theodore Roosevelt, coming from the same upper-class background, was powerfully influenced by Parkman's writings and perspectives, and when his own four-volume history, *The Winning of the West*, was published, he dedicated it to the recently deceased historian. Focusing on the role of US (read: white) "civilization" in forcefully and violently taking the land from the original inhabitants, Roosevelt explained to his readers: "It was wholly impossible to avoid conflicts with the weaker race, unless we were willing to see the American continent fall into the hands of some other strong power, and even had we adopted such a ludicrous policy, the Indians themselves would have made war upon us. It cannot be too often insisted that they did not own the land." Of course, Roosevelt was engaged in electoral politics in a later period than Parkman lived in, and he concluded that his own conservative upper-class sensibilities would be better served by pragmatically adapting to the temper of the times, which caused him to wear—with a characteristic flourish—the "Progressive" mantle in order to conserve, intelligently and effectively, traditional power relations. Yet the perspectives reflected in the way he interpreted history were no less racist and elitist than those of Parkman.[23]

The well-researched and eloquent corrections of the Parkman and Roosevelt view of history, in such works as Alvin Josephy's *The Patriot Chiefs* and Dee Brown's *Bury My Heart at Wounded Knee*, could be said to represent a history "from the bottom up"—except much of their focus is on famous Native American leaders (on individuals in powerful positions) such as Hiawatha, Pontiac, Tecumseh, Osceola, Crazy Horse, Chief Joseph, Sitting Bull, and Geronimo. In contrast to this, the work of Francis Jennings and Roxanne Dunbar-Ortiz—not focusing in leaders—casts the net wider into the realm of social history.[24]

The fact remains that "top-down" qualities in the accounts of Josephy and Dee hardly undermine their value, just as the genuine value of such works as Richard Hofstadter's *The American Political Tradition* and William Appleman Williams's *The Tragedy of American Diplomacy* is in no way negated because they focus on powerful political and economic figures and policymakers.[25]

The top-down version of US history had been given this kind of critical and left-wing twist much earlier, for example, in the 1911 account *Social Forces in American History*, written by A. M. Simons. One of the many intellectuals drawn to the Socialist Party of America (in the days when its central spokesman was Eugene V. Debs), Simons presented history as a succession of powerful upper classes making things happen at the expense of oppressed lower classes, with a projected socialist happy ending. Debunking the celebratory idealizations presented by mainstream historians, he emphasized "the commercial and plantation interests that brought about separation from Great Britain and formulated the Constitution, . . . the chattel slave owners that controlled the government and molded it for two generations, . . . the capitalist class that rode into power amid the blood and fraud and terror of civil war and Reconstruction." But now, he proclaimed, "the working class has become in its turn the embodiment of the spirit of social progress, and is fighting for victory with a certainty of success before it," destined to culminate in an industrial economy under the "common ownership by a democratically controlled government of the workers." This economic interpretation of US history not only influenced those inclined toward socialism, but even one of the central figures of US historiography, Charles A. Beard.[26]

Leo Huberman's *We the People*, published in 1932, took a qualitatively different approach, emphasizing the essential history-making role played by the great unwashed masses that had so horrified Parkman. "From its very beginnings, America has been a magnet to the peoples of the earth," he wrote, going on to emphasize the incredible racial, religious, and national diversity, and then adding to his list of diverse groups "farmers, miners, adventurers, soldiers, sailors, rich men, poor men, beggermen, thieves, shoemakers, tailors, actors, musicians, ministers, engineers, writers, singers, ditchdiggers, manufacturers, butchers, bakers, and candlestick makers." He went on to elaborate:

> It is a stirring account of the building of a nation through the efforts of men, women, and children of stout heart in the face of great odds. It is the story of tremendous economic expansion under the dominance of the corporate form of business enterprise. It is the saga of Big Business in America, its most congenial home. It is a tale of the growing power of monopoly. Not that this power went unchallenged. Opposition came from the farmers and from the industrial workers. The story of that opposition is included. So, too, is an account of the foreign adventurers of American Big Business, by which at the end of the nineteenth century it became a world force.

In the revised edition, he added chapters taking the story through the Great Depression, and through the Second World War, down to the immediate postwar period, concluding (in a muted and more conditional version of Simons's crescendo): "'America was promises.' But the promises have been fulfilled, in recent years, only for the men at the top. It is of crucial importance at this time that fulfillment of the promises should come for all of us."[27]

A careful examination of the "bottom up" historians reveals, in fact, that they are quite inclined to factor the "top down" aspects of our history (exploring the impact of powerful leaders and upper classes) into their understanding of what is going on from the bottom up. Staughton Lynd is quite explicit about his utter dissatisfaction with any so-called "bottom up" history

that "will give us the franchise for chimneysweeps who get cancer and seam-
stresses who burn to death when the foreman locks the door, so long as we
do not challenge the belief that American history is an exceptional story that
other nations should do their best to imitate." Rather, Lynd insists that celebrations of the status quo must be sharply challenged. While insisting that a
central aspect of "history from below" involves the notion that "participants
in making history should be regarded not only as sources of facts but as colleagues in interpreting what happened," he also insists that "we must be wary
of the notion that anything participants believe about their history is necessarily true"—the historian must use her or his own critical mind to come to an
interpretation about what *is* necessarily true, and how that can have use-value
for our own time.[28]

Zinn makes the same point as he argues "against 'history as private
enterprise' and for the idea that it is the social responsibility of the historian
to do work that will be useful in solving the critical human problems of our
time." He elaborates:

> History can untie our minds, our bodies, our disposition to move—to
> engage life rather than contemplating it as an outsider. It can do this by
> widening our view to include the silent voices of the past, so that we
> look behind the silence of the present. It can illustrate the foolishness of
> depending on others to solve the problems of the world—whether the
> state, the church, or other self-proclaimed benefactors. It can reveal how
> ideas are stuffed into us by the powers of our time, and so lead us to stretch
> our minds beyond what is given. It can inspire us by recalling those few
> moments in the past when men did behave like human beings, to prove
> that it is *possible*. And it can sharpen our critical faculties so that even while
> we act, we think about the dangers created by our own desperation.[29]

Wrestling with What Happened

This kind of activist-oriented history, undergirding the "history from below"
perspective, is by no means of recent vintage. Howard Zinn's outstanding and
influential contribution, *A People's History of the United States*, while reflecting
an immense flood of relatively new studies in US history (as well as standard
old works), offers interpretive elements reminiscent of what we have noted
in both A. M. Simons and Leo Huberman.[30] The "we the people" spirit in
Huberman is gloriously evident throughout; the "debunking" spirit in Simons
is very much there too, and it crops up especially in Zinn's accounts of times
of war—including the wars associated with the First American Revolution

(1775–83) and what some historians call the Second American Revolution (1861–65). In each case, Zinn demonstrates how rhetoric and ideals associated with freedom and democracy and human rights are thrown around freely to mobilize popular support for whatever war effort is on the table. The real reasons for whichever war was being fought, however, were to defend and expand the wealth and power of the upper classes; for Zinn, it was invariably "a rich man's war and a poor man's fight." And it is questionable whether the horrific killing and inhumanity of war can ever be justified. Basically, regardless of what the idealistic slogans are or how many lives are sacrificed, the fundamental reality remains: the lower classes (the great majority of us) remain oppressed and exploited by the upper classes.

There have been a number of efforts—from liberals (even left-liberals) as well as conservatives—to debunk the debunker, constituting a veritable Anti-Zinn Industry. While the accuracy of one or another presumed fact can be challenged, and the adequacy of one or another interpretation can be questioned—something that is true of any major work of history, especially one with the broad sweep and contemporary implications of *A People's History of the United States*—it seems to me that Zinn's history holds up fairly well. The basic structures of power that he refers to *have* existed (and continue to exist), with all of the kinds of inequality, oppression, exploitation, and forms of inhumanity associated with them. The basic social groups that make up the majority, that have so often been impacted by these power structures, and that have struggled to survive and, in some cases, have struggled for a better society—it cannot be honestly argued that such things are "made up." What Zinn has offered, if we are to be serious about our history, is an invaluable synthesis, contributing significantly to our understanding of the history of the United States.

Zinn's account is not, of course, the last word. The study of history is a collective and ongoing project. It appears that sometimes there is greater (and more interesting) complexity than Zinn seems to allow for in *A People's History of the United States*. My own inclination—imagining myself back into previous eras—is to support the democratic elements (represented by people such as Tom Paine) in the American Revolution, and also the democratic and antislavery currents (represented by such people as Frederick Douglass) in the Northern effort during the Civil War.

I am inclined to agree with Gordon Wood when he insists: "[T]he American Revolution . . . was as radical and revolutionary as any in history . . . In fact, it was one of the greatest revolutions the world had known, a momentous upheaval that not only fundamentally altered the character of American society but decisively affected the course of world history." In explaining what the "all men are created equal" phrase in the Declaration of Independence represented to those mobilizing for revolution, Wood notes:

> Equality became so important for Americans because it came to mean that everyone was really the same as everyone else, not just at birth, not in talent or property or wealth, and not just in some transcendental religious sense of an equality of all souls. Ordinary Americans came to believe that no one in a basic down-to-earth and day-in-and-day-out manner was really better than anyone else. That was equality as no other nation has ever quite had it.[31]

As Wood implies, the rhetorical force of the document pushed powerfully in the direction of asserting (independently of the Declaration signers' own particular notions) *human equality*—meaning "equal rights for all people," regardless of class, gender, race, or nationality. This has been the meaning embraced by variously oppressed multitudes. It is not erased by the fact that—as with all revolutions—the radical hopes of many "ordinary" people, in the midst of the enthusiasm of insurgency, were not fully realized in the revolutionary aftermath, and that (as Terry Boulton has put it) "the revolutionary elite had remade government to benefit themselves and to undermine the independence of ordinary folk." At the same time, Alfred Young has shown that in the wake of the Revolution there was a resurgence of "the popular movements of the revolutionary era of the cities and countryside," which forced the more conservative elite to "grant democratic concessions" to those "below"—with the "would-be rulers forced to make accommodations" of all kinds, certainly with the "middling sort" of "yeoman farmers and artisans," but also with the crowds of poorer laborers, sometimes even with "enslaved African Americans ... and with 'outsiders' to the system: women and Native Americans."[32] Such struggles to realize the promise of the Revolution have persisted for over two centuries, but the impetus provided by 1776 cannot be shrugged off.

I similarly find James McPherson persuasive when (referring to Isaiah Berlin's contrast between a relatively conservative "negative liberty" and a more radical "positive liberty") he asserts that during the Civil War "Abraham Lincoln played a crucial role in this historic shift in emphasis from negative to positive liberty," explaining:

> Positive liberty is an open-ended concept. It has the capacity to expand toward notions of equity, justice, social welfare, equality of opportunity ... With the "new birth of freedom" proclaimed in the Gettysburg Address and backed by a powerful army, Lincoln helped to move the

nation toward an expanded and open-ended concept of positive liberty.
"On the side of the Union," he said on another occasion, this war "is a
struggle for maintaining in the world, that form, and substance of government, whose leading object is, to elevate the condition of men—to
lift artificial weights from all shoulders—to clear the paths of laudable
pursuit for all"—black as well as white—"to afford all, an unfettered start,
and a fair chance, in the race of life." In "giving freedom to the slave,"
declared Lincoln, "we *assure* freedom to the *free*."[33]

Yet there is enough truth in Zinn's strictures to compel one to pause and
consider. One issue quite simply involves the question of whether, when, or
to what extent the killing of other people is justified, and whether war is a
reasonable means for bringing about anything positive.

Cutting even deeper into historiography, questions have been raised, for
example, about the American Revolution. Even a seemingly "mainstream"
historian such as Edmund Morgan was moved to shift from a fairly celebratory conceptualization (in *The Birth of the Republic, 1763–1789*) to a darker
conceptualization in his classic *American Slavery, American Freedom*. The Jef-
fersonian notion of freedom at the heart of the Declaration of Independence,
he argued, was inseparable from the centrality of slavery in the economy, and
in the social-political culture, by which Jefferson himself was shaped. This
has recently been extended to an argument, in Gerald Horne's *The Count-
er-Revolution of 1776: Slave Resistance and the Origins of the United States*, that
the American Revolution flowed from a commitment by Southern plantation
owners, with the complicity of Northern business interests that had a stake
in the plantation economy, to prevent developments emanating from Britain
that would undermine the slave trade and the slave system.[34]

On the other hand, we find such historians as C. L. R. James seeing
African Americans, and the freedom struggle of African Americans, as central to the wave of democratic revolutions from which the American Revolution was inseparable, with Benjamin Quarles adding important detail
regarding the active role of African Americans in the revolutionary struggle
which claimed "all men are created equal, and endowed by their Creator with
certain unalienable rights, and among these are Life, Liberty, and the Pursuit
of Happiness." This by no means allows for a dismissal of the points made by
Morgan and Horne—but it does indicate that there are contradictory realities
and levels of complexity, which are certainly suggested in a number of works
honoring the notion of "history from the bottom up" but which, nonetheless,
are inclined to see the American Revolution in a positive light.[35]

Those whose appetites are whetted by Zinn's *People's History of the United*

States should not stop there. There is more work to consider and factor in, more to wrestle with. The inclination to integrate the kinds of insights advanced by Wood, Young, McPherson, and James has become increasingly prevalent. Similarly, blended analyses of what has happened both from the top down and the bottom up, with consequent complexity and contradictions, can be found in such syntheses as Eric Foner's substantial *Give Me Liberty! An American History*, and—more succinctly—Paul Boyer's *American History: A Very Short Introduction.*[36]

I want to conclude this discussion of "history from the bottom up" by citing one of the earliest and most unusual examples of its practice. In 1933–34, the great Mexican revolutionary muralist Diego Rivera composed a remarkable set of portable frescos for the New Workers School in New York City, associated with a dissident Communist group led by Jay Lovestone and Bertram D. Wolfe. Although Lovestone and Wolfe later spectacularly de-radicalized, Rivera's art remained constant. These dramatic murals presented a Marxist interpretation of US history from the Colonial Era down to the early 1930s. They were reproduced in a book entitled *Portrait of America*, with a text by Wolfe.[37] Using the murals as my basis, I have put together a PowerPoint slideshow that I sometimes present to students in US history courses, in order to provide a visual portrayal of one way of interpreting history, and to generate discussion. Many students see it as one-sided, and some express shock at what to them as an anti-American vision of US history—seeming to show nothing but oppression, exploitation, violence, and ugliness. Some argue that, actually, the things portrayed are true, and that it is good to see "the other side" of the story typically presented in school. There are also some who argue that it is really pro-American—because it depicts many who struggled against the bad things (oppression, inhumanity, exploitation), and for freedom and equality and justice for all, for a better America.

It is especially interesting to consider Wolfe's description of the research and interpretive efforts that went into the creation of Rivera's murals. It gives a vibrant sense of the way history is written regardless of the historian's specific political orientation, but also a sense of what those seeking to produce a history from the bottom up are often reaching for:

> The theme of this mural is the history of this country—a portrait of the America of yesterday and today. It is interesting to record how the painter acquired an intimate insight into the history of a land not his own. Obviously, for the purposes of art, mere knowledge is not enough: it must be felt as well as known, reacted to as well as apprehended, absorbed until it becomes "second nature," before it can become the stuff of painting.

It was the task of the painter's assistants and members of the faculty and student members of the school to make this material accessible and vividly alive to Rivera. We avoided the standard histories in favor of contemporary documents and contemporary iconography; not alone for lack of confidence in professional historians, but more because only thus could the artist acquire a "feel" for the impact of living events upon sentient human beings.

We ransacked libraries, reference rooms, museums, for contemporary prints, wood cuts, oils, and news paper caricatures. We ran through the speeches and writings of each representative personage selected, viewed them through the eyes of their enemies, distilling the latter's hatreds, and through the eyes of their admirers, distilling their loves. And beneath and beyond we sought to dig to the moods of the nameless masses in which these men had inspired love or hatred, the masses who had followed them and in a sense created them as well.

How well this method succeeded at its best—thanks principally to Rivera's amazingly prehensile mind—is testified alike by the general sweep of the history of our land and by the beauty and vividness of such portraits as those of Ben Franklin and Tom Paine, Emerson and Thoreau, Walt Whitman and John Brown. Or by the brutal and savage power of such social caricatures as that of J. P. Morgan the First. Many may disagree with his interpretation of our history, but none can deny its impact or its power, nor regard it as a mere cold exercise in learning facts by rote. Indeed, whatever its shortcomings, there is no example by one of our own painters that comes anywhere near giving so complete and penetrating and moving a portrayal of our people, our history, and our land.[38]

What I Have Done

The foregoing explains the general framework within which the rest of this book was composed. The following indicates what I have done in this book, and it may help readers to decide if they want to meander through its pages, and if so, which path through the selections they want to take.

This introduction establishes an initial conceptual framework for what follows, giving an overview of the history of the United States and some sense of its general shape and dynamics.

The first essay discusses why there is no socialism in the United States, and to some extent why there is, giving considerable attention to those who wrestled with such matters—especially to early Marxist theorist Karl Kautsky.

The second essay looks at the amazing working-class revolutionaries (and martyrs) in Chicago who played a central role in the struggle for the eight-hour workday; who helped to establish the international working-class (and left-wing) holiday known as May Day; who considered themselves, equally, anarchists and socialists and communists; and who did some things that helped get them killed.

The third essay gives attention to a remarkable institution which the left-wing Christian A. J. Muste helped to create and run for about a decade—Brookwood Labor College. This relates to the fourth essay, which discusses different (in some cases fiercely competing) left-wing vanguards within the working class that helped to lead the immense working-class upsurge of the 1930s.

The fifth, sixth, and seventh essays focus on three very interesting heroes of the Left. One of these heroes, someone I knew personally and whom you probably never heard of, Ruth Querio, was part of the working-class upsurges of the 1930s. Another is the remarkable revolutionary intellectual whom many have heard about, C. L. R. James. The third is the best known, the Reverend Martin Luther King Jr. Following this is essay eight, which deals with the 1963 March on Washington for Jobs and Freedom, conceived of and organized by an amazing cadre of left-wing activists.

The ninth essay is a memoir of my own political experiences in the 1950s and 1960s.

Then, as a change of pace, I offer the tenth essay, outlining what those on the political right were doing—in reaction to all these struggles and changes—from the 1940s through the 1980s, when they brilliantly strategized and organized to take control of the United States.

In the eleventh essay I consider the incredibly broad upsurge of the 1960s New Left that I was part of, examining how important elements of that movement evolved in the direction of groups and individuals seeking to develop—in a variety of ways—a US manifestation of what some of them termed "Marxism-Leninism–Mao Tse-tung Thought." Although a New Leftist, I was not part of the Maoist development. Instead, I became part of the largest group in the United States attempting to follow in the footsteps of Leon Trotsky, the Socialist Workers Party, an endeavor that involved some good things but ended very badly, and those outcomes are explored in essays twelve and thirteen.

The fourteenth and final essay touches on one of the more recent manifestations of the Left in this country—the mobilization on behalf of "the 99%" against the rich and powerful "1%" known as the Occupy Wall Street movement, in which I participated from the vantage point of my native Pittsburgh. Here I don't attempt a blow-by-blow history of Occupy Pittsburgh (I hope someone writes that someday), but rather look at Occupy's ancestors and descendants.

Different readers will certainly have different reactions to one essay or another in this book, and not simply due to political tastes. The essays were produced in different contexts—some are more popularly written, some more academic. Rather than reading from beginning to end, some readers may want to pick and choose, depending on the special interest stimulated by the topic of one essay or the complexity in the argument of another.

My hope is that what I have written here will be interesting and useful even for those who fundamentally disagree with me politically. I like to think that some conservatives would want to read this in order to consider more carefully "what the other side thinks"—and I suspect that some of those who currently consider themselves on the right may discover (at some point) that they really belong on the left. But most people don't really tag themselves one way or the other, and I hope that they too (as well as others who *do* self-iden-tify as being on the left) may find something in these pages that will be useful to them as well. And if any of this contributes to a future for this country consistent with my own ideals, that would be best of all.

Pittsburgh
January 2017

1

Socialism in the United States
Absent and Latent

I s socialism possible in the United States? Why has there not been in this country the kind of massive socialist labor movement that arose, for example, throughout Europe? These questions have been debated and discussed for more than a hundred years. The initial impetus for this addition to that discussion was an invitation I received to contribute to a symposium, published in 2003, on Karl Kautsky's substantial review essay "The American Worker," which had just been translated into English. German sociologist Werner Sombart had discussed the matter in his well-known 1903 study *Why Is There No Socialism in the United States?*, and Kautsky's 1906 essay included a discussion of that book. (A secondary point of interest is the fact that this essay of mine also included an evaluation of Kautsky's Marxism close to that which would soon be advanced in Lars Lih's work on Lenin.) While subjecting what I wrote in 2002–2003 to some editing, mostly to condense and clarify, I have not altered its basic content, nor have I sought to update it with new material that has appeared since then.[1]

Marxists and American Realities

Our purpose here is to fit what Kautsky writes into a larger context. Specifically, we will explore the way in which a variety of thinkers and activists operating within the Marxist tradition for well over a century and a half have wrestled with the question posed by Werner Sombart: why is there no socialism in the United States?

Of course, Kautsky and the others sought to do more than that. They also struggled to comprehend the nature of capitalism in the United States, the peculiarities of the US working class, the specific dynamics of US history. And, as appropriate with Marxists, this was always within the context of seeing how socialism might be advanced in the "New World," in Europe, and globally. In a sense, we will be tracing a fluctuating but definite pattern in the

1

evolution of analyses—from *simplicity* to *complexity*. Woven through this are shifting patterns of optimism and pessimism regarding the straightforwardness—or even the possibility—of building a working-class movement capable of bringing a transition to socialism in the United States.

Sombart himself focused on what ex-Marxist economic historian Louis M. Hacker termed "the triumph of American capitalism," and we will want to explore ways in which this recurring and self-renewing triumph has influenced various analysts.[2] Actually, there are two counterposed strains of simplicity, and both operate from an assumption of inevitability (elements of each can be teased out in the early writings of Sombart): the inevitability of capitalist durability versus the inevitability of socialist revolution in the United States.

What tools did Marxists bring to the effort of joining with Sombart to comprehend the realities and possibilities of the United States? We will see that within the Marxist tradition (and within Kautsky himself) there was a tension between an activist and a fatalist dynamic—the former leading to greater sensitivity of complexities and openness to possibilities, the latter closing off possibilities and reducing reality to much simpler propositions (in a manner consistent with either a dogmatic optimism or pessimism).

Actually, within Marx himself (and, to a somewhat lesser extent, in his co-thinker Friedrich Engels and Marx's talented daughter Eleanor) we find a methodological approach that facilitates greater openness to complex and contradictory realities—with the result that we find fresh observations and flashes of insight regarding realities in the United States.

Such qualities were less apt to come into play as Marx's thought congealed into a simpler theoretical orthodoxy providing an ideological orientation for a mass movement in the international working class of the late nineteenth and early twentieth centuries. Essential elements of "open Marxism" tended to endure particularly among some of the more revolutionary theorists of international socialism. Kautsky himself, as he tilted toward the revolutionary dynamic in Marxism, was able to contribute useful elements (although not always a rounded and fully coherent analysis) that remain helpful today in studying the history and complexities of the US working class and were not surpassed—or even approached—by US co-thinkers employing the more standard (and fatalistic) version of what is known as "scientific socialism."

But the simple and optimistic assumptions of earlier socialists could not withstand the blows of "life itself."[3] The upward trajectory of working-class radicalism in the United States was reversed by World War I and the expansive capitalism of the 1920s. The resurgent labor militancy during the Great Depression of the 1930s, instead of generating the long-anticipated mass labor party and mass socialist consciousness, flowed into the New Deal pro-capitalist, liberal reform coalition of Democratic president Franklin D. Roosevelt. Since this seemed so divergent from European experience, efforts to define what made the United States so "exceptional" (and what was the meaning of this "exceptionalism") proliferated among stalwart Marxists and disillusioned ex-Marxists—sometimes in ways that pushed in the direction of simplified certainties, but sometimes in ways that added new insights and elements to an increasingly complex analysis. Additional lines of thought opened up with the awareness that the US experience might not be an exception to but instead a precursor of European (and global) capitalist developments. Consistent with present-day trends of "globalization," such lines of analysis include optimistic and pessimistic notions of what the future might bring.

The activist/fatalist dichotomy also emerges among US Marxists after World War II, with divergent ways of understanding distinctive aspects of the notion embedded in Marx and explicitly stated by his daughter—the existence of a "latent socialism" in capitalist America. This exists not only in the realities of capitalist society but in the consciousness (or, more accurately, in the subconsciousness) of working-class sectors experiencing oppression and exploitation in that society on a daily basis. An examination of the development of the labor process is one key to comprehending this, but so is an examination of popular culture. In both cases, we are dealing with the life-activity and self-expression of masses of people—how they spend their lives, how they make choices that shape the way society functions and history flows.

The fatalist or activist twist in this dichotomy (depending on which way one twists) can either nurture a sense of socialist inevitability or it can generate an intensified activism in order to help actualize socialist possibilities. The notion of a latent working-class socialism can also be given a twist that calls for the subordination of divergent and allegedly "diversionary" identities (such as race, gender, age, and sexual orientation) to class identity—a reversion to simplicity that (we will see) can slide into a variant of labor conservatism. It can also be approached with the complexity framework—giving attention to the ways in which "latent socialism" can be drawn out of the dynamically interpenetrating identities of class, race, gender, age, sexual orientation, and so on.

In any event, it seems likely that the persistence of capitalism will continue to sustain socialist commitments. It is noteworthy that Marxists in the early years of the twenty-first century should be reflecting over the work of the long-neglected Karl Kautsky, of all people. New ways of interpreting Kautsky have been developed by recent scholars, who urge us to push past the earlier dismissals. Here, too, there is more than one approach.

Kautsky and Dialectics

Kautsky, the orthodox Marxist who rejected Eduard Bernstein's reformist myopia—the new interpretation stresses—also rejected the destructive brutality of Lenin's Bolshevism. Subjecting the un-Marxist and undemocratic perniciousness of "the dictatorship of the proletariat" in Soviet Russia to critique, he also predicted the "ultra-imperialism" that would characterize the global economy later in the century. He preserved a serious-minded Marxism that future generations would have to find their way back to, given the historically demonstrated inadequacies of those to his right and to his left. It would make a considerable amount of sense, therefore, to turn our attention to the long-forgotten essay, "The American Worker," that Kautsky penned almost a century ago, even if it is time that we move beyond the orthodoxies that animated its author.[4]

This elegant reinterpretation has never quite erased the image of "the renegade Kautsky." His revolutionary rhetoric and theoretical "orthodoxy" during the glory days of the pre-1914 Second International masked the reformist corruption and impending collapse of social democracy in the face of an ascendant imperialism. Then came the murderous explosion of world war, and the embrace of the Kaiser's war effort by Germany's socialist majority. Kautsky distinguished himself with a stoic acceptance of the imperialist slaughter—only slightly modified by a belated and modest antiwar dissent. This pretentious "pope of Marxism" shook his finger at real revolutionaries (his martyred friend Rosa Luxemburg, Lenin, Trotsky) while clinging to a bureaucratized section of the labor movement that accommodated itself to the capitalist order. What can one expect from an old article by such a sorry figure? The answer: even Lenin, Trotsky and Luxemburg had thought highly of Kautsky in his earlier years.[5]

We owe it to Kautsky and to ourselves, however, to move beyond intellectual and political fashions—to confront the essay itself, and to understand its several contexts. One context has to do with the historical and sociological realities that Kautsky was writing about. Another has to do with the intellectual and political terrain of the socialist movement in 1906. Yet another context has to do with the tangled tradition of trying to explain "why there is no socialism in the United States."

There is no single, clever answer. Reality is too complex for that—this reality in particular. Kautsky certainly did not answer the question but instead made his own contribution to the cumulative process of trying to work out what brought socialism closer and what pushed it further away on the American scene. What we will want to look for is the sort of process John Rees once described in discussing "the algebra of revolution":

Society is taken to be in a process of constant change. Such change involves the totality of relations—economic, political, ideological, and cultural—of which the society is composed. This process of total change is a result of internal contradictions, manifested as class antagonism, which reconstitute society anew by both transforming and renewing the forces that first gave rise to the initial contradiction.[6]

"Ever-newer waters flow on those who step into the same rivers," Heraclitus emphasized in ancient Greece. Just as it is impossible, in a sense, to place your foot in the same river twice (since the water your foot went into has flowed far downstream by the time you step in again), so is the US working class in a dynamic state of flux. It is a different entity when Marx looks at it in the 1840s and again in the 1870s, when Engels engages with it in the 1890s, when Kautsky turns his attention to it in 1906, when Lukács and Gramsci discuss it in the 1920s, when Trotsky cheers it on in the 1930s, when Herbert Marcuse dismisses it in the early 1960s, and so on. At the same time, there are similarities, patterns, continuities, and an evolution within a definite (although contradictory, complex, dynamically evolving) social and economic context.

Triumphant Capitalism

Kautsky's essay was a critical review, first of all, of an important study by Werner Sombart, a prestigious student of Max Weber and an academic sympathizer of Germany's socialist labor movement. Sombart's work of 1905–6, *Why Is There No Socialism in the United States?*, sought to demonstrate why a socialist movement had failed to assume the mass proportions and political influence in America that it was attaining throughout Europe. True, Sombart predicted that the US socialists would soon catch up with their European comrades, and he promised a future study that would explain the reasons why. But the future study never appeared, and the future itself mocked the sociologist's prophecy.[7]

Sombart's analysis of socialism's failure on American soil consequently became one in a long succession of explanations of "why there is no socialism in the United States." Such explanations were produced, for example, by such disappointed socialists as Selig Perlman and Daniel Bell. Often these explanations show the influence of their authors' particular understandings of the Marxist method—involving a scientific concern for objective factors, shaping a deterministic outlook that dictated submission to the inevitabilities of history.

In Sombart, who was not assuming any predestined outcome, we find something better than that. He developed a searching and subtle analysis of political peculiarities having to do with the nature of political parties and of the state in this crudely democratic republic. He discussed somewhat speculatively but intelligently the impact of these peculiarities on working-class consciousness. He also sought the roots of the political peculiarities in the deeper peculiarities of American capitalism, and he reflected on how the economic factors—that provided relative prosperity ("roast beef and apple pie")—cut across the radicalization of the US proletariat.

While by no means rejecting such considerations, pioneering labor historian Selig Perlman emphasized other factors in his classic *Theory of the Labor Movement*, published in 1928. As a Marxist in the first decades of the twentieth century, he had considered revolution to be inevitable because capitalist society's majority class, the working class, was necessarily revolutionary thanks to the dynamics of capitalism as explained by Karl Marx. But by the conservative and prosperous 1920s, Perlman had turned this proposition on its head. The dynamics of capitalism, he had concluded, inevitably foster among workers an organic *job consciousness*, culminating not in socialist consciousness but in "pure and simple" trade unionism as represented by the American Federation of Labor under ex-socialist Samuel Gompers. While left-wing intellectuals want the workers to focus on the goal of proletarian revolution, real workers naturally prefer a capitalist economy in which they can seek guarantees of a job with improved wages, hours, and working conditions.[8]

Embracing both Sombart and Perlman, socialist-turned-sociologist Daniel Bell added his own updated scholarship and humorous insights, capped with a philosophical flourish. US socialism "was trapped by the unhappy problem of living '*in* but not *of* the world,' so it could only act, and then inadequately, as the moral, but not political, man in immoral society," Bell intoned in his 1967 text *Marxian Socialism in the United States*. "It could never resolve but only straddle the basic issue of either accepting capitalist society, and seeking to transform it from within as the labor movement did, or becoming the sworn enemy of that society like the communists." Of course, the enhanced political and economic opportunities of America "made a barren ground for a socialist movement," especially because Debsian Socialists as well as Communist militants were hampered by the "ideological blinkers" of Marxism. But Bell consistently reemphasized the assertion of Sombart's great teacher, Max Weber, that "he who seeks the salvation of souls, his own as well as others, should not seek it along the avenue of politics."[9]

This approach became associated in the 1950s and early 1960s with the "end of ideology" current in intellectual life represented by Bell, Louis Hartz,

Seymour Martin Lipset, Nathan Glazer, Sidney Hook, Lewis Feuer, and other ex-leftists who gravitated to Cold War liberalism (and finally, in some cases, to neoconservatism).[10]

There were others who were by no means inclined to abandon "ideology" (i.e., Marxism) yet also viewed capitalism as being even more triumphant, materially and ideologically, than those to their right would allow. Most prominent among these was Herbert Marcuse. By the early 1960s, Marcuse was suggesting that "advanced industrial society is capable of containing qualitative change for the foreseeable future," making "technology and science its own . . . for the ever-more-effective domination of man and nature, for the ever-more-effective utilization of its resources." In sum: "Domination—in the guise of affluence and liberty—extends to all spheres of private and public existence, integrates all authentic opposition, absorbs all alternatives."[11]

James Boggs came up with a similar theorization from his own experience in the late 1950s and early 1960s as a radical Black autoworker from Detroit: "The sons of the factory workers and coal miners have become teachers, engineers, draftsmen, scientists, social workers. . . . The working class is growing, as Marx predicted, but it is not the old working class which the radicals persist in believing will create the revolution and establish control over production. That old working class is a vanishing herd."[12]

Elaborating on this claim, Marxist economist Paul Sweezy noted that within such an increasingly differentiated proletariat "occupational and status consciousness has tended to submerge class consciousness," that the working class as a whole becomes a "non-revolutionary majority." Sweezy tentatively suggested a historical generalization that would challenge a central Marxist tenet: "If the early opportunities of the early period of modern industry are missed, the proletariat of an industrializing country tends to become less and less revolutionary." Nonetheless, Sweezy, Boggs, and Marcuse argued that certain elements—a majority of African Americans in the United States, and the oppressed laborers of the "third world" of Asia, Africa, and Latin America—still constituted a revolutionary force with the potential to overthrow capitalism.[13]

But possibilities for revolutionary socialists in the United States would be limited if the working class under "mature" capitalism is necessarily nonrevolutionary. While building on elements of Marxist analysis, the analytic-strategic conclusions reached by Marcuse and others represented a dead end for Marxism as such. And in fact, it could be argued, a more open Marxism—free from both optimistic and pessimistic varieties of fatalism, and from both de-radicalized and radical notions of what workers will "inevitably" decide—is necessary for comprehending the development of capital and labor in the United States. This open Marxism is consistent with the revolutionary-activist current one can find in the work of Antonio Gramsci and of Georg Lukács from 1919 to 1929, as well as the contributions of Luxemburg, Lenin, and Trotsky. And Kautsky's 1906 perspective can be identified with that tradition as well.

Kautsky's Journey—Revolutionary Activism to Evolutionary Fatalism

A number of scholars have documented that, at the very time when his "American Worker" essay appeared, Kautsky's Marxism was most consistent with the orientation dominating the revolutionary wing of international socialism. From 1905 through 1909, Kautsky's thinking converged with that of Trotsky, Luxemburg, and Lenin, as indicated by their shared views on the dynamics of the Russian revolutionary struggle, which were in sharp contrast to the more "orthodox" but dogmatic-fatalist emphasis of such Menshevik leaders as Plekhanov, Martov, and Dan that Russia's upcoming "bourgeois-democratic" revolution required a worker-capitalist alliance to overthrow tsarist absolutism.[14]

Kautsky's radicalism reached a crescendo with his *Road to Power* (1909), where he thundered against class collaborationism: "To want the Social Democratic Party to link itself with bourgeois parties through an alliance policy now, at the very time when those parties have prostituted and utterly compromised themselves; to want the Party to link itself with them in order to further that very prostitution—that is to demand that it commit moral suicide." Challenging the deepening reformism of trade union bureaucracy and of those party leaders who sought gains through "selling [the party's] strength to a bourgeois government," Kautsky insisted on a radically different vision:

> The vanguard of the proletariat today forms the strongest, the most far-sighted, most selfless, boldest stratum, and the one united in the largest free organization, of the nations of European civilization. And the proletariat will, in and through struggle, take up into itself the unselfish and far-sighted elements of all classes; it will organize and educate in its own bosom even its most backward elements and fill them with understanding and the joy of hope. It will place its vanguard at the head of civilization and make it capable of guiding the immense economic transformation that will finally, over the entire globe, put an end to all the misery arising out of subjection, exploitation, and ignorance.[15]

But when Rosa Luxemburg pressed the struggle against the non-revolutionary standpoint of the Social Democratic leadership even more sharply, to the extreme displeasure of the party and trade union apparatus,

Kautsky—initially closely allied with her—finally chose to back off. In 1910 he turned his polemical guns against Luxemburg. Contrasting the "strategy of attrition" (patiently struggling for reforms) to the "strategy of overthrow" (revolution), and promising that the first strategy in the near future "must go over" to the second (probably—he suggested optimistically—"in the next Reichstag elections"), he warned Luxemburg that one must not "be carried away by impatience into premature actions and fire our last rounds in the opening skirmish."[16]

Each in his own way, Lenin and Trotsky were inclined to align themselves with the prestigious Kautsky rather than Luxemburg in this debate, but Lenin's Menshevik opponents (also wanting to enhance their Marxist credentials with Kautsky's authority) viewed the debate as a vindication of their own fatalistic "orthodoxy" in the Russian socialist movement, which—in contrast to the views of Lenin and Trotsky—posited the need for a worker-capitalist alliance in overturning a semifeudal tsarism. Moira Donald notes: "Trotsky and Riazanov both informed Kautsky that the Mensheviks welcomed his stand as evidence that he was drawing closer to Menshevism. Riazanov explained that the Mensheviks wanted to prove that Kautsky was 'a real Menshevik and Rosa a Bolshevik.'" While Kautsky initially held back from endorsing this view, his reluctant acceptance of the First World War in 1914 and rejection of the Bolshevik Revolution in 1917 brought him into an alignment with the Mensheviks, and he accepted the linkage of Luxemburg with the Bolshevism that he had come to abhor.[17]

This political evolution brought to the fore fatalistic elements in his Marxism. In *The Materialist Conception of History* (1927), he connected the notion that "the advance and progress of the proletariat is irresistible" with the conviction that "evolution advances to ever-higher forms," that "the special laws of the development of society . . . do not contradict the laws of natural evolution, but form . . . their natural extension," in a manner operating "independently of men's volition and knowledge." Hence: "We must count on the advance and ultimate victory of the non-European proletariat as much as on that of the European one (in which are also to be included the North American and Australian). Here as well as there, this process will take place on the basis of the same laws of industrial capital, which is more and more taking hold of the whole world."[18]

Such fatalistic elements can certainly be found in Kautsky's earlier works, and in the Marxism of the Second International, influencing—as we have noted—subsequent Marxist theorists of the late twentieth century. "The scientism and positivism which characterized Kautsky's interpretation of Marx's writings," notes sympathetic critic Dick Geary, were "part and parcel of a widespread *Weltanschaung* [worldview] in nineteenth-century Europe, which looked to natural sciences for a model . . . of human history." At certain points, Geary points out, Kautsky rejected a fatalistic interpretation of Marxism, but "when confronted by any specific tactical question the [German Social Democratic Party's] leading theorist produced innumerable arguments to justify inaction. The proletariat invariably had to *wait* upon the laws of capitalist development." Geary adds that, at such points, Kautsky's "Marxism was not, as it was for Lenin, 'a guide to action' but rather a recipe for 'inaction.'"[19] But in Kautsky's most interesting and revolutionary period, the period in which "The American Worker" appeared, a different and more open quality comes to the fore.

Open Marxism and American Realities

"The overall vulgarization of Marxism," according to Antonio Gramsci, has generally taken the form of "deterministic, mechanistic, fatalistic elements." We have seen that such determinism also left its marks on disillusioned ex-Marxists and even (at moments) on critical Marxists who are inclined to be neither vulgar nor mechanistic. To hold that one or another aspect of capitalist development inevitably assigns to the mass of working-class individuals any specific consciousness (whether revolutionary or nonrevolutionary) is problematical. "We should, I think, prepare a funeral elegy on the concept of fatalism," Gramsci concluded, "praising its usefulness in a certain historical period but burying it once for all—with full honors." Gramsci—like his contemporary Georg Lukács—saw future possibilities as being conditioned by "objective" economic and social realities. But the thinking of these Hegelian Leninists was also alive to multiple possibilities—grounded in the understanding that not only are "objective" factors too complex and fluid to be fully grasped in analysis, but that the consciousness and actions of human beings (especially when informed by revolutionary theory and focused through effective organization) can alter the "objective" factors.[20]

Marx's thought was similarly animated by a passionate and critical-minded optimism—engaged with and shaped by a multiplicity of new realities generated by the democratic and industrial revolutions that were having an explosive impact on his world. He was by no means constructing a parochial and fatalistic dogmatism, but rather a critical analysis open to the experience of global developments. "Socialism and communism did not originate in Germany," he commented in 1847, "but in England, France, and North America." There were several elements in this American contribution to the emergence of scientific socialism. One element was the deepening of class oppression that was part of the growing industrial capitalist order. A second element involved the growth of a working-class political movement that had profoundly radical implications. A third element involved the rise—within this context—of transcendentalist, radical-democratic, and utopian-socialist currents. All of this preceded, was studied by, and helped shape the thinking of the young Marx.[21]

Drawing on perceptive studies of US realities by Alexis de Tocqueville, Gustav de Beaumont, and especially Thomas Hamilton, Marx in the early 1840s grappled with the collisions of capitalist industrialization and a democratizing political order, out of which a working-class radicalization seemed to be arising. As Maximilien Rubel has commented, "In becoming an economist, Marx [gave] to Thomas Hamilton's premonitory warnings the theoretical coating in the famous chapter of *Capital* entitled 'Historical Tendency of Capitalist Accumulation.'"[22]

Marx was also alert to countervailing tendencies in the United States that blocked the realization of the revolutionary socialist scenario. Drawing together the different strands of Marx's thought from the 1840s through the 1850s suggests this analysis: the radicalism inherent in the early working-class movement of capitalist America had little hope of being triumphant as long as slavery continued to exist and as long as the "safety valve" of Western lands remained available. With the end of slavery (1865) and the conclusion of a forty-year period of population growth and westward expansion (occurring in the 1880s), an upsurge of labor radicalism could be expected to alter the political landscape, placing socialism on the agenda.[23]

Marx himself was never able to observe American realities firsthand, and he died before this forty-year deadline had passed. But a speaking tour of the United States by Marx's daughter several years after his death generated impressions and evidence that seemed to justify his optimistic forecast. In 1886–87, many Americans had a half-formed set of perceptions, inclinations, hopes, and values that added up, in the opinion of Eleanor Marx and Edward Aveling, to a sort of "unconscious socialism." In the United States of the 1880s, the two visitors discovered scores of working-class and pro-labor newspapers, reflecting vital working-class and labor-radical subcultures.[24]

Eleanor and her companion saw insurgent working-class, oppositional, and dissident elements of the United States as the 1880s were fading into the 1890s. A formidable proletarian challenge to the bourgeois status quo that would—they were certain—soon be generated by the still-mushrooming Knights of Labor, the still-radical American Federation of Labor, the militant struggles for an eight-hour workday, the widespread labor party efforts, and the growing clusters of organized socialists. Of course, what Marx and Aveling wrote about the United States could not be more than the vivid impressions gained from a brief tour. The reality was far more dynamic than even these perceptive observers could see.

Marx and Engels had commented in the *Communist Manifesto* of 1848 that capitalism involves the "constant revolutionizing of production, uninterrupted disturbance of all social conditions, everlasting uncertainty and agitation," in which—over and over again—it seems that "all that is solid melts into air." The United States, which by 1890 would be the world's foremost manufacturing nation, was undergoing remarkable changes fundamentally altering the realities which these insightful optimists sought to describe. "The structural changes that transformed United States society in the half century from 1865 to 1920," writes labor historian Melvyn Dubofsky, "continuously reshaped the composition of the working class," to the extent that in retrospect it gives the impression of being "in a state of permanent flux rather than a class in process of formation." The Marx-Aveling account is like a single frame, or at most a brief scene, from a motion-picture. It provides a partial indication that Marx's analytical prediction was on target. But further developments showed that other factors would have to be identified as powerful obstacles to the realization of socialist hopes in America.[25]

The initial labor party stirrings failed to yield any durable alternative to the pro-capitalist Republican and Democratic parties. In 1887 Friedrich Engels—sharing the hopes expressed by Marx-Aveling—had hailed the first political steps through which "the laboring masses should feel their community of grievances and of interests, their solidarity as a class in opposition to all other classes," expecting that the embryonic labor party would "find the common remedy for these common grievances" and eventually advance this remedy (socialism) in its party platform. Such hopes were bitterly disappointed: not only did the mass political insurgency fail to embrace socialism, but it also soon collapsed and was largely reabsorbed by the Democratic and Republican parties. In an 1893 letter, Engels sought to explain why "American conditions involve very great and peculiar difficulties for a steady development of a workers' party." The three factors he identified—imperfectly grasped in the Marx-Aveling account—became ingredients in the analyses of innumerable historians seeking to explain the absence of a labor party and socialist movement in the United States:

> First, the Constitution, based as in England upon party government, which makes it appear as though every vote were *lost* that is cast for a candidate not put up by one of the two governing parties. And the American, like the Englishman, wants to exert an influence on his state; he does not want to throw his vote away.

Then, and more especially, immigration, which divides the workers
into two groups: the native-born and the foreigners, and the latter in turn
into (1) the Irish, (2) the Germans, (3) the many small groups—Czechs,
Poles, Italians, Scandinavians, etc.—who understand only their own language. And in addition the Negroes. Very powerful incentives are needed
to form a single party out of these elements. There is sometimes a sudden
strong élan, but the bourgeoisie need only wait passively, and the dissimilar elements of the working class will fall apart again.

Third. Lastly the protective tariff system must have enabled the
workers to participate in the sort of prosperity which we in Europe (apart
from Russia, where, however, not the workers profit from it but the bourgeoisie) have not seen for years.[26]

The poisonous impact of ethnic hatreds and pervasive racism—touched
on in Engels's brief comments but inadequately comprehended in the
Marx-Aveling account—continues to be felt down to the present day. Complex specifics of the *intersection* of class, racial, and gender identities—and the
decisive meaning of this for the experience, consciousness, and struggles, and
the future evolution, of the US working class—were generally beyond the
grasp of even the most sophisticated nineteenth-century socialists. They have
eluded the comprehension of many latter-day Marxists as well.

Less surprising is the relative inattention of Eleanor Marx, Aveling, and
Engels to the rising Populist movement among hard-pressed farmers in the
South and the Midwest. After all, their concern was with the *working-class*
movement (the movement of those whose living was based on the sale of
labor-power for wages), whereas the small farmers who formed the Populist
base have generally been seen as a "petty bourgeois" layer—small-scale landowners engaged in petty commodity production—destined to be crowded
out by larger and more efficient business interests as the capitalist economy
continued to develop along lines of growing productivity. The Populist revolt
against such capitalist progress was seen by many deterministic leftists (and
also many influential historians) as "reactionary" by definition.

The fact is, however, that in the 1890s a powerful challenge was mounted
by these embattled small farmers, in alliance with sections of the labor movement (the Knights of Labor, the American Railway Union, trade union activists in Chicago and other Midwestern urban areas) and with various radical
and maverick currents, to defend democracy (rule by the people) from plutoc-
racy (rule by the rich), a challenge which was deflected into the Democratic
Party and then decisively crushed by a Republican Party electoral effort that
was massively financed by big business interests in the presidential campaign
of 1896. In fact, some Marxist-influenced labor activists of the time scornfully

rejected the notion that they should make common cause with the "petty bourgeois" farmers.

What is intriguing is that almost two decades earlier, in a comment to his friend Engels about the violent nationwide labor uprising of 1877, Karl Marx had suggested the possibility of the predominantly white working-class movement merging with the struggles of African American agricultural labor in the South (just betrayed by the Republican Party sellout that dismantled Reconstruction) and the hard-pressed small farmers who would eventually spearhead the Populist movement.[27] This was, however, a fleeting insight in Marx's massive intellectual output. Such fertile speculation about the possibility and desirability of far-reaching social alliances was beyond the range even of his thoughtful daughter in 1887, or even of his shrewd co-thinker in 1893.[28]

The failure of majority sectors of the US laboring population to make common cause enabled political representatives of the big-business robber barons to divide and conquer the various lower-class challengers, consolidating the control of industrial and financial corporations over the nation's economic development and political life. The Democratic Party—based on an alliance of Southern agrarian interests and political machines catering to immigrant communities in Northern urban centers—claimed to be the party of labor. So did the Republican Party, which favored high tariffs facilitating the forward march of industry that would bring jobs and prosperity for all. And when push came to shove, both were dedicated to the triumph of American capitalism that was making the United States a great world power. An additional factor beyond the scope of Engels's comments was the consequent overseas economic expansion through the Open Door Policy—backed by "dollar diplomacy" and "gunboat diplomacy"—designed to secure foreign markets, raw materials, and investment opportunities that were vital to the future of America's dynamic market economy. The overwhelming triumph of corporate capitalism, no less than the ethnic and racial fragmentation of the US working class, had a profound impact on the manner in which the US labor movement developed.

By the dawn of the twentieth century the movement that Marx and Aveling had described was pulling into increasingly conservatized and radicalized components. The labor radicals reflected the socialist commitments and inclinations identified in this study, with many "unconscious socialists" (one thinks of Eugene V. Debs, "Big Bill" Haywood, and others) becoming sufficiently conscious to organize the Socialist Party of America (1901) and the Industrial Workers of the World, or IWW (1905), both mass organizations which would in some ways represent the high point of US labor radicalism. The labor conservatives—including some who had also been influenced by socialism—sought to guide organized labor into a "realistic" accommodation with the triumphant capitalist order. Within this order a moderated and narrowly economic "pure and simple" trade unionism might secure, at least for the more skilled and organized sectors of the labor force, better working conditions, a shorter workday, and higher wages at the workplace. Radicals saw this not only as a betrayal of the labor movement's lofty ideals, but also as a short-sighted betrayal of the majority of the less skilled and less organized workers. Such a tension and division in the ranks of labor, never fully resolved one way or the other, shaped the history of the US working class throughout the twentieth century.[29]

Kautsky and His Comrades

Reading Karl Kautsky's 1906 essay "The American Worker," one finds an admirable thoughtfulness well served by a clarity of expression, characteristic of his best writing. In some ways, the essay is disappointing—more a survey with suggestive ideas rather than a rounded analysis. It combines the qualities of a lengthy review (here, the book being critiqued is Sombart's *Why Is There No Socialism in the United States?*), a sophisticated polemic against German reformism, and an unfinished study of the American working class. But its virtues cannot be shrugged off: rich comparisons of the particular nature of capitalism and the distinctive qualities of the working class in the United States with those in Russia, England, and Germany; insightful points regarding immigration and the dialectic of class and ethnicity; shrewd comments on both industrial and agricultural development; the presentation of illuminating statistical material on a variety of questions.

The apparent triumph of democracy and prosperity in the capitalist United States posed a challenge for Kautsky and other socialists. "Why become a socialist, why struggle for a distant future, if a considerable part of the socialist aims had become a reality in America, at least until quite recently?" he wrote. The starkness of this challenge is only partly mitigated by the three final words of that question.[30]

But he shared Sombart's expectation that "all the factors that till now have prevented the development of Socialism in the United States are about to disappear or to be converted into their opposite," and from that standpoint he took the offensive, as a revolutionary socialist, against reformist-socialist efforts to reorient the German Social Democratic Party and the Second International. From this standpoint he applauds Sombart's critical contrast of capitalist trade unionism—the moderate "pure-and-simple unionism, focused only on wages, hours, working conditions," and "carved from the same wood as capitalism itself"—and socialist trade unionism, "also tailored to success in the present, but at the same time [not losing] sight of the proletarian class-movement against capitalism."[31] From the same standpoint, he sharply asserts (with words as relevant to labor supporters of liberal capitalist politicians as to working-class parties that would form governmental alliances with them): "Only those who have forgotten the fundamental difference between Social Democracy [i.e., socialism] and liberalism can be of the opinion that a trade-union leader, or any other leader of the proletariat, can represent its interests from a post he owes to the liberals."

There was a potential in the Kautsky/Sombart distinction for justifying the newly formed IWW, or even the earlier sectarian project of Daniel De Leon's Socialist Labor Party, to establish a Socialist Trade and Labor Alliance competing with the American Federation of Labor (AFL). But, for the substantial number of socialists in the AFL, predominating in about one-third of the Federation's affiliates, it meant helping more and more AFL members, and eventually the Federation as a whole, move beyond "pure and simple" unionism, break definitively from all pro-capitalist political parties (Democrats and Republicans alike), and embrace the cause of socialism.

More stimulating for scholars, however, are Kautsky's less polemical comments—especially his marvelous comparisons. "If the American capitalists constitute a much more homogeneous class than in England," he points out, "nowhere is the working class more heterogeneous than in the United States."[32]

Kautsky's failure to focus on the centrality of racism in the working-class fragmentation is striking but not surprising given its absence in the book that he is reviewing and the relative backwardness of both US and European socialists on this question. Another obvious limitation is the failure to discuss more fully something that was intimately experienced by all American workers—the nature of, and the ongoing transformation of, the labor process. Both of these realities, we will see, must be comprehended if we wish to understand the working class of the United States.

There are other slips. Kautsky offers an interesting generalization on the absence of a precapitalist class of aristocratic and militaristic landowners (most dramatically the Prussian Jünkers), adding the qualification that "I am ignoring here the Southern planters, whose regime came to an end when that of the capitalists began," presumably with the conclusion of the Civil War.[33] This is open to more than one challenge. Did not a regime of the capitalists exist in the United States from the very beginning of the republic? Did not the slavocracy constitute a peculiar variation of and faction within the bourgeoisie? Did not much of the former slavocracy end up, with the defeat of Reconstruction, maintaining its control of much of the land and reclaiming much of its political power in the South and nationally? Did not the political culture of the United States continue to feel the impact of this reactionary, authoritarian, militaristic stratum that Kautsky shrugs off?[34]

Nonetheless, there is much that holds up well—especially with the dramatic Russia-US comparisons. "In America we can speak more than anywhere else about the dictatorship of capital. In contrast, nowhere has the fighting proletariat reached such significance as in Russia, and this significance must and will increase, because this country has just now begun to take part in the modern class struggle." His next layer of comparison was no less intriguing: "Germany's economy is closest to the American model; its politics, on the other hand, is closest to the Russian."[35] And, obviously, such comments as these would endear him to such Russian revolutionaries as Lenin and Trotsky, as well as such leaders of Germany's revolutionary Left as Rosa Luxemburg.

Returning to the Russia/America contrast, Kautsky notes that "as a capitalist land [the United States] is not older than Russia," but that capitalist development in Russia has been more dependent on foreign investment, while in the United States "a very considerable section of the industrial proletariat comes from abroad, indeed from the four corners of the world, whereas its capital is totally indigenous and almost completely confined to the circle of interests of industrial capital." Consequently, in Russia capital is weaker and the proletariat is stronger, while in the US capital is stronger and the proletariat weaker "than what they should be according to the degree of industrial development of the country."[36]

Kautsky goes on to tell us that a larger number of Russian workers are filled with "revolutionary romanticism," while a much greater proportion of US workers follow the leadership of practical-minded moderates dealing "only with the nearest and most tangible things."[37] He links this contrast to differences in the intelligentsia of the two countries.

The point Kautsky articulates here—associating the development of working-class consciousness with the intellectual and cultural efforts of the intelligentsia—represents one of his most original contributions to theorizations about the absence of a substantial socialist movement in the United States, overlapping with analytical orientations associated with Lenin, Lukács, and Gramsci. Deserving a separate essay in itself, Kautsky's striking suggestion should at least be highlighted in some of its specific elements.

Thanks to the repressive and restrictive peculiarities of the tsarist system, "in Russia the intelligentsia, because of its social position, has become the indispensable agency through which revolutionary consciousness is brought to the proletariat, which it resembles in many respects."[38]

In stark contrast, the intelligentsia in the United States "represents the connecting link between the proletariat and the capitalist class." This is related to the level of US capitalist development—if one generalizes (as Kautsky himself seems inclined to do) a comment he makes on Russian capitalism. "As long as capital is scanty, and its profit small, the capitalist is stingy in his personal consumption, he is puritanical and full of contempt, not only for senseless luxury and pomp, but also for serious art and science." Such is the case in backward Russia, he implies—although one can find similar limitations among US industrialists up to the 1870s. "But the more capital and the rate of exploitation grow, the easier it becomes for the capitalist to let accumulation go ahead at full speed and at the same time to increase his personal consumption and feed an army of unproductive workers, lackeys of all sorts, learned and unlearned, aesthetic and unaesthetic, ethical and cynical." This helps to generate a corporate capitalist culture that infiltrates innumerable aspects of working-class life and consciousness.[39]

In fact, writes Kautsky, "many proletarians enter politics, journalism, and the legal professions, which because of the conditions of the country constitute vast sources of enrichment, ladders through which a man can escape from the ranks of the propertyless. The American intelligentsia is therefore dominated by the desire to get rich, filled with the most unscrupulous capitalism of the soul."[40]

Workers in the United States, while often responding critically to certain specifics of their oppression, have not been inclined toward "inquiring into and opposing the totality of the existing social order." The development of "a resolute class-consciousness, as well as . . . the setting of great goals involving the transformation of the entire society," cannot—as in tsarist Russia—be advanced by the bulk of the US intelligentsia. "From this intelligentsia the worker can receive no enlightenment about his interests or about the historical tasks of his class. The American intellectual knows nothing about these matters, and when he knows something, he takes pains to hide it carefully."[41]

There is another noteworthy contribution by Kautsky, but it is one he articulated only incompletely so it required more careful development, particularly by Lenin and others building on Lenin's perspective.[42] It involves the understanding that capitalism had been developing "more and more," by the turn of the century, into a new stage—"the stage of private monopoly, of the trusts." (The terms "trusts" and "monopoly" refer to the rise of big-business corporations—involving, as Lenin put it, "the concentration of production" and "the merging or concrescence of banks with industry.")[43] Kautsky characterizes this as a system "of capitalist feudalism that gives to a few families absolute domination over the whole capitalist economy and oppresses more and more even the small capitalists, making completely hopeless any aspiration of the proletariat to enter the ranks of the bourgeoisie." He seems somewhat uncertain, however, over precisely how this fits with other aspects of his survey, and it seems to remain one item on a list rather than a key dynamic in an analysis.

Related to this, we find no serious discussion of imperialism—an issue he did take up three years later in *The Road to Power.* The points made in that later work are illuminating. Noting that "capitalism constantly expands further and must constantly expand, if exploitation is not to become completely intolerable," Kautsky remarks: "Everywhere in Asia and Africa, the spirit of rebellion is growing. There, the use of European weapons, too, is spreading; resistance to European exploitation is growing. Capitalist exploitation cannot be transplanted into a country without the seed of rebellion against this exploitation being sown there." Such struggles, he concludes, "are weakening European capitalism and its governments and introducing an element of political unrest into the whole world."[44] This makes all the more disappointing Kautsky's failure in "The American Worker" to explore, in the era of Teddy Roosevelt's "big stick" diplomacy, connections between imperialist dynamics and the conditions and consciousness of the US working class.

Kautsky does suggest that the rise of corporate power, intensifying the exploitation of the US working class, undermines the analyses of the reformists. But first he reviews the exceptional conditions that—one would expect—made the United States the ideal location for a successful reformist strategy. "Nowhere are the conditions, which according to our revisionists can assure the economic progress of the working class within the capitalist mode of production," he notes, "more highly developed than in the United States: complete democracy, the greatest freedom of organization and the press, the highest possible social equality of rights."[45] (It is indicative, however, of Kautsky's limited understanding that he does not comment that this "social equality of rights" did not extend to African Americans and other people of color.)[46] Kautsky adds that "though the reserve of free land has shrunk, it has not yet been completely exhausted. And on top of that comes also a strong development of the trade unions." He points out that from 1896 to 1904 the membership of the AFL grew from 271,315 members to 1,672,300 members. But the power of the big-business trusts, "whose rise in the United States began simultaneously with the already mentioned strengthening of the trade unions, but whose force has grown more rapidly," has blocked the further growth of the unions, even bringing a decline in union membership.[47]

While some of the AFL unions have been able to continue improving their situation, "the progress of some strata" has been "more than counteracted

by the retrogression of the great masses." This means "an absolute deteriora-
tion in the situation of the American working class." Thanks to the power of
"private monopoly," the proletariat's "participation in the product of national
labor has declined enormously," regardless of the historical exceptions that
benefited US workers in the past.[48]

Flowing from this came an expectation of working-class radicalization
and a forecast brimming with revolutionary optimism—a future "flourishing
of socialism in America" and an expectation that "perhaps America will give
us, even before Europe, the example of a proletariat conquering political and
economic power." In Kautsky's opinion, "the Golden Age for the American
worker within the capitalist mode of production [lies] not *before*, but *behind*
him; that his social position vis-à-vis capital—and that is the decisive thing—
is continually worsening."[49]

Today, after a century's worth of experience, one might argue that this
perspective proved to be far too linear. Another (in some ways even greater)
Golden Age for the US working class opened up four decades after Kautsky
wrote these lines—and with the passage of a few more decades much of
what had been won was again lost. The dynamics of modern capitalism have
resulted in multiple successions of composition, decomposition, and recomposition—of the working class, of the labor movement, of living and working
conditions. Of course, at the dawn of the twenty-first century "the flourishing
of socialism in America" seems as far away as ever.

Unfortunately, none of Kautsky's American comrades came close to sur-
passing his contribution. Isaac Hourwich was able to produce an outstanding study of *Immigration and Labor*, but this made no pretense of offering
the analytical sweep one finds in Kautsky's essay. A. M. Simons fashioned
an interesting socialist history of the United States—*Social Forces in American History*—but its economic determinism and fatalistic optimism about
a socialist future provide little insight into why socialism failed to become
a greater force in American life. Most of Morris Hillquit's classic *History of
Socialism in the United States* holds up quite well—but, in dealing with the past
failures of US socialism, he offered nothing that cannot be found in Engels
and less than can be found in Kautsky's suggestive comments. Austin Lewis's
The Militant Proletariat is the product of a creative thinker, far more inclined
than the other Americans mentioned here to explore fault lines within the
US labor movement and the working class (especially those separating skilled
workers and craft unions from the rest of the working class)—but here, too, at
a certain point, critical analysis is engulfed by revolutionary optimism. Only
the brilliant William English Walling offered a comprehensive orientation
going beyond the boundaries of Kautsky's analysis (in his trilogy *Socialism as*

It Is, *The Larger Aspects of Socialism*, and *Progressivism—and After*). But Walling's seemingly idiosyncratic notions—emphasizing (as did Austin Lewis) the "class struggle within the working class," decrying the "idealization of the industrial working class," advocating a cross-class alliance of "the human race" against the ruling class—combined with his unstable character and commitments to place him, unfortunately, pretty much outside the Marxist dialogue and debates of his time.[50]

In this period, it appeared that the Socialist Party of America and the IWW were in the process of bringing an end to socialism's absence on the American scene. The fact remains that there were no US Marxists of that time who were able to build on Kautsky's contributions in order to deepen and advance his analysis. Only in later decades would they be matched and surpassed.

American Exceptionalism—and Beyond

One must look in the ranks and the dissident fringes of the Communist movement to find new contributions to understanding the realities with which Kautsky grappled. Disappointments and defeats seasoned such efforts with important new insights.

The socialist upsurge of the Progressive Era (1900–1920) was brought to an end with the super-patriotic repression and "Red Scare" of World War I and its aftermath. Varieties of "100 percent Americanism" were employed to push back the earlier socialist influences. Socialism and other aspects of Marxist thought were, in one way or another, found to be "foreign" imports inconsistent with both reality and morality in the United States of America. Residues of this outlook remained powerful even during the "Red Decade" of the 1930s and beyond. In a 1939 essay designed to introduce a broad US readership to Marx's *Capital*, Leon Trotsky complained:

> In certain American circles there is a tendency to repudiate this or that radical theory without the slightest scientific criticism, by simply dismissing it as "un-American." But where can you find the differentiating criterion of that? Christianity was imported into the United States along with logarithms, Shakespeare's poetry, notions on the rights of man and the citizen, and certain other not unimportant products of human thought. Today Marxism stands in the same category.[51]

Trotsky went on to emphasize that Marx's classic account of capitalism in some ways is more relevant to the United States than to Europe. "Although *Capital* rests on international material, preponderantly English, in its theoretical foundation it is an analysis of pure capitalism, capitalism in general, capitalism as such," he noted. "Undoubtedly, the capitalism grown on the virgin, unhistorical soil of America comes closest to that ideal type of capitalism."[52]

This begs the question of why, in contrast to Europe's capitalist societies, a mass socialist workers' movement failed to arise in the most purely and highly developed capitalist United States. Since the development of capitalism results in the development of an increasingly large working class, and since—according to Marx—the workers are the gravediggers of capitalism and the agency for the coming socialist order, one would expect that the most highly developed capitalist society would have the most highly developed working-class socialist movement. The opposite seems to be the case.

Those seeking to apply Marxist generalizations to US specifics have more than once emphasized "exceptional" realities of American history that may require modifications in the revolutionary Marxist orientation. Lewis Corey, an independent Marxist theorist of the 1930s, asserted that an essential aspect of "Americanizing" Marxism involves developing an "analysis of the special problems created by peculiarities in the development of the American economy, class relations, and labor movement."[53]

This was a tenet of what had come to be known as "American exceptionalism." In a common latter-day variant, this refers to the notion that the United States is inherently better than the rest of the world and has a mission to transform it. In its original Marxist formulation, the meaning was quite different. The left-wing variant was developed by a current in the Communist Party led by Jay Lovestone, a current with which Corey informally identified after it was expelled from the Communist International for differing with the alleged "greatest living theoretical and political leader of the working class," Joseph Stalin. A pamphlet-length critique of Corey's ambitious 1934 study *The Decline of American Capitalism*, published in the same year, minced no words. "Especially it should be remembered that it was Stalin who led the fight against the theory of American exceptionalism, as far back as 1928, when Lovestone had begun to defend it," noted V. J. Jerome and Alexander Bittelman. "Since then the Communist Party of the United States has been waging its main theoretical battles on the basis of Stalin's analysis of American capitalism against all bourgeois and social-reformist theories of American exceptionalism."[54] Bertram D. Wolfe aggressively defended the theoretical views of the Lovestone group:

> Yes, we consider that conditions in America are different from conditions in Germany or Spain or the Soviet Union. We are more than "American exceptionalists." We are "exceptionalists" for every country of the world!

And in pleading guilty to considering the conditions of each country different from those of the rest, peculiar, "exceptional," we are in good company—the company of Marx and Lenin.[55]

If the general theory of Marxism is the result of vast powers of generalization distilled from the investigation of concrete reality, it becomes a guide to action only in so far as it is concretely applied to living situations and realistically grasped and analyzed. . . . This requires, in the first place, an analysis of the special development and peculiar features of American capitalism, and in this sense, except for fragmentary hints from the pens of Marx, Engels and Lenin, and partial beginnings made by certain American Marxians, the development of "American Marxism" (in the sense of the application of Marxian theory to the analysis of American conditions) has scarcely begun.[56]

Unfortunately, neither Corey nor Wolfe was able to go very far in making original or durable contributions to this project before they themselves drew away from Marxism. By the 1940s, their disillusionment over the failure of the US working class to live up to revolutionary expectations, and their conclusion that the USSR had become an irredeemably and dangerously totalitarian force in the world, resulted in their abandonment of Marxism. But there was certainly nothing wrong in their challenge that US Marxists—and other Marxists—must develop a serious understanding of the specifics and peculiarities of US realities.[57]

Yet in a friendly but critical review of *The Decline of American Capitalism* George Novack complained about "Corey's habit of treating the development of American capitalism not as an integral part of the evolution of world capitalism, but apart from it." In fact, according to Corey, "capitalism in the United States came to real power with the Civil War and the progressive forces expressed and invigorated by that struggle." Novack disagreed. "From its origins the American economy has been either capitalist in character or a subsidiary part of the world capitalist economy," he insisted. "American capitalism, no less than European capitalism, had an international foundation throughout all the stages of its evolution."[58]

Novack stressed that the "exceptional" features of American capitalist development could only be understood as part of a global dialectic:

In reality, the special peculiarities of American capitalism were a product of the given constellation of economic forces constituting the world market, in which the economic forces of the United States were throughout this period a subordinate factor. The peculiarities of its economic development were not spontaneously generated from within itself alone, but were the outcome of the interactions between the national and the international productive forces and relations.[59]

It should not be surprising that Novack's internationalist emphasis was rooted in the orientation of his intellectual and political mentor Leon Trotsky. In a 1939 essay designed to introduce Marx's ideas to the US reading public, Trotsky also sought to place American "peculiarities" in global context. He noted that capitalism developed in Europe not only through the ruination of artisans, craftsmen, and peasants but also through overseas conquests. "The exploitation of classes was supplemented, and its potency increased by the exploitation of nations." Colonialism, an essential element in emergent capitalism in Europe, had enabled the capitalists of the "mother countries" to create "a privileged position for its own proletariat, especially the upper layers, by paying for it with some of the super-profits garnered in the colonies. In its expanded manifestation bourgeois democracy became, and continues to remain, a form of government accessible only to the most aristocratic and the most exploitative nations." US capitalist development fit precisely within this Bolshevik-Leninist analysis. "The United States, which formally has almost no colonies, is nevertheless the most privileged of all the nations of history," wrote Trotsky. "Active immigrants from Europe took possession of an exceedingly rich continent, exterminated the native population, seized the best part of Mexico and bagged the lion's share of the world's wealth."[60]

Similarly, contemporary US historian Eric Foner has suggested that "a preoccupation with the exceptional elements of the American experience obscures those common patterns and processes that transcend national boundaries, most notably the global expansion of capitalism in the nineteenth and twentieth centuries and its political and ideological ramifications." Foner suggests that "because mass politics, mass culture, and mass consumption came to America before it did to Europe," socialists in "exceptional" America have been merely "the first to face the dilemma of how to define socialist politics in a capitalist democracy."[61]

We should recall Georg Lukács's late 1920s observations of prominent bourgeois currents in Europe in regard to their attraction to the US model of democracy, "in which every possibility for the free development, accumulation and expansion of capital is given, while at the same time the external forms of democracy are preserved—but in such a way that the working masses cannot exert any influence whatever on the actual political leadership."[62]

In the same period Antonio Gramsci, in an article entitled "Americanism and Fordism" (written from a prison in fascist Italy), discussed the implications for Europe of the socioeconomic development of US capitalism.

"Fordism" referred to a dynamic combination: the use of technology and the modern assembly line (increasing productivity and thus lowering costs and prices), and at the same time increasing workers' wages (made possible by rising productivity) so that the proletarians could afford and become a ready-made market for these cheaper mass-production commodities. As Gramsci put it, "an ultra-modern form of production and of working methods" in which industrial and commercial life, freed from "parasitic sedimentations" of Europe's precapitalist traditions, is able to develop on "a sound basis," allowing increased efficiency and productivity. "These economies affected production costs and permitted higher wages and lower selling prices," which was combined with "various social benefits" and "extremely subtle ideological and political propaganda" promoting capitalism among the workers. Also involved, however, were greater ideological, cultural, and social controls over the working class—especially including control over the labor process through which capitalists "maintain the continuity of the physical and mus-cular-nervous efficiency of the worker." Gramsci raised the possibility that "America, through the implacable weight of its economic production . . . will compel or is already compelling Europe to overturn its excessively antiquated economic and social basis," thereby generating "'a new culture' and 'new way of life' which are being spread around under the American label."[63]

As I noted in my earlier discussion of "triumphant capitalism," the somber post–World War II analyses of such theorists as Herbert Marcuse concluded that the combined economic-technological-ideological onslaught of modern capitalism—with a consumerist "mass culture" pioneered in the United States but engulfing "advanced capitalist" societies of other lands—was creating a "one-dimensional" society in which the consciousness of the working-class majority was being inexorably pulled into a de-radicalized and nonrevolutionary orbit. The absence of socialism in the United States was possibly the precursor for the absence of socialism globally.

Latent Socialism

The notion that capitalist mass culture was brainwashing workers was sharply challenged as "a conception totally unhistorical" by the Black Marxist historian and cultural critic C. L. R. James. "To believe that the great masses of the people are merely passive recipients of what the purveyors of popular art have given to them is in reality to see people as dumb slaves," James pointed out. He went on to emphasize the need "to examine more closely the conditions in which these new arts, the film, and with it the comic strip, the radio and jazz have arisen, in order to see exactly why they become an expression of

mass response to society, crises, and *the nature and limitations of that response.*"
Writing in the United States of the early 1950s, he stressed that "the mass is
not merely passive. It decides what it will see. It will pay to see that." This
means that in important ways it is not capitalist "culture moguls" that manip-
ulate the working class, but the tastes and desires of the masses that shape
popular culture: "The makers of movies, the publishers of comic books are
in violent competition with each other for the mass to approve what they
produce. Any success tends to be repeated and squeezed dry, for these people
are engaged primarily in making money. *Huge and consistent successes are an
indication of mass demand.*"[64]

This dovetails with the 1956 perceptions of Harry Braverman, who like
James was trained intellectually and educated politically in the Trotskyist
movement, and like James was now trying to stretch beyond "traditional"
theory in order to comprehend new realities. He identified positive shifts in
popular consciousness regarding "a certain body of elementary ideas about
race, politics, cooperation, sex and women's rights, our heritage of freedom
and independence, civil liberties, art, culture, humanism, and the promise
of the future." Since the 1920s the new sensibilities had "seeped through the
land—unevenly, vaguely, and in still limited doses, but noticeably." There
were multiple sources: "The unions, the New Dealers, the last generation
of radicals all had a lot to do with it. But even the regulation instruments
of information and culture—the newspapers with their reports of strange
new events around the world, the flood of paperback books, some motion
pictures, increased secondary and higher education especially for veterans,
and so forth—had a hand in the gradual change." In Braverman's opinion,
"the result has been a considerable and growing body of humanism, toleration, sophistication, cosmopolitanism, and a general spread of a more mature
mood and approach."[65]

Braverman connected such observations on popular culture with an
argument that the allegedly "middle class" transformation of the US working
class—while having an element of truth—was greatly overstated, and that in
some ways "the workers have achieved a greater consciousness of class than
ever before." He elaborated:

> The worker has been conservatized by his higher standard of living, but it
> is a surface change which can be sloughed off with great rapidity when he
> realizes his income is threatened. Moreover, the worker by and large has
> not too much real confidence in this prosperity as a permanent affair—
> not because he is an economist but because the conditions of the factory,
> with layoffs and rumors of layoffs even in the best years and the basic

insecurities of a proletarian life constantly refresh his recollections. . . .
The worker . . . knows he is an interchangeable part in mass industry, and
nothing else. His car and house don't change that in his mind, and in that
respect his illusions are modified.[66]

In Braverman's opinion, the realities he was pointing to demonstrated
that "it is wrong to get too exclusively preoccupied with the problems and
harassments of the moment, to the point where the big and slow-moving
changes are forgotten." He added: "Future crises will be met by a generation
unlike any that came before, better prepared in many ways, and able to move
forward to great progress in short periods of time."[67]

The line of thought developed by James and Braverman brings to mind
the comments made in the 1880s by Eleanor Marx and Edward Aveling about
the "unconscious socialism" prevalent in the perceptions, inclinations, hopes,
and values of growing numbers of US workers. And it certainly opens analytical paths between Kautsky's discussion of US workers and the work of
present-day scholar-activists who see the continuing relevance of socialist
struggles for the working-class labor movement.

The notion of a latent socialism existing within the actually existing
working class has recurred, in various forms, among those examining the
relationship between workers and socialist ideas in the United States. As we
will see, however, this can go in either radical or conservative directions—
with James and Braverman both insisting on analytical elements that are
more or less absent from Kautsky's analysis, but that are necessary if the revolutionary edge of his 1906 orientation is not to be blunted.

In the Depression years of the early 1930s, an idiosyncratic leftist named
Leon Samson argued that a popular ideology of "Americanism"—which
embraced radical-democratic and egalitarian values, similar to those underlying Marxism—had taken the place of, and in some ways blocked the development of, a socialist-oriented working-class consciousness. In the economic
affluence and political conformism of the early 1950s, ex-Marxist historians,
political scientists, and sociologists developed this notion by concluding that
this was all for the best: American capitalism, blended with democratic traditions, had more or less fulfilled the hopes and needs that were supposed to
have propelled the masses toward socialism.[68]

In the 1950s and 1960s, many in the Socialist Party of America gave this
view a seemingly more radical twist. For example, ex-Trotskyist Max Shachtman—taking off on the post-socialist reflections of Daniel Bell—commented:
"The socialist movement lives in but is not of this world because the proletariat which is its bearer lives in but at the same time is not of this—that is, of

the capitalist—world!" Insisting on the central importance of the trade unions (whose "bureaucratic-conservative" leadership was denounced by more radical critics), Shachtman emphasized that "the working class and its natural movement, the unions, are the social force and mainspring from which we draw our inspiration when every trifler and dilettante finds it fashionable to sneer at it."[69]

For Shachtman and other Socialist Party leaders this necessarily meant enlisting in the pro-capitalist Democratic Party, whose social-liberalism had long made it the home of the American Federation of Labor and Congress of Industrial Organizations (AFL-CIO). As Shachtman protégé Michael Harrington explained, the liberal-labor wing of the Democratic Party was actually—although "invisibly"—a force for socialism. The actual "progressive" social policies of ostensibly pro-capitalist labor leaders like George Meany added up to creating "socialist definitions of capitalism." For some Socialist Party adherents, the very distinctions between capitalism and socialism became blurred. William Bohn, once a partisan of the IWW and the Socialist Party's revolutionary wing, as a columnist for the semi-socialist New Leader in the 1950s could concede that under US capitalism "there are some who are too rich while others are obviously too poor," but nonetheless: "The system is flexible. We have changed it. We are changing it. We shall continue to change it. That is why it works and will continue to work."[70]

C. L. R. James drew quite different conclusions from his studies of popular consciousness within American civilization. He believed revolutionary elements in the consciousness of the US working class were destined to shift from "unconscious" to conscious socialism (not to be confused with the reformism of moderate socialists) as difficult economic shifts once again sharpened contradictions between, on the one hand, the actual development of capitalism and, on the other, the democratic and egalitarian elements deeply rooted in the popular culture of the United States.[71]

One of the essential elements of James's outlook was a radical understanding of the centrality of racism in undermining class consciousness and class struggle within the US working class. It was his view that an independent African American movement for Black liberation "has got a great contribution to make to the development of the proletariat in the United States, and that it is in itself a constituent part of the struggle for socialism." This outlook identifies what a significant current of analysts—including Alexander Saxton, David Roediger, Noel Ignatiev, Karen Brodkin, and Michael Goldfield—see as a fundamental explanation for the failure of socialism in the United States.[72]

Goldfield's analysis is the most elaborate and is explicitly developed as an explanation for why the US working class has been unable to advance toward the creation of an effective socialist movement. He notes that there have been a number of historic turning points in American history that involved mass insurgencies, opened up possibilities for new directions in historical development, and resulted in a restructuring or redefinition of social relationships and politics. Through each of these turning points Goldfield sees the persistence of a system of white supremacy and racist ideology, rooted in the culture and economic structure of American capitalism, whose function is not only to control and exploit African American and other "nonwhite" labor, but also "to control white workers, isolating them from their potential allies among nonwhites." While this racism has often undermined the immediate economic interests and organizational strength of white workers, the pervasiveness of white supremacy has been buttressed by "many economic, political, ideological, and other institutional supports." Noting the recurrent instances of white racism that lead to fragmentation and defeat, Goldfield also emphasizes "highlights of labor struggle . . . when class consciousness and organization seemed to be blooming," stressing that maintaining such gains is linked to "placing the fight against racial discrimination at the top of the agenda."[73]

As James pointed out, this consciousness could be expected to come not from a white-dominated labor movement but from an independent Black struggle that "would be able to hit the bourgeoisie a tremendous blow, and by hitting the bourgeoisie a tremendous blow it would bring the proletariat on the scene and break up the Democratic Party."[74]

Another divide between James and the moderates was his emphasis on the vital importance of life and struggle at the workplace—a contested terrain where many millions of workers spend at least half of their waking lives, with their labor making possible the existence of human society, but also where they experience an ongoing exploitation of their labor for the purpose of enriching a minority of wealthy capitalists.[75]

One of James's closest collaborators, Martin Glaberman, noted what he saw as three characteristics of working-class struggles: 1) they are generally not public but occur at the workplaces, "and unless you're there, you don't know what's going on"; 2) they take place over extended periods of time, often changing form as changes are introduced into the labor process; and 3) "it's a slowly maturing thing with a sudden explosion at the end." In the view of James and his co-thinkers, many would-be Marxists who failed to recognize these characteristics of struggle degenerated into sectarian arrogance and irrelevance. But the leadership of the trade unions had also grown increasingly distant from day-to-day workplace realities and from the experience of rank-and-file workers. The result was that "a bureaucratic structure, divorced from its own membership and unable to carry out even the most common and traditional functions of conservative unionism: the protection of jobs and living standards."[76]

Harry Braverman would have been in substantial agreement with such views. But his pioneering studies of the labor process in the US capitalist economy—particularly *Labor and Monopoly Capital*—identified yet another factor contributing to the erosion of the working-class power, cohesion, and consciousness necessary for the triumph of socialism.

As Marx taught, employers purchase labor-power (the ability to work) from the employees, but to maximize their profits they must squeeze as much *actual labor* as possible from the workers. In order to do this, they have—over and over again—introduced new technologies and managerial strategies to secure greater control over the labor process and the laborers. This involves eroding the power, the skills, and the dignity of their employees—sometimes driving them down into broader and less-skilled job categories, sometimes replacing them altogether with machines or cheaper labor or more lucrative investment opportunities. The consequence may be radicalization of the workers, but it can also involve disorientation and demoralization. Braverman observed that as a result of these dynamics of capitalism, "classes, the class structure, the social structure as a whole, are not fixed entities but rather ongoing processes, rich in change, transition, variations, and incapable of being encapsulated in formulas, no matter how analytically proper such formulas may be." The consequent dynamic of repeatedly decomposing and recomposing aspects of the labor process and of sectors of the working class itself has had an impact on the consciousness, culture, and organization of the working class in ways that have sometimes cut across the development of a working-class socialist movement.[77]

The contributions of James and Braverman—particularly in regard to race and the labor process—draw the notion of "latent socialism" away from the optimistic simplicity that Shachtman was inclined to settle for and into a deeper appreciation of complex realities, more consistent with the revolutionary approach of Marx.

Conclusions

In Karl Marx's reflections on the United States, he very much saw socialism not as a doctrine that must be imported to enlighten the ignorant US workers, but rather as something arising organically out of the realities of American capitalism and society, inherent in the experience and perceptions and struggles of US workers, and also logically developing out of American democracy. This was so much the case that he viewed modern socialism as being, in part, a product of the American experience.

Marx also saw certain blockages to the development of mass socialist consciousness within the growing working class—particularly the existence of slavery before 1865, and also the availability of so much land that would provide many laborers with opportunities to avoid wage-slavery and with hopes for relative prosperity within the capitalist order. He also felt that these obstacles would be cleared away, after which socialist consciousness would flourish within the growing US working class. He anticipated important alliances of the radicalizing labor movement with poor farmers, as well as with oppressed African Americans.

While Eleanor Marx and Edward Aveling more or less shared Marx's general orientation, and especially believed that fundamental aspects of socialism were embedded in much of the popular consciousness and would naturally, organically evolve within the consciousness of US workers, it was Engels who added new and significant elements to Marx's analysis. In particular, he identified three additional obstacles to the development of a strong socialist movement in the United States, although two of these involved an extension of issues identified by Marx. One was that the possibility of a relative prosperity for workers provided by free land in the 1840s was now being provided, instead, by industrial development (with high tariffs and rising productivity). A second was that the fragmentation of those who toiled—even though the divergence of slave labor and wage labor was ended by the Civil War—was continued due to ethnic diversity brought by waves of immigration, plus continued anti-Black racial prejudice. Third, Engels had concluded that the way US democracy was structured (and limited) constituted not something that would logically and naturally flow into socialism but, instead, as something that would tend to block such a development.

Kautsky felt a new concern, in the years that followed Engels's observations, to combat the idea that American realities had made socialism unnecessary. Related to this was his concern, in the years before World War I, to polemicize in favor of revolutionary socialism (and in favor of what he termed "socialist trade unionism") in the face of a strong reformist challenge that had arisen within the international socialist movement. When one reviews the additional points he makes, partly building on the ideas of Engels, one is struck by the dramatic shift that his thinking represented for the Marxist movement. He gives significant attention to the racial/ethnic diversity that—he argues— weakens the US working class, and he comments that the relative prosperity has had the effect of inculcating among workers a narrow pragmatism rather than a heroic romanticism which he finds more common among workers in Europe.

Kautsky emphasized how strong the capitalist class was in the United States, although he expressed the view that the proletariat would, in the foreseeable future, become stronger yet. He saw a relative prosperity enjoyed by only a minority of the workers, but he seemed to conclude that—rather than fragmenting the working class between the more and the less privileged—this would propel the working class as a whole toward socialism. While much of Kautsky's essay may strike one as less coherent and compelling than what one would expect from Marx, it is unambiguously articulated within a revolutionary Marxist framework, and it is graced with a breadth, coherence, and critical-minded openness that places it above the contributions of his US contemporaries.

Post-Kautsky theorists following the current within his approach that is "open" (non-fatalist)—far from providing a sense of positive or negative inevitabilities—wrestled with issues of "exceptionalism," universality, and the global relevance in the American experience. Far more than Kautsky, some of them considered elements of socialism latent in working-class experience and consciousness. Some identified aspects of race and racism that have in some ways obstructed and in other ways furthered radicalization within the working class. A few have also stressed the centrality of developments in the labor process that have undermined but also sharpened aspects of the class struggle. Greater attention has been given to issues of culture and consciousness, as well as to the debasement of democracy in the United States (with diverse views on how this affects class consciousness and class struggle).

The most capable analysts have comprehended all such things as part of a contradictory totality in the process of change—with the outcome of such change not determined in advance. The outcome is dependent on the interpenetration of "subjective" elements (the consciousness and actions of revolutionaries, workers, the oppressed) with the "objective" realities of US capitalism.

2

Haymarket Revolutionaries
Albert Parsons and His Comrades

The life and death of Albert Parsons and his comrades, known as the Haymarket Martyrs, resonated throughout the United States for many decades, and into the twentieth century as prominent left-wing spokespeople told their story over and over again, stirring emotions and teaching lessons. This was especially so among the radical-labor vanguards whose struggles were to transform in the United States in the 1930s.[1]

As militant strikes and factory occupations (sit-down strikes) were forging the Congress of Industrial Organizations in 1937, the most prominent trade union figure in the Communist Party was emphasizing the connection of these struggles with those of half a century before. "Parsons and his comrades were revolutionary trade unionists," wrote Communist leader William Z. Foster in 1937, and in the early 1880s "when they developed their great mass following, the mass of workers were just learning to organize to resist the fierce exploitation of a ruthless capitalism." Emphasizing the link between their successes and their martyrdom, Foster concluded: "The great eight-hour strike movement led by the 'Chicago Anarchists' gave an enormous impulse to trade union organization everywhere, and it was for this that the employers' interest had them hanged."[2]

The story of the Haymarket Martyrs reached around the world. The revolutionary Mexican muralist Diego Rivera had seen often their faces on posters at rallies and marches in Mexico, and in the early 1930s, when he created a mural history of the United States at the New Workers School in New York City for his friends of the Communist Party Opposition (a dissident group led by Jay Lovestone and Bertram D. Wolfe), he placed Parsons and his comrades in a central panel depicting the birth of the US labor movement. Wolfe explained:

The eight-hour strikes of May Day 1886 aroused the workers throughout Europe. The Haymarket victims consecrated the struggle with their blood. Thus originated International May Day ... and each year on the First of

33

May the workers of all lands go out on strike in memory of the Chicago
martyrs, in emulation of the great American labor struggle of 1886, and in
token of the solidarity of the workers throughout the world.[3]

Parsons was no less essential to another central leader of US Communism, James P. Cannon, expelled from the Communist Party in 1928 by his
comrades Foster and Wolfe for opposing the Stalinist degeneration of their
movement. A year after, amid the 1929 stock market collapse, he wrote a
poem, unpublished in his lifetime, entitled "Parsons":

> They say he was defeated, he went down
> To everlasting failure and disgrace,
> On that gray morning when they woke the town
> To see him hanging in the market place;
> No more will he rebel, long has he lain
> In somber silence in the graveyard gloom;
> His words and deeds and dreams were all in vain,
> The dust of forty years is on his tomb.
> And yet his footsteps on the gallows' stair
> Resound like drumbeats, quickening the feet
> Of men who hear and even now prepare
> The march of stern avengers in the street;
> And blazoned on their banners overhead
> Is the accusing silence of the dead.

Cannon became a leader of the Socialist Workers Party, whose members were followers of Leon Trotsky. Their open opposition to imperialist
aspects of the US war effort during the Second World War resulted in prison
sentences. From Sandstone Prison, Minnesota, in 1945, Cannon wrote to a
friend: "Of all the literary projects laid out, the one closest to my heart is
the book on labor leaders, and of that, the chapter on Parsons. I have long
felt a strong compulsion to do justice to the memory of 'the dear little man'
who stands above all others in my affection."[4] While this was a project never
finished, the example and ideas of Parsons and his comrades have continued
to resonate.

Something to Learn

Among radical labor activists of the 1870s and 1880s, Parsons was almost
without equal. An effective trade union and political organizer, orator, writer,
and editor, he would inevitably have played a major role in making the left

wing of the labor movement a force to reckon with throughout the United States, as he was already doing in Chicago. The forces of capitalist "law and order" recognized this. Not only were he and three of his comrades executed, but the movement he led in Chicago was savagely repressed.

Characteristically, liberal writers have been inclined to deplore the killing of the Haymarket martyrs but to also argue that they were hardly a threat to anyone since "scarcely more than fifty or seventy-five 'wage slaves' attended their 'mass meetings.'"[5] In fact, they regularly drew hundreds and sometimes thousands to their activities, and they led demonstrations for the eight-hour workday which brought Chicago to a standstill. More than simply honoring their memory, perhaps we can learn something from them.

In 1883 Albert Parsons was invited to address the West Side Philosophic Society of Chicago. He was well known as a leading labor radical. The society's members were the "elite": millionaires, judges, and generals, and their beautifully dressed wives and daughters. Perhaps those who invited him thought this a splendid opportunity for a dialogue. Or perhaps it was merely an unusual entertainment. Surveying his audience, Parsons began:

> I am not in the habit of speaking to men and women dressed in such fine raiment. The men I speak to nightly are the hard-fisted, greasy mechanics and laborers of our city, with the smell of shavings about their clothes. They wear no broadcloth—their constant struggle is to keep the wolf from the door. The women I speak to are those who work from ten to twelve hours a day for a pittance, and must be satisfied with an ordinary dress. But it is these greasy mechanics and these poor women that weave your broadcloth, your silk and satin; that shape into form your costly bonnets and feathers, and grind into exquisite beauty and shape the jewels I see about me, but which *they* cannot wear.

An eyewitness later recalled: "With these preliminary remarks, he secured the closest attention to one of the most eloquent, cutting, and defiant speeches I ever heard."[6]

The Making of a Revolutionary

This remarkable person had a remarkable past. Born in 1848, Parsons grew up in Texas and as a teenager joined the Confederate Army during the Civil War. But when the war ended, he became an outspoken Radical Republican, defending Black people's rights and the social reforms of Reconstruction. (In later years he commented that a key reason he took this stance was that after his parents' death when he was five years old, the woman who became his surrogate mother in his older brother's home was a slave known as "Aunt Ester," whom he loved and respected.) In 1872, Parsons married a beautiful dark-skinned woman named Lucy Gonzales, who claimed Spanish and Indian ancestry and who may also have been partly African American. After a few years, however, the Republican Party betrayed Blacks and poor whites by abandoning the Reconstruction program and allowing the well-to-do white racist elites to return to power throughout the South. An important aspect of this development was the use of massive violence through groups like the Ku Klux Klan. In 1874, Albert and Lucy Parsons fled Texas.

Arriving in the booming industrial city of Chicago, Parsons found work as a printer. A talented speaker and organizer, he soon became a leader in his local of the typographical workers union. He was also drawn into the Knights of Labor, the eight-hour movement, and the Workingmen's Party of the United States (WPUS), the first significant socialist party in this country, founded in 1876. Lucy also joined the WPUS and began to participate in the work of the labor movement.

There is a common misconception that the socialist movement of this time was made up exclusively of German immigrants who spent their time wrangling over radical doctrines brought from the old country, isolating themselves from American workers and ignoring American realities. It is true that a majority of those in the left wing of the labor movement were German, but the American working class was made up largely of immigrant workers, and the largest immigrant group in the US at this time was German American. A careful examination of the history of this period confirms Nathan Fine's assessment: "The intelligent and educated German worker and the idealistic intellectual brought their socialism with them to America. Immediately upon landing they set themselves the task of organizing their fellow-countrymen and then reaching out for the native and English-speaking workers . . . That socialism did not make greater strides in the leading capitalist country is no fault of the tireless and conscientious German-American wage earners, the pioneers of Marxism in America."[7]

One commentator has suggested that the influence of such people on Parsons "is an early example of the tendency of American leftists to look outside themselves for revolutionary guidance."[8] One could argue that there is also a strong tendency among some American leftists to denigrate "foreign doctrines" and glorify "native pragmatism." With Parsons we have the case of a Texan who came to Chicago where he was influenced by P. J. McGuire (a socialist speaker from New York City), George Schilling (a Chicago-based German American), Thomas J. Morgan (originally from Wales), and others who were influenced by the theories of Karl Marx and Ferdinand Lassalle

(German Jews), by the experiences of the German and British labor movements, et cetera. Because he was not a closed-minded provincial, Parsons became a socialist. Because the realities of capitalism, against which he was rebelling, were confined neither to Texas nor Chicago nor the United States, this openness to "outside influences" made sense.

The great labor uprising of 1877, a spontaneous mass strike, drew many thousands of working people into its vortex in cities and towns throughout the country. It had a profound impact on Parsons. The Chicago WPUS called a rally at the height of the upsurge, and Parsons found himself addressing a crowd of twenty thousand. He skillfully drew upon the rage and excitement of the assembled workers, integrating it with a class-struggle analysis, and outlined a clear and dramatic strategy:

> Let us reduce the hours of labor to one-half and then form a combination, and then demand what wages we want. In order to do this we have to combine in some kind of labor organization. . . . Let us understand our position. If we reduce our hours of labor, the bosses and capitalists will immediately purchase another machine to replace us. Let us then, immediately, reduce the hours of labor once more, and in that way we can keep pace with them. [Voices: "We can, every time."] . . . Let us remember that we are the working classes of America. Let us give the politician to understand that we don't want him about. We have no votes to give to the Republican or Democratic Party. [Voices: "Or the greenbackers either."] Let us remember that Democratic, Republican and Greenback parties are composed of the bosses of the country. [Voices: "you bet," and "hear, hear."] . . . Let the grand army of labor say who shall fill the legislative halls of this country.

Parsons concluded by emphasizing the revolutionary nature of this strategy:

> We take out of their hands the means by which they now enslave us. Let us not forget the fact that all wealth and civilization comes from labor, and labor alone. Let us not forget that while we work ten hours a day the capitalist puts the value of seven hours of it in his pocket. It rests with you to say whether we shall allow the capitalist to go on, or whether we shall organize ourselves. Will you organize? [Cries: "We will."] Well, then enroll your names in the grand army of labor, and if the capitalist engages in warfare against our rights, then we shall resist him with all the means that God has given us.[9]

Yet in Chicago, as elsewhere, the police and army violently suppressed the uprising. Parsons was promptly fired and blacklisted, then briefly arrested. He was told to "go back where you came from" and that if he tried to "make trouble" in Chicago he might be strung up on a lamppost. Instead, Parsons and his comrades increased their efforts. Thanks to the strong base they had in the trade union movement, the Chicago socialists actually elected four socialists to city council in 1878 and got twelve thousand votes for their mayoral candidate in 1879. The capitalist politicians began to respond by using fraud to eliminate socialist candidates. Workers were also severely pressured to "vote the right way" by their employers.

The socialists faced a challenge of a different kind with the election of Democrat Carter Harrison as mayor. A very rich and highly sophisticated businessman, Harrison actively sought support in the immigrant working-class neighborhoods. He assumed a pro-labor posture, and on occasion referred to himself as "somewhat of a socialist" (though, he added, of "the red-white-and-blue variety").[10] Although he was a strongly pro-business mayor, and allowed his police force to use strong-arm tactics against striking workers "when necessary," he backed some labor reforms and was not above appointing certain "respectable" socialists to positions in his administration. Not surprisingly, some Chicago socialists went over to the Democratic Party.

A majority held firm, however, and even became more militant. Parsons was among them. They wanted socialism, not crumbs and rhetoric. Yet by 1880 the socialist movement was facing a crisis. In 1877 the WPUS had been transformed into the Socialist Labor Party (SLP), after some members split away in order to concentrate exclusively on trade union organizing. Some who remained believed that simply through utilizing the electoral process, socialism could be voted into being. When it became clear that this could not be easily achieved, they decided to make an electoral deal with the reform-capitalist Greenback Labor Party. Many, including Parsons, believed that this was a betrayal of principle. They also began to argue that the workers would never achieve socialism—or even successfully resist the repressive measures of employers and the government—unless the workers armed themselves, a step which they openly began to advocate and carry out. The SLP split, with the bulk of the Chicago socialist movement sharing the standpoint of Parsons and the man who would become one of his closest comrades, August Spies, the editor of the socialist daily *Arbeiter-Zeitung*.

In the fall of 1883 a convention was held in Pittsburgh to form a new organization uniting the revolutionary-minded activists who had left the SLP. Its name was the International Working People's Association (IWPA), which within two years had eighty-nine sections in seventeen states, with a membership of twelve thousand. It also had eight newspapers—a majority in German, one in English—with over twenty-one thousand subscribers. Its strongest centers were in Chicago, where Parsons and Spies were the dominant personalities, and New York City, under the sway of Johann Most.

Anarchists or Marxists?

Johann Most was a German refugee, formerly a member of Parliament from the German Social Democratic Party. Critical of the party leaders' moderation, he carried on a factional fight that soon degenerated into personal attacks, bloodcurdling phrase-mongering, and violations of party discipline. Upon his expulsion from the party, Most gravitated toward the followers of the anarchist Mikhail Bakunin. He incorporated into his positions support for individual terrorism ("propaganda of the deed"), denunciations of organizational centralism, and a demand for the total abolition of the state. Upon arriving in the United States, Most presented himself as the most revolutionary interpreter of the ideas of Karl Marx, yet he also played a major role in popularizing many anarchist notions within the American movement.[11]

At the Pittsburgh convention, the "Pittsburgh Manifesto" was adopted, a statement blending ideas from the Declaration of Independence, the *Communist Manifesto*, and anti-centralist conceptions of Bakunin, all in an intransigently revolutionary tone. Yet there were differences in attitude within the IWPA. As one leading member of the Chicago IWPA later recalled: "One time the Pittsburgh program with which many were unsatisfied was discussed. Spies explained: 'The Pittsburgh program is secondary, our program is the *Communist Manifesto*.' . . . Spies had Parsons, Gorsuch and other Americans around him in the office of the *Arbeiter-Zeitung* on whom he impressed the basic teachings of the booklet."[12]

Parsons himself argued that "the IWPA was not founded by Bakunin." He traced its ancestry back to the International Workingmen's Association (the First International, headed by Marx), adding: "The distinctive feature of the manifesto of the Pittsburgh Labor Congress was opposition to centralized power, abolition of authoritative, compulsory or force government in any form. This is why we were, and are, designated anarchists . . . The IWPA is *not* in opposition to Marx . . . The first publication ever issued by the IWPA was written by Marx and Engels"—the *Communist Manifesto*, of which twenty-five thousand copies were distributed in one year.[13]

A study of the *Alarm*, the English-language paper of the IWPA, reveals many more positive references to Marx than to Bakunin. Parsons noted: "We are called by some Communists, or Socialists or Anarchists. We accept all

three of the terms." He defined anarchy as "a condition of society which has
no king, no emperor, president or ruler of any kind. In other words anarchy is
the social administration of all affairs by the people themselves."[14]

Another revealing text regarding Parsons's views on Marx is *Anarchism:
Its Philosophy and Scientific Basis*, a posthumously published volume that Parsons prepared. The book is divided into two parts. The first offers an explicitly Marxist analysis of capitalism, with lengthy extracts from the *Communist
Manifesto* and *Capital*. It also offers an outline of American history from colonial times to 1886, in which Parsons attempts to apply Marx's materialist conception of history to the United States. The second half of the book contains
extracts from speeches of Parsons and his codefendants at the Haymarket
trial, followed by several anarchist essays by Peter Kropotkin and others, con-
demning the institution of the state and describing a stateless communism.
These explicitly anarchist selections were undoubtedly appealing because the
Marxist analysis of the state—set out briefly in Marx's *Critique of the Gotha
Program* (published in the 1890s) and reconstructed in Lenin's *State and Revolution* (1917)—was not available to most socialists in this period, among whom
the statist orientation of Lassalle had some influence.

Thus, it's misleading to simply label people like Parsons and Spies "anarchists." The word had a different connotation for them than it does today.
The sharp differentiation between socialism and anarchism developed only
in later years. In fact, the so-called anarchists were far closer to revolutionary
Marxism than were the moderate leaders of the SLP. Perhaps more useful
than reflecting over labels is to look at the living movement that these revolutionaries helped to lead.

The Chicago Movement

Friedrich Sorge, a German American comrade of Marx and Engels, was
fiercely critical of both the SLP and of the IWPA as represented by Johann
Most. But his attitude toward the Chicago IWPA was different:

> Only the Chicagoans maintained a certain agreement of views and tac-
> tics, stayed in close touch with the trade unions and other organizations,
> and secured themselves great respect and importance among the working
> population of the city. This they took advantage of on various occasions
> and made the bourgeois authorities very uncomfortable ... At the head of
> the Chicago anarchists, indeed of the Chicago workers at that time, stood
> intelligent and energetic people. The Germans August Spies and Michael
> Schwab, the American Albert Parsons, the Englishman Samuel Fielden,
> supported by many others, were active and untiring agitators and the first

three also served as writers and editors of the *Arbeiter-Zeitung* and *Alarm*. To the aforementioned characteristics must also be added great courage, loyalty of conviction, and untouchable personal honor.[15]

The approach of the Chicagoans—a revolutionary rejection of electoralism and of the state, combined with a focus on building a mass working-class movement through trade union efforts and other struggles for economic justice—came to be tagged by historians as "the Chicago idea."[16]

The Chicago IWPA had thirteen hundred members (with perhaps three thousand at its high point), including an English-language section of about ninety people. Parsons and Spies estimated that it had about twenty thousand supporters in the city. The twice-monthly *Alarm* had a regular circulation of two to three thousand per issue, not counting ninety thousand free copies distributed each year.

The *Alarm* was a lively paper, filled with reports on strikes, demonstrations, and meetings; extensive correspondence and articles from working-class readers; stirring and fact-filled social commentaries; speculative opinion pieces; and educational articles on revolutionary theory. A variety of outlooks jostled each other in its pages. Parsons later explained: "They sent in their articles—Tom, Dick, and Harry; everybody wanted to have something to say, and I had no right to shut off anybody's complaint. The *Alarm* was a labor paper, and it was specifically published for the purpose of allowing every human being who wore the chains of monopoly to clank those chains in the columns of the *Alarm* . . . It was a free speech paper."[17]

While this made the *Alarm* an exciting paper to read, it also meant that many incendiary statements—including openly terroristic threats against the capitalists—were printed. The defenders of capitalist "law and order" later made use of this to victimize the movement.

The Chicago IWPA distributed about four hundred thousand books, pamphlets, and circulars over the course of one year. In addition, it often sent leading members on agitational tours as far west as Omaha, as far east as Pittsburgh, and as far south as St. Louis. In Chicago itself there were frequent open-air meetings on the lakefront—public lectures, parades, rallies, picnics, concerts, and festivals. These were often organized with great creative flair and an audacious and militant humor that appealed to large numbers of working people. Unlike many currents in the early labor movement, the IWPA was not for men only. "The trouble with these damned socialists," commented Police Captain John Bonfield, "is that they always have their wives and children with them. I wish I could have three or four thousand of them in a bunch, without their families, and then I would make short work of them."[18] But the revolutionaries didn't operate like that. The Chicago IWPA encouraged women to participate fully in the movement, and among the most visible of whom were Lucy Parsons and the assistant editor of the *Alarm*, Lizzie M. Swank.

One factor that gave the revolutionary movement great weight in Chicago was its deep roots in the trade union movement. There were about 250,000 wage workers in the city, perhaps 30,000 of whom were organized. About half of these were in the twenty-two unions affiliated with the Central Labor Union (CLU). Founded by members and supporters of the IWPA, its goal was the "destruction of the existing class rule by all means necessary—i.e., by energetic, relentless, revolutionary, and international action."[19] While the CLU's membership consisted primarily of immigrants, it should be remembered that over 40 percent of the working class and almost 70 percent of all union members in Illinois were foreign-born. Not satisfied with working exclusively among skilled workers of the craft unions, however, the IWPA also pioneered in reaching out to unskilled workers and the unemployed.

According to Friedrich Sorge, Chicago had "a very cosmopolitan population, one-third of which is German, almost as many Irish, and also Scandinavians, Italians, Poles, Czechs, French, and so forth. It is the undeniably meritorious accomplishment of the Chicago anarchists to have brought into this marvelous mixture of workers of all nationalities and languages a certain order, to have created affinity, and to have given the movement at that time unity and goals."[20]

Radical Labor Subculture

In the history of left-wing movements throughout the world, one finds— invariably and necessarily—the emergence of radical labor subcultures. In addition to significant socialist and communist and anarchist formations (in this case the IWPA), there is often an array of organizations formed around a variety of issues—groups and coalitions for labor rights and democracy, against war and militarism, against racial or gender oppression, against poverty and unemployment, et cetera. Educational classes and forums, books and pamphlets, newspapers and magazines, novels and short stories, songs and poems, plays and paintings, picnics and socials, marches and rallies— all blend together to create an expanding and deepening pool of ideas and sensibilities, of human relationships and a sense of solidarity, of insight and understanding. It was, in fact, a subculture (involving what the anthropologist Melville Herskovits called a "total body of belief, behavior, sanctions, values, and goals") that generated and nourished the kind of consciousness necessary for the sustained struggles that brought about a genuine power shift in US society to the benefit of the working-class majority.[21]

As Paul Avrich has put it, the revolutionaries of Chicago "developed a rich libertarian counterculture, deeply rooted in the working classes and totally at odds with the values of the prevailing system," reflecting instead the vision of "an alternative society, based on freedom, brotherhood, and equality, as opposed to the authority and privilege of the established order." Bruce C. Nelson, in the best study of this aspect of the Chicago movement, emphasizes that "what I am describing as a movement culture was not synonymous, numerically or institutionally, with working-class culture. Rather movement culture, which tried to draw upon or from the larger class culture, was always smaller." He notes that the largest event the IWPA movement was able to organize drew thirty-five thousand in a city of eight hundred thousand. He also stresses that "the socialist movement was too diverse and pluralist to have imposed any one ethnic culture on its membership."[22]

This movement subculture had many facets. There was, of course, literature—including several IWPA-connected newspapers in various languages (a total of fourteen if the entire country is included), including the German-language daily *Arbeiter-Zeitung*; plus a rich array of leaflets, pamphlets, and books. There were regular public forums and lectures on a variety of topics related to labor, socialism-communism-anarchism, and various problems of society; concerts and poetry recitations; plays; and more. Nor was this cultural scene merely something for spectators. Avrich tells of "a network of orchestras, choirs, theatrical groups, debating clubs, literary societies, and gymnastic and shooting clubs involving thousands of participants." Nelson notes, "The supposedly unwashed, wide-eyed, bomb-throwing anarchists held family picnics and went to dances." Sometimes there would be festivals combining all of these elements, plus special features such as "living tableaux," in which costumed men, women, and sometimes children would pose as living statues, representing stirring revolutionary scenes of the past. Attendance at smaller gatherings might number several dozen or several hundred, sometimes as many as three thousand, and the number at larger gatherings might number twenty thousand or more. Nelson observes that such events created a bond among the participants, a bond "produced and reinforced by a sense of pride in craftsmanship—of socialist songs well sung, of plays well acted, of pageants well staged."[23]

According to Nelson, there was ongoing discussion, an interchange of ideas, and circulation of and reading aloud from left-wing newspapers among especially the skilled workers who gathered in their workplaces, and Nelson comments on "the educational value of little forums existing in each shop." No less important, however, were places they could gather after work. "Saloons and beer-gardens—Grief's Hall, Zepf's Hall, Steinmueller's Hall, Neff's Hall—became bustling centers of radical life." Here one could find left-wing literature (in some cases articles were read aloud) and meeting rooms where radical workers held discussions. The public, and in particular the hostile capitalist press, often stressed the prominence of alcohol at the events. The focus in the news stories could be benign—a description of a socialist picnic might mention that the participants "enjoyed themselves much as any other band of picnickers largely composed of foreigners would have done, and went home in beery good nature." Or, in accounts of a march or demonstration, the focus could take a more menacing tone: "With the smell of gin and beer, with blood-red flags and redder noses, and with banners inscribed with revolutionary mottoes, the anarchists inaugurated their grand parade and picnic yesterday." (Yet Nelson argues that "these were not rag-tag marches but ordered and orderly processions.") The parades, marches, and processions were an essential IWPA activity—affording the movement "its greatest degree of public visibility," as Avrich observes, "designed above all to display the strength of the movement to its opponents and at the same time to encourage its supporters with a sense of their collective power."[24]

Avrich describes a typical parade in June 1885, which started off with two thousand workmen and their families marching through the center of Chicago with three bands playing, the Stars and Stripes in front, followed by twenty-three red flags. Innumerable banners had such slogans as these: "Poverty Is a Crime," "Exploitation Is Legalized Theft," "Anarchy," "Workingmen of the World Unite" and "No Rights Without Duties, No Duties Without Rights." By the time they had reached a picnic area, the crowd was four thousand strong. Before the picnicking began, there were brief speeches by Samuel Fielden in English and Michael Schwab in German, making the point that workers must organize and take their rights by force. Then the bands struck up "The Workers' Marseillaise"—

Ye sons of toil, awake to glory!
Hark, hark, what myriads bid you rise;
Your children, wives and grandsires hoary
Behold their tears and hear their cries!
Shall hateful tyrants mischief breeding,
With hireling hosts, a ruffian band
Affright and desolate the land,
While peace and liberty lie bleeding?

To arms! to arms! ye brave!
Th' avenging sword unsheathe!
March on, march on, all hearts resolved
On Victory or Death.

With luxury and pride surrounded,
The vile, insatiate despots dare,
Their thirst for gold and power unbounded
To mete and vend the light and air,
Like beasts of burden, would they load us,
Like gods would bid their slaves adore,
But Man is Man, and who is more?
Then shall they longer lash and goad us?

To arms! to arms! ye brave!
Th' avenging sword unsheathe!
March on, march on, all hearts resolved
On Victory or Death.

O, Liberty! can man resign thee?
Once having felt thy generous flame,
Can dungeon's bolts and bars confine thee?
Or whips, thy noble spirit tame?
Too long the world has wept bewailing,
That Falsehood's dagger tyrants wield;
But Freedom is our sword and shield;
And all their arts are unavailing!

To arms! to arms! ye brave!
Th' avenging sword unsheathe!
March on, march on, all hearts resolved
On Victory or Death.[25]

Such activities "provided a source of inspiration and promoted a feeling of solidarity and strength, of their own dignity and worth, which many had previously lacked," Avrich writes. "Within the bosom of a society that they detested, they found a spirit of camaraderie and warmth, of devotion to a common cause." The very same activities "sent shivers of fear through the propertied classes" he points out. "The extremism of the [IWPA's] opposition to existing institutions, the totality of its commitment to the overthrow of the established order, could not but alarm the city's prosperous residents."[26]

Free Speech, Violence, and "Diversity of Tactics"

We have seen that Parsons viewed the paper he edited as "a free speech news-paper," since "everybody wanted to have something to say." He and August Spies also saw as their duty the task of making available to readers and com-rades the thinking of a broad range of revolutionary thinkers.

Among those thinkers were Mikhail Bakunin, who romantically extolled the liberating qualities of violence, and his disciple Sergei Nechayev, who composed a *Catechism for Revolutionaries*, advocating grotesque uses of vio-lence and manipulation. Johann Most composed *Revolutionary War Science*, showing how to make and use dynamite bombs and other destructive devices, with the rationale: "Our enemies have never been fastidious in their methods of the people . . . Let us therefore have an eye for an eye . . . We say murder the murderers. Rescue mankind through blood, iron, poison, and dynamite."[27]

All of this appeared in *Arbeiter-Zeitung* and the *Alarm*, along with a much larger number of qualitatively different writings by (or influenced by) the cre-ative anarchist theorist Peter Kropotkin—who thoughtfully theorized what the hoped-for future society would look like—and the American antistat-ist Benjamin Tucker (who would soon evolve rightward to develop positions contributing to contemporary pro-capitalist libertarianism), not to mention those by socialists Karl Marx, Ferdinand Lassalle, and others, as well as more practical reports and analyses of experiences, struggles, and questions facing workers in Chicago and beyond.[28]

Workers who latched on to one or another idea in this heady mix were given the space to speak their minds in the pages of the *Alarm*. Some might offer thoughts on the positive qualities or limitations of trade unions or con-sumer cooperatives or socialism. But there was also room for local activist Gerhard Lizius to enthuse: "Dynamite! Of all the good stuff, this is the stuff." Lizius went on to fantasize: "Stuff several pounds of this sublime stuff into an inch of pipe, gas or water pipe, plug up both ends, insert a cap with fuse attached, place this in the immediate neighborhood of a lot of rich loafers who live by the sweat of other people's brows, and light the fuse. A most cheerful and gratifying result will follow."[29]

At the same time, a more serious consideration of revolutionary violence was percolating among many socialist-communist-anarchist labor activists, such as Spies and Parsons. What were the implications that flowed from their deepening conception of the class struggle as well as the nature of capital-ism and of the capitalist state? Violence is built into the very nature of cap-italism, and most capitalists will not hesitate to use violence and killing to advance their interests and to maximize their profits. The state is basically controlled by the capitalists and operates (again using violence and killing) to perpetuate and expand the ability of capitalists to maximize their profits at the expense of everyone else. What does this mean for serious working-class activists wishing to create a society of the free and the equal, liberated from all oppression and exploitation and violence?

They honestly wrestled with such questions, testing out ideas and considering options. In seeking to honestly communicate their evolving notions with others, Parsons and his comrades were not inclined to be diverted into using "defensive formulations" that might offer protection from powerful civil authorities. Because they were new to some of the questions and ideas they were wrestling with, some of their writings and speeches also had a "thinking out loud" quality that suggested dramatic short cuts in logic and reasoning, inconsistent with their more mature perspectives and, for that matter, with reality. Historian James Green has cogently elaborated on this:

> The Chicago anarchists fell in love with the idea of dynamite as the great equalizer in class warfare. "One man with a dynamite bomb is equal to one regiment," wrote one of the *Alarm*'s correspondents in a typically exaggerated claim. On several occasions in public speeches and newspaper articles, Parsons and Spies advocated its use in revolutionary warfare; they seemed enamored of its scientific mystique, but they also valued dynamite because its potential power promised to instill a sense of courageous manhood in workers intimidated by the police and the militia. No one outdid Lucy Parsons in her fantastic claims for the importance of explosives: "The voice of dynamite is the voice of force, the only voice that tyranny has ever been able to understand," she proclaimed.

"If anarchists like Spies and Albert and Lucy Parsons indulged in 'bomb talking' to frighten the authorities and to encourage their followers," Green added, "there were, among their comrades, other men, men of few words, frustrated militants who were prepared to make and use bombs in the showdown they expected to come."[30]

This approach was reflected in the Lehr und Wehr Verein (Educational and Defense Society), paramilitary workers' militia units—originally organized in the late 1870s for "self-defense" in struggles against the various armed forces of capitalism—that would regularly engage in target practice and military drills. Although they never actually took action in real-life battles, some comrades saw them as an important reserve for the revolutionary future. It is estimated that four hundred or so IWPA members were involved in such units.[31] The drift toward revolutionary violence was reflected even more in the increasingly industrious making and distribution of bombs (pioneered by

Johann Most in the New York area, but most notoriously carried out in Chicago by Louis Lingg, a recently arrived working-class immigrant).

At the same time, there were currents within the IWPA arguing that people such as August Spies and Michael Schwab (and, of course, Parsons) were far too moderate and insufficiently "serious" about the actual need for revolutionary violence. George Engel, Adolph Fischer, and Gottfried Waller were among the leaders of a left faction that controlled the North-West Side Group of the IWPA and had the support of less than one-fourth of the Chicago IWPA's German-speaking members. Paul Avrich refers to this faction as the Intransigents and has described them this way:

> What they lacked in numbers . . . they made up in revolutionary zeal. Their adherents were anarchists of an implacable and ultra-militant stamp . . . Where Spies and Schwab concentrated on building a solid base of support among the workers, Engel and Fischer pinned their hopes on small, independent action groups, devoted to armed insurrection and propaganda by the deed. Impatient for the social revolution, which they expected at any moment, they called for the complete destruction of the established order by force.[32]

Although a majority of workers in the movement were not inclined to turn away from Spies and Parsons to follow Engel and Fischer, the message of this minority faction had some resonance among radicalizing workers who were drawn to the banners of the IWPA. Despite their minority status, the Intransigents represented an ongoing pressure on the movement led by Spies and Parsons. To avoid being outflanked by the Intransigents, leaders of the IWPA majority undoubtedly felt a need to utilize extreme rhetoric, thereby buttressing their revolutionary credibility as they sought to maintain their majority—also trying to pull Engels and Fischer back from a destructive direction. Ideologically, as well, they felt a pressure to allow for a diverse set of libertarian tactics.

There are numerous indications, however, of sharp tensions. They are reflected in remarks by William Holmes, a Parsons confidante who was married to the *Alarm*'s coeditor Lizzie Swank. Referring to an earlier demonstration, he commented, "Several of our comrades were armed and prepared to defend themselves to the death against any onslaught by the police," and he wrote that there were those looking for "the opportunity to carry out desperate projects already conceived." He later observed "there was a movement afoot to precipitate the social revolution," and he wrote to a friend on the eve of the massive demonstration of May 1, 1886:

These are stirring times, but it is my humble opinion there are still more desperate days to come *very soon*. I hope the revolution will not come too soon—or rather the revolt—of course the revolution cannot come before a reality before its time. But what I fear sometimes is that we may grow too impatient and endeavor to hasten it; which will only result in disastrous failure.[33]

During the unfolding of the momentous events of early May, there is a record of sharp differences, and (as it turns out) only partial reconciliation, between Fischer and Spies around key tactical issues—in part flowing from a May 3 meeting of the Intransigent faction. Spies complained to one of his comrades that an implementation of some of Fischer's proposals would mean "there will be trouble, and I don't want that. That will break up our organization."[34] As it turned out, this is what happened—although at first the mass action orientation of Spies and Parsons seemed on the verge of triumph.

May Day, 1886

May Day, the international workers' holiday, originated on American soil. In 1884 and 1885 the Federation of Organized Trades and Labor Unions, the immediate forerunner of the American Federation of Labor (AFL), had passed resolutions demanding "that eight hours shall constitute a legal day's labor from and after May 1, 1886," and calling for a nationwide general strike on that day to force the realization of the demand.[35]

Some of the leaders of the federation—Adolph Strasser, Samuel Gompers, P. J. McGuire—had been part of the socialist movement and had not yet abandoned all of their radical convictions. Yet their federation was then a relatively weak alliance of unions with a combined membership of only 50,000. The far more prestigious 700,000-member Knights of Labor also favored the eight-hour workday. But this organization was led by the domineering Grand Master Workman Terrence V. Powderly, who was anxious to preserve the "respectability" of the Knights and therefore used all of his influence to prevent the local assemblies of his organization from participating in this militant action.

Yet the demand caught the imagination of growing numbers of American workers. They generally worked from ten to sixteen hours a day and experienced deteriorating working conditions and living standards as the robber barons of industrial capitalism transformed the US economy in the decades following the Civil War. The enthusiasm for the May Day proposal was part of a general labor upsurge that swept many into the struggle. The table below tells much of the story.

Year	Strikes in the US	Establishments Struck	Number of Workers Involved
1884	443	2,367	147,054
1885	645	2,284	242,705
1886	1,411	9,891	499,489

An increasing number of workers' strikes and demonstrations in the United States were for the eight-hour day. By the second week in May 1886, 340,000 workers were united in the "eight hours" battle, and 190,000 actually put down their tools and went on strike for it. Of these, 80,000 struck in the city of Chicago.[36]

At first the Chicago International Working People's Association (IWPA) had been inclined to follow the lead of Johann Most in New York City, who dismissed the eight-hour movement as an "unrevolutionary" reform that probably couldn't be won anyway. The only reasonable course of action, Most preached, was social revolution. He urged workers to arm themselves, make dynamite bombs, and prepare to kill the tyrants who oppressed them. But this was irrelevant bombast with little mass appeal. The enthusiastic response of the working class to the eight-hour demand, on the other hand, forced the thoughtful revolutionaries of Chicago to reconsider the question and finally to throw themselves into the upsurge.

The moderate wing of the Chicago labor movement had sought to make the eight-hour movement eminently respectable. The moderates denied that the demand was in any way revolutionary (they were happy to agree with Most on that), and they tried to make it more palatable to the business community by calling for eight hours' work with a consequent reduction in pay. But the radical wing of the movement, led by the IWPA, insisted on eight hours' work with no pay reduction. Historian Henry David notes that the revolutionaries' "labors were extensive, and were to some degree responsible for the scope and vigor of the movement in Chicago." According to Friedrich Sorge, they virtually "took over the leadership of it in Chicago."[37] Indeed, the city was unique because it had the best organized labor movement and the most effective revolutionary working-class leaders in the country.

Albert Parsons and other IWPA leaders had concluded that, with the uncompromising demand they advanced, this struggle *did* have revolutionary implications. The *Alarm*, describing a meeting that the IWPA organized for unskilled workers, reported:

Parsons thought the organization of the vast body of unskilled and unorganized laboring men and women a necessity, in order that they might formulate their demands and make an effective defense of their rights. He thought the attempt to inaugurate the eight-hour system would break down the capitalist system and bring about such disorder and hardship that the Social Revolution would become a necessity. As all roads in ancient times lead to Rome, so now all labor movements of whatever character inevitably lead to socialism.[38]

Parsons and his comrades were explicit about their views and intentions, but they had built up substantial authority among a large sector of Chicago's workers over the years. Meetings and demonstrations throughout March and April drew tens of thousands of participants. On the target day of May 1, over thirty thousand Chicago workers were on strike demanding ten hours' pay for eight hours' work. At least sixty thousand were in the streets, demonstrating peacefully but militantly for this demand. And the struggle showed every sign of escalating.

While some employers were beginning to capitulate to the intensifying pressure of the workers, most were resisting and preparing a counterattack. Leading businessmen formed a special committee of the so-called Citizens' Association of Chicago, a committee that met in almost continuous session "for the purpose of agreeing upon a plan of action in case the necessities of the situation should demand intervention in any way."[39]

Haymarket

The capitalists had substantial resources, in addition to their massive economic power. As Henry David has shown, the Chicago police force had been "long used as if it were a private force in the service of the employers."[40] This was augmented by Pinkerton detectives, units from the state militia, and federal troops if necessary. Then there were the newspapers which they controlled and used to shape public opinion.

On May 1, the Chicago *Mail* editorialized: "There are two dangerous ruffians at large in this city; two sneaking cowards who are trying to create trouble. One of them is named Parsons; the other is named Spies . . . Mark them for today. Keep them in view. Hold them personally responsible for any trouble that occurs. Make an example of them if trouble does occur."[41]

May Day passed, but the struggle was clearly not resolved. On May 3, a clash between police and workers took place at the McCormick Harvester factory. The police fired into the crowd of workers, wounding many and killing at least two (while suffering no serious injuries themselves). This attack set off a wave of indignation in Chicago's labor movement.

On the evening of May 4, a hastily organized protest meeting was held in Haymarket Square. Spies, Parsons, and Samuel Fielden addressed a crowd of about three thousand. Rain clouds began to gather as the final speaker, Fielden, neared the end of his speech. Many began to leave at that point, including Spies and Parsons. As Fielden was drawing his remarks to a close, a force of 180 police, led by the much-hated John ("Black Jack") Bonfield, appeared in order to break up the rally. Fielden asserted that the gathering was peaceful, then stepped down from the platform. At this point, someone threw a dynamite bomb, which exploded in the ranks of the police. They, in turn, opened fire on the workers. Some workers had guns and shot back. Seven policemen and at least seven workers died; many more were injured on both sides.

With this, the capitalist counteroffensive began in earnest. Neither the revolutionaries nor the moderates in the labor movement were prepared for what was in store for them.

Labor's "friend," Mayor Harrison, issued a proclamation declaring that since crowds, processions, and public gatherings were "dangerous," he had authorized the police to break them up if they occurred. The police did much more than this. By May 7 dozens of left-wing offices, meeting halls, saloons, and private homes had been raided, and over two hundred arrests had been made. Police Captain Michael J. Schaack, who headed these operations, boasted that "a series of searches kept up night and day for two weeks, and no house or place where an Anarchist or Socialist resided escaped police attention."[42] Indeed not. As historian Harvey Wish later commented: "Homes were invaded without a warrant and ransacked for evidence; suspects were beaten and subjected to the 'third degree'; individuals ignorant of the meaning of socialism and anarchism were tortured by the police, sometimes bribed as well, to act as witnesses for the state."[43]

The capitalist press whipped up a hysterical campaign. For example, the *Chicago Tribune* of May 6 declared: "These serpents have been warmed and nourished in the sunshine of toleration until at last they have been emboldened to strike at society, law, order, and government." With the exception of a few labor journals, the reportage and editorials of newspapers throughout the country were the same. Even some of the moderate labor spokesmen were gripped by panic, denouncing "the cowardly murderers, cutthroats and robbers, known as anarchists . . . They are entitled to no more consideration than wild beasts."[44]

In the wave of reaction, hysteria, and fear that followed the Haymarket tragedy, the revolutionary movement was crushed, and the eight-hour and trade union movements were thrown into disarray. Strikes were broken, eight-hour struggles petered out, and state legislatures began passing anti-labor bills.

Several years later, Captain Schaack's superior—Chief of Police Ebersold, with whom Schaack was then feuding—revealed that the brave captain had "wanted to keep things stirring. He wanted bombs to be found here, there, all around everywhere . . . After we got the anarchist societies broken up, Schaack wanted to send out men to organize new societies right away . . . He wanted to keep the thing boiling, keep himself prominent before the public."[45] For a while, at least, Captain Schaack got his way, with the blessing of his friends in the business community. Schaack freely acknowledged that he received "funds . . . supplied to me by public-spirited citizens who wished the law vindicated and order preserved in Chicago."[46]

Trial and Execution

In this atmosphere, eight men were tried for murder—Albert Parsons, August Spies, George Engel, Adolph Fischer, Louis Lingg, Michael Schwab, Samuel Fielden, and Oscar Neebe. All pleaded "not guilty" and offered an eloquent defense of their actions and beliefs. But a hostile judge and a well-chosen jury were unmoved. The prosecution, and also the newspapers, made ample use of the most terroristic IWPA utterances to "prove" that the unknown Haymarket bomb-thrower had simply been carrying out the instructions of the defendants. It was proved that Louis Lingg was a maker and distributor of bombs. Several IWPA members of the Intransigent faction of the IWPA (such as Gottfried Waller) were broken and became witnesses for the prosecution, testifying that there had been discussions about taking the struggle to a "higher level" and intentions to use violence against the police. Nor was their cause helped by the grand jury testimony of Intransigent Gerhard Lizius, who responded with a decisive "yes" when asked whether he believed that "the man who threw the bomb over there did right" and that "it was a righteous act in shooting down policemen." Lizius then added: "The only mistake the Anarchists made was in not using enough bombs." (Being a man already dying of consumption saved Lizius from himself being brought to trial.)[47]

Much of labor's mainstream recoiled in fear and horror at the rhetoric, the violence, and the onslaught of repression and red-baiting aimed at "the Chicago anarchists." Defenders of the status quo aggressively sought to link bombs and violence to the labor movement in general. Soon, however, the labor movement as a whole rallied to support the Haymarket defendants. Even moderate Samuel Gompers of the AFL felt that "labor must do its best to maintain justice for the radicals or find itself denied the rights of free men." By December the official journal of the Chicago Knights of Labor asserted

that "public opinion has turned completely around regarding the eight con-
victed anarchists . . . within the past few months."[48]

But little mercy and no justice would be granted—or at least this was
the most widespread twentieth-century verdict among scholars familiar with
the case, largely influenced by the judgment of Governor John Peter Altgeld
exonerating the Haymarket martyrs several years later. A more recent conclusion has been advanced by a scholar, Timothy Messer-Kruse, who sifted
through evidence and trial records—"that Chicago's anarchists were part of
an international terrorist network and did hatch a conspiracy to attack police
with bombs and guns that May Day weekend," and that "by the standards of
the age, the trial was fair, the jury representative, and the evidence establishing most of the defendants' guilt overwhelming."[49]

Messer-Kruse is able to demonstrate what the prosecution demonstrated.
Bakunin, Nechayev, and Most, as well as a number of "propagandists of the
deed" who had assassinated monarchs and other perceived tyrants in various
countries, definitely existed and influenced the IWPA—hence the Chicago
activists can be linked to "an international terrorist network." Bombs were
made and distributed, men with guns performed drills in the paramilitary
Lehr und Wehr Verein, incendiary rhetoric was common, and the Intransigent faction gathered to discuss ways and means of taking the struggle to
a "higher level." Such realities were established earlier by such historians as
Henry David, Paul Avrich, and James Green (although Messer-Kruse, unfortunately, gives the impression that this is not the case).

What Messer-Kruse is not able to demonstrate is that Parsons, Spies,
Schwab, and Fielden were actually connected with the specific discussions
or plans of the Intransigents, a faction that was, in fact, extremely critical of
them for being too "moderate." Nor is he able to demonstrate some clear plan
on the part of the Intransigents—aside from revolutionary posturing, sloppy
thinking, and half-baked tactical discussions, culminating in irresponsible
actions. Nor does he even try to refute, or to seriously address, the question of
whether the defenders of capitalism and the corporations intended to use the
Haymarket events to smash what they saw as a growing threat to the smooth
functioning of their system. Nor is he inclined to address seriously the point
made by Governor Altgeld regarding the more general and persistent context
established by the violent repression of the status quo: "While some men
may tamely submit to being clubbed and to seeing their brothers shot down,
there are some who will resent it, and will nurture a spirit of hatred and seek
revenge for themselves."[50]

Yet, as Avrich points out, "Fielden, in all probability, never touched a
pistol or saw a bomb in his life," and "as for Parsons, Spies, and Schwab, they

were men of ideals who, especially in time of economic distress, made rash and provocative statements, but themselves did nothing more violent than assist in the arming of the workers in preparation for what they regarded as the inevitable confrontation with capital."[51]

Neebe, a minor figure in the Chicago movement, was sentenced to eighteen years in prison. The others were sentenced to death. Schwab and Fielden appealed for clemency, and their sentence was changed to life imprisonment. Parsons and Spies seemed to have felt that it was wrong to separate themselves from the Intransigents, and that—while insisting on their innocence—they should be prepared die for their revolutionary convictions. Lingg died under mysterious circumstances while awaiting execution—it seems he committed suicide with a bomb that was smuggled in to him. On November 11, 1887, Spies said on the scaffold: "The time will come when our silence will be more powerful than the voices you strangle today!" Engel and Fischer shouted a couple of slogans. The trap was sprung when Parsons was attempting to say his final words, and the four men plunged into their final moments of strangulation.[52]

Two days after the executions, a funeral cortege followed the victims' caskets to Waldheim Cemetery. Six thousand marched behind the coffins, and a quarter of a million lined the streets. Fifteen thousand attended the burial exercises.

In 1893, as new governor, John Peter Altgeld freed Schwab, Fielden, and Neebe. In his 17,000-word message of pardon, Altgeld demonstrated that the martyrs had been railroaded by a hostile court because of their revolutionary beliefs.

The Legacy

In Nevada in 1886 there was a seventeen-year-old miner who often talked with a coworker named Pat Reynolds, a veteran member of the Knights of Labor. "It was some time before I got the full significance of a remark that he made, that if the working class was to be emancipated, the workers themselves must accomplish it," the young miner said. "Early in May, 1886, this thought was driven more deeply into my mind by reading in the newspapers the details of the Haymarket Riot, and later the speeches that were made by the men who were put to trial. The facts and details I talked over every day with Pat Reynolds . . . It was a turning point in my life. I told Pat that I would like to join the Knights of Labor."[53] This young miner was William D. ("Big Bill") Haywood, who later led the Industrial Workers of the World (IWW).

By 1898 so prominent a trade union leader as Eugene V. Debs was saying of the Haymarket martyrs: "I would rescue their names from slander. The slanderers of the dead are the oppressors of the living."[54] Debs soon went on to help organize the Socialist Party of America, and as the leader of its revolutionary wing he helped to spread the martyrs' ideas.

When Lucy Parsons joined Debs and Haywood at the founding convention of the IWW in 1905, she voiced the same commitments for which she and Albert Parsons had given so much twenty years before. She now called it revolutionary socialism and concluded, "I hope even now to live to see the day when the first dawn of the new era of labor will have arisen, when capitalism will be a thing of the past, and the new industrial republic, the commonwealth of labor, shall be in operation."[55]

This vision, the ideas, the example of Albert Parsons and his comrades remained vibrant long after they died—and they continue to reverberate down to our own time. Just as conscious workers have, over the past century, pondered their meaning, so must we.[56]

Parsons and Spies were among the finest that our working class has produced. But what is more, from a close reading of what they actually said and wrote and did, we see how they represented a revolutionary socialist current that had far more in common with the later revolutionary Marxism of Rosa Luxemburg's *Mass Strike* and Lenin's *State and Revolution* than has been generally assumed. The influence of Johann Most, Bakunin, and others caused them sometimes to veer toward individual-terrorist rhetoric and sectarian "purism," *but at decisive moments* they veered back to their touchstone: a commitment to dynamically linking, in practice, the immediate struggles of the working class with the struggle for socialism. They grappled with revolutionary perspectives far more seriously than did other labor radicals of their time, and for them its connection with practical politics was intimate.

Their outlook contained not only an inspiring vision but also considerable sophistication, which made them a force to be reckoned with. Yet it also contained fatal ambiguities and even primitiveness, which helped the authorities to reckon with them in a murderously successful fashion. Their hope that the eight-hour movement would generate a revolution did not take into consideration the lack of revolutionary leadership outside of Chicago. Their decentralist predilections helped guarantee that the successes of the Chicago IWPA would not be duplicated in other cities. Their failure to break with and openly challenge the terroristic bombast of Johann Most (violent rhetoric not backed up with real working-class strength), presumably respecting a diversity-of-tactics silence (not *openly* taking issue with what one sees as self-defeating rhetoric or tactics of other activists), contributed to the irrelevance of the IWPA outside of Chicago, and helped make it vulnerable to repression in Chicago itself. Sometimes open debate is essential for building a genuinely revolutionary movement.

While it can be argued that these revolutionary activists made serious mistakes, they clearly had great strengths. One of their finest qualities was a deep thoughtfulness that enabled them to learn from mistakes and move forward. The tragedy is that certain of their mistakes helped the defenders of the status quo destroy them before they had time to continue their growth, which had been steady up to 1886. Those who have embraced their legacy can and must learn from their strengths as well as their weaknesses. But it would have made a profound difference if Parsons and his comrades themselves had enjoyed the opportunity to deepen their revolutionary understanding and continue their work beyond 1887. It is conceivable that this would have resulted in a stronger, more radical working-class movement than what actually developed in the United States.

With deterministic "wisdom," many labor historians have seen the revolutionary activists' failure as inevitable: they failed because they had to fail. Reality has spoken.

Yet reality often contains more than one possibility. Had these amazingly perceptive and energetic and talented leaders not been eliminated, if they had been able to continue developing, is it a foregone conclusion that they would have been either utterly conservatized (as the leaders of the AFL were) or without influence in the labor movement? The rise and influence of labor radicals in the two decades following the Haymarket Riot—Debs, Haywood, and others—suggests that this should not be a foregone conclusion. If they had remained a potent force in Chicago, with consequent growing national influence, how would this have altered the course of American labor history? What would have happened if Debs and Haywood had been able to join an already strong left-wing labor current rather than trying to forge one themselves?

This also poses a serious philosophical question: Can the elimination of a handful of individuals, particularly a man like Albert Parsons, really alter history's course? Determinists of both conservative and radical persuasion answer "no" with equal satisfaction. This, however, may be a question to be resolved not by philosophers, but by activists.

3

Brookwood Labor College

B rookwood Labor College, one of the outstanding educational institutions in the United States, played an essential part in the training of labor activists—intellectually and organizationally—who in the 1930s revitalized the labor movement through the creation of the Congress of Industrial Organizations (CIO). Established in Katonah, New York, in 1921, it was animated by the tension between (a) an institutionalized union movement functioning as part of a capitalist economy and (b) the vision of democratic and militant workers' struggles to create a future free from oppression and exploitation. The tension increased and culminated in fissures among the school's founders and faculty, and finally in Brookwood's closing in 1937.

Workers' Education and Brookwood's Beginnings

In the wake of the radicalization that issued from the disillusionment over World War I and the hopes generated by the Russian Revolution, many left-wing trade unionists and radical educators in the United States—in part influenced by workers' education efforts in England—moved to establish "labor colleges" across the United States. In 1921, a Workers' Education Bureau was created to help coordinate such efforts, and its first president was James Maurer, who explained that "the underlying purpose of workers' education is the desire for a better social order . . . and the ultimate liberation of the working masses." He urged that it not be utilized to help students rise out of the working class, but rather that it help them to "serve the labor movement in particular and society in general."

Some workers' education efforts took the form of evening classes sponsored by unions and central labor councils, whereas others involved summer schools, such as the Bryn Mawr Summer School for Women or the Wisconsin School for Workers (affiliated with the University of Wisconsin). A third form consisted of residential labor schools, of which Brookwood Labor College was the most prominent.

At the end of World War I, well-to-do pacifists William and Helen Fincke, deeply influenced by Walter Rauschenbusch's Christian Socialist

Social Gospel perspective and by John Dewey's approach to progressive education, had sought to establish a school for working-class children in Westchester County, on a beautiful wooded estate about forty miles from New York City. After consulting with their close friends Toscan and Josephine Bennett and concluding that the effort should be shifted in the direction of workers' education, the Finckes called a conference of left-wing labor activists to discuss such a project at the proposed site in Katonah, New York.

Even at the start of the relatively conservative 1920s, the time seemed right for the convergence of radicalized labor activists and socially conscious educators. Veteran labor militant James Maurer complained that in the mainstream educational system "our children are being trained like dogs and ponies, not developed as individuals." He denounced "uniformity of thought and conduct, no originality of self-reliance except for money-making schemes, a worshipful attitude toward those who have wealth and power, intolerance for anything that the business element condemns, and ignorance of the great social and economic forces that are shaping the destinies of all of us." In the opinion of idealistic teacher Josephine Colby, "the labor movement is more and more a factor in democracy and if we hold to our slogan, 'Education for Democracy,' we will have in some way to acknowledge that the labor movement is one of the most, if not the most, important factors in progress." With Shakespearean flourish, she reflected: "Education for democracy without education for service in the labor movement is presenting the play of Hamlet with Hamlet left out."

Among those who gathered at Katonah were John Brophy, president of District 2 of the United Mine Workers of America; Jay Brown, president of the International Timber Workers Union; Fannia Cohn, education director of the International Ladies' Garment Workers' Union; John Fitzpatrick, president of the Illinois Federation of Labor; Charles Kutz, head of Pennsylvania Railroad employees in the International Association of Machinists; Abraham Lefkowitz, vice president of the American Federation of Teachers; James Maurer, president of the Pennsylvania Federation of Labor; A. J. (Abraham Johannes) Muste, president of the Amalgamated Textile Workers of America; Joseph Schlossberg, secretary-treasurer of the Amalgamated Clothing Workers of America; and Rose Schneiderman, president of the Women's Trade Union League. They agreed on four basic points that would be the basis for the establishment of Brookwood Labor College:

1. A new social order was needed and was coming—in fact, it was already on the way.
2. Education would not only hasten its coming, but would also reduce to a minimum and perhaps entirely eliminate the need to resort to violent methods.
3. The workers themselves would usher in the new social order.
4. There was an immediate need for a workers' college with a broad curriculum, located amid healthy country surroundings, where the students could completely apply themselves to the task at hand.

A socialist perspective lay at the core of Brookwood's philosophy, but it was intimately intertwined with a commitment to practical trade union organizing within the AFL framework. "Socialist ideas were not offered as a substitute for trade unionism, but rather as a supplement, a means of strengthening the union," John Brophy explained. He and the others formed a board of directors for the Brookwood Labor College, and they selected A. J. Muste to head the school. A tall, lean thirty-six-year-old who had been an effective leader of the 1919 Lawrence Textile Strike, Muste had been a scholarly pastor, associated with the pacifist Fellowship of Reconciliation, and animated by the Social Gospel and by an enthusiasm for the socialism of Eugene V. Debs.

Although day-to-day activities at Brookwood would be determined by the faculty in consultation with the students, policy was set by the ten-person board of directors. The board would be made up of labor representatives, with a nonvoting Educational Advisory Committee, and with representatives of the faculty having four votes and of the students having two votes.

Fifteen students enrolled in 1921, and eventually the yearly number of students would average fifty. This was the beginning of a venture that would eventually educate close to five hundred organizers and activists who would later help transform the American political scene.

A. J. Muste's Faculty and Students

With a few significant exceptions, the workers enrolled at Brookwood Labor College were young labor radicals who were either open to or already influenced by various currents of left-wing thought. One early Brookwood student, Len De Caux, later described Brookwood's director in this way:

A. J. Muste was the man who ran Brookwood, resident labor college, of the Twenties. We could not then have imagined his later career as militant activist in radical and pacifist causes—in his eighties he matched

the youth as man of action against the Vietnam war. To us young Brook-
wooders, A. J. was essentially the moderate. We respected his counsels of
caution, practicality, a relative labor conformism. But our favorite crack
was that he always looked for the center with his "On the one hand . . .
But on the other hand . . ." I would have expected him to progress ever
rightward, a typical social-democrat. Youthful impatients, we didn't suspect that fires like our own might burn beneath the diplomatic calm of
this lean and eager man.

Muste's own evaluation of the faculty, staff, and students at Brookwood
is also revealing. "Above all, the men and women . . . with whom I worked
closely for a decade or more at Brookwood, in the general field of workers'
education, and in various phases of labor organization and strike activity, were
people of integrity," Muste later recalled. "They had their shortcomings, in a
few cases distressing or irritating ones, but they were solid and clean, incapable
of playing cheap politics, though by no means political babes or bunglers."
   Muste himself taught courses in the history of Western civilization and
the United States. Specializing in US and international labor history was
David J. Saposs, who had been a student and associate of John R. Commons
and had co-authored with Commons, Selig Perlman, and others the classic
History of Labor in the United States. His minor classic *Left-Wing Unionism:
A Study of Radical Policies and Tactics* (whose arguments against radical "dual
unionism" coincided with those of William Z. Foster) was published by the
Communist Party's International Publishers in 1926—though Saposs was not
a member of the Communist Party (Brookwood students remembered him
as being more moderate than Muste) and was destined to become a member
of the National Labor Relations Board. Mark Starr, who taught economics
and labor journalism, had been involved in the National Council of Labor
Colleges of England; he would later become education director of the International Ladies' Garment Workers' Union and co-author of a standard popular text, *Labor in America* (1944), for use in high schools and labor education
classes in the late 1940s and 1950s. He met his future wife, Helen Norton (a
rail worker's daughter and college graduate from Kansas), on the Brookwood
faculty, where she trained students in labor journalism and helped them produce a periodical, the *Brookwood Review.*
   One of the most popular and most radical of the teachers was Arthur
W. Calhoun. Calhoun had an undergraduate degree from the University of
Pittsburgh and a PhD from the University of Wisconsin, and teaching experience at Clark University; he was also the author of the pioneering three-volume *Social History of the American Family from Colonial Times to the Present*

and taught sociology, economics, and even courses in Marxism (reflected in his 1927 volume *A Worker Looks at Government*), while his wife Mildred taught courses in English. Calhoun was replaced in 1929 by an instructor from the Seattle Labor College, John C. Kennedy. Another popular Brookwood stalwart was Josephine Colby, a high school teacher with a degree from the University of California; she was an instructor in English (also teaching English as a second language to many of the immigrant workers who came to Brookwood), literature, and public speaking, and directed many of the plays put on by the Brookwood Labor Players. Tom Tippett, who developed as an energetic labor educator during his years as a radical mineworkers' organizer, served as director of Brookwood's extension program, organizing classes for central labor councils, state labor federations, and local unions. According to one student, he was "a stimulating and colorful teacher who correlates theory with practical activity"; he also became involved in union organizing efforts in the South, which he described in the classic *When Southern Labor Stirs* (1931).

Workers from mostly urban and largely industrial environments were not brought in to a well-organized and beautiful campus in a rural setting for the purpose of duplicating normal "higher education," which Brookwood supporter Jean Flexner described as catering to "the inexperienced, impressionable dilettante, who drifts with open and colorless mind through a kaleidoscope of courses to emerge without deep convictions or definite objectives." Seasoned labor radical Clint Golden—Brookwood's field secretary, who raised money, secured union support, and scouted for students—explained that workers needed "expert knowledge as a weapon in their struggle for justice," emphasizing: "By developing and controlling our own institutions of learning, for the men and women of our movement, we will educate the workers into the service of their fellow workers rather than away from the labor movement, as is so often the case when the ambitious unionist enters the average university." Yet, according to Cara Cook (the librarian who also oversaw much of the administrative work and also did tutoring), a distinctive characteristic of Brookwood was that students and faculty "were always singing." One of the songs gave a humorous sense of faculty and staff:

> There's A. J. Muste, a teacher,
> He used to be a preacher . . .
> And Polly Colby makes them speak,
> With phrases smooth and manner neat . . .
> Dave Saposs tells them stories,
> About past union glories . . .
> And Helen Norton makes them write,

For labor papers day and night . . .
Tom Tippett teaches classes,
In the field to union masses . . .
While J. C. Kennedy does his stuff, and
Makes them learn their Marx enough . . .
Mark Starr does British labor,
With considerable British flavor . . .
And Cara Cook does this and that,
and runs the Secretariat . . .

Singing, socializing, putting on plays, playing baseball, communing with nature—all were essential elements of the Brookwood experience. So was physical labor, with all students and faculty expected to help with the work that was necessary to prepare meals, wash dishes, do the laundry, clean the various facilities of the institution, maintain the grounds, repair and expand the school's buildings, and so on. "The importance and dignity of hand work and head work are both fully appreciated," Brookwood's founding committee affirmed.

Another aspect of the Brookwood curriculum was "fieldwork." This involved practical experience assisting unions (sometimes in strike situations or assisting in the efforts of union reformers) or engaging in other campaigns—such as participating in the struggles to save the lives of the famous Italian anarchists sitting on death row, Nicola Sacco and Bartolomeo Vanzetti, or participating in antiwar activities. Faculty as well as students were expected to do such fieldwork.

Students could attend Brookwood for either one or two years. The first year offered basic courses and the second (for those returning) offered more advanced training. In addition to courses designed to give a background in history, sociology, economics, and other academic areas, there were courses designed to teach practical skills for labor activists: Trade Union Organization; Structure, Government, and Administration of Trade Unions; Labor Journalism; Labor Legislation and Administration; The Strategy of the Labor Movement; Public Speaking; Labor Dramatics; and Training in Speaking and Writing. A typical first-year student might, for one term, study Economics two mornings a week, English three mornings a week, and in the afternoons have Drama twice a week and Sociology three times a week. A typical second-year student might have morning courses in Public Speaking and Drama twice a week, Journalism twice a week, and Labor Issues twice a week; with the afternoons involving intensive Labor History and Social Psychology courses.

The evenings might involve social or cultural activities—or educational discussions with guest speakers: novelist Sinclair Lewis, labor historian

Norman Ware, A. Philip Randolph of the Brotherhood of Sleeping Car
Porters, Norman Thomas of the Socialist Party, Father John A. Ryan of
the Catholic Social Welfare Council, Communist Party educator Bertram
Wolfe, philosopher John Dewey, economist Scott Nearing, Fenner Brockway
from the British Labor Party, Jeanette Olson of the Norwegian Labor Party,
Socialist Party educator and journalist Oscar Ameringer, Roger Baldwin of
the American Civil Liberties Union, John Keracher of the Proletarian Party,
historian Harry Elmer Barnes, and many others.

Diversity was a hallmark of Brookwood's student body, which ranged
in age from teens to people in their fifties (though a majority were between
twenty-one and thirty years old). About one-third of the student body was
female (much higher than the percentage of women in the labor movement
of that time). A survey of forty-two students in 1927 reveals that about 52 percent were native-born and 48 percent foreign-born, with the great majority
(thirty-three students) coming from families of industrial workers; and that
half had completed no more than eight years of school (and some significantly
less). Although the industrial Northeast drew the largest number of students,
many came from the South and Midwest, and some from the Far West as well
as from other countries. There was also significant ethnic diversity, including
African American workers and activists. Ideological diversity was also represented in different religious backgrounds and different political orientations.
A mixture of socialists from various organizations (and from no organization
at all) mixed with anarchists and "pure and simple" trade unionists, as well as
workers who didn't identify themselves with such labels.

Gompers and Lenin

Debate and discussion were encouraged at Brookwood, and all were urged to
see themselves as part of the effort to revitalize the labor movement. Dominant currents within the AFL increasingly saw this approach as a threat;
as the 1920s unfolded, they were increasingly inclined to become even more
conservative than the ex-socialist, "pure and simple" AFL president Samuel
Gompers had been. They certainly did not want to be "revitalized." Ultimately, this tension deepened and finally tore Brookwood apart.

Along with Gompers and many others in the labor and socialist movements, most of Brookwood's faculty, staff, and students threw themselves
into the 1924 third-party presidential campaign of Progressive Robert M. La
Follette. La Follette netted an impressive four million votes, but the AFL
leadership reared back from what it considered a terrible failure. In contrast,

Brookwood spokespeople continued to advocate the creation of an independent labor party. They also were increasingly inclined to criticize the exclusive craft-union focus on skilled workers favored by the dominant forces in the AFL, calling instead for new industrial unions that would organize unskilled mass production workers. Moreover, they were tolerant of or even actively sympathetic toward various forms of labor radicalism that challenged the AFL's top leadership.

The list of guest speakers, as we have seen, included a large percentage of left-wing figures, some of whom were members of or close to the Communist Party, which was anathema to the AFL leadership. For that matter, several of the faculty members—Calhoun, Saposs, Colby, and Tippett—were identified (falsely) by some AFL conservatives as being Communist Party members.

The school staged memorials to commemorate the deaths not only of AFL founder Samuel Gompers, but also of Russian Communist leader Vladimir Ilyich Lenin and US Socialist Party leader Eugene V. Debs. May Day celebrations featured portraits of all three, along with such others as Rosa Luxemburg and Leon Trotsky. Some songs sung at Brookwood may also have proved offensive to labor conservatives. One of them was written by student Edith Berkowitz and contained, in part, the following words: "They've refused to heed our suffering. But they'll hear our marching feet! We have the workers' Red Flag unfurled. We come to take back our world."

In 1928, after several years of fruitless efforts to force Brookwood to submit to its more conservative labor orientation, the AFL leadership—relying on informants placed within the student body—released a sensational public denunciation of Brookwood Labor College as Communistic and called on its affiliates to sever relations. Many of them refused to do so when Brookwood denied the charges, and many prestigious pro-labor liberals and radicals rallied to the college's defense. (When the esteemed liberal educator John Dewey spoke out in favor of Brookwood, AFL president Matthew Woll shot back that "Dewey went to New York City for the purpose of planting the germ of Communism in our educational institutions.") The situation created terrible tensions—which were complicated by the Communist Party's attacks on Brookwood in the same year.

Among the Communists attending the college were Sylvia Bleeker and her companion Morris Lewit, who—in the factional disputes within the Communist Party at that time—were aligned with William Z. Foster against the organization's general secretary, Jay Lovestone. Factional infighter that he was, Lovestone made a point of having the party press attack Brookwood in 1928 as "class-collaborationist," serving as "a cloak for the reactionary labor fakirs." He publicly berated the "Fosterites" at the college for co-signing a

Brookwood statement allegedly "denouncing the communist movement and kowtowing to the American Federation of Labor bureaucracy." This began an irreversible development of Communist Party hostility to Brookwood that continued well after Lovestone lost his factional fight. (Under the influence of Soviet dictator Joseph Stalin, US Communists from 1929 through 1934 would attack all socialist groups and labor organizations not controlled by the Communist Party.)

Adding to the tangle was the fact that Brookwood faculty member Arthur Calhoun publicly disassociated himself from the college's defensive statement. While insisting that he was not a member of the Communist Party, he argued that Brookwood should openly break from reactionary AFL leadership and politically align itself with the revolutionary orientation that the Communists represented. In response, Muste and the majority of the faculty (including those who had been red-baited by the AFL leaders) urged the board of directors not to renew Calhoun's contract. This created new dissension among Brookwood's remaining supporters.

And then the Great Depression came. This, combined with the attacks from the AFL, caused Muste and some of the others associated with Brookwood to assume a more radical trajectory. Since 1924, the Socialist magazine *Labor Age*—edited by labor activist Louis F. Budenz—had become increasingly associated with Brookwood, and by 1929 Muste was working with Budenz and others in the milieu of the magazine and college to establish the Conference for Progressive Labor Action (CPLA). A number of Brookwood graduates and supporters became involved in the new venture—which began with a call for (1) organizing the unorganized workers into unions, (2) working to transform the craft unions of the AFL into more inclusive industrial unions, (3) breaking down all exclusion from union membership for racial, political, economic, social, or religious reasons, (4) launching government programs providing unemployment benefits and other forms of social insurance, (5) creating a labor party based on the trade unions, (6) persuading the US government to recognize the Soviet Union, and (7) encouraging anti-imperialist and antimilitarist policies by the US labor movement, which would lead to "a closer union of all workers of the world."

With the coming of the Depression, a majority of activists in the CPLA became more intensely involved than ever in the struggles of the unemployed (building militant unemployed leagues), as well as in desperate strike actions. Through the early 1930s, a powerful dynamic of radicalization drew Muste and a number of CPLA members to the conclusion that—in competition with what they saw as the "sectarian" Communist Party and the hopelessly compromising Socialist Party—the CPLA should evolve into a revolutionary vanguard party that operated according to the principles of democratic centralism. This would mean that its members would be "workers and fighters in the revolutionary movement"—with "the policies which they carry out in a disciplined manner . . . worked out by these members themselves on the basis of the most democratic discussion." Muste urged that "Brookwood be transformed into a training base" for "CPLA fighters" and that it focus less on general education and more on "action and direct involvement in the labor struggle."

A majority of Brookwood's faculty (including Colby, Norton, Saposs, and Starr) and the board of directors decisively rejected this version of the CPLA in 1933. The break was painful. Muste and his supporters left the college to pursue their radical course. Brookwood continued for almost four more years under the capable and energetic leadership of Tucker P. Smith, who was recruited not from the labor movement but from the pacifist Fellowship of Reconciliation. Among the new faculty was Roy Reuther, who with his brothers Walter and Victor (both of whom also visited Brookwood) would play a key part in the creation of the United Auto Workers. Those remaining sought to adhere to Brookwood's original goals, yet the college's spirit was altered and its base significantly eroded by what had taken place. Lack of funds forced it to close its doors in 1937.

Legacies

Brookwood Labor College was a vital moment in the history of the American labor movement; though itself unable to endure, it left an enduring legacy. Many Brookwood veterans played an essential role in the battles, strikes, and organizing efforts that created the Congress of Industrial Organizations. Many of them went on to assume important posts in the CIO (and after 1955 in the AFL-CIO) and its various union affiliates, as well as in the fields of education, politics, and government. While many of these former radicals became very much a part of the trade union establishment, younger labor radicals seeking to revitalize the labor movement have often looked to the Brookwood experience for inspiration and useful lessons.

Muste and those who followed him away from Brookwood with the CPLA went on, during the early years of the Depression, to militant actions of the unemployed leagues and "class struggle" activities. One of the most dramatic of these activities was the Toledo Auto-Lite Strike of 1934. The CPLA evolved into the American Workers Party at the end of 1933, and then it merged with the Communist League of America (followers of Leon Trotsky) at the beginning of 1935. Some of Muste's comrades stayed with the Trotskyists for many years, others ended up in other groups, and some dropped out of left-wing politics altogether. Muste himself soon returned to his radical pacifist and Christian roots in the Fellowship of Reconciliation, where he played a leadership role in antiwar and antiracist struggles for many years afterward.

The Brookwood experience influenced other radicals who had a major impact on the civil rights movement of the 1950s and 1960s. Myles Horton visited and studied Brookwood as a partial model for the Highlander Folk School, which he and other radical educators established in Tennessee during the 1930s and which shifted from training labor activists to training civil rights activists in the 1950s. One Highlander associate who was centrally involved in establishing both the Southern Christian Leadership Conference of Martin Luther King Jr. and the Student Nonviolent Coordinating Committee was Ella Baker—who had also been a student at Brookwood Labor College.

The old Brookwood faculty had formed Workers Education Local 189 of the American Federation of Teachers, which expanded beyond Brookwood during the 1930s to embrace labor educators in many locations, although internal differences later led to a shift in affiliation to the Communication Workers of America. In 2000, Local 189 merged with the University and College Labor Education Association to create the University Association for Labor Education, which has become a focal point for labor educators in the twenty-first century.

Bibliography

Allen, Devere. *Adventurous Americans*. New York: Farrar and Rinehart, 1932.

Altenbaugh, Richard J. *Education for Struggle: The American Labor Colleges of the 1920s and 1930s*. Philadelphia: Temple University Press, 1990.

Bernstein, Irving. *The Lean Years: A History of the American Worker, 1920–1933*. Boston: Houghton Mifflin, 1966.

Bloom, Jon. "Workers Education." In *Encyclopedia of the American Left*, edited by Mari Jo Buhle, Paul Buhle, and Dan Georgakas, 898–99. New York: Oxford University Press, 1998.

Brameld, Theodore. *Workers' Education in the United States*. New York: Harper and Brothers, 1941.

Breitman, George, Paul Le Blanc, and Alan Wald. *Trotskyism in the United States: Historical Essays and Reconsiderations*. Atlantic Highlands, NJ: Humanities Press, 1996.

Brooks, Thomas R. *Clint: A Biography of a Labor Intellectual, Clinton S. Golden*. New York: Atheneum, 1978.

Calhoun, Arthur W. *A Social History of the American Family from Colonial Times to the Present*. 3 vols. Cleveland: Arthur H. Clark Co., 1917–19.

———. *The Worker Looks at Government*. New York: International Publishers, 1927.

Conference for Progressive Labor Action. *CPLA Program-Policies*. New York: Futuro, n.d.

Danielson, Leilah. *American Gandhi: A. J. Muste and the History of Radicalism in the Twentieth Century*. Philadelphia: University of Pennsylvania Press, 2014.

De Caux, Len. *Labor Radical: From the Wobblies to CIO, a Personal History*. Boston: Beacon, 1970.

Dewey, John. *Democracy and Education*. New York: Macmillan Co., 1916.

Faulkner, Harold U., and Mark Starr. *Labor in America*. New York: Harper and Row, 1949.

Foner, Philip S. *The T.U.E.L. to the End of the Gompers Era*. Vol. 9, *History of the Labor Movement in the United States*. New York: International Publishers, 1991.

Hentoff, Nat. *Peace Agitator: The Story of A. J. Muste*. New York: Macmillan, 1963.

Howlett, Charles F. *Brookwood Labor College and the Struggle for Peace and Social Justice in America*. Lewiston, NY: Edwin Mellen, 1993.

Kates, Susan. *Activist Rhetorics and American Higher Education, 1885–1937*. Carbondale: Southern Illinois University Press, 2001.

Le Blanc, Paul. *Marx, Lenin, and the Revolutionary Experience: Studies of Communism and Radicalism in the Age of Globalization.* New York: Routledge, 2006.

Le Blanc, Paul, and Michael Steven Smith. "Morris Lewit: Pioneer Leader of American Trotskyism (1903–1998)." In *Revolutionary Labor Socialist: The Life, Ideas, and Comrades of Frank Lovell,* edited by Paul Le Blanc and Thomas Barrett, 272–94. Union City, NJ: Smyrna, 2000.

Lovell, Frank. "Sylvia Bleeker (1901–1988): Union Organizer, Socialist Agitator and Lifelong Trotskyist." In *Revolutionary Labor Socialist: The Life, Ideas, and Comrades of Frank Lovell,* edited by Paul Le Blanc and Thomas Barrett, 295–301. Union City, NJ: Smyrna, 2000.

Lovestone, Jay. *Pages from Party History.* New York: Workers Library, 1928.

Muste, A. J. "My Experience in Labor and Radical Struggles." In *As We Saw the Thirties: Essays on Social and Political Movements of a Decade,* edited by Rita James Simon, 125–50. Urbana: University of Illinois Press, 1967.

———. "Sketches for an Autobiography." In *The Essays of A. J. Muste,* edited by Nat Hentoff, 1–174. New York: Simon and Schuster, 1970.

Ransby, Barbara. *Ella Baker and the Black Freedom Movement: A Radical Democratic Vision.* Chapel Hill: University of North Carolina Press, 2003.

Rauschenbusch, Walter. *Christianity and the Social Crisis.* New York: Macmillan Co., 1907.

Robinson, Joanne Ooiman. *Abraham Went Out: A Biography of A. J. Muste.* Philadelphia: Temple University Press, 1981.

Ryan, Alan. *John Dewey and the High Tide of American Liberalism.* New York: W. W. Norton, 1995.

Saposs, David J. *Left-Wing Unionism.* New York: International Publishers, 1926.

Schneider, Florence Hemley. *Patterns of Workers' Education: The Story of the Bryn Mawr Summer School.* Washington, DC: American Council on Public Affairs, 1941.

Tippett, Tom. *When Southern Labor Stirs.* New York: Jonathan Cape and Harrison Smith, 1931.

Wong, Kent. "Draft History of UALE," United Association for Labor Education, http://uale.org/about.

4

US Labor Vanguards in the 1930s

There are two riddles that I want to explore. The answers have practical implications for us today. The answer to the first riddle is suggested in this presentation. Perhaps the answer to the second riddle—touched on all too briefly here—can be further explored not only by scholars, but also by activists. In fact, the activists' contributions would be especially useful.

The 1930s, in US labor history, have been seen as "the Turbulent Years" and as the decade of "Labor's Giant Step" in the words of Irving Bernstein and Art Preis, the respective authors of books with those titles. These classic histories cover the rise of the Congress of Industrial Organizations and the heroic struggles of working people that resulted in the creation of the big unions, which formed the base of the CIO.[1] But some statistics almost seem to suggest that this was an optical illusion. That's the first riddle.

It is irrefutable that enormous gains were made by US workers, despite the effects of the devastating economic Depression and the tyranny of the corporations. The growth of the CIO and the revival of the AFL directly affected millions of people. The number of unionized employees more than tripled, from 2.8 million in 1933 to 8.4 million in 1941. This yielded positive changes in wages, hours, working conditions, and dignity on the job, plus valuable social legislation and a deep transformation of the political climate, giving working people a greater measure of control over their world.[2]

On the other hand, another respected labor historian, Melvyn Dubofsky, combing through the statistics on union organizing drives and strikes in the 1930s, observed that the overwhelming majority of working people during this period were simply not involved in these union struggles. He focused attention on two years of the most intense struggles—1934 and 1937.[3]

The year 1934 saw general strikes in three cities: Toledo, Ohio; San Francisco, California; and Minneapolis, Minnesota. In Toledo workers at the Auto-Lite Company, and their allies in the militant Lucas County Unemployed League battled the company and the National Guard, with the support of the city's central labor council and under the leadership of A. J.

Muste's left-wing American Workers Party. In San Francisco longshoremen and other workers, following a left-wing leadership—especially militants of the Communist Party—also were backed be the city's central labor council, fought company goons and local police, and confronted the National Guard. In Minneapolis and neighboring St. Paul, the radicals providing leadership to the workers' battles were members of the Communist League of America, followers of Leon Trotsky. The city's teamsters, supported by the central labor council and masses of unorganized and unemployed workers, and nearby small family farmers, faced down the city's powerful employers, fought police, and—here too—engaged in struggles that brought in the National Guard.[4]

The stunning union victories in these cities generated the mass organizing drives of industrial workers and launched the CIO. The year 1937 saw the mass sit-down strikes and other militant working-class actions through which the CIO-sponsored United Auto Workers and the Steel Workers Organizing Committee conquered the mighty General Motors and United States Steel corporations.[5]

Only a Minority in the Big Union Drives

The fact is, however, that in 1934 and in 1937, only about 7 percent of employed workers were involved in strikes. We have to ask what the other 93 percent of the labor force were doing during the great strike waves of 1934 and 1937, and throughout the decade.[6]

The perceptive radical journalist Louis Adamic, covering labor and other issues during that era, explained why so few workers participated in strikes: "I know, or have known, hundreds of unskilled workers, particularly in the small industries, whose apathy and resignation are something appalling. Where no union has appeared to rouse them, most of them are basically indifferent to the conditions they have to endure. Because certain conditions exist, they see no possibility of having them altered. There is a dead fatalism."

Adamic denied that capitalist oppression would naturally breed militant class consciousness. "The exploitation is outrageous, but the workers merely grumble," he wrote. "When unionization is suggested, they oppose it: it might lose them their jobs! Yet they hate their jobs. That hate expresses itself in subversive talk, sabotage, defeatism." Adamic added: "Most American workers have little or no conception of jobs outside their fields. They are unaware of the interdependence of the workers' functions, and so ignorant of their importance, to the indispensability of their work. Many tend to deprecate their functions, if not orally, then to themselves and perform listlessly, as workers, as human beings . . . and the general public, as uninformed as they are concerning what makes the wheels go round, tends to agree with them."[7]

"Kinship-Occupational Clusters"

I think it may be useful, also, to look at some of the findings of a social historian named John Bodnar, who studied and interviewed individuals from what he calls "the masses of rank-and-file toilers who were reared in strong, family-based enclaves" of largely immigrant working-class communities, plus many Blacks as well as some whites who migrated from the South.

Particularly as employers were developing mass-production techniques in the early decades of the twentieth century—largely to eliminate the power of potentially radicalizing skilled workers—recently arrived unskilled immigrant laborers were absorbed as mass-production workers, and often they found jobs in their workplaces for needy friends and relatives as well. Family and ethnic ties became intertwined with occupational patterns, creating what Bodnar calls "kinship-occupational clusters" in which "familial concerns were strongly reinforced." This cut across the competing ideologies of capitalist upward mobility through "rugged individualism" on the one hand and a revolutionary proletarian class consciousness on the other. "Clearly," Bodnar writes, "family obligations dominated working-class predilections and may have exerted a moderating influence on individual expectations and the formulation of social and economic goals."[8]

This family- or kinship-focused orientation "muted individual inclinations and idealism in favor of group survival." While people in this situation might respond to union organizing drives under certain conditions, more often they would not be in a position to initiate militant class struggles.

Vanguard Layer of the Working Class: Radicals and Union Militants

In a sense, the answer to the riddle we have posed is as obvious as the answer to the question of why the chicken crossed the road. A majority of workers did not engage in the big class battles of the 1930s because they did not feel able to. We can refer to the minority of workers who were actually involved in taking "labor's giant step" of the 1930s as the vanguard layer of the working class—those who, for a variety of reasons, were able to see themselves and their situation in a certain way, and were in a position to make certain life decisions, that enabled them to move forward before most of the others.

Within this vanguard layer, however, we find two different components. One has been a smaller network of working-class organizers identified by

Staughton and Alice Lynd in their excellent book *Rank and File*. The Lynds write: "The rank and filers in this book felt . . . that there had to be basic social changes. They were both militant, in demanding changes in their unions and workplaces, and radical, in the sense that they tried to democratize the larger society. They imagined both a union and a society which were more just, more humane, more of a community."[9] In fact, most of the veteran working-class activists they interviewed had been members of Socialist, Communist, or Trotskyist organizations.

A different and larger component of the vanguard layer was made up of those who may have had brief flirtations with larger social visions, but were inclined to a more or less "pure and simple" trade unionism. Melvyn Dubofsky brings our attention to the dialectic between diverse working-class militants and the larger rank and file. He writes: "More often than not, action by militant minorities (what some scholars have characterized as 'sparkplug unionism') precipitated a subsequent collective response." His portrait of a multilayered working class is worth presenting at length:

> Even the most strike-torn cities and regions had a significantly inter-
> nally differentiated working class. At the top were the local cadres, the
> sparkplug unionists, the men and women fully conscious of their roles in
> a marketplace society that extolled individualism and rewarded collective
> strength. These individuals, ranging the political spectrum from Social
> Democrats to Communists, provided the leadership, the militancy, and
> ideology that fostered industrial conflict and the emergence of mass-pro-
> duction unionism. Beneath them lay a substantial proportion of workers
> who could be transformed, by example, into militant strikers and union-
> ists, and, in turn, themselves act as militant minorities. Below them were
> many first- and second-generation immigrant workers, as well as recent
> migrants from the American countryside, who remained embedded in a
> culture defined by traditional ties to family, kinship, church, and neigh-
> borhood club or tavern. Accustomed to following the rituals of the past,
> heeding the advice of community leaders, and slow to act, such men and
> women rarely joined unions prior to a successful strike, once moved to
> act behaved with singular solidarity, yet rarely served as union or political
> activists and radicals.[10]

The reality of the working class was even more complex than this, though Dubofsky's rough categorizations are useful as an initial approxima-tion. The piece of the analysis that I want to focus on, at this point, is the militant minority that we can subdivide into political radicals and militant but non-socialist trade union activists, who together played an indispensable "vanguard" role. Even among the autoworkers in Flint, Michigan, during the 1937 sit-down strike, according to seasoned participants, at the start of the strike only one-third were actively engaged in the union struggle, while another third were hostile to it and the final third were holding back to see how things would go. What could be called the "militant minority" included activists of the organized Left, plus workers who had a union consciousness, a social consciousness, a sense of class consciousness—but were not inclined to commit, at least for the present, to a conscious struggle against capitalism.[11]

The political radicals were members of various Communist and Socialist groups and splinter groups, plus anarchists and old-time Wobblies (members of the Industrial Workers of the World, the IWW), who altogether represented a vital left-wing subculture that existed within the US working class in the first half of the twentieth century. The ideas, the vision, the confidence, the organizational know-how provided by these left-wing working-class organizations constituted an essential part of the chemistry for the great labor upsurge of the 1930s.

Role of the Communist Party

It is necessary to go beyond this generalized recognition of a vanguard layer, however, to emphasize the role of members of the Communist Party, whose prominence is suggested by their numbers within left-wing organizations during the mid-1930s. The Trotskyists—even after they merged with A. J. Muste's American Workers Party—only had about seven hundred members. The rightward-leaning Communist dissidents following Jay Lovestone had perhaps one thousand. Even the Socialist Party, fluctuating around ten thousand members, had only thirteen hundred who belonged to trade unions—including in the garment and auto industries, where many were in the process of leaving the Socialist Party. The Communist Party, on the other hand, had about thirty thousand people, of whom fifteen thousand were union members—and in both cases their numbers were growing. In any event, the Left was essential for the workers' triumph of the 1930s.[12]

This brings us to the second riddle: if the Left was really so essential to the growth of the new labor movement, how could it be smashed within a fairly short period? From the mid-1930s to the late 1940s it had considerable influence within the CIO and much influence (social, cultural, political) in the larger society. By the early 1950s, this influence was demolished.[13]

It seems unlikely that a communist or socialist or proletarian revolution could have been brought about in the United States in the 1930s. I'm not talking about that. I'm talking about the survival of an effective left-wing force in the labor movement, which would have set the stage for more effective struggles in the future.

Some labor historians have argued that it was impossible for the Communist labor activists to do qualitatively better than they did, that the triumph of conservative anticommunism was inevitable, that the Left could do little to prevent marginalization and elimination. There are reasons to question this argument, however. In his memoir entitled *Labor Radical,* former CIO publicity director Len De Caux explained that the early CIO was not simply a new trade union federation but "a mass movement with a message, revivalistic in fervor, militant in mood, joined together in class solidarity." De Caux elaborated:

> As it gained momentum, this movement brought with it new political attitudes—toward the corporations, toward police and troops, toward local, state, national government. Now we're a movement, many workers asked, why can't we move on to more and more? Today we've forced almighty General Motors to terms by sitting down and defying all the powers at its command, why can't we go on tomorrow, with our numbers, our solidarity, our determination, to transform city and state, the Washington government itself? Why can't we go on to create a new society with the workers on top, to end age-old injustices, to banish poverty and war?[14]

By the early 1950s the US labor movement had been mostly de-radicalized—with the vision indicated by De Caux replaced by the notion that capitalists and workers are "partners in progress." Would it have been possible for a socialist left wing to survive as a significant force in the United States? Given the years of Cold War anticommunism and capitalist prosperity, was the smashing of the Left inevitable?

I would suggest that it was not. But if that is so, then we must turn our critical attention to the one organization on the Left that was in the best position to make a difference: the US Communist Party. The point is not to scapegoat the many dedicated and idealistic activists who were part of that party and who played an often heroic role in building the CIO. But if their defeat was avoidable, or if it could have been less damaging and thoroughgoing, then it is important for us to understand the various reasons why. We must explore this in order to learn from the fatal shortcomings, so that similar mistakes are not made in the struggles of the future. I will offer a few of my own thoughts in conclusion.

It is conceivable that an organization of the size and with the resources of the US Communist Party at the beginning of the 1930s could have been guided somewhat differently than in the way it was. If this different program had been applied intelligently—with a sensitivity to, an ability to learn from, and a respectful interaction with various layers of the US working class—then it is possible that a more durable working-class left-wing movement would have emerged from the Depression decade.

What was needed was not only a flexible and energetic united-front policy in building the new industrial unions, which the Communist Party certainly worked to implement, but also five other components: (1) a greater internal democracy and less sectarianism among left-wing groups; (2) a critical independence from the bureaucratic-authoritarian and murderous Stalin regime of the USSR: (3) an independence from the Democratic Party and consistent support for the development of an independent labor party—while recognizing and living with the fact that many friends and allies in the labor movement would be drawn into the Democratic Party (at least for a time); (4) an understanding of the revolutionary but relatively independent character of the African American struggle, which—far from being subordinated to the needs of a liberal-labor coalition—should be supported as essential for the radicalization of the working class as a whole; and (5) persistent education and recruitment of newly unionized workers and others to reach an understanding of the class struggle and the need for working-class political power and socialism.[15]

As we look to create the labor movement that is needed in the future, the approach suggested by these five components may be helpful in guiding a left-wing vanguard that is poised to effect genuine change.

5

Remembering Ruth Querio

The first Trotskyist I came to know and love was Ruth Querio, a down-to-earth working-class revolutionary who inspired me and many others.

I met her when I was eighteen, in October 1965, during the International Days of Protest against the War in Vietnam. A small group of us were in a roving caravan, picketing at a succession of draft boards in the Pittsburgh area. In Mount Oliver there was an old lady (or so this fifty-nine-year-old seemed to me) waiting for us. She was wearing an antiwar button and arguing with members of a drunken mob that had gathered to attack us. She proved as brave (and as scared) as the rest of us, as we tried to stand our ground before making a speedy exit. In March 1966 she stood with us again—when there were more of us—at an outdoor rally of about three hundred people in freezing weather, when I made my first public speech clutching a scribbled text in the wind, and she helped to warm my hands afterward. She explained her Trotskyism to me as we drank wine at a party that night, sitting on the floor after a spaghetti dinner, and we hugged each other as we shared our dreams of peace and justice.

I left town that summer to work in the national office of Students for a Democratic Society, and after I returned, I didn't even try to maintain contact with her—blame the foolish, thoughtless, unintentional cruelty of youth. I should have stayed in touch; I knew it would mean a lot to her, but I didn't. I simply went about my life and my activism, with an occasional thought or memory of her (about which I did nothing, in part, perhaps, out of guilt for being out of touch with her for so long). After a year or so, I saw her at some antiwar event that I helped to organize, and I went up to her saying: "Hi, Ruth!" She looked back at me, embraced me, and whispered in my ear: "You traitor!" And she forgave me. After which I didn't allow myself to be quite so thoughtless.

When I finally joined the Trotskyist movement in 1973, she told me she believed from the start I'd get around to that eventually. She regularly came to Socialist Workers Party (SWP) events when she could, delighted that the struggles of her youth were being continued by a growing number of activists who were the same age that she and her comrades had been when they were building the movement in the old days. In 1976 I left Pittsburgh to help build the SWP in Albany, then moved to New York City where I made the "turn to industry" that the SWP was carrying out in that period in order to establish a base in the industrial working class. I stayed in touch this time, and spoke with her on the phone when she was in the hospital. Whenever I spoke to her on the phone, she would always end the call with a warm and loving: "Bye-bye for now." But she didn't say those words this time.

Ruth died in 1978. A sense of her comes through in this article from the January 26, 1979, issue of the *Militant*:

Ruth Querio, Veteran Trotskyist
By Kipp Dawson

PITTSBURGH—After forty-five years as a socialist fighter, Ruth Querio died here November 26 at the age of seventy-two. On December 13 many of her comrades, family, and friends met at the Socialist Workers Party hall to celebrate her life.

Frank Lovell, a national committee member of the Socialist Workers Party, spoke of Querio's first experience with politics in Allentown, Pennsylvania.

"Like many thousands of working-class families, Ruth, her husband, and young daughter were destitute in 1933 when this country was in the depths of the depression.

"Her husband had been a mill worker, a silk weaver. When the workers began to organize for their own protection against overwork and low pay, the mill owners at first blacklisted those they thought were ringleaders and later began closing down the mills altogether."

With no work available and no money to pay rent, the Querios were evicted from their home.

"Members of the National Unemployed League learned about the eviction of the Querio family and came to their aid," Lovell said. "This taught Ruth that she and her family were not alone."

Lovell described how Ruth became an activist in the unemployed movement and through her work there came into contact with the Conference for Progressive Labor Action, then led by A. J. Muste.

Querio became involved in the CPLA's discussions about the need for a working-class political party. In a 1973 interview, she said she learned during the depression that since nothing is given to working people, "you have to fight every inch of the way. I believe that workers must have their own world."

"Ruth was no idle dreamer," Lovell continued. "She wanted to make things happen." This propelled her to joining the Workers Party of America. The Workers Party, forerunner of the Socialist Workers Party, was formed in November 1934 when the CPLA [which had changed its name to the American Workers Party] fused with the Trotskyist Communist League of America.

Querio helped steer the Allentown branch of the Workers Party through difficult times, including a raiding action by agents of the Communist Party.

In a message to the meeting here, SWP leaders Farrell Dobbs and Marvel Scholl recalled that "Ruth lived in and for the party. Despite years of untold suffering from several physical ailments, she never let her illness stand in the way of self-imposed assignments—unable to march in antiwar demonstrations she often stood in the cold of a Pittsburgh winter to sell the *Militant*.

"For many years Ruth helped keep the idea of socialism alive in Pittsburgh, working in almost total isolation, after the former Pittsburgh branch was dissolved. And then, when she found a few young people responsive to her revolutionary ideas, she contributed as much as possible to the building of a new branch."

One of those young people was Paul Le Blanc, who helped to found the new Pittsburgh branch of the SWP in 1973.

Le Blanc told the memorial meeting, "Through the 1950s and early 1960s the Trotskyist movement and the organized left in general had shrunk down to almost nothing in Pittsburgh. There were intense pressures to conform to the seemingly affluent and all-powerful capitalist status quo. But Ruth refused to give up the insights, the understanding, or the hopes that she had developed in the revolutionary socialist movement....

"It was such a joy for those of us who were young radicals in the mid-1960s to discover that there was an old fighter like Ruth who hadn't been beaten, who hadn't given up, who was still there—expecting us, waiting for us, an older person ready to join us and encourage us and share with us as much knowledge and energy as she could in the fight against war, racism, and all forms of injustice.

"And the fact that a new generation was ready to struggle for a better world was, I know, a source of great joy for her too. It was a case of love at first sight."

Many of Querio's comrades sent messages to the meeting. Some described her enthusiasm over the new women's movement and the Socialist Workers Party's active participation in it. Veteran Trotskyists, including Sam Gordon, Anne Chester, and Regina Shoemaker, hailed Querio's long and ever-optimistic dedication to her party.

Le Blanc summed it up. "Ruth was lucky to be so valued. But she was lucky, also, to be a revolutionary socialist.

"It adds a rich meaning to a person's life to struggle for socialism—a society in which our class, the masses of working people, are in charge of the economy and running the government to make sure that *each* person is valued and has the opportunity to grow and develop for himself or herself a richly meaningful life, a community in which each person gives according to their abilities and receives according to their needs.

"Ruth was lucky to have been animated by this goal. And so are we. And we're very lucky to have known and been a part of the life of this fine and wonderful person."

There are some important facts that did not find their way into Kipp's article. Ruth's daughter Charmaine had been involved with her, as a comrade, in meetings and struggles from the old days, but then moved on to marry a working-class militant who—as the 1940s turned into the 1950s, and the 1950s dragged on—became a relatively well-off union member, working for Greyhound, leaving his militancy far behind as he embraced "the American Dream." He and Ruth were quite critical of each other, with Charmaine serving as a buffer—which was important, because Ruth lived with them in the house they'd bought. There were two grandchildren, neither of whom was political. I regret being unable to remember their names. The boy ended up being drafted and sent to Vietnam, and he died there—which made Ruth hate the war even more. The girl struck me, from the very little contact I had, as a "typical" moody teenager (at least when she was around the grown-ups). But she came with her mother to the memorial meeting and seemed amazed with all that was being said about her grandmother.

I remember Ruth often speaking with great affection about her many comrades of years gone by. Art Preis, a young leader of the Lucas County (Ohio) Unemployed League, had come to her rescue when she was about to be evicted; later she became the organization's treasurer and helped to organize militant demonstrations that converged at the state capitol in Harrisburg; in Preis's *Labor's Giant Step* he mentioned her by name (it made her so proud!). Sam Gordon, who moved to England, was definitely one of her favorites; he later wrote her about the British Labour Party, recommending a book that she very much wanted to read. Other names often rolled off her tongue— Regina Shoemaker, Louise Simpson, Anne Chester, and others. Her daughter once told me that Ruth had a soft spot in her heart—almost in spite of herself—for Max Shachtman, but I know she also had bitter feelings for some of the Trotskyist intellectuals such as James Burnham and Dwight Macdonald who, she felt, used to look down on working-class rank-and-filers like herself, preferring instead to socialize with their own kind. C. L. R. James had appealed to her until, during a 1939 visit to her Allentown home, he suggested that perhaps Trotsky was getting a bit senile (or so she interpreted his remarks), at which point she threw him out. She always spoke glowingly of Farrell Dobbs and Marvel Scholl, but SWP leader James P. Cannon was without a doubt the party figure for whom she felt the greatest enthusiasm. She would often talk of her memories of "Jim" relaxing at the party-owned Mountain Spring Camp, rolling up his sleeves in the midst of a factional conflict at a party convention, cracking jokes with close comrades, passionately explaining the meaning of socialism at a public meeting, or taking time to reach out to an individual comrade.

One of Ruth's most prized possessions was a letter that Cannon wrote to her in the 1930s when she still lived in Allentown. She let me have a photocopy of the letter, and reading it gives a sense of the movement to which she committed her life:

New York, January 17, 1936
Ruth Querio
Allentown, Pa.

Dear Comrade Querio:

I received your letter and was glad indeed to hear from you. I fully appreciate the extraordinary difficulties which confront the comrades in the Allentown situation,[1] and have the warmest admiration for those who persist in the struggle to develop the branch into a revolutionary organization, worthy of the name. Nobody is born a Bolshevik. It takes time and great effort and travail to weld a group of people of different personalities and temperaments into a homogeneous organization. When, as is the case in Allentown, one has to begin with a membership which, as a whole, is comparatively new to the political movement, the difficulties are only magnified. That is what we always have to keep in mind about the Allentown situation. It excludes a quick solution of the difficulties; similarly, it makes it impossible for the Political Committee to solve the problem by means of single decisions or disciplinary measures. Time and education and experience are all necessary factors.

On the other hand, it is very obvious to us that we are making headway. The fact that you have succeeded in organizing 20-odd comrades into a grouping which really attempts to face the political issues, and to carry out the party line, and that this group grows in political understanding and self-confidence as the struggle develops—this is a positive gain. You must not underestimate it. Whatever happens, we are now assured of a serious political nucleus in Allentown. In the end it is bound to prevail. For political ideas and a political line are far more powerful than all the intrigues and tricks and prejudices of a transitory majority. If our group there really assimilates the ideas and methods of Bolshevism, we need have no fear for the future.

We are now going thru [sic] a period of the richest political experience, and we are all learning from it. Perhaps we, ourselves, were not free from mistakes in the Allentown situation. It seems to me that some very good comrades, who have the making of Bolsheviks, have taken a position against us in Allentown. We must hope that their antagonism is temporary and we must aim to win them over. Above all, we have to convince them by our personal attitude that we do not pursue personal aims and that we are not animated, in any way, by sentiments of personal antagonism or personal revenge. On the contrary, we have to make it clear, we have to convince those comrades who have good faith, that we want to advance a political line which is necessary for the building of the party and the mass movement, and that we want to unite every possible comrade on the basis of that line. We must look ahead; we have a long [period of] work before us. It will do us no good to lose our heads and cry for immediate and final solution of the situation, which is still maturing. We must persist and persevere and take consolation in the fact that we are gaining, and will continue to gain as long as we act like Bolshevik politicians and not like chickens with their heads cut off. Danton said that audacity was the first merit of revolutionists. He might have added that patience comes next in order. Please don't think that I am simply lecturing you. I am really directing this just as much at myself, because impatience is my own fault, also.

We are going to have a party convention February 28th. It will be a historic affair, a turning point in the development of our movement. We want to keep our movement united, if it is possible. The trend of the national party sentiment is on our side. That will make its influence felt in Allentown and will help you. We do not want any explosions or splits before the convention, if we can avoid them. We will have the majority and that will impose upon us the duty of conciliating the minority. Once the political line is established by the convention—and we must not make any compromises when it comes to a question of principled lines—then we must try to keep the movement united on the basis of that line. Above all, we must not let personal antagonisms reach the point where they provoke artificial splits.

In this next period, as I have suggested to comrade Gordon, much attention should be devoted to the caucus group which we have organized around our political platform. You should have frequent meetings, devoted to a discussion of political problems, so that the group will become further strengthened and consolidated, on a political basis. That is the most profitable work that can be done now, and it is also the best way to insure [*sic*] your eventual victory in the branch and in the mass movement. I hope to come to Allentown, at least once, before the convention for a branch discussion meeting and also for a discussion meeting with the group. I also hope that the most active comrades will begin to plan far in advance to attend the party convention which will be open to all party members.

With Bolshevik greetings and personal regards,
J. P. Cannon[2]

This admirable working-class radical, Ruth Querio, was a vital part of history (as we all are) and a dear friend. I could ask her questions like what should I do about a pair of shoes I had that were really starting to smell bad, and learn from her that wiping them out with witch hazel might work. I am saddened now that I saw her as "an old lady." Once when she asked what I thought her age actually was, she was visibly shocked when I said she was seventy-five or so. She was still in her sixties—but life had been hard. I remember seeing a photo of her and Charmaine from the late 1940s, when Ruth looked as though she were Charmaine's older sister, two vibrant young women on a picket line. And I still can hear her warm and loving voice saying "Bye-bye for now."

6

The Marxism of C. L. R. James

From the late 1980s into the twenty-first century, Cyril Lionel Robert James (1901–89) has enjoyed a remarkable revival among US, European, and Caribbean intellectuals, who are spreading his influence more widely than it reached at any time during his life. He is best known for his magnificent history of the Haitian Revolution, entitled *Black Jacobins* (first published in 1938 and reprinted often since then), and for pioneering contributions in the theorization of the Black liberation struggle in the United States, but many other facets of his work have also attracted attention.[1]

James's contributions are an essential source for those in any way concerned with the relevance or application of Marxism in the United States and beyond. At the same time, in order to be politically and theoretically serious, we must approach what he did with critical minds. For anyone who identifies with the Leninist and Trotskyist traditions—as I do and as James once did—there is a responsibility to in some way come to terms with James's rejection, or partial rejection, of those traditions.

What follows are, essentially, two essays, which I have labeled Part One and Part Two. The first part offers an introduction to the work of C. L. R. James, and while it attempts to integrate profound criticisms of what some who had been close to him saw as his limitations, it focuses on what I term "the James Accomplishment," which strikes me as considerable. The second part includes an appreciation for the remarkable insights and creative impulses that permeated his work, but it essentially constitutes a critique of qualities I find to be problematical in his work.

Part One: The James Accomplishment

"Everyone produces his/her own James," commented one of his closest comrades and most thoughtful interpreters, Martin Glaberman. "People have, over the years, taken from him what they found useful and imputed to him what they felt necessary."[2] This is not surprising, given the quality and breadth of his thought. Yet the driving force in his thought—aside from James's own

dynamic personality and passion—was a commitment to the global triumph
of a working-class majority and the creation of a society of the free and the
equal, and a commitment to helping further the processes that might make
this so.

Scott McLemee has captured the reality beautifully. "Shakespeare and
Lenin, cricket and Victorian literature, Hegel's Science of Logic and wildcat
auto strikes, Pan-Africanism and the democratic polis of Greek antiquity—a
unique combination of interests unfolds across the decades of C. L. R. James's
life and work." Far from reflecting "mere eclecticism," McLemee stresses,
"James's writings display something all too rare: a genuinely open and responsive intelligence, a cosmopolitan sensibility which, although intensely concerned with the past and with cultural traditions, also possesses an acute and
visionary feeling for 'the future in the present' as it emerges from the struggles
of ordinary people around the globe for a better life."[3]

James is generally acknowledged to have been one of the most original
Marxist thinkers to emerge from the Western Hemisphere, though essential aspects of his identity came from the other side of the Atlantic, from
Europe and Africa. As he explained to one African American scholar, "I
am a Black European, that is my training and outlook."[4] Yet his intellectual
breadth is global. He offered penetrating analyses on the interrelationships
of class, race, and gender, and his discussions of colonialism and anti-co-
lonialism were sometimes brilliant. But C. L. R. James also embraced the
heritage of the Enlightenment and the French Revolution, the working-class
and socialist movements of Europe and North America, and the Bolshevism
of Lenin and Trotsky that transformed Russia and promised to liberate the
world from all oppression. At the same time, his writings on sports deserve
special emphasis—which is something that can be said of few Marxist theorists. James began his writing career by writing about baseball's English-born
cousin, cricket, first in the West Indies and later in England itself.

Paul Buhle, following James's insight, tells us that such sports are a means
of "expression for ordinary genius," adding that James regarded cricket as "a
fully fledged art form equal to theatre, opera and dance. To this claim James
added a populist amendment: 'What matters in cricket, as in all the finer arts,
is not the finer points but what everyone with some knowledge of the elements
can see and feel.' It embodied the elemental human movement which . . . constituted the basis and the source of renewal for all arts." (One can imagine such
insights might be applied to modern-day basketball, music and music videos,
films, television, computer games, websites, blogs, texting, and much else.)[5]

Such things—James felt—come from the same deeply creative
sources that generate both more-conventional great art and also genuinely

revolutionary politics. The mass popular response to such things, similarly, has something in common with the emotions and sensibilities associated with social revolutions, in which masses of people creatively transform reality.

James's Political Involvements

James moved to England in 1932 from the West Indian island of Trinidad. In England he quickly made contact with the British working-class movement, becoming part of the radical Independent Labour Party and of a small Trotsky-ist organization within it called the Marxist Group. He learned his Marx-ism within this context and made some of his most enduring contributions to Marxism while he was part of the Trotskyist movement in Britain and the United States. James also became involved in the Pan-Africanist movement, becoming associated with such figures as George Padmore, Paul Robeson, W. E. B. DuBois, Jomo Kenyatta, and Kwame Nkrumah. In 1938, reflecting this involvement, James wrote a pioneering pamphlet, *A History of Negro Revolt*, for publication by the Independent Labour Party, in which he was also involved.[6]

It was in 1938 that James helped to found the Fourth International, the worldwide organization of revolutionary socialists associated with Trotsky, and was elected to its International Executive Committee. In the same year, at the strong urging of James P. Cannon, he moved to the United States and became part of the Socialist Workers Party. Frank Lovell has offered this recollection:

> When C. L. R. James came to this country from Britain, where he was a leader of the Trotskyist movement, he was welcomed into the Social-ist Workers Party and given leadership responsibilities. James was an impressive speaker with his British accent and his poise. He was a tall, handsome Black man . . . He spoke without notes, standing aside from the podium on the speakers' platform. It was as if he were a great actor delivering a famous oration.
>
> At his first appearance he shared the platform with [the top leaders of the SWP, Max] Shachtman and [James P.] Cannon in the Irving Plaza meeting hall where Trotskyist meetings were often held. Shachtman was the first speaker and was not brief. James came on next and even though his talk was longer than Shachtman's, he completely captivated his audi-ence and received a big ovation. Cannon was the last speaker. Although he was the national secretary of the party and had been announced for a major speech, Jim had no intention of standing on his dignity or trying to hold the audience so late at night in order to have his turn. He put aside his notes, congratulated James on his speaking ability and welcomed him to the Socialist Workers Party.[7]

James remained part of the Trotskyist movement until 1951, adopting the party name "J. R. Johnson." In 1940, when Shachtman and many others split from the SWP and set up the rival Workers Party, James initially lined up with the Shachtmanites. At the same time, along with a vibrant theorist-in-the-making named Rae Spiegel, later known as Raya Dunayevskaya, who took the party name "Freddie Forest," James formed a very distinctive political current: the Johnson-Forest tendency.

The Johnson-Forest tendency, which never had more than a few dozen adherents, mapped out an ambitious project for US revolutionaries: to develop an Americanized Marxism, and an Americanized Bolshevism, that would involve a dynamic interpenetration of the US and international revolutionary traditions.

This was to include intellectual efforts that have had an impact on later scholars and social critics: the development of substantial analyses of US history, studies of modern culture (including a serious attitude toward popular culture), historical and sociological labor studies, the development of Marxist economic analysis, and an embrace of dialectical materialism which involved an immersion in the philosophical writings of Hegel. Among the contributions of the Johnson-Forest tendency was the first English-language translation of Marx's important *Economic and Philosophical Manuscripts*, which were published in the early 1840s.

As early as 1940, Cannon expressed a concern that James was focused on establishing "an independent political line for himself and his followers" inside the Socialist Workers Party. In the same year, a major split *did* take place in the SWP, focused on how to characterize the Soviet Union—as a bureaucratically degenerated workers' state (needing a political revolution to democratize it, but also critical defense from the capitalist world) or as a new form of class society tagged "bureaucratic-collectivism" (no better than capitalism). A slim majority around Cannon held to the first position, while the second was that of Max Shachtman, who led a split to establish a new Workers Party. James and his co-thinkers, within the Workers Party, viewed the Soviet Union as representing a variant of capitalism—"state capitalism"— and also had their own distinctive views on other questions. These attracted some of the more energetic young comrades and—among other things— inspired them with the ambition to master the complexities of Marx's *Capital* and Hegel's *Phenomenology of the Mind*. Shachtman, and those close to him had little patience for such stuff. As one veteran of the Shachtmanites later recalled: "You would see these 17 year olds who could barely spell, and they were carrying Hegel." A one-time Shachtmanite youth leader agreed: "In the youth group, with Hegel, they would get up and start espousing Hegel, and it was utterly incoherent."[8]

Three other sins of the Johnson-Forest tendency, prominently emerging after the split, also aggravated Shachtman and his co-thinkers: 1) the position that the African American struggle, rather than being subsumed under the general struggle of the working class, had a powerful dynamic of its own and would be central to the socialist revolution in the United States; 2) the position that the American working class was far more radical, having a greater revolutionary character, than many of the Shachtmanites imagined; and, at a certain point, 3) that the Socialist Workers Party of James P. Cannon was much better than Shachtman and others were willing to admit, and that the two groups should reunify.

This finally led to a split from the Workers Party in 1947, after which the Johnson-Forest group returned to the SWP. While many SWPers were not inclined to accept much of the Johnson-Forest theoretical output, and especially rejected the Johnson-Forest notion that the Soviet Union was a "state-capitalist" society, the tendency's members were seen as serious and hardworking revolutionaries. The contributions that James had to make regarding the so-called "Negro Question" were also highly valued. And yet disappointed hopes regarding the failure of the US working class to turn in a revolutionary direction, growing difficulties and frustrations brought on by the Cold War and McCarthy periods, and deepening political differences, caused James and his followers to leave the SWP in 1951. In doing this, they also openly rejected Trotskyism and any commitments to building a Leninist-type party in the United States.

Shortly after this split, James—who was not a US citizen—was arrested and thrown out of the country because of his revolutionary politics. In 1955, Raya Dunayevskaya and others split away from James's group to establish their own "Marxist-Humanist" News and Letters group (named after their newspaper); in 1962 the Johnsonites—known by the name of their own paper *Correspondence*—suffered yet another split led by James Boggs and Grace Lee Boggs. James and his co-thinkers regrouped around the name "Facing Reality" (the title of a major Johnsonite document). By the end of the 1960s, the remnants of the Facing Reality group (led by James's close associate Martin Glaberman) decided to dissolve. "The movement which we started has been broken up almost to bits," James lamented from London. He confided to his former wife and still friend, Constance Webb, feelings of sorrow that (in her words) "he had wasted his strength, his time, and his health on something absolutely useless."[9]

In the meantime, however, two of James's protégés in other countries—Kwame Nkrumah in Ghana and Eric Williams in Trinidad—assumed state power, and welcomed their mentor's support and assistance. In Ghana and,

to a much greater extent, in Trinidad, James contributed what he could—
especially important writings—to advance the revolutionary struggle. In both
cases, he was forced to break with the political course adopted by Nkrumah
and Williams, each in their own way veering off from the revolutionary-democratic and socialist perspectives that he represented.[10]

In the final decades of his life, James was able to see his influence grow in
England, the United States, and in the Caribbean among activists who were
attracted to these revolutionary perspectives.

Human Limitations . . .

Before surveying some of James's significant theoretical contributions, it is
worth giving sustained attention to what some have seen as major political
and personal limitations—though, as we shall see, some of these involve
qualities that might seem more complex and contradictory than some critics
have been inclined to acknowledge.

Several people who had been central figures in James's US group—
Freddy and Lyman Paine, Grace Lee and James Boggs—and who broke with
him in 1962 agreed, looking back after a dozen years, that James had become
what they called "a Marxist egocentric" who became all too inclined to "bal-
lyhoo" C. L. R. James.[11]

In a similar vein, British writer Ethel Mannin offered a brief portrait
of James as an "eminent Trotskyist" (in late 1930s England) who was "an
extremely handsome young Negro" with "a dark rich beautiful voice." In her
portrayal (based on her own experience with him), James is a brilliant and eloquent speaker entering a well-wisher's London apartment while in the midst of
explaining to a couple of his co-thinkers that "the Permanent Revolution and
International Socialism must form the base of all revolutionary strategy." He
takes a moment to greet his hostess: "How are you, my dear?" without waiting
for her reply. Draping himself on her sofa, he goes on to elaborate on the situations in France, Spain, Abyssinia while critiquing—among other things—the
People's Front and the nature of imperialism. So wrapped up is he in a nonstop
discourse on theoretical, political, and historical matters, addressed to his two
admirers, that—aside from graciously accepting tea and sugar, sandwiches and
cake with a gracious "thank you, sister" and a few nods—he ignores his hostess
(who is able to speak a total of twelve words during his one-hour presence).
Frank Rosengarten suggests that James "was never quite able . . . to make his
theory of human equality into a living reality" in his own life.[12]

On the other hand, Kent Worcester argues that the Johnson-Forest
group of the 1950s "sought to create a democratic form of organization that

would encourage the active participation of all members and 'prefigure' social relations in the 'new society.'" Yet a disgruntled member has very critically described how this was implemented:

> The real proletarians were put in the first layer, people of mixed status, like housewives, in the second, and the intellectuals were put in the third. Our meetings consisted of the now highly prestigeful first layer spouting off, usually in a random, inarticulate way, about what they thought about everything under the sun. The rest of us, especially we intellectuals in the third layer, were told to listen.[13]

Although James and a few others might, on occasion, passively "listen" if sitting in on such meetings, the actual development of revolutionary theory was deemed too important to leave to such a process. James and a couple of others did the serious, intellectual heavy lifting, and then articulated the correct line. "He injected a climate into the entire group where his subordinates didn't have any dialogue either," recalled Steve Zeluck, a participant in such discussions. "There was a pecking order, an instruction order, someone gave you the line and that was it. If that was not your style, you were not long for that group." Susan Drake-Raphals, another participant, confirmed that "rank-and-file women who lacked the credentials of a Grace Boggs or a Raya Dunayevskaya were shunted off to the margins, and were not taken seriously by the leadership."[14] In addition, Constance Webb later recalled dynamics not uncommon among left-wing groups, but vibrantly reflected in the Johnson-Forest group, about which she, in looking back, was sharply critical:

> Our tiny group had noble and grand ideas of creating a better life for people worldwide, but as individuals they led narrow, circumscribed lives. They made every sacrifice—financial, physical, and personal—and there wasn't much energy left to simply enjoy themselves. Even our parties were political. They were to raise money or gain new members. Some people enjoyed themselves by getting a little drunk, but of course never the leading members. If the few who drank too much were working class, comrades were tolerant, because in our political view a worker could do no wrong . . .
>
> When I was a member I was as righteous and all-knowing as any member of a sect. Never again will I believe that I or anyone else is in *sole* possession of the truth: about what to think; how to live; what to do or be. It is dangerous to think that only you are right, that you know the truth and all whom you know must agree or something is wrong with them.[15]

Anna Grimshaw has traced a deep-rooted discrepancy—which even James is sometimes aware of—"between what [he] calls 'essence' and 'appearance,' between his internal state (chaos, the demons) and his external presentation (order, restraint, commitment)." Even among closer comrades in his own factional current, many found problematical interpersonal dynamics. "Despite his choice of female collaborators and intimate colleagues in revolutionary politics—indeed he regarded three of them ([Raya] Dunayevskaya, [Grace] Lee and [Constance] Webb) as among his greatest 'pupils'—he still acknowledged the depth of his resistance to admitting women into his life on equal terms," writes Grimshaw. "At best, James dealt with them as colleagues and collaborators (though he always sought to incorporate them into *his* vision of the world); at worst, he used them as domestic servants." At the same time, however, it is important to register something remarkable. "The leadership of the Johnson-Forest Tendency consisted of a West Indian Negro and two women, one of them Chinese-American," Martin Glaberman has pointed out. This was highly unusual at a time when, even on the Left, white male predominance was the norm. "This diversity was a configuration quite unique on the Left and at every other point on the political spectrum."[16]

Yet gender tensions were prevalent here as well. Those close to Raya Dunayevskaya—who had been one of James's closest, hardest-working, and most brilliant collaborators, yet who began to develop her own distinctive perspectives—believed that James "was indifferent and even hostile to the political implications of her work" to the extent that it was independent of his. On the other hand, James explained some of his hostility in a 1955 letter to her, focusing on the issue of authoritarian leadership: "While our contact with workers through the paper [of the Johnson-Forest group] should be as flexible as possible, you want it tightened . . . This attitude is the horrible *domination* that you feel you *must* exercise over the rank-and-file" [James's emphasis]. Yet this could cut two ways. A James stalwart, Lyman Paine (who would eventually break with him in 1962), wrote to James Boggs in 1961: "With regard to C. L. R., we had experiences dating back some time, in my case to 1955–56. We had tried to talk, to discuss, to explore. What we got was just what you have received now, a threat and a warning and an imposition of past authority, but no help, no discussion, no equality, no motion."[17]

Being a "Marxist egocentric," in the opinion of some of his comrades, sometimes undermined the quality of James's own thinking. One of his admirers, Walter Goldwater, was surprised by his "inability to look at himself objectively" and by his need to "always be at the center of attention." Goldwater saw aspects of James's theories as "arcane" and out of touch with reality—although those close to him shared James's own view (at least for a time) that his particular Hegelian-Marxist orientation resulted in placing them in a unique position for "facing reality." In the late 1940s, an irate Workers Party comrade, Irving Howe, sharply challenged what he perceived as James's "vague and irresponsible" inclination to see "soviets in the sky"—envisioning a revolutionary working class in the United States when, in fact, "America is the only country in the world today where the masses still retain their essential faith in the workability of the capitalist system, though they desire reforms and amelioration." Howe added that James "constantly speaks of the 'self-activity' of the working class as if that were some magical panacea." In 1950, before an SWP meeting at which James was speaking, Bert Cochran (at the time a prominent figure in the Socialist Workers Party) asked his wife and comrade Cynthia to attend because he was ill and unable to go himself. At his request, she brought him a report on what James had to say. She later recounted:

> I sat there ... he was a very handsome guy, very attractive ... I listening very carefully to every word he was saying. And then I start panicking about a third of the way through. I said [to myself], "What I am going to tell Bert?" I'm really listening to report it, and he didn't say much of anything, is what it added up to. But he said it beautifully. In other words it was more air than substance, was what *I* got out of it ... I went home and—Oh God!—I didn't know what to tell him. I told him two or three things [James] said, and then I couldn't think of anything else, and I thought I'd missed everything ... I ... told Bert "I'm sorry, that's all I can report." It was one of the few times he laughed and he said, "That's all right. *That's* C. L. R. James."[18]

An even closer comrade, Selma James, insisted, after breaking with him, that James's idiosyncrasies during the 1960s were manifested in "his sporadic Black nationalism, his defense of the vanguard party [in relation to the "third world"], and his glorifying and fawning over heads of state [in relation to Williams in Trinidad, Nkrumah in Ghana, and Castro in Cuba]."[19]

... and Strengths

Yet, the idiosyncrasies and egocentrism—one might argue—were, in some ways, inseparable from a self-conception that James theorized in the early 1960s, in a searching examination of the decline and disintegration of the organized tendency he represented:

> The leader of a Marxist organization must himself be a well-educated Marxist and be able, if not necessarily to work out the fundamental problems, at least to know what they are and seek some sort of answer with

some sense of historic continuity and the perspectives of a socialist movement . . . Marxism is above all the leadership and, if not the material, the
ideological leadership of the working-class movement and of those who
consider themselves Marxists. We have to lead. That does not mean being
placed in a position with an army or body of followers behind you. In
what you do, in the way you pose your problems and your solutions, you
show that you recognize your role.[20]

Three points can be drawn from this.

First of all, it seems to stand in stark contrast to the anti-Leninist and
anti-elitist notions that many who are superficially drawn to James want to
attribute to him. (Of course, James, despite his rejection of the so-called
"Leninist vanguard party," was in no way inclined to reject Lenin—whom
he held in a more or less uncritical embrace, the same as he did with Marx.)

Second, it seems to privilege the "ideological" (political ideas) over the
"material" (social forces). This came down to working out the ideas, the theory, the analysis independently of practical concerns of how such things are to
be utilized, implemented—even communicated—in the actual, material class
struggle. The Johnson-Forest group, when it was on its own, never had more
than one hundred members, and most of the working class had no awareness
even of its existence, let alone of its carefully worked out ideas. It was a "leadership" that lacked a significant followership.

Third, there is the question of who is a "well-educated Marxist." Those
who did not measure up, in James's estimate, naturally included the central
leaders of the US Trotskyist movement (Cannon, Shachtman, and others).
But they also included the remaining US leadership of the Johnson-Forest
group after his 1953 exile to England. James's various efforts to guide (or
micro-manage) his comrades from London generated resentments and fed
into splits.

As time went on, however, more than one knowledgeable person commented that James developed "a remarkably self-critical attitude concerning
his behavior with women and a willingness to learn."[21] Nor is it clear that he
was simply out of touch with those to whom he spoke. A younger friend in
Britain, Farrukh Dhondy, describes a presentation James gave to nine leading
activists in London's Black Panther Movement. "He was fluent, insightful,
penetrative and immediate," Dhondy recounts. "He said nothing obvious,
nothing patronizing. He knew to whom he was talking and brought all his
erudition to bear." He elaborated:

C. L. R. had a more direct demeanor than most lecturers I had heard.

When he spoke, he engaged with the small problems that his audience was grappling with and spread them on a larger canvass; giving them a history, significance and importance. He never spoke about a subject without assessing in a shrewd and instinctive way what his audience would want from him. In subsequent lectures and in later years I heard him do this again and again. He would penetrate the preoccupation of an audience having assessed them at a glance, and give their worries and wants deep historical depth.[22]

Nor was this interactive dynamic something manifested simply when James spoke to groups or crowds. "He had a wonderful way of getting people to talk to him, even the most shy," noted Constance Webb, a critical-minded confidant who was in a position to observe his interactions with people over a significant length of time. "And it wasn't a tactic or something planned in advance; it was a genuine interest in everyone to whom he spoke." She added: "He made people feel special, that what they thought or did was important. They were also left with a feeling that they could accomplish anything they set out to do." This contrasts with Ethel Mannin's humorous account of her experience with—one must note—a significantly younger James. The more mature political leader could (Webb emphasizes) "listen to others for hours and inspire them and make them feel they could accomplish miracles."[23]

The fact remains that politically, in his own mind, James was "the leader"—this never seems to have changed. While that can be seen as representing unmitigated arrogance, there is also a strong element of truth in it, which must be grasped if we are to understand James's significance and achievement. While James's style proved too autocratic for some, his intellectual contributions and the intellectual pursuits he inspired in comrades were invaluable. James himself, while corresponding with Martin Glaberman and other co-thinkers in 1962, elaborated on the Johnson-Forest tendency's impressive output.[24] Before examining that comment, it is worth considering a point made in the 1970s by some of the comrades who sharply broke with him:

> By 1936 C. L. R. James had thought about all the important things in European civilization and then he wrote *World Revolution*. Having written it, it crystallized in him the idea that the ideas in that book were permanent. So he became a preacher of world revolution, something like Trotsky. But he was a man of extreme breadth. He knew European history, he knew literature, he knew music, he wrote plays. Without C. L. R. James none of us would be talking the way we are talking today . . .
> In the years after the [1940] split from Cannon [and the SWP], the Johnson-Forest tendency was actually an intellectual faction within

the Workers Party. Throughout the World War II years we made an intensive effort to understand Marx in the light of European history and civilization, German Classical Philosophy, English Political Economy, and French politics in and after the French Revolution. We carried on studies that were fantastic: Adam Smith, Ricardo, and *Capital* in light of the development of German Classical Philosophy and English Political Economy, dialectics, Shakespeare, Beethoven, Melville, the Abolitionists, Negro history, Marcus Garvey.

We did a huge intellectual work during these years because we thought it was necessary to the American Revolution and because we saw the American working class as heirs to all this. Raya Dunayevskaya is still living on this work today. Only C. L. R. James could have given us the leadership in this.[25]

In his 1962 letter on the accomplishments of the Johnson-Forest group in this period, James usefully specified the material the group was able to publish:

a) a complete study of the Russian Question, the most comprehensive that has been done to my knowledge in the Marxist movement so far;
b) the economic-philosophical manuscripts of Marx . . . ;
c) I wrote for our education and understanding, including my own, some eighty thousand words on dialectic applied to Marxism . . . ;
d) The *American Worker*, one of the first serious studies of the actual life of a worker in the plant. . . . It showed the deep and profound comprehension we had of what constitutes Marxist politics;
e) made a fundamental analysis of our politics in terms of social forces in the country. Those in reality constitute the essence of the two *Balance Sheets*;
f) an analysis of world politics in *The Invading Socialist Society*.[26]

James also noted *State Capitalism and World Revolution*, written during the brief return to the SWP, as well as his own remarkable study of Herman Melville's *Moby Dick* entitled *Mariners, Renegades and Castaways*, plus *Indignant Heart: A Black Worker's Journal* by Matthew Ward. (Ward was the pen name of a Black autoworker also known as Charles Denby—his actual name was Si Owens. In this literary effort Constance Webb's central involvement, unfortunately, would go unacknowledged for decades). James additionally put together an impressive list of works that he believed *might* have been produced had he not been forced to leave the United States and if the Johnson-Forest group had, instead, remained intact under his leadership.[27]

What comes through here is the sense of an incredibly rich collective process that James initiated, orchestrated, and was at the center of. His contributions from the 1940s onward are largely a product of that process. It is certainly marked by personal limitations and striking contradictions, but these do not negate the value of many of his contributions.

James on Black Liberation in the United States

Among James's most substantial contributions was his role in helping to make revolutionary Marxists aware of the centrality of "the Negro Question"—to the class struggle and to any genuinely revolutionary perspective in the United States. First of all, he insistently demonstrated that the history of Blacks in the Americas was not simply a history of poor victims of oppression, but of a vibrant and conscious people that found innumerable ways to resist their oppression, assert their humanity, and periodically struggle for their own liberation.[28]

But James went much further than this. On the basis of in-depth study and experience in Black communities of the United States, creatively utilizing Lenin's views on oppressed nationalities, and in collaboration with Trotsky (with whom he had extensive discussions in Mexico), James developed a profound theoretical orientation to help guide the practical work of US revolutionaries.[29]

"The American Negroes, for centuries the most oppressed section of American society and the most discriminated against, are potentially the most revolutionary elements of the population," James explained in one resolution he wrote in 1939. "They are designated by their whole historical past to be, under adequate leadership, the very vanguard of the proletarian revolution." He added that "the broad perspectives of [Trotsky's theory of] the permanent revolution will remain only a fiction" unless revolutionary socialists can find their way to the African American masses.[30]

The implications of this analysis were that a consistent, uncompromising struggle for the democratic rights of African Americans (largely proletarianized) would necessarily challenge bourgeois power and capitalism, with a potential for growing into a struggle for working-class power and socialism. Yet James did not leave things at that. A second resolution noted that African Americans might feel moved, on the basis of their own historic oppression, to advance the demand "for the establishment and administration of a Negro state." He explained that "in a revolutionary crisis, as they begin to shake off the state coercion and ideological domination of the American bourgeois society, their first step may well be to demand the control, both actual and symbolical, of their own destiny."[31]

Rejecting schematic definitions having to do with whether Blacks in the US constituted "a nation," James pointed out that "the raising or support of the slogan by the masses of Negroes will be the best and only proof required." Under such circumstances, revolutionary socialists should support the demand, the realization of which could constitute, as James put it, a "step forward to the eventual integration of the American Negroes into the United Socialist States of America."[32]

James added: "The advocacy of the right of self-determination does not mean advancing the slogan of self-determination. Self-determination for Negroes means that Negroes themselves must determine their own future."[33] It is worth noting that there are, in fact, two meanings attached to the term "self-determination" here. One meaning involves separation, setting up a politically distinct nation—which may or may not take place, depending on what Blacks themselves wish to do. The other meaning involves the right of an oppressed people to define what they shall be and to determine their own future—which, James insisted, must be a constant principle for revolutionary Marxists.

He also observed that "the awakening political consciousness of the Negro not unnaturally takes the form of independent action uncontrolled by whites. The Negroes have long felt, and more than ever feel today the urge to create their own organizations under their own leaders and thus assert, not only in theory but in action, their claim to complete equality with other American citizens. Such a desire is legitimate and must be vigorously supported even when it takes the form of a rather aggressive chauvinism." James's next point is of particular interest: "Black chauvinism in America today is merely the natural excess of the desire for equality and is essentially progressive while white American chauvinism, the expression of racial domination, is essentially reactionary."[34]

This general orientation was so advanced for its time that the SWP proved incapable of fully assimilating it, and even today many socialists, even some who identify with Trotskyism, don't accept it. But in the 1960s James's position provided a basis for understanding the rising tide of militant struggles and nationalist consciousness in the Black community. While these new developments proved to be unexpected by and utterly confusing to many observers, Trotskyist analyst George Breitman was able to draw on the earlier perspectives to provide a revolutionary Marxist explanation. Especially important was Breitman's ability to highlight, document, and help popularize the profoundly revolutionary meaning of the ideas and life of Malcolm X—which would have been impossible without the kind of analysis pioneered by James a quarter of a century before.[35]

Part Two: James, Lenin, Trotsky—Critique

James is someone from whom one can learn much, sometimes even as one is challenging him and clarifying a disagreement. Before touching on problematical aspects of his thought, it makes sense to focus on strengths and insights that can be beneficial for social analysts as well as revolutionary socialists.

James's general approach to reality seems to me very dynamic and exciting. An essential aspect of his method is to make links between seemingly diverse realities, sometimes to take something that is commonly perceived as being marginal and to demonstrate that it is central; for example: the relation of the Haitian Revolution to the French Revolution and later to the fortunes of Napoleon Bonaparte; the relation of Blacks to world history, Western civilization, and the class struggle; the relation of popular culture—sports, movies, hit songs, dancing, pulp fiction, comic books, et cetera—to more "refined" culture, to social realities, and to class consciousness. James focuses on these so-called marginal realities in a manner that profoundly alters (rather than displaces) the traditionally central categories.

The attentive reader will find that such a methodological approach generates innumerable fruitful challenges that help to move one's thinking forward on a variety of issues. His approach to the world around him was comprehensive, multifaceted, and penetrating. As a revolutionary internationalist, he concerned himself with revolutionary events in Europe, Asia, Latin America, Africa—and also with the real struggles of working people and the oppressed in the United States, in which he saw genuinely revolutionary qualities. There is a profound continuity in how he viewed these struggles and the manner in which he defined socialism. This comes through in this passage from a 1947 pamphlet of the Johnson-Forest tendency entitled *The Invading Socialist Society*:

> The struggle for socialism is the struggle for proletarian democracy. Proletarian democracy is not the crown of socialism. It is its basis. Proletarian democracy is not the result of socialism. Socialism is the result of proletarian democracy. To the degree that the proletariat mobilizes itself and the great masses of the people, the socialist revolution is advanced. The proletariat mobilizes itself as a self-acting force through its own committees, unions, parties and other organizations.[36]

An essential aspect of James's approach is not that members of small revolutionary socialist groups need to persuade the working class to become such a "self-acting force." Rather, he insisted, the working class already is such a force, carrying out innumerable forms of resistance and struggle in everyday life in their own workplaces and communities and personal lives, which—while not necessarily conforming to the blueprints and schemata of revolutionary socialist groups, and often not noticed by these groups—effectively combat, undermine, and subvert capitalist power, creating elements of a new democratic-collectivist society within the shell of the capitalist society around us.[37]

In 1943 James expressed this outlook in a brilliant polemic against Sidney Hook (a pioneering post-Marxist whose 1943 volume *The Hero in History* is often echoed today in fashionable ex-leftist critiques of Marxism and Leninism). Here James writes eloquently about the relationship between the working class and genuinely revolutionary socialist groups. Noting that one aspect of Lenin's strength was that he was an organic part of Russian culture, he goes on to say:

> As to the outstanding role Lenin played inside his own party, even Marxist histories tend to give it a false significance. Lenin fought for the Bolshevik principles in 1903 and won. He was constantly winning, which means that he expressed ideas which stood the test of practice. The proletariat as a whole, at all critical moments, followed the Bolsheviks.
>
> More important than this, however, is the fact that the Russian proletariat taught and disciplined Lenin and the Bolsheviks not only indirectly but directly. Basically the organization of the party paralleled the organization of the productive power of the proletariat in revolution. In 1917, Lenin thought the struggle hopeless, and was thinking of giving it up. A few weeks later came the massacre of January, and the magnificent response of the Russian proletariat revived the faltering leader. The proletariat created the soviets [democratic workers' councils]. The Bolsheviks learned here to understand the vitality and creative power of the proletariat in revolution. . . . The great change in policy in April was only a manifestation of the essential policy of the Bolshevik Party, to express and organize the instinctive desires and aims of the proletariat. . . .
>
> The proletariat repeatedly led the Bolsheviks and gave Lenin courage and wisdom. Between 1890 and 1921 the interrelation between leader, party, class and nation was indivisible. The transformation of Bolshevism into totalitarianism is adequately dealt with in the literature of Trotskyism. The analysis is embodied in history, and the lessons are plain. With the proletariat or against it, that is the future of every modern nation. The secret of Lenin's greatness is that he saw this so clearly, and he saw this so clearly because this choice was the inescapable product of the whole past of Russia.[38]

We have here a vision of revolutionary organizations being organically connected with the history and culture of their own countries, and especially with their own working classes. Such a vision yields the insight that a revolutionary organization must be able to learn from the working class if it hopes to have anything to teach the working class, that it must follow the workers in order to lead, that the relationship between the revolutionary group and the working class must be profoundly interactive. Twenty years later, in 1963, James presented an equally positive notion of what constitutes authentic Leninism, one consistent with more recent scholarship:

> The theory and practice of the vanguard party, of the one-party state, is not (repeat not) the central doctrine of Leninism. It is not the central doctrine, it is not even a special doctrine. . . . Bolshevism, Leninism, did have central doctrines. One was theoretical, the inevitable collapse of capitalism into barbarism. Another was social, that on account of its place in society, its training and its numbers, only the working class could prevent this degradation and reconstruct society. Political action consisted in organizing a party to carry out these aims. These were the central principles of Bolshevism. The rigidity of its political organization came not from the dictatorial brain of Lenin but from a less distinguished source— the Tsarist police state. Until the revolution actually began in March 1917, the future that Lenin foresaw and worked for was the establishment of parliamentary democracy in Russia on the British and German models. . . . Bolshevism looked forward to a regime of parliamentary democracy because this was the doctrine of classical Marxism: that it was through parliamentary democracy that the working class and the whole population . . . was educated and trained for the transition to socialism.[39]

Marxism for Our Time

Some of the most interesting of James's writings related to the issue of building a revolutionary party can be found in the collection edited by Martin Glaberman, *Marxism for Our Times*. Of particular interest is a document that James presented to the Workers Party in 1944—"Education, Propaganda, Agitation: Post-War America and Bolshevism."[40] This document contains formulations that James would probably not have used in later years, but it is worth taking it in its own terms. We need to recall the context—the Great Depression had given way to the Second World War, but throughout there was an upswing of working-class insurgency and militancy, a general growth of left-wing organizations and movements, and a leftward tilt in national politics.[41]

Within this context, it was quite conceivable that "the working class could be educated and trained for the transition to socialism," as James had put it, but this would not happen if there was not, in the United States, an equivalent of the Bolshevik party that was able (again to use his words) "to express and organize the instinctive desires and aims of the proletariat." He added, "All studies of dialectic, of historical materialism, of political economy, of the history of the working class and of the revolutionary movement are for the most part meaningless if they do not concretely contribute to and culminate in the theoretical analysis of party building."[42]

James was absolutely in favor of the decision by the Workers Party to move the great majority of its members into industry and to work at "incorporating itself into the broad workers' movement." He argued that "no party, no group, can grow and develop unless the majority of its members function and function intelligently among the workers in industry." But he also argued that his comrades should not fool themselves as to what they had been able to accomplish by making this shift. "To have 75% of our membership in the unions did not transform us into a mass party," he lamented. "We became a propagandist sect in the unions. That is all."[43]

To illustrate his point, James compared the Workers Party, with a membership of no more than one thousand, to its greatest rival on the Left, the US Communist Party, which had a membership at that time of approximately eighty thousand (it had more than doubled its numbers over a several-year period, and now had a periphery of sympathizers several times that number). Despite the Stalinist deformation of Marxist theory and political practice, it was the kind of "small mass party" that the Workers Party aspired to be, as James pointed out in "Education, Propaganda, Agitation":

> Ten members of the CP could distribute 10,000 copies of the Sunday *Worker* in any area and confidently hope to reap results. Their paper has behind it the international power and prestige of a great modern state. The party is nationally recognized. In various spheres its actions materially affect the wages and working conditions and political life of large bodies of workers. Periodically its nationally known speakers can visit the area and capitalize on such a mass distribution policy. It can, at a given time, throw in organizers and pull its contacts together by activity and special concentration on the area in the pages of the paper. All that was and is entirely beyond our strength.[44]

Ten comrades working to distribute the Workers Party weekly paper, *Labor Action*, would not be able to have the same impact. "Workers in any numbers are repelled from small insignificant groups," he tells us. "The perspectives of one-by-one building up of a party to have an effect in ten or twenty years have little sense to a worker in a country where organized labor

is 14 million strong and the NAACP has half a million members."[45] James
integrates this into a more sweeping analysis of the situation facing the facing
the Workers Party:

> It is a highly specialized situation; a country ripe for socialism, a working
> class in a highly charged and explosive national and international situa-
> tion, but without even the education that is given by the political practice
> of a mass reformist party. Finally, there is another party, the Communist
> Party, representing Bolshevism in the eyes of the masses, pushing them
> as hard as it can back into bourgeois-democratic illusions, perverting and
> distorting all the fundamentals of Marxism and skimming off the cream
> of the revolutionary workers as they emerge from the broad masses.[46]

James does not, however, offer any clear explanation as to how the Workers Party is to overcome this dilemma (that is, the obstacles to replacing the
Communist Party with a genuinely revolutionary party capable of leading
the struggle for socialism). Instead, his train of thought shifts to a different,
though perhaps related, question.

Labor Action, in his opinion, despite its strengths, was hampered by a
misconception. "The world in which we live makes it imperative for us to concentrate all our best energies into making the paper an agent for the training
and recruiting of conscious Marxists," but the Workers Party was inclined
to believe "that the general level of consciousness of a working class movement forbids the strong and vigorous teaching of Marxism," that instead the
workers must be eased in the direction of class consciousness and class mobilization around more immediate struggles and issues. This, James argued,
"is contrary to the whole theory and practice of the Marxist movement for a
hundred years." His examples were not simply Lenin, Trotsky, and the Bolsheviks, but also the pre–World War I mass socialist movement in the United
States. The struggles of the 1930s, with a militancy carrying over into the
1940s, suggested that to limit one's self to a least-common-denominator level
makes no sense—for then "in *Labor Action* . . . we did not tell these thousands
of workers what they could not learn in any other way or from any other
source."[47] He wrote:

> The present writer believes that the American working class does not
> need its combativity stimulated. Any such approach on our part in partic-
> ular is not only ridiculous but presumptuous. Neither need there be any
> fear that the working class will not create mass political organizations.
> Without any assistance from *Labor Action* or the Bolsheviks, these are
> going to come with a violence and range which, as usual, will astonish

nobody more than the radicals themselves. The whole history of labor
and of labor in this country is indicative of the fact that what the American working class needs is the history and practice of Bolshevism. That is
what it needs, and that is what it can get only from us.[48]

The question of how to build a mass revolutionary party, he argued, was
something to be discussed, explored, and developed in the pages of *Labor
Action*. "Lenin insisted that the problems of party building should be discussed not only among the leaders and the intellectuals, but in the press
before the workers." In addition to this, James argued that it was not the
case that the Workers Party would, in fact, be able to transform itself into
the mass revolutionary party that the working class needed. "The American
mass party will not be built by us or by the Cannonites," he wrote. "Groups
of Virginia miners, West Coast sailors, Southern sharecroppers, Pittsburgh
steel workers, all sorts of 'left' formations will coalesce in time and hammer
out a unified organization. They will bring their qualities." This sense of a
multifaceted process (which may strike some of us as especially relevant to
early twenty-first-century realities in the United States) may have been too
open—too "non-vanguardist"—for James at this particular moment, for he
added that "our task is to form such a strong nucleus that the coalescence will
take place around us." But then he immediately shifted back to a more open
conceptualization—"or even if that does not take place, our special contribution will be Marxism and the theory and practice of Bolshevism."[49]

Perhaps James's failure to clarify and work through this tension and
partial contradiction provides a clue to his later dramatic shift—a shift that
involved its own contradictions and (what seems to me, at any rate) its own
lack of political clarity.

As Kent Worcester asserts: "By the late 1940s, the Johnsonites had implic-
itly rejected this conception of building a 'small mass party' in favor of an
emphasis on the masses' capacity for independent mobilization." Martin Glaberman put it this way: "James could see, as Lenin and Marx could see, that to
think that only with the guidance of a vanguard party could the working class
be fit to make a revolution was utopian nonsense."[50] Exactly what this means,
practically speaking, is not clear, and we shall return to the matter at the conclusion of this essay. But it will be worth lingering a bit longer over James's
1944 document in order to consider additional rich insights that it offers.

The Americanization of Bolshevism

"To Bolshevize America," James asserted, "it is necessary to Americanize Bolshevism." He explained that Marxist ideas had to be fully integrated with Russian traditions and experience in order to have resonance among revolutionaries and radicalizing workers of early twentieth-century Russia. "The Bolshevik Party was rooted in the day-to-day work, in industrial and mass struggles, to a degree compared to which our modest efforts can claim comparison only in good intentions," James noted. "Only an armor-plated ignorance could think of the Bolshevik leader as anything else but an advocate of mass activity." Yet inseparable from this was the Russification of Marxism. Lenin "considered it his special task" to help provide necessary intellectual resources for thousands of activists in his native land—and, in an impressive range of books, articles, and polemics—he applied philosophical, social, economic, and political perspectives of Marx to Russian realities and struggles. He accomplished this "with a grandeur, breadth, and vision that are astonishing," and it was necessary to do the same for the United States.[51]

"It is impossible to build an American mass party with our propaganda consisting of Marx on France and Germany, Lenin on Russia, and Trotsky on Stalinism and Spain; supplemented by the present *Labor Action* [with topical articles on the class struggle]," James argued. "It is impossible for a number of average workers to become Bolsheviks unless on the basis of some systematic penetration into American development." He insisted: "We have to begin now, not to write a few pamphlets but to build up the American counterparts of the *Communist Manifesto*, *The 18th Brumaire*, and perhaps even more important, the American counterpart of *What Is to Be Done*." James kept hammering away at this point: "In fact and in truth, only until one has dug the principles of Marxism for himself out of his own familiar surroundings and their historical past that the Marxism of Marx and Engels, Lenin or Trotsky and the famous European Marxists truly stand out in their universal application . . . Unless it is rooted in the American environment and in such terms as the American worker can grasp, we cannot lift them above the instinctive class struggle, sharp as that will become."[52]

James traced a line of exploration from the abstract to the specific. "Every principle and practice of Bolshevism needs to be translated into American terms," he wrote. "Historical materialism, the Marxian economic analysis, the role of the party, the relation between democracy and socialism, the relation between the trade union and the party, reformists and revolution, the role of Social Democracy, the theory of the state, the inevitability of socialism, every single one of these can be taught, developed, demonstrated from the American economic, social, and political development." This suggested an amazing set of research and education projects:

> The American Revolution, the Civil War, the Knights of Labor, the Populist Movement, the Southern economy, the tremendous history of the CIO, the development of the two major parties, the political and social contributions of Paine, Jefferson, the Wilson administration, the New Deal, the NRA, the American dollar civilization, the rise and decline of the Socialist Party, Eugene Debs, John L. Lewis, the Marxist analysis of all this is the material of our education, of our propaganda, of the creation of a Bolshevism which will break a path for us to the American masses. The ideas of Marxism must be boldly and uncompromisingly presented to the American workers. The great European classics must be used, not only for their own sake, but as a means of explaining American development.[53]

Later in the essay—as one would expect from the author of the path-breaking "Revolution and the Negro"—he adds:

> The Negro Question. Here, as Marxist interpreters, the field is ours, Negroes and populism, Booker T. Washington, Frederick Douglass, the Garvey movement, whatever serious work we do here will not only educate ourselves but will be gobbled up by the Negro people, masses and intellectuals alike. And progressive white workers.[54]

There are certainly gaps in what James lays out, nor does he connect all the dots in this swirl of arguments on the ways and means of creating a US equivalent of the Bolshevik party. Yet one senses that he is on to something when he writes: "With such a party, we shall not only be able to educate our members and give to those with whom we come in contact what they will increasingly be looking for." He sees this not only as an aspect of party-building, but as "our special contribution to the labor movement," concluding: "The two complement each other to complete what is known as scientific socialism. If one aspect is ignored, neglected, or superficially dealt with, then the other assumes an unchecked momentum of its own and does not even bring the rewards which the efforts lead us to expect."[55]

What is striking to a Leninist admirer of James is that this incredibly challenging and seemingly fruitful party-building agenda of 1944 was abandoned. The historical record indicates that James and his followers became frustrated by experiences in Shachtman's Workers Party, then by experiences resulting from their return to Cannon's Socialist Workers Party, and that they subsequently gave up on the party-building project altogether. One can certainly find valuable residual elements of this abandoned agenda in subsequent Johnson-Forest perspectives and efforts (which lived on in the two fragments after the separation of Johnson and Forest). But the disjunction between ideological and material, noted in Part One of this contribution, became a more central element in their political practice.

It could be argued—probably persuasively—that neither the Workers Party nor the Socialist Workers Party was capable of carrying out even half of what James was proposing in "Education, Propaganda, Agitation: Post-War America and Bolshevism." James himself had identified some of the reasons why it wasn't feasible in that very document. The yawning gap between theoretical ambition and actual material reality—to some extent captured in Irving Howe's polemical jibe about "soviets in the skies"—was never resolved.

In order to "move on" with the kind of theoretical work that it wanted to do, it became necessary for the Johnson-Forest Tendency to abandon the two Trotskyist party-building contenders in the United States—and the party-building perspective altogether. There was more than one way to theorize this decision. The way that James chose—as we shall see—involved the development of some sweeping generalizations (not devoid of insights) about the working class, class consciousness, and the relation of Marxism to the working class, intertwined with a full-scale rejection of Trotsky himself. The results were highly problematical.

A Challenge to Revolutionary Marxists

There are a number of challenges that James poses—many that are stimulating and suggestive, others that are problematical. In order to take James seriously, we owe it to him (and to ourselves) to give attention to an example of what is problematical.

By 1951 the Johnson-Forest Tendency (with James leading the way) had consciously and explicitly broken not only with the formal Trotskyist movement, but also what they had concluded was Trotsky's flawed theoretical and organizational approach. Well after the breakup of his group, James continued to counterpose his perspectives (which he continued to identify with Marx and Lenin) to the perspectives of Trotsky—and this is what he presented to an audience of left-wing and radicalizing activists in London in 1963, in comments that would be read over the coming years by significant numbers of younger radicals.

James commented: "What has happened to the revolutionary movement under the guidance of Trotsky" was "nothing else but an absolute disaster."[56] He went on to prove this, to his satisfaction, by taking a brief quote by

Trotsky—out of context—which he easily demolished and ridiculed, before triumphantly comparing what he saw as Trotsky's understanding of things with Lenin's (and James's own). Here is the passage, from Trotsky's *History of the Russian Revolution*, that James attacks:

> To overthrow the old power is one thing. To take power is another. The bourgeoisie may win power in a revolution not because it is revolutionary but because it is bourgeois . . . Quite otherwise with the proletariat. Deprived in the nature of things of all social advantages, an insurrectionary proletariat can count only on its numbers, its solidarity, its cadres, its official staff.[57]

James aptly notes the words *cadres* and *official staff* refer to "party" and "party leadership," going on to imply that Trotsky is saying that the working class cannot do anything unless led by a revolutionary party. He then triumphantly responds: "The things that matter in Britain, the proletariat is responsible for. To mention two, the end of the Empire, and the end of unemployment as a necessary part of society." Regarding Trotsky's presumed notion of working-class sterility that consequently requires a revolutionary party, James scoffs: "That is his conception, that is what he is writing in 1932. And that is what he wrote until he died."[58]

There are five problems with what James does here.

First of all, he omits Trotsky's explanation of the power of the bourgeoisie: "It has in its possession property, education, the press, a network of strategic positions, a hierarchy of institutions." All true. Trotsky then points out, accurately enough: "Quite otherwise with the proletariat." Second, James makes his job of dismissing Trotsky easier by ignoring several pages of detailed discussion meant to clarify what Trotsky means in the quoted passage.[59] To act as if relatively important elaborations and explanations are absent is not the same as actually refuting them.

Third, he ignores the fact that Trotsky is simply paraphrasing Marx's 1864 Inaugural Address of the International Workingmen's Association—not developing his own distinctive view but simply embracing and repeating that of Marx. In the 1864 address, Marx says of the working class: "One element of success they possess—numbers; but numbers weigh only in the balance, if united by combination and led by knowledge." And in preceding remarks, Marx links the need for the workers "to conquer political power" with the fact that "efforts are being made at the political reorganization of the workingmen's party." In challenging Trotsky here, James is challenging a position that Trotsky adopted from Marx.[60]

Fourth, while Trotsky (like Marx) is referring to the ability of the working class *to take political power*, James shifts to a somewhat different question of whether the working class can pressure the capitalists to change the way capitalism functions—for example, to end the colonial empire, and to implement welfare-state reforms designed to decrease the effects of unemployment. (Because the working class did *not* actually *take political power* in Britain, some would argue, British imperialism merely shifted to different—non-colonial—outlets, and working-class unemployment was by no means forever eliminated.)

Fifth, not only does James distort what Trotsky said in *History of the Russian Revolution*, but he attributes this distortion to Trotsky as though it were permanent, insisting that he maintained it for the rest of his life—even though there is much in Trotsky's later writing to indicate otherwise. In his writings about Germany, for example, it is quite clear that Trotsky believed a multifaceted labor movement, created by the working class, had become a powerful political force, with a potential for forming a transition to socialist revolution—which was why it was targeted by the Nazis and their bourgeois supporters. Trotsky offered a theorization in early 1933 that was inconsistent with what James attributes to him, as he sought to persuade workers in the Social Democratic and Communist parties to join together in preventing the imminent Nazi victory:

> Within the framework of bourgeois democracy and parallel to the incessant struggle against it, the elements of proletarian democracy have formed themselves in the course of many decades: political parties, labor press, trade unions, factory committees, clubs, cooperatives, sports societies, etc. The mission of fascism is not so much to complete the destruction of bourgeois democracy as to crush the first outlines of proletarian democracy. As for our mission, it consists in placing those elements of proletarian democracy, already created, at the foundation of the soviet system of the workers' state. To this end, it is necessary to break the husk of bourgeois democracy and free from it the kernel of workers' democracy. Therein lies the essence of the proletarian revolution.[61]

One of the complexities in all of this is that Trotsky is actually being criticized for attempting to apply Lenin's party-building perspectives—a strategy that in 1944 James himself enthusiastically elaborated on in "Education, Propaganda, Agitation." From the late 1940s onward, however, it was James's contention that this strategy no longer makes sense (and he seemed to feel that Lenin would have agreed with him on this). James never altered his analysis of and admiration for Lenin and the Bolshevik party. But he discarded the conception of building a revolutionary vanguard party in the United States because he felt this conception—as understood by most US Leninists—got in the way of cultivating the necessary interactive relationship between revolutionary Marxists and the actually existing, self-acting working class.

In a related development, he came to the conclusion that Trotsky and other revolutionary Marxists had been wrong about believing that, after a working-class revolution, a transitional period between capitalism and socialism would be necessary. He felt that before the working class made its revolution it would already have created—spontaneously, or semi-spontaneously, through its own activity—democratic, collectivist, socialist relations through its resistance to capitalist oppression. Even if the working class did not put a "socialist" label on its own consciousness, activities, and relationships, these were developing in a socialist direction within the very framework of capitalist society, through the class struggle that—as noted in the *Communist Manifesto*—is "now hidden, now open." The transition to socialism, he felt, is taking place now in the consciousness and struggles of working people in their workplaces and in their communities, and the transition will be completed (not begun) by a working-class revolution.

James—in *Notes on Dialectics*, a highly abstract document written for his followers in 1948—sought to interweave the ideas of Hegel, Marx, and Lenin in order to provide an orientation based on these notions. "The task today is to call for, to teach, to illustrate, to develop *spontaneity*—the free creative activity of the proletariat." While historically "organization has been the backbone of the proletarian movement, . . . there comes a time when organization and the maintenance of the organization become ends in themselves in the most direct conflict with the essential movement of the proletariat." Contrasting the "constantly breaking out impulses, activity, spontaneity of the workers and the implacable bureaucracies of Stalinism," he concluded: "If the free activity of proletariat is to emerge, it can emerge only by destroying the communist parties. It can destroy these parties only by free activity. Free activity means not only the end of the communist parties. It means the end of capitalism."[62]

We have noted James and his co-thinkers saw the socioeconomic system in the USSR and similar countries simply as a form of capitalism—which they termed "state capitalism." We should also acknowledge that their approach was grounded in the general global context that James perceived in the late 1940s:

> As I write the German people are being fought over as dogs fight over a bone. France is being torn to pieces. Britain lives by blood-plasma from the United States. The world moves to civil war and imperialist war, or imperialist civil war. They are being prepared openly before the people.

The Stalinists are overrunning China. They aim at Burma, Korea, Indonesia, Indo-China and then India. Year by year for thirty years this is the course bourgeois society has taken.[63]

What is described here is certainly not our world in the twenty-first century (and one could raise questions about how accurately it captures James's world in the mid-twentieth century.) In any event, the perspectives James and his co-thinkers advanced in major documents of 1950 and 1958—*State Capitalism and World Revolution* and *Facing Reality*—flow from this historically specific understanding of reality.[64] In the year preceding James's 1948 analysis, he and others had developed some of these concepts, which are highlighted by the very title of that earlier document, *The Invading Socialist Society*, emphasizing that socialism would inevitably flow from socialist elements that were already seen in ideas and activities within the working class in the "here and now" of the late 1940s.

Conclusion

I believe that there is some truth in the ideas James put forward. The notion that socialism (the actual impulses, if not the actual label) is latent in the present society strikes me as particularly fruitful. But he took it too far. Socialism is not inevitable. There are countervailing tendencies—anti-socialist, anti-democratic, anti-humanist tendencies—in our society, in our culture, and within the working class. The genuinely revolutionary and socialist tendencies that James points to are there in the consciousness, the struggles, and the everyday life of those who are part of the working class. But these can become triumphant only to the extent that they become conscious, are organized and mobilized—and there are no guarantees that this will happen on its own. Elements *within* the working class, including people like ourselves, will need to *work hard to help make it happen.*

To be effective, we will need to organize ourselves, we will need to learn how to work collectively and carry out activities, aligned with a coherent plan, that contribute to the growth of a working-class socialist movement, creating organizational structures that can facilitate all of this. Those who do this in the United States, contrary to what James argued in the 1950s and afterward (but consistent with what he argued before), are moving in the direction of creating a US variant of the Bolshevik-Leninist party.

Those who are doing that, however, will be well served by critically drawing from the rich contributions offered to us by our comrade C. L. R. James. There is much that recommends him to us—his great intellectual breadth, which is reflected in the quality of his Marxism, combining a serious concern with philosophy, history, economics, culture, and practical political work. There is also his capacity to see things that aren't quite "there" yet, but which are in the process of coming into being.

Related to this is his capacity to identify fruitful connections between seemingly disparate phenomena, and his consequent ability to take what is "peripheral" and show that it is, in fact, central to an adequate understanding of politics and society. In addition, there is the deep humanism that is essential to revolutionary Marxism but which James makes very much his own, which opens to us a crucial insight: socialism is not something that is simply thought up by brilliant intellectuals—it is an integral part of the reality around us. Essential elements of it can be found in the thinking, the perceptions, the values, the desires, the everyday-life activities, the many ongoing struggles of the human beings who are part of the working-class majority.

7

Martin Luther King
Christian Core, Socialist Bedrock

The life and example of Martin Luther King Jr. are central to any quest for a better world—in part because he so effectively illuminated and helped people struggle against the realities of racism, highlighting the link between issues of racial and economic justice. I will argue here that his outlook represents a remarkable blending of Christian, democratic, and socialist perspectives.

As a Christian, King rejected the humanist atheism of Karl Marx, which held that "man, unaided by any divine power, can save himself and usher in a new society." He insisted that "there is a God in the universe who is the ground and essence of all reality," who is "a Being of infinite love and boundless power," and the "creator, sustainer, and conserver of values" that are essential to humanity. "Man cannot save himself, for man is not the measure of all things and humanity is not God," King tells us. "Bound by the chains of his own sin and finiteness, man needs a Savior." King scholar Keith Miller has observed, however, that he also "refused to repudiate Marxism wholesale."[1]

In fact, King had a radical orientation from the very beginning of his political career. His widow, Coretta Scott King, noted that "within the first month or so of our meeting," in 1952, King "talked about working within the framework of democracy to move us toward a kind of socialism," arguing that "a kind of socialism has to be adopted by our system because the way it is, it's simply unjust."

She commented that "democracy means equal justice, equity in every aspect of our society," and that King "knew that the basic problem in our society had to do with economic justice, or . . . the contrast of wealth between the haves and the have-nots. Believe it or not, he spoke these words to me when I first met him. It wasn't something that he learned later and developed." She added: "I think Martin understood from the very beginning that this goal could not be accomplished all at once . . . I had enough training and background myself to appreciate where he was in his thinking."[2]

This was a person who was centrally important to King's life. It may be worth lingering for a few moments on her training and background, which is generally passed over in silence by those discussing King's life and ideas.

Coretta Scott was born into a poor family in rural Alabama, whose proud and hardworking patriarch—through working in a lumber mill, truck farming, and barbering on the side—was able to secure for his loved ones a more secure life than had been experienced by many Southern Blacks enmeshed in the sharecropping system.

Coretta herself was no stranger to hard physical labor, tending crops and picking cotton. Poignantly aware of the many aspects of racism that shaped her family's and her own experience, she was also somewhat protected by living in a rural "all-black community of three generations of land ownership," which "helped to instill in us racial pride, self-respect, and dignity which inevitably gave us the proper self-image."[3]

Excelling in school, she was able to secure a scholarship to Antioch College in Yellow Springs, Ohio. The experience at Antioch was positive in many ways, but her experience of racism in the North helped to propel her into student activism in the late 1940s.

"Antioch had a chapter of the NAACP and a Race Relations Committee and a Civil Liberties Committee. I was active in all of them," she recounted in her memoirs. "From the first, I had been determined to get ahead, not just for myself, but to do something for my people and for all people."

The liberal and socially conscious values inculcated through the academic program at Antioch "reinforced the Christian spirit of giving and sharing which had been taught to me by my parents, particularly my father." Her studies and experiences "reaffirmed my belief that individuals as well as society could move toward the democratic ideal of brotherhood."[4]

Through her musical activities in a choir she had an opportunity to meet and appear on the same program as the famous African American baritone Paul Robeson, a left-wing icon for many progressive-minded Blacks and whites. Swept up in the radical social idealism of the 1948 presidential campaign of Henry Wallace (who argued that peace, prosperity, racial equality, and social justice required a break from the big business–dominated Democratic and Republican parties), she attended the founding convention of the Progressive Party.

Robeson and the Progressives were severely red-baited in these early Cold War years for being influenced by the Communist Party, but this didn't stop Coretta from exploring and sharing socialist ideas. King was aware of her interests, as shown in a 1952 letter to her where he discusses his positive reaction to an old socialist classic, Edward Bellamy's utopian novel *Looking*

Backward, which she had obviously already read before him: "I welcome the book because much of its content is in line with my basic ideas," he wrote. "I imagine you already know that I am much more socialistic in my economic theory than capitalistic."[5]

Before he met Coretta, King attended Crozer Theological Seminary in Chester, Pennsylvania, from 1948 to 1951. It was clear to one of his teachers and closest associates there, Reverend J. Pious Barbour, that King "believed Marx had analyzed the economic side of capitalism right" and that "the capitalistic system was predicated on exploitation and prejudice, poverty, and that we wouldn't solve these problems until we got a new social order." In this period he studied the *Communist Manifesto* and *Capital*.[6]

He also immersed himself in the works of left-wing Protestant theologians, of whom, King noted more than once, Walter Rauschenbusch and Reinhold Niebuhr were the most important to him. Rauschenbusch, whose 1907 *Christianity and the Social Crisis* reveals a powerful Marxist influence, proclaimed that "the working class is now engaged in a great historic class struggle which is becoming ever more conscious and bitter," and that "socialism is the ultimate and logical outcome of the labor movement."[7]

Rauschenbusch argued that "the new Christian principle of brotherly association must ally itself with the working class if both are to conquer," since "the force of religious spirit should be bent toward asserting the supremacy of life over property."[8] Niebuhr, whose 1932 classic *Moral Man and Immoral Society* critically integrates not only Marx but even more the "brutal realist" Lenin into what was (in that period) a quite radical version of the "Christian realist" synthesis, approvingly quoted from Lenin's *State and Revolution*:

> In their sum, these restrictions (of middle-class democracy) exclude and thrust out the poor from politics and from active share in democracy. Marx splendidly grasped the essence of capitalistic democracy, when, in his analysis of the spirit of the commune, he said the oppressed are allowed, once every few years, to decide which particular representatives of the oppressing classes are to represent and repress them in politics.[9]

According to Niebuhr, "a certain system of power, based upon the force which inheres in property, and augmented by the political power of the state is set against the demands of the worker." In his opinion, "conflict is inevitable, and in this conflict power must be challenged by power."[10]

Even while attending Morehouse College in Atlanta, Georgia, King was exposed to liberal and radical religious and political influences through Dr. Benjamin Mays, the college's president and a King family friend. A key figure among Black and white socially conscious clergy, Mays insisted that "if the gospel of Jesus Christ cannot solve the race problem, Christianity is doomed." This orientation, Mays's association with such left-of-center figures as Reinhold Niebuhr and Paul Tillich, as well as W. E. B. Du Bois and Paul Robeson—together with his visionary and precisely articulated speaking and preaching styles—influenced his colleagues and students, King no less than others.

But there were other influences that King had been exposed to every Sunday as he grew into manhood. Deeply rooted in African American preaching traditions are profoundly radical elements—what Keith Miller has called "a system of knowledge and persuasion created by generations of black folk preachers, including [King's] father and grandfather"—that would later find dramatic reflection in his life and thought.[11]

Elements of this "system" were also reflected in the works of the radical Black theologian Howard Thurman, who in his 1949 work *Jesus and the Disinherited* (which influenced King and many others) explains that "the basic fact is that Christianity as it was born in the mind of this Jewish thinker appears as a technique of survival for the oppressed." Thurman added: "The striking similarity between the social position of Jesus in Palestine and that of the vast majority of American Negroes is obvious to anyone who long tarries over the facts."

That Christianity "became, through the intervening years, a religion of the powerful and the dominant, used sometimes as an instrument of oppression, must not tempt us into believing that it was thus in the mind and life of Jesus," Thurman insists. "His message focused on the urgency of a radical change in the inner attitude of the people."

This analysis ran parallel to the earlier assertion of Rauschenbusch that "Jesus proceeded from the common people. He had worked as a carpenter for years and there was nothing in his thinking to neutralize the sense of class solidarity which grows up under such circumstances. The common people heard him gladly because he said what was in their hearts . . . Jesus was not a mere social reformer . . . He has been called the first socialist."[12] The analysis certainly ran parallel to King's later comments:

We have the power to change America and give a kind of new vitality to the religion of Jesus Christ . . . He initiated the first sit-in movement. The greatest revolutionary that history has ever known . . . You don't have to go to Karl Marx to learn how to be a revolutionary. I didn't get my inspiration from Karl Marx; I got it from a man named Jesus, a Galilean saint who said he was anointed to heal the broken-hearted. He was anointed to deal with the problems of the poor. And that is where we get our inspiration. And we go out in a day when we have a message for the world, and we can change this world and we can change this nation.[13]

During his childhood, King—perceiving the effects of the Great Depression—recalled how he questioned his parents "about the numerous people standing in the breadlines," and reflected over "the effects of this early childhood experience on my present anticapitalistic feelings." While in his teens he worked for two summers in a factory with a Black and white workforce where "the poor white was exploited just as much as the Negro," planting the thought that "the inseparable twin of racial justice was economic justice."[14]

Socialist Roots of the Civil Rights Struggle

Decisive for the development of the modern civil rights movement were several important left-wing institutions and key activists that had a substantial Marxist influence and socialist-orientation, and whose impact on King was substantial.

Aldon D. Morris, in his fine study *The Origins of the Civil Rights Movement*, has emphasized the role of what he calls "movement halfway houses." He describes these as having "a relative isolation from the larger society" and not having a mass membership, but as "developing a battery of social change resources such as skilled activists, tactical knowledge, media contacts, workshops, knowledge of past movements, and a vision of a future society."

Among those institutions that he identifies in this manner, and as playing a vital role in the origins of the civil rights movement, are the Fellowship of Reconciliation, Highlander Folk School, and the Southern Conference Educational Fund.[15]

The Fellowship of Reconciliation (FOR) was the country's foremost pacifist organization, influenced by Christian and socialist currents and by the example of Mohandas Gandhi's nonviolent campaigns to free India from British colonial rule. Its executive director was the venerable Reverend A. J. Muste.

Muste began as a Christian pacifist who, under the impact of Social Gospel currents personified by Walter Rauschenbusch and others, had shifted from preaching to union organizing to functioning as the director of the left-wing center of labor education of the 1920s and '30s, Brookwood Labor College.

Absorbing a considerable amount of class-struggle experience plus the ideas of Marx, Lenin, and Trotsky, he became a leader of the homegrown socialist American Workers Party, then merged with the Trotskyists of the Communist League of America to form the Workers Party of the United States. Muste returned to Christian pacifism in the late 1930s but never shed essential elements of his Marxist understanding.

It was FOR that attracted a young Black radical, James Farmer, to help found the Congress of Racial Equality. Others involved with FOR included Howard Thurman, as well as two young ministers and Gandhian radicals who would play key roles in the civil rights movement, James Lawson (prominently active in the Southern movement beginning in 1957, and a leader of the 1968 Memphis struggle of striking sanitation workers) and Glen Smiley (a key white supporter during the Montgomery Bus Boycott), as well as Bayard Rustin, who helped lead the first Freedom Rides in 1942.[16]

Highlander Folk School was founded in rural Tennessee during the early 1930s by Myles Horton, Don West, Elizabeth Hawes, James Dombrowski, and others committed to establishing a progressive labor education center in the South. Blending religious and Marxist perspectives, they attracted support from such figures as Reinhold Niebuhr, Norman Thomas, and John Dewey.

Highlander was designed "to educate rural and industrial leaders for a new social order," particularly in union organizing efforts that would advance what Horton called "conscious class action." West explained that Highlander "educates for a socialized nation" in which "human justice, cooperation, a livelihood for every man and a fair distribution of wealth" would replace the present system of "graft, exploitation, and private profit."

Hawes noted the school's "revolutionary purpose" to help bring its students to an awareness of the need for, and the skills needed to struggle for, "a classless society." At the same time, as Horton later explained, it was informed by the insight that "people have to believe that you genuinely respect their ideas and that your involvement with them is not just an academic exercise."[17]

From the early 1930s the school viewed the necessity of cooperation among Black and white workers in order to advance the needs of both. Highlander's central role as a school for CIO workers in the South from the late 1930s through the late 1940s was disrupted by the Cold War, when labor's mainstream drove out Communist-influenced unions, as well as dramatically marginalizing left-wing influences in general.

By the early 1950s, Highlander shifted "to extend its activities into wider fields of democratization," and in the wake of the Supreme Court's 1954 decision on school desegregation it became a center for education and training to assist the civil rights movement. Among those attending Highlander workshops were people who initiated the Montgomery Bus Boycott, such as NAACP activists Rosa Parks and E. D. Nixon.

Highlander staff member Septima Clark, who became director of those workshops in 1954, developed a Citizenship Education Program that combined teaching literacy and voter registration information with holding fundamental discussions on social, economic, and political questions.[18]

Highlander pioneer James Dombrowski also played a central role in creating the Southern Conference Educational Fund (SCEF). Dombrowski, whose 1936 study *Early Days of Christian Socialism in America* remains a minor classic, was a protégé of Rev. Harry F. Ward, furthest to the left of all the faculty at Union Theological Seminary (eventually gravitating too close to the Communist Party to be tolerated by most of his seminarian colleagues).

Dombrowski served as director of the left-liberal Southern Conference for Human Welfare and was a prominent supporter of the Progressive Party campaign of 1948. When he initiated SCEF in the late 1940s, he was able to attract such prominent African American supporters as Benjamin Mays of Morehouse College, who served as SCEF vice president until 1954.

Several years later, Rev. Fred Shuttlesworth, centrally involved in the Birmingham, Alabama, civil rights struggles and a close associate of Martin Luther King, would become SCEF's president, defending SCEF staffers Carl and Anne Braden when they were attacked by the House Un-American Activities Committee. The Bradens were independent-minded socialists who had worked for left-led unions, been involved with the Progressive Party, and courageously challenged segregated housing where they lived in Louisville, Kentucky.

They edited the SCEF monthly journal the *Southern Patriot*, which played a significant role in the early civil rights movement. It was Anne Braden who drove King from a 1957 conference at Highlander Folk School, where, among other things, he first heard the song "We Shall Overcome," sung by Pete Seeger. King commented, "There's something about that song that haunts you."[19]

One of the most authoritative figures in the Black community on the national stage was A. Philip Randolph, whose political career began as a Socialist Party member and who published a radical magazine, the *Messenger*. His discovery of Marxism, he later commented, was "like finally running into an idea which gives you your outlook on life," which now included the view that "when no profits can be made from race friction, no one will longer be interested in stirring up race prejudice."

Running as a Socialist Party candidate in 1918, he proclaimed: "The new Negro is here, and there will be many more of them to enrich the socialist movement in the United States." Hailing the Russian Revolution, the *Messenger* asserted: "We want a patriotism not streaked with race, color, or sex lines. What we really need is a patriotism of liberty, justice, and joy. This is Bolshevik patriotism, and we want more of that brand in the United States."[20]

While Randolph turned against what he considered to be a sectarian and manipulative dynamic inherent in the Communist movement during the Stalin era, there is no indication that he ever repudiated his support for the earlier incarnation of Bolshevism. His longtime aide Bayard Rustin commented many years later that "democratic socialism" was "the political system which was the foundation of his strategy and tactics in the trade union movement, and in the civil rights movement."[21]

During the 1920s and 1930s he played a central role in organizing and building the Brotherhood of Sleeping Car Porters, a modest but vital bastion of Black strength in the labor movement and of down-to-earth radicalism in the Black community.

In 1941 Randolph built an effective March on Washington movement to protest racial discrimination in the armed forces and war industries. This forced President Roosevelt (as a condition for calling off the march) to sign an executive order banning discrimination in war industries, government training programs, and government industries.

"Power and pressure are at the foundation of the march of social justice and reform . . . power and pressure do not reside in the few, and intelligentsia, they lie in and flow from the masses," Randolph commented, adding: "Power is the active principle of only the organized masses, the masses united for a definite purpose."[22]

In the decades leading up to the emergence of the modern civil rights movement, Randolph had a profound impact. Among many contributions, he gave immediate and substantial backup to Sleeping Car Porters local union president and Montgomery, Alabama, NAACP leader E. D. Nixon when the 1955–56 Montgomery Bus Boycott began. It was Randolph (with Rustin) who initiated and oversaw the organization of the 1963 March on Washington for Jobs and Freedom where Martin Luther King gave his "I Have a Dream" speech.

Particularly important in conceiving of and helping to found the organization that King would lead after the victory of the Montgomery Bus Boycott, the Southern Christian Leadership Conference (SCLC), were three capable Northern activists who also had an important influence on King—Stanley Levison, Ella Baker, and Bayard Rustin.

All were part of a loose but significant left-liberal group formed in 1955 known as In Friendship, designed to provide Northern assistance for school desegregation. Levison, a New York attorney, had been active in the Communist Party from the 1930s until the early 1950s—then seems to have concluded (while maintaining his socialist orientation and not becoming an anti-Communist) that it no longer was an effective vehicle for social change.[23]

Ella Baker was never a member of the Communist Party but had attended radical Brookwood Labor College in 1931. She worked in New York City for many years for the NAACP—absorbing and interacting with various left-wing currents. During the 1930s she was in or close to the Communist

Party Opposition, a dissident left-wing group headed by Jay Lovestone and
Bertram D. Wolfe, and unlike some of the group's leaders after its dissolution,
she never shed her left-wing perspectives. "We won't be free until we've done
something to change society," she once commented, and "the only society
that can serve the needs of large masses of poor people is a socialist society."[24]

Bayard Rustin had been a shining light in the Young Communist League
in the late 1930s, then sharply broke from the Communist Party with profound
political differences in 1941. He worked closely with A. Philip Randolph in
the March on Washington movement of 1941, was attracted to the Gandhian pacifism of FOR, and became a prominent figure in the War Resisters
League and CORE. "He was like a superman," recalled Stokely Carmichael,
"hooking socialism up with the black movement, organizing blacks."

Rustin never abandoned his Marxist orientation and when he became
executive director of the A. Philip Randolph Institute in the late 1960s was
still citing the *Communist Manifesto* as essential reading for those wishing to
understand contemporary social issues and strategies for social change.[25]

King's development, strengthened by such influences as these, resulted in
an orientation not typically associated with Black Southern preachers. Actor
Ossie Davis, a prominent figure among left-wing African American intellectuals, later remembered that King's "philosophy of nonviolence seemed dangerous nonsense to many of us in the North." But King had a powerful impact
on Davis and his milieu when he came to speak to them in person.

"Here was something more than Reverend 'Pork Chops'—more than
hellfire and brimstone." Speaking in "that mellifluous, rolling baritone of
his" with impressive eloquence and mounting passion, "erecting one tower
of rhetoric after another," moving the crowd to enthusiasm, "it was perfectly
clear—nonviolence notwithstanding—that we in the black church, and in the
black community, had found ourselves a leader."

Left-wing lawyer Conrad Lynn, closely associated with Davis, was no
less skeptical of King's pacifism but concluded that "in retrospect, it is clear
that the nonviolent strategy and tactics of Martin Luther King were the best
available weapons for the black people in the period of the sixties," adding:
"Martin Luther King, by his strong stand against the Vietnam war and his
final alliance with the union garbage collectors of Memphis, showed that he
was capable of growth into the most significant leader the black people have
had in this century."

The seasoned Black revolutionary C. L. R. James also concluded—after
intensive discussions with King—that King was "a man whose ideas were as
advanced as any of us on the Left."[26]

King's Strategic Orientation

Describing the civil rights movement, King asserted that "we are engaged in a social revolution," explaining: "It is a movement to bring about certain basic structural changes in the architecture of American society. That is certainly revolutionary." At the beginning of 1964 he noted that while African Americans were "making progress . . . in the middle classes," the realities of everyday life for "the masses remain about the same."[27]

He shared with key figures A. Philip Randolph, Bayard Rustin, Stanley Levison, and others a strategic vision of how racism is to be overcome. The achievements and tragedy of the modern civil rights movement cannot be understood unless we consider that vision. This involved a Marxist-influenced analysis emanating from various sources—the Socialist Party, Highlander Folk School, and SCEF, activists formerly relating to the Communist Party, Christian Socialists connected with A. J. Muste's Fellowship of Reconciliation, and others.

King and his co-thinkers had a profound grasp both of individual racism (conscious and unconscious) as well as institutional racism (the legal form predominant in the South and the de facto form prevailing in the North). They recognized that it made sense to focus the antiracist struggle where racism was most vulnerable (given the new national and world situation after World War II)—against the Southern Jim Crow system.

If the struggle was both militant and nonviolent, it would be possible to win victories and at the same time to help increasing numbers of whites to push back various forms of conscious and unconscious racism.

King perceived a dividing line between the very rich and everybody else, between the blue-collar and white-collar working-class majority (which included the working poor and the unemployed), and the elite of business owners and executives above them who seek to control and profit from their labor.

Of course, divisions of race and racism cut across this class divide. But the majority of Blacks and whites happened to be part of this broadly defined working class, having common economic interests. Shifts in identity-consciousness among whites—involving a further erosion of racism—would potentially come to the fore only when the civil rights movement transcended the focus on legal segregation in the South to take up a broader agenda involving the entire nation.

And at a certain point, King and his co-thinkers believed, simply in order to push back the effects of racism on African Americans, it would become necessary to challenge the de facto form of institutionalized racism prevalent in the North. This could only be done effectively by attacking its underlying economic roots, which in turn could only be done effectively by developing a broader program for economic justice.

While such a program would be initiated by Blacks, it would be powerfully relevant to a majority of whites. The resulting interracial coalition for economic justice would have the dual function of eliminating the roots of institutional racism and creating an atmosphere of idealism and common struggle that would help to further push back various forms of individual (conscious and unconscious) racism.

This orientation was advanced at a conference held just after the 1963 March on Washington for Jobs and Freedom. The post-march conference was organized by activists in and around the Socialist Party. "One began to understand what was meant by a march for 'jobs and freedom,'" noted independent journalist I. F. Stone. "For most Negroes, civil rights alone will only be the right to join the underprivileged whites."

A. Philip Randolph pointed out: "We must liberate not only ourselves, but our white brothers and sisters." Stone's report continued in this way:

> The direction in which full emancipation lies was indicated when Mr. Randolph spoke of the need to extend the public sector of the economy. His brilliant assistant on the March, Bayard Rustin, urged an economic Master Plan to deal with the technological unemployment that weighs so heavily on the Negro and threatens to create a permanently depressed class of whites and blacks living previously on the edges of an otherwise affluent society. It was clear from the discussion that neither tax cuts nor public works nor job training (for what jobs?) would solve the problem while automation with giant steps made so many workers obsolete. The civil rights movement, Mr. Rustin said, could not get beyond a certain level unless it merged into a broader plan of social change.[28]

In 1966 A. Philip Randolph issued a pamphlet titled *A "Freedom Budget" for All Americans,* endorsed by over two hundred prominent civil rights, labor, social activist, and academic figures. He described the Freedom Budget as being dedicated "to the full goals of the 1963 March." One of its strongest supporters was Martin Luther King, Jr., who insisted that "the ultimate answer to the Negroes' economic dilemma will be found in a massive federal program for all the poor along the lines of A. Philip Randolph's Freedom Budget, a kind of Marshall Plan for the disadvantaged."[29]

Randolph himself elaborated on the Freedom Budget's specifics (involving a ten-year federal expenditure of $180 billion) and its meaning:

The "Freedom Budget" spells out a specific and factual course of action, step by step, to start in early 1967 toward the practical liquidation of poverty in the United States by 1975. The programs urged in the "Freedom Budget" attack all of the major causes of poverty—unemployment and underemployment; substandard pay, inadequate social insurance and welfare payments to those who cannot or should not be employed; bad housing; deficiencies in health services, education, and training; and fiscal and monetary policies which tend to redistribute income regressively rather than progressively. The "Freedom Budget" leaves no room for discrimination in any form, because its programs are addressed to all who need more opportunity and improved incomes and living standards—not just to some of them.[30]

Randolph explained that such programs "are essential to the Negro and other minority groups striving for dignity and economic security in our society," but that "the abolition of poverty (almost three-quarters of whose victims are white) can be accomplished only through action which embraces the totality of the victims of poverty, neglect, and injustice."

He added that "in the process everyone will benefit, for poverty is not an isolated circumstance affecting only those entrapped by it. It reflects—and affects—the performance of our national economy, our rate of economic growth, our ability to produce and consume, the condition of our cities, the levels of our social services and needs, the very quality of our lives." In Randolph's opinion the success of this effort would depend on "a mighty coalition among the civil rights and labor movements, liberal and religious forces, students and intellectuals—the coalition expressed in the historic 1963 March on Washington for Jobs and Freedom."[31]

The realization that such a course was necessary to achieve the goals of the civil rights movement propelled King and the SCLC to begin focusing more sharply on economic struggles from 1965 to 1968. A 1965–66 campaign in Chicago touched off revealing explosions of racist hatred and violence from white working-class and "middle class" neighborhoods, and it was ultimately outmaneuvered with all manner of far-reaching verbal "concessions"—by the powerful political machine of Mayor Richard Daley.

But some of this experience helped to inform and fuel a much more ambitious Poor People's Campaign, designed to mobilize a massive interracial movement in an uncompromising struggle to eliminate poverty throughout the United States. Involving what one of King's biographers has described as "a proletarian assault on Washington,"[32] and in part operating under the impact of the Vietnam War, the campaign had a far more radical tone than what Rustin and Randolph had articulated.

King appealed for "the dispossessed of this country" to "organize a revolution" that would eliminate poverty:

> I can't see the answer in riots. On the other hand, I can't see the answer in tender supplications for justice. I see the answer in an alternative to both of these, and that is militant nonviolence that is massive enough, that is attention-getting enough to dramatize the problems, that will be as attention-getting as a riot, that will not destroy life or property in the process. And this is what we hope to do in Washington through our movement.
>
> We feel that there must be some structural changes now, there must be a radical reordering of priorities, there must be a de-escalation and a final stopping of the war in Vietnam and an escalation of the war against poverty and racism here at home. And I feel that this is only going to be done when enough people get together and express their determination through that togetherness and make it clear that we are not going to allow any military-industrial complex to control this country.
>
> One of the great tragedies of the war in Vietnam is that it has strengthened the military-industrial complex, and it must be made clear now that there are some programs that we can cut back on—the space program and certainly the war in Vietnam—and get on with this program of a war on poverty. Right now we don't even have a skirmish against poverty, and we really need an all out, mobilized war that will make it possible for all of God's children to have the basic necessities of life.[33]

For King, a militant union organizing drive and strike by Black sanitation workers in Memphis, Tennessee, was an essential prelude to the Poor People's Campaign: "The road to Washington goes through Memphis." He hailed that struggle for "highlighting the economic issue" and "going beyond purely civil rights to questions of human rights."

Noting at a workers' rally that "along with wages and other securities, you're struggling for the right to organize," King commended the strikers: "This is the way to gain power. Don't go back to work until all your demands are met." He saw the strike and the militant demonstrations in support of the strike as constituting "a rejuvenation of the movement."[34]

It was in this context that King was killed. His death coincided with a deeper political defeat for the movement that he led—and also for the country as a whole. This defeat was rooted in some of the same realities that had contributed to the movement's earlier victories.

Beyond Defeat

The successes of the civil rights movement in overcoming the racist segregation of the South had, after all, been related to decisions of key elements in the US political-economic establishment. In Northern urban areas during the 1950s and 1960s, with the northward shift of the African American population, liberal politicians in both the Democratic and Republican parties were, of course, increasingly concerned to appeal to the growing number of Black voters.

No less significantly, such politicians and the powerful economic interests they were associated with felt the pressures of the Cold War—especially the competition between the United States and the USSR for influence among the overwhelmingly nonwhite populations of Asia, Africa, and Latin America. Such realities required that the US political establishment appear to be supportive and responsive as civil rights activists mounted nonviolent assaults on the South's Jim Crow system.[35]

But the same political-economic elite was hardly prepared to embrace any serious challenge to the nation's economic structures and distribution of wealth. The reliance on "friends" in the Democratic and Republican parties proved to be fatal to the radical strategy represented by Randolph and King. Laboring to win political support for Randolph's economic program, Bayard Rustin found, according to his biographer, that "the Freedom Budget 'didn't sell'—not under the Lyndon Johnson presidency and surely not under his conservative successor, Richard Nixon." Randolph could only complain: "This system is a market economy in which investment and production are determined more by the anticipation of profits than by the desire to achieve social justice." In the last year of his life, King, refusing to set aside his radical commitments (as Randolph and Rustin chose to do), struggled to push beyond this limitation.[36]

The final defeat suffered by King and the movement he led is instructive—but so are the earlier victories. The radical ideas that he expressed so eloquently, and the strategic orientation flowing from them, were rooted in a broader political culture in which Christian values and democratic principles merged with socialist insights. It is a legacy that remains relevant at the dawn of a new century.

8

Revolutionary Road, Partial Victory
The March on Washington for Jobs and Freedom

The year 1963 was a high-water mark for the civil rights movement—the year of the great March on Washington for Jobs and Freedom, which drew hundreds of thousands to march for civil rights. But the march also set the stage for the opening of what was perceived as a second, far more radical, phase of the civil rights strategy, developed by the march's organizers. This led to the development, over a three-year period, of the proposed *"Freedom Budget" for All Americans*. It projected nothing less than the elimination of all poverty and unemployment in the United States before the end of the 1970s.

A Frightening Left-Wing "Conspiracy"

In light of the now iconic standing the March on Washington has in the history of the twentieth century, it is all too easy to forget the intense hostility (and fear) that powerful forces felt regarding the rally. The prestigious *Herald Tribune* voiced these fears when it editorialized: "If Negro leaders persist in their announced plans to march 100,000-strong on the capital . . . they will be jeopardizing their cause. . . . The ugly part of this particular mass protest is its implication of uncontained violence if Congress doesn't deliver. This is the kind of threat that can make men of pride, which most Congressmen are, turn stubborn."[1]

Even greater hostility emanated from J. Edgar Hoover and his Federal Bureau of Investigation. A Justice Department lawyer of the time later commented: "Everything you have read about the FBI, how it was determined to destroy the movement, is true." Accounts indicating that "the Bureau and its Director were openly racist" and that "the Bureau set out to destroy black leaders simply because they were black leaders" have been carefully investigated and frankly corroborated by historian David Garrow, who adds: "The Bureau was strongly conservative, peopled with many right-wingers, and thus it selected people and organizations on the left end of the political spectrum for special and unpleasant attention."[2]

Pulitzer Prize–winning journalist Russell Baker states that Hoover was "a terrifying old tyrant whose eyes and ears were everywhere," who explained to a skeptical Attorney General Robert Kennedy that "the brains of black people were twenty percent smaller than whites," and who gloated—once tapes were later secured about Martin Luther King Jr.'s "amatory" indiscretions—that "this will destroy the burrhead." Since the emergence of the Black freedom movement in the 1950s, Hoover had been warning that "the Negro situation is being exploited fully and continuously by Communists on a national scale." FBI activities—in part reflecting such attitudes and in part reflecting a need to find justification for continued funding—found ample justification for investigating, spying on, and at times attempting to disrupt or discredit the activities of protest groups and leaders (such as key figures in the movement's activist wing like King and Bayard Rustin).[3]

"Bureau officers exchanged information about African American protest with local police in the South," notes Rustin biographer John D'Emilio. "The practice sustained an atmosphere in which Southern sheriffs who suppressed demonstrations knew they had friends in the Bureau, while FBI agents saw the protection of civil rights activists as outside their mission." Over a thousand civil rights activists (including Rustin) were tagged as security threats by the FBI. "With the knowledge it secretly acquired, it could disrupt events, sow dissension in organizations, ruin relationships, and destroy the credibility of individuals."[4]

Hoover did what he could to discredit the 1963 March with fears of violence and Communist infiltration. Identifying South Carolina segregationist Senator Strom Thurmond as "one of our strongest bulwarks in the Congress," the FBI shared with him a tremendous amount of information about key march organizer Rustin's explicit radicalism, homosexuality, and former membership in the Young Communist League—as well as a considerable accumulation of negative judgments about the projected march. Leading up to the protest, Thurmond used this information to launch a full-scale attack on the Senate floor, while Attorney General Kennedy, fed similar information, viewed the march as "very, very badly organized," with "many groups of Communists trying to get in."[5]

As it turned out, the march was brilliantly organized, and participation was incredibly broad and "respectable." The kernel of truth in Hoover's vicious interpretation of the march, however, was that central to the entire effort was an influential core of socialists who sought, as they themselves more than once asserted, a revolutionary transformation of society—although they also seemed committed to a *nonviolent* revolution.

Socialist Origins

The earliest beginnings of the March on Washington arose among socialist activists clustered around A. Philip Randolph, organizer of the Brotherhood of Sleeping Car Porters and the country's foremost African American trade union leader.

It is likely that the idea for the march was never far from the consciousness of Randolph himself, who in the 1940s had projected four different marches on Washington and canceled them each time. These earlier aborted marches had yielded significant gains, such as an executive order eliminating segregation and racist policies in war-related industries before the Second World War and the elimination of racial segregation in the US Armed Forces as the Cold War was developing. He had been denounced by Attorney General A. Mitchell Palmer in 1919 as one of "the two most dangerous Negroes in the United States" (the other was Randolph's friend and fellow socialist Chandler Owen).[6] And Randolph never abandoned the basic Marxism that he had absorbed from the Socialist Party of Eugene V. Debs. He consistently emphasized the link between racial justice and economic justice.

Over the years Rustin worked closely with Randolph, whose political orientation he fully shared. He was also, off and on, a close and trusted advisor to King. After leaving the Communist movement in 1941, Rustin had become a radical pacifist. He associated himself first with the Fellowship of Reconciliation and then the War Resisters League. He was later a founder of the Congress of Racial Equality (CORE), led by fellow socialist James Farmer.

Indeed, from the late 1940s onward King himself, as Clayborne Carson observes, adhered to a version of Social Gospel Christianity, which "incorporated socialist ideas as well as anti-colonial sentiments spurred by the African independence movements." Carson emphasizes that "the works of Karl Marx had reinforced his [King's] long-held concern 'about the gulf between superfluous wealth and abject poverty.'"[7] In all of this, he shared common ground with Rustin and Randolph.

Rustin became an inspiration and mentor for radicalizing young activists in the late 1950s. As Stokely Carmichael (later a key leader of SNCC, the Student Nonviolent Coordinating Committee) recalled: "Bayard was one of the first I had been in direct contact with [of whom] I could really say, 'That's what I want to be.' He was like superman, hooking socialism up with the black movement, organizing blacks."[8] In 1956 socialist writer and activist Michael Harrington introduced two socialist teenagers, Tom Kahn and Rachelle Horowitz, to the charismatic Rustin. Kahn and Horowitz soon became key figures in the Young People's Socialist League (YPSL, the youth group of the Socialist Party), resulting in a set of political partnerships that would last for many years and would intersect with SNCC and CORE.

In 1958 the Socialist Party absorbed the Independent Socialist League, a political group led by Max Shachtman, a one-time aide to the exiled Russian Communist revolutionary Leon Trotsky. The merger revitalized the Socialist Party and especially its youth group. These were, in the words of historian Maurice Isserman, "people with political skills, a sense of mission, and a willingness to devote long hours to the movement." As Michael Harrington later recalled, the new recruits included "some of the most important militants of the second generation of the SNCC leadership—Stokely Carmichael, Courtland Cox, and Ed Brown [older brother of H. Rap Brown]," among others. Their discussions took up such questions as "why our various struggles would have to converge someday into the battle for socialism itself."[9]

Looking back on the YPSL's involvement in the civil rights movement, Kahn, writing in 1980, commented that "YPSLs [i.e., members of the YPSL] were the backbone of the 1958 and 1959 Youth Marches for Integrated Schools," adding that they "helped staff numerous defense committees, played an important role in CORE, participated in direct action projects, marched in the South, and went to jail." He concluded: "Out of our efforts, in large part, came the 1963 March on Washington." In all of this, Rustin and Kahn became close friends, co-thinkers, and for a time lovers. But their particular brand of socialist politics was the target of hostile characterization, in 1963, by Stanley Levison (himself a former Communist, an erstwhile friend of Rustin's, and a close advisor to King): "Tom Kahn is the Lenin of the Socialist Party . . . and Bayard is absolutely manipulated by him. This was Bayard's downfall years ago." Stokely Carmichael and other young activists saw things quite differently from the view conveyed in Levison's contemptuous remark: "Tom was a shrewd strategist with by far the most experience of us all in radical political organizing, having, as it were, studied with Rustin."[10]

"The Deepest Implications"

In 1960 the twenty-two-year-old Kahn produced the influential pamphlet *The Unfinished Revolution*. It offered a vivid, passionate description of the activist upsurge of that year but also pushed for a broadened strategic orientation capable of bringing about positive reforms—and with it a fundamental power shift in society. "The Negro without a vote and without a union card has little to say about his wages and is up against a take-it-or-leave-it proposition," he wrote. "In addition, the presence of a politically disenfranchised and economically uprooted Negro population would represent a threat to the poor whites because if the latter sought to improve their economic status, their bosses could always threaten to turn them out and give the job to Negroes who, in desperation, would work for less." He envisioned a scenario in which civil rights forces and struggles associated with Randolph and King joined with unions to help lay the basis for a mass political party of labor, one "committed to the fight of the Negro for equality, of the workingman for improved living conditions, of the farmer for the fair share of his produce."[11]

The pamphlet was graced with a laudatory foreword by Socialist Party icon Norman Thomas, but more significantly, another foreword was written by James Lawson (a militant black minister leading the nonviolent struggle in Nashville and a close ally of King), who commented: "In the heat of the struggle, it often happens that the deepest implications of a mass movement are not understood. . . . This pamphlet, written by a young man who has worked on the Youth Marches for Integrated Schools and in a number of other important civil rights projects, makes a unique contribution in filling this void."[12]

One of the key elements in the orientation of this dynamic cluster of socialists was the link they saw, and always emphasized, between the struggles for civil rights and economic justice. This was reinforced in 1962 when Michael Harrington's *The Other America* became a best seller. He stunned thousands of readers by his informative and sensitively written account of "the other America" in which between forty and fifty million people lived in poverty, close to a quarter of the US population. What he had to say had powerful impact:

> To be sure, the other America is not impoverished in the same sense as those poor nations where millions cling to hunger as a defense against starvation. This country has escaped such extremes. That does not change the fact that tens of millions of Americans are, at this very moment, maimed in body and spirit, existing at levels beneath those necessary for human decency. If these people are not starving, they are hungry, and sometimes fat with hunger, for that is what cheap foods do. They are without adequate housing and education and medical care.[13]

In the autumn of 1962, left-wing union organizer Stanley Aronowitz quietly surveyed labor circles on Rustin's behalf. The purpose was to gauge support for a mass demonstration, focused on the issue of jobs, during the centennial year of the Emancipation Proclamation. In December 1962 discussions between Randolph and Rustin crystallized on the concept of a mass action in Washington, DC, to advance this aspect of the civil rights strategy. The old trade unionist asked Rustin to develop a detailed proposal.

For assistance, the experienced organizer reached out to some of his closest young Socialist Party comrades—Kahn and Norman Hill, the latter a seasoned African American socialist, associated with the Shachtman tradition and active in the leadership of CORE. By January 1963, Rustin was able to present Randolph with a finished proposal.

Quite pleased, Randolph secured adoption of the proposal by the Negro American Labor Council and then sought support from both King's Southern Christian Leadership Conference (SCLC) and SNCC as a prelude to seeking participation from the NAACP and the Urban League. For various reasons, King's initial reaction was lukewarm. The NAACP and the Urban League were noncommittal. The projected date was shifted to October, and Randolph reached out to the AFL-CIO. Its president, George Meany, was exasperated by Randolph's criticism of racist policies in some unions and had complained during the 1959 AFL-CIO convention: "I would like Brother Randolph to stay a little closer to the trade union movement and pay a little less attention to outside organizations that pay lip service rather than real service." At the same convention he exploded: "Who the hell appointed you as the guardian of all the Negroes in America?" Still standoffish several years later, Meany viewed the March on Washington as "an unwise legislative tactic," rejecting the proposal for AFL-CIO endorsement. Walter Reuther, the ex-socialist liberal leader of the United Auto Workers, was the only member of the AFL-CIO executive board to respond positively.[14]

It was not clear if this proposed march would get off the ground.

Civil Rights Upsurge

A succession of events in the first half of 1963 totally changed the landscape within the civil rights movement and caused King to become a strong advocate. "Birmingham was a turning point in the Southern struggle; it eventually changed the face of the South and awakened the nation," Anne Braden observed in a lengthy 1965 report titled "The Southern Freedom Movement in Perspective," written for the *Monthly Review*. "The immediate objectives of the Birmingham campaign were a beginning on desegregation of public accommodations and a beginning on opening up job opportunities." The arrest of King (which resulted in his eloquent "Letter from a Birmingham Jail") was part of a larger phenomenon in which "thousands joined the movement and went to jail," and even "the children of Birmingham became involved." Police Commissioner Bull Connor, who "had been breaking up integrated meetings since the 1930's," remained true to form—he did not hesitate to bring out "the police dogs, clubs, and fire hoses." In contrast to previous years, however, now it was televised and widely reported in the national and international media. "The nation and the world were shocked and moved to action."[15]

A firestorm of protests swept through the South. "No state remained untouched. In a single month, there was mass direct action in at least 30 cities," according to Braden. "Some surveys placed the figure at 100 communities for that entire hot summer of 1963."[16] The backlash of white racist violence assumed murderous proportions, most dramatically with the assassination of Medgar Evers, the outstanding NAACP leader in Mississippi. This, on top of Bull Connor's brutality, was too much. President John F. Kennedy, as leader of the "free world" in the midst of the Cold War era, felt compelled at last to introduce civil rights legislation.

It was now an entirely new situation, and the thinking of King and his advisors shifted dramatically. "We are on a breakthrough," King insisted. "We need a mass protest." They decided to contact Randolph and work out a common perspective. One point of agreement was that civil rights must be coequal with economic justice—the march was now "for Jobs and Freedom."[17]

Rustin eloquently gave a sense of the militant spirit of this historical moment:

> The Negro community is now fighting for total freedom. It took three million dollars and a year of struggle simply to convince the powers that be that one has the right to ride in the front of the bus. If it takes this kind of pressure to achieve a single thing, then one can just as well negotiate fully for more, for every economic, political, and social right that is presently denied. That is what is important about Birmingham: tokenism is finished.
>
> The Negro masses are no longer prepared to wait for anybody: not for elections, not to count votes, not to wait on the Kennedys or for legislation, nor, in fact, for Negro leaders themselves. They are going to move. Nothing can stop them from moving. And if that Negro leadership does not move rapidly enough and effectively enough they will take it into their own hands and move anyhow. . . .
>
> Birmingham has proved that no matter what you're up against, if wave after wave of black people keep coming prepared to go to jail, sooner or later there is such confusion, there is such social dislocation, that white people in the South are faced with a choice: either integrated restaurants or no restaurants at all, either integrated public facilities, or none at all. And the South then must make its choice for integration, for it would rather have that than chaos.[18]

This is from Rustin's preface to Kahn's pamphlet published in spring 1963, *Civil Rights: The True Frontier.* Kahn and his comrades envisioned a transition from the initial phase of the struggle against the Jim Crow system to the more radical struggle for economic justice. "We are socialists," Kahn affirmed. "Ultimately, we believe, the elimination of all forms of prejudice, of all the subtle, psychological and emotional products of centuries of racism, awaits the creation of a new social order in America—a social order in which political democracy passes from shibboleth to reality, and in which economic democracy guarantees to each individual that he shall be judged as a person, not as a commodity. This, we are convinced, is a democratic socialist order." But his focus was on the here and now. "To those who reject our socialist vision we therefore reply: Very well, but at least live up to your own vision. . . . Give all moral and material support to the Negro struggle for equality," because "the elimination of Jim Crow, with all its legal, administrative and political supports, is an immediate possibility." He concluded: "To those whose commitment knows no compromises we pledge our full, vigorous and loyal cooperation."[19]

Militancy and Moderation

The young militants of SNCC were absolutely on board with the perspectives articulated by Rustin and Kahn, and with Randolph's call for a march on Washington. Increasingly frustrated with and critical of the failure of the Kennedy administration to provide clear support on either issue, or adequate protection for civil rights activists in the South, they were especially eager for militant action in the nation's capital. Along with Rustin, they envisioned the march as a massive and radical flashpoint of protest. Cleveland Sellers, one of a number of leading SNCC activists drawn into helping to organize the action, recalls the way Rustin outlined it to them:

> The march, which was [to be] sponsored by SNCC, CORE, SCLC, the NAACP and the Urban League, was being conducted to emphasize the problems of poor blacks. It was to be a confrontation between black people and the federal bureaucracy. Rustin told us that some people were talking about disrupting Congress, picketing the White House, stopping service at bus and train stations, and lying down on the runways at the airports.[20]

One of Rustin's biographers emphasizes that he saw the Gandhian method of civil disobedience as being "near the heart of [the march's] conception," without which the action would be "little more than a ceremonial display of grievance." And as Rustin himself put it, the Washington action would be followed by "mass demonstrations continuing in this country for the next five years, covering wider and wider areas, and becoming more intense."[21]

Things turned out somewhat differently. It was a one-day action—August 28, 1963—with the civil disobedience, the confrontations, and most of the explicit radicalism combed out as a condition for the support of the NAACP, the Urban League, the Catholic clergy, Kennedy supporters, and others.

There had been concerted efforts to prevent Rustin from playing the role of directing the march. Randolph had no tolerance for this exclusion, believing that "Rustin is Mr. March-on-Washington himself," and he maneuvered skillfully and successfully to ensure his central organizing role (by assuming the position of director of the march, and then appointing Rustin as his deputy director).[22] Rustin, in turn, appointed trusted members of the Socialist Party as his key aides, and they drew together—to assist with their organizing work in Washington, DC, and in cities throughout the country—a very substantial network of activists in or near the Socialist Party: the YPSLs; members of Students for a Democratic Society (then still the youth group of the Socialist Party educational front, the League for Industrial Democracy); staff members of the Socialist Party–linked Workers Defense League; SNCC activists; and members of CORE, a number of whom were in and around YPSL and the Socialist Party.

The perspectives of the Socialist Party were also advanced in lengthy congressional testimony by Norman Thomas, reprinted in a special March on Washington supplement of the weekly Socialist publication *New America*. The testimony emphasized the need to strengthen President Kennedy's proposed civil rights legislation and included provisions for full and fair employment to wipe out poverty and economic inequalities. The same issue of the paper included a statement by Randolph lauding the Socialist Party's platform: "The revolution for Freedom Now has moved into a new stage in its development. Its demands have necessarily become not only the end of all discrimination against black Americans, but for the creation of a new society—a society without economic exploitation or deprivation."[23]

There were, of course, more moderate elements that were drawn, finally, into support for the March on Washington. The NAACP, led by Roy Wilkins, had made countless contributions to the civil rights struggle over the years, had actually been started by socialists (including the great African American historian, sociologist, and educator W. E. B. Du Bois), and included in its ranks some of the outstanding civil rights activists of recent years (Rosa Parks, E. D. Nixon, and Medgar Evers being only some of the better known). But as an organization it favored a far more moderate stance, not only veering away from radical and socialist ideology, but also preferring legal and educational pathways, and working, when possible, with establishment politicians while tending to look down on protest demonstrations. The National Urban

League, led by Whitney Young, had embraced an even more moderate orientation and had consequently enjoyed an even closer relationship with the Kennedy administration.

Urban League sponsorship meant that a greater aura of "respectability" would be associated with the action—which meant little to some, but much to many others. And the NAACP—with its massive membership, significant resources, and dense network of branches throughout the country—had a capacity to mobilize large numbers. Yet if these organizations were to support the march, they would insist on far greater moderation than the initial organizers had projected. There is ample evidence that they did just that.

While Wilkins and Young did not always get their way (for example, they had intended to block Rustin from being the central organizer of the march), they were able to force the weeding out of one radical aspect of the initial plan after another.

Criticism and Justification

Rustin aide Rachelle Horowitz "regarded the compromise as a terrible sellout. . . . Roy Wilkins and Whitney Young weren't going to join anything that would be embarrassing to John F. Kennedy, because they were very close to the President. I was in a funk for days." King himself was dismayed over dropping each and every possibility of civil disobedience.[24]

Rustin saw things differently. "The march will succeed if it gets a hundred thousand people—or one hundred fifty thousand or two hundred thousand more—to show up in Washington," he insisted. "Bayard always knew we would have to trade in militancy for numbers," Norman Hill suggested later. "He probably let us put in militant actions [in the original plan] so he could trade it away. Four things mattered—numbers, the coalition, militancy of action, and militancy of words. He was willing to give up militant action for the other three."[25]

As it turned out, however, even the militancy of words was contested terrain: major forces of the march's leadership insisted on censoring the speech by John Lewis of SNCC. The speech had been a collective product of the young militants who had considered themselves to be "Bayard Rustin people." Horowitz had loved the initial draft, and Kahn had worked with SNCC leaders to help sharpen it. There are indications that the Kennedy administration had gotten a copy of it and applied pressure on moderate elements to have the speech killed. Washington, DC, archbishop Patrick O'Boyle, who had agreed to deliver the invocation at the beginning of the march, threatened to pull all Catholic clergy out of the event. Reuther and even King joined forces with Wilkins and Young to demand either a rewrite or yanking Lewis from the speakers' list. Randolph and Rustin ran interference for the indignant SNCC activists but also persuaded them to cut and soften the speech—although much of its radicalism remained (and, according to some, was even covertly sharpened).

The questions remain: To what extent did the march live up to the revolutionary hopes and expectations that animated its key organizers? To what extent had that been compromised away? The most unrelenting criticism came from Malcolm X, in a speech titled "Message to the Grass Roots":

> The same white element that put Kennedy into power—labor, the Catholics, the Jews, and liberal Protestants—the same clique that put Kennedy in power, joined the march.
>
> It's just like when you've got some coffee that's too black, which means it's too strong. You integrate it with cream, you make it weak. But if you pour too much cream in it, you won't even know you ever had coffee. It used to be hot, it becomes cool. It used to be strong, it becomes weak. It used to wake you up, now it puts you to sleep. This is what they did with the march on Washington. They joined it. They didn't integrate it. They infiltrated it. They joined it, became part of it, took it over. And as they took it over, it lost its militancy. It ceased to be angry, it ceased to be hot, it ceased to be uncompromising. Why it even ceased to be a march. It became a picnic, a circus. Nothing but a circus, with . . . clowns leading it, white clowns and black clowns. . . .
>
> No, it was a sellout. It was a takeover.[26]

Some critics of the compromise had second thoughts. "I came to recognize that the decision to scale down the militancy of the march was a sensible one," Horowitz later commented. "After all, we wanted the demonstration to be as broad-based as possible, reflecting a coalition of American conscience. We couldn't have achieved that objective if we had insisted on a program of radical confrontation with the government."[27]

The march, however, involved, as Malcolm X emphasized, an accommodation with the US government (insisted on by the march moderates), which in some cases—ranging from an agreed-upon post-march meeting with President Kennedy to vital last-minute assistance in repairing a sabotaged sound system for the rally—eased over into a degree of government assistance, which some argued finally meant a high degree of government control. Indeed, Randolph, King, Farmer, Wilkins, Young, and Reuther all met with President Kennedy on June 22 in order to iron things out and secure his support. Initially, Kennedy sought to compel them to call off the march.

Persuaded that this was impossible, but assured that these leaders were committed to keeping the action moderate and not antagonistic to his administration, he indicated his tacit support.

Stokely Carmichael voiced the disappointment of many militant activists about "the price" being too high; the march's militancy was diluted to fit the demands of the White House. "Which is not to say that Bayard and Mr. Randolph do not deserve credit," he added. "They surely did. For their initiative and persistence had forged that alliance that made the march possible. And the march itself? It was a spectacular media event . . . a 'political' event choreographed entirely for the television audience."[28] Of course, the fact that millions of people throughout the United States and the world were watching an unabashedly pro–civil rights spectacle in 1963, when powerful legal and extralegal forces were fighting to save the racist Jim Crow system by any means necessary, had a profound impact on the course of events.

Cleveland Sellers shared much of Carmichael's sourness over the de-radicalization of the march. But there was another aspect to the event. "The people who got the most out of the march were the poor farmers and sharecroppers whom SNCC organizers brought from Mississippi, Alabama, and southwest Georgia," Sellers concluded. "The march was a tremendous inspiration to them. It helped them believe that they were not alone, that there really were people in the nation who cared what happened to them."[29]

Next Steps

The great novelist and essayist James Baldwin caught the challenge posed by critics: "The day was important in itself, and what we do with this day is even more important."[30] The fact is that Randolph, Rustin, and their socialist comrades were concerned, precisely, with *what to do with the day*. Their plan all along had been to utilize the momentum of the march, the coalition it represented, and the militant grassroots struggles against Jim Crow that it reflected, to move forward on what they saw as a revolutionary path.

The game plan of the Socialist Party was to draw a number of activists into a major conference that would map out and help propel forces into the future of the civil rights struggle—a future that would fundamentally change the structures of power in US politics and in the economy. A special trifold flyer was mimeographed and distributed, inviting those interested to a Conference on the Civil Rights Revolution, to be held in Washington, DC, for two days following the March on Washington. The sponsor was the Socialist Party. According to *New America*, over four hundred people attended this conference whose purpose was to engage in "discussions of the strategy and politics of this unfinished revolution," with the participants including "many young civil rights activists from the North and the South."[31] The independent journalist I. F. Stone was powerfully impressed:

> Far superior to anything I heard at the monument [i.e., the Lincoln Memorial, where the march's speeches were given] were the discussions I heard the next day at a civil rights conference organized by the Socialist Party. On that dismal rainy morning-after, in a dark union hall in the Negro section, I heard A. Philip Randolph speak with an eloquence and humanity few can achieve.... He reminded moderates that political equality was not enough. "The white sharecroppers of the South have full civil rights but live in the bleakest poverty." One began to understand what was meant by a march "for *jobs* and freedom." For most Negroes, civil rights alone will only be the right to join the underprivileged whites. "We must liberate not only ourselves," Mr. Randolph said, "but our white brothers and sisters."
>
> The direction in which full emancipation lies was indicated when Mr. Randolph spoke of the need to extend the public sector of the economy. His brilliant assistant on the March, Bayard Rustin, urged an economic Master Plan to deal with the technological unemployment that weighs so heavily on the Negro and threatens to create a permanently depressed class of whites and blacks living precariously on the edges of an otherwise affluent society. It was clear from the discussion that neither tax cuts nor public works nor job training (for what jobs?) would solve the problem while automation with giant steps made so many workers obsolete. The civil rights movement, Mr. Rustin said, could not get beyond a certain level unless it merged into a broader plan for social change.
>
> In the ill-lighted hall, amid the assorted young students and venerables like Norman Thomas, socialism took on fresh meaning and revived urgency. It was not accidental that so many of those who ran the March turned out to be members or fellow travellers of the Socialist Party....
>
> "In days of great popular uprising—like today's civil rights revolution—with their tensions, tumult, and fermentation," Randolph intoned, "the frontiers of freedom, equality, social justice, and racial justice can be advanced." Emphasizing the centrality of demonstrations for forcing the drafting and passage and implementation of civil rights legislation, Randolph argued that there was a necessity for deeper change, that to solve the economic issues related to racism, "the public sector of the economy must be expanded, the private sector of the economy must be contracted," and that "we need some organization in the country that will carry on and maintain sound exposition of the economic qualities that are to obtain in the nation, and this can only be done by . . . the Socialist Party, which is dedicated to democracy, and which believes that political democracy requires economic democracy, and that the two must go hand in hand."[32]

Hope and Defeat

Three years later, in 1966, Randolph and others would present *A "Freedom Budget" for All Americans*. The aging activist described it as being dedicated "to the full goals of the 1963 March." It was designed to eliminate poverty and unemployment within a ten-year period, to "attack *all* of the major causes of poverty—unemployment and underemployment; substandard pay, inadequate social insurance and welfare payments to those who cannot or should not be employed; bad housing; deficiencies in health services, education, and training; and fiscal and monetary policies which tend to redistribute income regressively rather than progressively." He added that it would leave "no room for discrimination in any form, because its programs are addressed to *all* who need more opportunity and improved incomes and living standards—not just to some of them."[33]

This remarkable ten-year proposal, with a price tag of $200 billion, had been developed with the assistance of Leon Keyserling (a leading economist associated with Franklin D. Roosevelt's New Deal—serving at a high level in various government agencies and drafting legislation—as well as Harry Truman's administration), and in conjunction with Harrington, Kahn, Rustin, AFL-CIO economists, and others. It was endorsed by over two hundred prominent figures associated with the civil rights movement, the labor movement, academia, and the religious community. In Randolph's opinion the success of this effort would depend on "a mighty coalition among the civil rights and labor movements, liberal and religious forces, students and intellectuals—the coalition expressed in the historic 1963 March on Washington for Jobs and Justice."[34] King, one of its leading proponents, explained:

> The journey ahead requires that we emphasize the needs of all America's poor, for there is no way merely to find work, or adequate housing, or quality-integrated schools for Negroes alone. We shall eliminate slums for Negroes when we destroy ghettoes and build new cities for *all*. We shall eliminate unemployment for Negroes when we demand full and fair employment for *all*. This human rights emphasis is an integral part of the Freedom Budget and sets, I believe, a new and creative tone for the great challenge we yet face.[35]

Within two years, King himself was dead—struck down as he sought to bring life to the principles embedded in the Freedom Budget through the Poor People's Campaign and the sanitation workers' strike in Memphis, Tennessee. By that time, the Vietnam War was raging, and the leaders of the Democratic Party—not to mention the Republicans who would soon sweep into power under Richard Nixon—made it clear that they would not support such seemingly radical policies. Worse, the embryonic coalition crystallizing around the March on Washington, which Randolph and his co-thinkers had envisioned as decisive to the effort, was now deeply fractured. The Socialist Party itself was being torn apart over diverging positions on the war.

The 1963 March on Washington continues to stand as a great achievement, which—combined with hard-fought nationwide struggles—helped to secure meaningful civil rights and voting rights legislation, and impressive shifts in consciousness. Yet the promise and expectations of King, Randolph, and Rustin for a full realization of their goals for interlinked racial and economic justice remained unfulfilled. Twenty years after Randolph's 1966 launch of the Freedom Budget, Rustin lamented:

> In Randolph's view, perhaps the most important contribution he attempted was a failure. That was his introduction of the Freedom Budget for all Americans. While he got the signatures of many, many liberals in all walks of life and civil rights leaders to endorse the Freedom Budget, they never considered it a priority. Randolph foresaw the further decline of the black family—and all the consequent pathology, including drugs, crime, illegitimacy, etc.—and the creation of economic "untouchables" in the black, Hispanic, and white communities, and general decline of the working class should the Freedom Budget not be accepted.[36]

9

A Reluctant Memoir of the 1950s and 1960s

have been asked to write a memoir that would give a sense of the Old Left/ New Left realities of the 1950s and '60s. That seems quite odd to me (why would I be writing such a thing?), until I look in the mirror and see this old guy looking back at me. As I reflect, it does seem to me that I experienced a lot, met a lot of people, and perhaps learned from all that, so I will share some of my story.

This fragment can make sense, I think, only by placing it in a larger context, the aspects of which I have attempted to sketch out myself in various writings, and others have done likewise (one of the best recent efforts is Van Gosse's compact 2005 study *Rethinking the New Left: An Interpretative Essay*).[1] And there are the memoirs of others whose journeys through this era can open up a rich variety of "universes" that intersect with this one.

I grew up in a rural area outside of Clearfield, Pennsylvania (population 10,000). My parents moved there in 1950 when I was three years old because my father was the District 2 director of the United Stone and Allied Products Workers of America, a small industrial union affiliated with the Congress of Industrial Organizations (CIO).

Clearfield was located in the middle of District 2, with some very large plants of the Harbison-Walker Corporation (then a Fortune 500 outfit), which made firebrick for the kilns of the steel industry. Many of these plants were organized by the Stoneworkers (which began many years before as a union of quarry workers in granite-rich Vermont, under the leadership of an old-time Socialist and Scottish immigrant, John Lawson, who remained secretary-treasurer for many years).

When John L. Lewis led those committed to industrial unionism in a break away from the de-radicalized and bureaucratized American Federation of Labor (AFL) to form the CIO amid the big strikes and organizing drives of the 1930s, the Stoneworkers followed Lewis. The main priority, in the CIO ethos, was to organize workers—all workers. Hence the quarry workers' union diversified into "stone and allied products workers," drawing in those who labored in many different occupational categories.

This also helps explain why among my earliest memories is being at meetings and on picket lines of workers of the Clearfield Cheese Company, who fought a militant battle for the right to organize. When asked why the Stoneworkers union was trying to organize cheese workers, my father quipped: "Well, they make brick cheese, don't they?" (The workers were defeated—but some years later my father helped organizers of the Amalgamated Meat Cutters and Butcher Workmen to unionize that plant.)

The labor movement was like a religion to my parents. "Union" was a holy word: it signified workers coming together to help each other, to protect each other, and to make things better for themselves and their families (all of them), in necessary and inevitable struggle with the powerful bosses who sought to enrich themselves by exploiting the workers.

This was not an abstraction for us. Often there were meetings that filled our small house with cigarette smoke (both my parents were smokers, as were most of the union members who met there), there were larger meetings in union halls, there were picnics and sometimes picket lines, there were intense discussions during and after negotiating sessions around union contracts. There were Labor Day events that my parents helped to organize in Clearfield County, there were trips the family took—often related to union work—in which we sometimes whiled away the boring stretches of road by playing Twenty Questions but also by singing union songs (my favorites being "Solidarity Forever" and, especially, "Union Maid").

Among my favorite relatives were those, in Massachusetts and New York, who seemed to embrace the same warm and glowing ideals of a better world for all the workers. There were Eve and Adrian, an aunt and uncle (my father's brother) who had once been involved with the United Electrical, Radio and Machine Workers of America, for which my mother had also briefly worked before becoming pregnant with me.

On my mother's side of the family there were George and Rose, an uncle and aunt of hers (he working in the printing trades but also a veteran of something important called the Spanish Civil War, she a pioneer in the field of social work), and my great-grandpa Harry Brodsky, a retired garment worker who long ago had helped organize and lead an early local of the International Ladies' Garment Workers' Union.

There were some things in my house and my family that seemed not to be in the houses and families of my other friends in Clearfield. The artwork, on the walls and in some books we had, was different—Rembrandt, Goya, van Gogh, various impressionists, more modern folks—especially Picasso and Mexican muralists such as Rivera and Siqueiros and Orozco. The music included a few Broadway musicals but also union songs from the Almanac Singers, the Weavers, as well as a lot of classical music and some jazz. And, of course, there was the rich and wonderful voice of Paul Robeson.

One of the biggest differences was that there were so many books (including, I later learned, some that were kept relatively hidden, and even some that were quietly destroyed). Among my mother's favorite novelists were Russians, Tolstoy and Dostoyevsky, but perhaps her favorite American writer was Howard Fast. His compellingly written and profoundly idealistic novels—*Spartacus, Conceived in Liberty, Freedom Road, Citizen Tom Paine, The American*—were precious items, which I was to devour during my teenage years.

There were many attitudes in my home that were different from some that I found outside it. In school, I ran into a lot of anti-union sentiment, of course, and as time went on I found myself arguing with teachers and some students who expressed such sentiments. But there were other things. My parents were very clearly opposed to racism, for example—my mother wouldn't let my older sister, Patty, participate in the regular high school minstrel show; she pulled me out of a third-grade puppet show called "Little Black Sambo."

My father refused to join a number of working-class social clubs (the Loyal Order of Moose, the Sons of Italy, et cetera) because they excluded Blacks. There weren't many Black families in Clearfield, but my mom's best friend in town, Esther, was African American and very beautiful, very clever and funny, and a very strong personality; she had four kids who were very much a part of my growing-up years. Such friendships were not the norm in towns like Clearfield in the 1950s.

The term "feminism" was not commonly used in my home—but the reality of it permeated my early years. There wasn't much feminist literature available then—though I remember books by Eve Merriam and Elizabeth Hawes, creative and strong-minded women who, I later learned, had been around the Communist Party. The family also revered Ibsen's play *A Doll's House* (my younger sister, Nora, was named after the play's heroine) and delighted over the strong women in the plays of George Bernard Shaw.

My mother was obviously very intellectual, very much on a par with my father, though each brought different qualities to grappling with issues and realities that they faced. They talked and worked as equals, which was something that my father obviously valued. When at home (he was on the road a lot), he helped with the housework—as did my two sisters and I. The discussion and implementation of strategy and tactics to advance positive developments, in the local labor movement and within the Stoneworkers union nationally, was very often something that my parents carried out jointly.

A woman's place was definitely not in the home—and when my mother found herself, at times, predominantly in the "housewife" role, her profound depression was absolutely palpable. For her, the purpose of getting jobs outside the home—helping with odd tasks for one or another union, then working as a full-time secretary—was probably, as I look back, to help her keep her sanity as much as to bring in much-needed additional income. She finally "found herself," by the early 1960s, as a caseworker in the Department of Public Assistance, and (with my father's full support) ended up going back to graduate school for a master's degree in social work.

Another big difference between us and other families was around religion. My father was an angry ex-Catholic, my mother a secular Jew, and, as my mother put it, "We don't believe in God—we believe in the Brotherhood of Man." This obviously wouldn't fly among my playmates and their parents, and initially I came up with an excellent solution. My dad being Catholic and my mom Jewish—that must make me a Protestant, like many of my friends! (There was, of course, no genuine logic behind this—aside from allowing me to self-identify with the majority.)

Later I tended to identify as half-Jewish, or plain old Jewish, but without any clear religious sense. In my mid-to-late teens, I worked out my own theology (partly influenced by Tolstoy's *War and Peace*), which I called "pantheist-humanist." Since that made little sense to most people, I later switched to calling myself an atheist (though I've stopped doing that now, since I've never lost the sense of God roughly equivalent to that of my teenage reflections).

There's something else that occurs to me—something that my family shared, to a large extent, with many, many others in the United States—and worth reflecting on. We saw ourselves as basically "middle class." This is an incredibly fuzzy term, but whatever it might mean, in the 1950s and early '60s, we felt it defined us.

My father had been a worker, laboring for wages under one or another employer in the 1920s and '30s (including as a WPA worker, where he was involved in the left-wing Workers' Alliance)—but now he earned a salary, working as a union staff member. My mother had come from an extended family that had been mostly working class—but her father, in fact, was a small businessman, her parents enjoyed an increasingly upscale standard of living, and she herself (unlike my father) had gone to, and graduated from, college.

We owned a home, one and then two cars, a TV set, and enjoyed summer vacations. This was not seen as the traditional working-class lifestyle. My parents assumed that my sisters and I would go to college and end up as some kind of white-collar professionals. Throughout the 1950s our finances were tight, our debts sometimes high, our circumstances relatively impoverished. But my father's rising salary and my mother's finally secure employment, first as secretary and then as case worker, truly placed us at a middle-income level by the '60s. Like growing numbers of others in the US working class, we didn't apply Karl Marx's definition of the working class to ourselves: those who make their living by selling their ability to work (labor power) to an employer. No, although we identified fiercely with the labor movement and with the working class, in our consciousness we ourselves were middle class.

Discovering the Old Left

One of my parents' finest qualities was their restraint in imparting their own ideas to me. I could see the example of who and what they were, and they would certainly tell me (for the most part) what they believed and why, but they encouraged me to develop my own understanding of things and to find my own way. I certainly felt a need to do that, given how jarring the difference sometimes was between some of the ideas in my own home and the ideas in the larger community.

In many homes, and also in school, President Eisenhower was seen in a very positive light—but not in my home. Vice President Richard Nixon and the fierce Secretary of State John Foster Dulles were even worse, though lower yet was Senator Joseph McCarthy, who claimed to be leading a crusade against the insidious evils of Communism. I remember my parents being glued to the black-and-white TV in our home in 1954, watching what seemed to me never-ending "hearings" (in which, I later learned, McCarthy was finally being politically cut down).

On the other hand, some things that were clearly seen as bad elsewhere seemed to have the glow of goodness in my home. People like Alger Hiss, indicted for espionage, or the executed "atom spies" Ethel and Julius Rosenberg (the photos of their sons, little boys like me, were burned into my young mind) were presumed innocent by my parents. Those who refused to cooperate with congressional investigating committees that sought to root out "un-American activities" stood as heroes.

Nor were the Soviet Union and Red China seen as evil. In 1956, when there was an anti-Communist uprising in Hungary, my parents' attitude also seemed inconsistent with the positive outpourings that were the norm all around us. They seemed subdued, distrustful, critical. Yet I remember watching newsreels, then and a bit later, of clusters of Hungarians, some seeming close to my own age, students and working-class kids—intense, determined, turning to look into the camera, right into my own eyes, holding guns that they were preparing to use on some unseen enemy associated with inhuman, armored tanks—and I felt a profound sense of identification with them.

I vaguely remember, in the same period, my parents' concentration on some revelations from Soviet leader Nikita Khrushchev published in the *New York Times*. (According to Khrushchev, Joseph Stalin, the highly revered leader of the Soviet Union from 1929 to 1953, had actually been a murderous tyrant—something which Communist Party members had always denied.) They also pored over an issue of a small cultural magazine I didn't commonly see in our home—it was called *Mainstream*, and it contained an important article by our beloved Howard Fast explaining that he had changed his mind about something important (his membership in the Communist Party) and wouldn't write for that magazine anymore. My parents were very disappointed and discussed this, and related matters, with friends who lived in another Pennsylvania town.

When I turned thirteen my parents sat me down to tell me something important. They believed in socialism, and so did all of my favorite relatives. This made me very uneasy, because I had a sense that this was seen as something "bad" in the larger culture. They explained that instead of everyone competing to make a living, and instead of a few people privately owning the economy that all of us were dependent on (for jobs, food, clothing, shelter, all necessities and luxuries), the economy should be owned together by everyone, working together to provide the things they would all need and want.

This sounded very nice—similar to their conception of unions, but on a bigger scale and more thoroughgoing. It also sounded impossible to me, given the world that I knew around me. But when I asked critical questions, they had what seemed to me reasonable-sounding answers, so I concluded that this was something worth thinking about.

A more shocking revelation followed not long after. They sat me down again. Both of them had once been members of the Communist Party. Some of my favorite relatives had been members of the Communist Party. They were not sorry that they had been members—they still believed in the things that had caused them to be Communists. Those things had to do with the Brotherhood of Man, fighting for unions and the dignity of workers, opposing all forms of racism and oppression, and believing in the socialist vision.

Some bad developments had been occurring in the Communist Party that had caused them to leave quietly around the time we moved to Clearfield, and some bad developments had obviously taken place in the Soviet Union and in the larger Communist movement. But there was also a lot of good in these entities, they felt, and they did not reject any of them in their entirety.

The kicker was that I was absolutely prohibited from sharing any of this information with anyone at all, even my friends. In an atmosphere pervaded by fervid Cold War anti-Communism, hostile people would use such exposure to destroy all of the good things my parents had been working for. They would very likely lose their jobs, many people (including friends) would turn against us or be afraid to associate with us, and we would have to leave Clearfield. This had happened to other people, other friends—even to Uncle Adrian.

The weight of this terrible burden of secrecy was a difficult and damaging thing. Especially given the larger culture's seemingly unremitting assault on my own particular "family values," on my roots, on each and every one of my favorite relatives, I think it made me at least a little crazy. Especially when my ninth-grade history teacher urged anyone in class who wanted to know about the dangers of Communism in the United States to get the true facts from *Masters of Deceit* by J. Edgar Hoover.

I immediately bought a brand new copy for only fifty cents, popular paperbacks being incredibly inexpensive back then. This vicious little book by the director of the Federal Bureau of Investigation horrified me—and helped to propel me into an intensive, almost obsessive search for the real truth. More than ever, I became a voracious reader and, in some ways, a compulsive searcher.

Truth-Seeking

My guiding principle, initially, was that "the truth is somewhere in between." That is, it was in between the Communism of my parents and the right-wing anti-Communism, reflected in what J. Edgar Hoover had to say, that permeated so much of the world around me. And for me, this happy medium quickly came to be defined by what I read in the centrist-liberal *New York Times* and in a good left-liberal magazine (safely, though not viciously, anti-Communist) that came to our home each month, *The Progressive*.

Yet there were other influences as well. Also arriving to our home were two important left-wing periodicals. One was the very readable "independent socialist" *Monthly Review*, edited by Paul Sweezy and Leo Huberman (which, combined with a number of Monthly Review Press pamphlets and books, would play a key role in my education as a socialist). The other was a "progressive newsweekly," the *National Guardian*—in which was blended a somewhat diluted Communist Party influence with various other, more independent, sometimes more critical-minded, radical elements.

Not long after, I also discovered *I. F. Stone's Weekly* and also stumbled across Dorothy Day's *Catholic Worker*, both of which further expanded my political horizons. My seeking "the truth somewhere in between" caused me to read the well-written but hostile *American Communist Party: A Critical History* by "moderate socialists" Irving Howe and Lewis Coser, on the one hand,

and at least portions of the more turgid "official" account by Communist leader William Z. Foster, *History of the Communist Party of the United States*.

More vibrant than either were the "insider" essays of *The God That Failed*, a copy of which was among my parents' books. I was especially impressed by the passionate essay of Ignazio Silone, whose story, I later learned, was sadder and murkier than he felt able to admit (the fascists had broken him, he had informed)—but whose novel of the 1930s, *Bread and Wine*, seeming to blend Marxism with Christianity, helped me decide, at the age of sixteen, that I was, indeed, a socialist.

No less important were the writings of the acidly anti-Stalinist but staunchly socialist George Orwell, whose satirical jab at Stalinist Russia, *Animal Farm*, and devastating vision of totalitarianism in *Nineteen Eighty-Four* were topics of intense conversation among my closest high school friends and me. A high school classmate introduced me to Arthur Koestler's *Darkness at Noon*, about an Old Bolshevik revolutionary destroyed by (but perhaps partly responsible for) Stalin's purges in 1930s Russia, which was incredibly disturbing.

More to my liking was Albert Camus's *The Plague*, an allegory in which— it seemed to me—ex-Communists remain true to the struggle for humanity's future.

I was also fortunate to stumble upon two gems in unlikely places. In the upper-middle-class home of my mother's parents in Brooklyn, New York, I found a rare copy of Victor Serge's 1937 classic, *Russia Twenty Years After*, purchased by the eager teenager that my mother was when she got it, only to be quickly abandoned after a Stalinist lecture by her beloved Uncle George (who explained that Serge was a phony, a "Trotskyite," an enemy of the Soviet Union).

Permeated by the spirit of revolutionary socialism, this neglected book eloquently explained many things—clearly distinguishing the heroic Communism of Lenin, Trotsky, and the early Bolsheviks from the bureaucratic and murderous realities associated with the Stalin regime—that have stayed with me ever since. (Many years later, I was pleased to facilitate the republication of this book in the Revolutionary Studies series I edited for Humanities Press.)

The other gem had been acquired for some reason by my high school library—the short, readable, amazingly affirmative *Story of an American Communist* by John Gates, a Spanish Civil War veteran like my Uncle George, as well as a former editor of the *Daily Worker*, who seemed proud of much that he and the US Communist Party had stood for and done but was sharply critical of its failure to break with old Stalinist norms and its defense of the 1956 Soviet invasion of Hungary.

The John Gates of 1958 (not yet a bitter anti-Communist) and the Victor Serge of 1937 offered accounts that inspired hope for the future. I would later discover similar qualities in the revolutionary pacifist memoir by A. J. Muste, an amazing leader of labor, antiracist, and antiwar struggles for many decades, included in his anthology, *The Writings of A. J. Muste*, and also in the fascinating reminiscences of another old-timer, Trotskyist leader James P. Cannon, in *The First Ten Years of American Communism*.) It seemed to me, as I read the books by Serge and Gates (and later by Muste and Cannon), that one could learn from the positive as well as the negative lessons from the past, in a way that would not try to duplicate what had gone before. Rather, one could build on that experience toward something better.

In 1962, another important book appeared, *The Marxists*, by C. Wright Mills, which included a clearly written and critical yet relatively sympathetic presentation of Marxism (including selections from the writings of Marx and others) by a wonderful, independent-minded sociologist who had just died. It was available in Clearfield as a cheap popular paperback—only twenty-five cents more than *Masters of Deceit*, and worth every penny! I learned from it, and through it discovered Isaac Deutscher, whose informative writings on the history of revolutionary Russia and the bureaucratized Soviet Union I also began to read.

From an ad in *The Progressive*, I learned about a magazine (I can't recall the name) briefly published by the Young People's Socialist League, which led me to some Socialist Party publications, but also to the magazine *New Politics*, to which I became an early subscriber. There I became more acquainted with left-wing polemics often associated, later, with the Old Left—with a flourishing anti-Stalinism that came in a variety of flavors, reformist Social Democrats jostling with still-revolutionary "third camp" socialists, and other elements that fit into neither category.

I forget when I first became aware of Eugene V. Debs, the wonderful and inspiring working-class socialist leader of the twentieth century's first two decades, when the Socialist Party that he led had a mass base throughout much of the labor movement, throughout our cultural life, and in communities throughout the United States. Its membership was in the hundreds of thousands, it inspired millions, it had powerful impact. But when I went looking for the writings of Debs in the early 1960s, I discovered that none were in print.

A visit to the small national office of the Socialist Party–Social Democratic Federation in New York City brought me face to face with a young secretary who told me that Debs's writings were old and out of date, and she sent me to the Tamiment Library, where a kindly librarian gave me a pleasant, rather innocuous little pamphlet about Debs by an old Social Democrat named August Claessens.

Going through boxes of files, pamphlets, magazines, and other materials that were rotting away near our house in an abandoned chicken coop, where my parents had "stored" all of that stuff, I first became aware of the immense and pervasive influence of the Communist Party (CP) and its periphery in the 1930s and '40s (whose last gasp seemed to be the hopeful crusade and disastrous defeat of the Henry Wallace Progressive Party campaign of 1948)—it was all there. During the mid-to-late '30s, in the midst of the Depression decade, the CP had been a mass movement, with a dubious Popular Front ethos (tied so closely into the pro-capitalist Democratic Party) that, nonetheless, had a powerful residual radicalism and that, again, had inspired and influenced millions. In the 1940s, the movement briefly was given a special push by the World War II alliance of the United States and the Soviet Union against Hitler.

Hoping to find something of that earlier magic by going to the biggest bookstore of the Communist Party in the United States—the Jefferson Bookstore in (again) New York City—I found myself face to face with portraits of Marx, Engels, and Lenin; lots of old books and magazines; some shiny new things from the Soviet Union; and some less shiny new things that were published in and for our own country but that seemed flat, inward-looking, and unimpressive compared to what had existed in those earlier decades.

In my final years of high school, I longed for something akin to Divine Intervention that might somehow bring back those Glory Days of mass radicalism, challenging the status quo of seemingly "affluent," culturally conformist, politically repressed Cold War America, and opening up pathways for creating, in fact, the kind of world that my parents and favorite relatives, and so many other good people, had dreamed about.

Stirrings beyond the Printed Page

But at this time there were, in fact, radical stirrings affecting the lives and consciousness of millions. First and foremost were musical influences. I am afraid that the often subversive and liberating elements that many found, at the time, in a variety of important genres (whether jazz, rhythm and blues, rock 'n' roll, soul, or country and western) were at that time beyond me. Others can give firsthand accounts of their importance.

What did grab me was the so-called "folk music revival," which professional anti-Communist Herbert Romerstein warned against as a pernicious Communist-inspired plot, in a small book titled *Communism and Your Child* (1962), also available in my high school library. There were old union songs and even older work songs, spirituals, the left-wing songs of Woody Guthrie, songs of the Spanish Civil War, amazing and haunting old ballads going back for many generations, clever new protest tunes, humorous and often apolitical folk tunes, and more—from the Weavers, Harry Belafonte (and the Belafonte Folk Singers), the Kingston Trio, Theodore Bikel, Pete Seeger, Malvina Reynolds, Joan Baez, Odetta, Dave Van Ronk, and many others.

For a small youthful clutch of us in Clearfield (as in so many other places in the early 1960s), especially important were the wonderful compositions, records—and even the persona—of a young Bob Dylan. More than such musical stirrings were the underlying realities that were helping to generate a response to such music among many who seemed to have no left-wing connections in their family backgrounds.

This went far beyond the stultifying superficiality and creeping boredom associated with the cultural conformism of the '50s and early '60s, against which there was the cultural rebellion of the so-called beatniks (Allen Ginsberg, Jack Kerouac, Diane di Prima, et cetera), but also an amazing proliferation of stand-up comics that we could watch on our black-and-white TVs, such as Jonathan Winters, Mike Nichols and Elaine May, Dick Gregory, Mort Sahl, Godfrey Cambridge (and even Lenny Bruce, fleetingly)—not to mention the slyly subversive cartoons of *The Rocky and Bullwinkle Show*.

For that matter, there was an accumulation of movies that seemed to challenge the status quo. (Off the top of my head, I remember *On the Beach*, *The World, the Flesh and the Devil*, *The Defiant Ones*, *Spartacus*, *Dr. Strangelove*, *Raisin in the Sun*, and *To Kill a Mockingbird*.)

This status quo seemed dominated by realities that disturbed more and more of us, and a growing number of struggles against these things increasingly attracted our attention and inspired more and more of us. We were all keenly aware of "the Bomb," the nuclear weapons systems that both sides were building up in the Cold War that could destroy all life on our planet several times over (there was even a word for this—"overkill"), and nuclear tests that were polluting our atmosphere with radioactive particles and something called strontium 90.

There was also the obvious fact that the United States, in its Cold War crusade that was presumably for "freedom," willingly supported a large number of vicious and unpopular dictatorships, just so long as they were anti-Communist. It also became evident that various popular struggles against such right-wing dictatorships were being fought against by the government of the United States in the name of "anti-Communism."

There were growing criticisms and protests—not in Clearfield, Pennsylvania—but we got word of mass protests in Britain led by the aged philosopher Bertrand Russell and other prominent intellectuals, and also word of the

US formation of other groups that organized smaller but no less important protests, groups such as Committee for a Sane Nuclear Policy (commonly known as SANE), Women Strike for Peace, the Student Peace Union.

Even earlier, and in many ways going far deeper (deeper into my emotions, deeper into the problems afflicting the day-to-day reality of US society), there was the amazing emergence of the civil rights movement. My earliest recollections of the proliferating images of this movement blur together: the Supreme Court's 1954 decision that declared racial segregation in public schools to be unconstitutional; the howling white mobs, replete with Confederate flags, in the streets of Little Rock, Arkansas, being subdued by federal troops there to protect young Black students; a jailed Rosa Parks in Montgomery, Alabama, sparking a bus boycott led by a young minister named Martin Luther King Jr.; Southern white policemen with snarling dogs, fire hoses turned on peaceful marches, the politely worded bigotry of the White Citizens Councils and the burning crosses of the Ku Klux Klan; the howling mobs again, with Black and white Freedom Riders who challenged segregation on Greyhound buses going South, being beaten and one of the buses burned; many hundreds, then thousands, of dignified African Americans, along with a growing number of white allies, picketing and rallying and sometimes going to jail for committing nonviolent civil disobedience against racist segregation laws; and in 1963 hundreds of thousands converging on Washington, DC, in an interracial protest for "Jobs and Freedom," a gathering once again bathed in the eloquence of Rev. Martin Luther King Jr.

Growing numbers of us, in high schools throughout much of the country, individually and in small handfuls were powerfully inspired by what was happening. We vowed to ourselves that as soon as we could, we would join in. I deeply regretted that I had been born a couple of years too late to be able to go south in 1964, in response to the call of the Student Nonviolent Coordinating Committee (SNCC), Congress of Racial Equality (CORE), and others to join in the Freedom Summer campaign.

For me, the next best thing was what I actually did in the summers of 1964 and 1965— got a summer job as a counselor at Camp Henry, an interracial camp run by the Henry Street Settlement of New York City, bringing out to the countryside of upstate New York waves of young boys (ages six to sixteen) from impoverished neighborhoods of New York City's Lower East Side. It was an experience from which I learned much—including much that I had not expected.

The kids were largely African American and Puerto Rican, and for the most part they had a great time. The counselors were largely white, but with significant numbers of Blacks and a couple of Puerto Ricans. The top administrators were white. Those of us working there were almost all very, very liberal—with one or two open-minded conservatives, and a few who were much more left-wing than liberal (although there was a vague kind of socialist or left-wing sensibility and background that seemed to permeate the liberalism even at the top administrative levels).

It seemed to me that working with these kids was truly important work (I still think so), and that it was truly a manifestation of the wonderful and inspiring changes that, I thought, would be transforming the United States more and more through the Black-led but interracial "freedom struggle," personified by Martin Luther King. But I discovered that life was more complicated than that.

In the summer of 1964, I think there were powerful elements at Camp Henry that reflected the spirit of the interracial "beloved community" that seemed to characterize the civil rights movement at that particular historical moment. Yet beneath the surface—and by 1965 very much coming to the surface—I was able to see growing racial tensions, aspects of which involved cultural differences that were poorly understood on the part of some of the whites, and also some resentments among some African Americans regarding white and Black status and power differentials.

Even more obvious to me by 1965 was an unconscious paternalism and elitism among the top white administrators—a belief that a primary responsibility of Camp Henry was to introduce these kids to superior forms of culture, as reflected in the tastes and sensibilities of these white, urban, liberal-Democrat, largely Jewish public school teachers from New York City who were proud members of the United Federation of Teachers (UFT). During the 1968 strike of the UFT, a disastrous confrontation erupted—led by the union's "moderate socialist" president Albert Shanker against local control of the schools by the Black and Puerto Rican communities—and at that moment I vividly recalled the escalating tensions that had rattled my naïve notions while working at Camp Henry three years before.

A More Radical Edge

In a sense, the truth I sought was not somewhere "in between" the Communist Left and the reactionary Right, and certainly not in the left-liberal zone in which I sought intellectual-political comfort. It could be far more complex and unsettling than I had imagined.

One of the most unexpected influences on me, in this period, was the sharp, absolutely uncompromising Black nationalism associated with Malcolm X. He was portrayed in the media as a powerful Black racist who advocated a hatred of whites among increasingly receptive numbers of African Americans, in stark contrast to the interracial harmony represented by Martin Luther King and the civil rights movement. This horrified me, yet I saw how aspects of Malcolm X's ideology resonated among some of the people I knew at Camp Henry—which disturbed me, but which also now made a certain kind of sense.

What really impressed me when I actually read some of what Malcolm X had to say, in interviews that found their way into one or another "mainstream" outlet, was the quality of his thinking. In the same period I discovered James Baldwin's novel *Another Country*, which beautifully revealed many of the sharp edges and complex dimensions of racial and sexual politics of which I had not been fully aware.

I also read positive discussions of Black nationalism in the pages of *Monthly Review*, and not long after his death read *The Autobiography of Malcolm X* and *Malcolm X Speaks*. This opened new realms of thought and understanding. It seemed to me, more and more, that powerful historical and contemporary realities pointed to the necessity of the core principle in Malcolm X's outlook: Black self-determination, that is, Black control of the Black struggle, and Black control of the Black community.

I was, in these years, becoming increasingly disenchanted with the profound limitations of the mainstream liberalism with which so much of the organized Old Left (particularly those in and around the Socialist Party and those in and around the Communist Party) had come to identify. Liberalism's incompatibility with powerful insights represented by Malcolm X was only one reason. Another had to do with foreign policy.

The pillars of Democratic Party liberalism, it had seemed to me, were Eleanor Roosevelt and her own favorite candidate (following the 1945 death of her husband, President Franklin D. Roosevelt), the two-time loser of 1952 and 1956, Adlai Stevenson. Of course, in 1960 Stevenson was shunted aside by the youthful John F. Kennedy—whose shining liberal luster had beguiled me into becoming one of his most ardent thirteen-year old campaigners. And in rapid succession, President Kennedy—defended by his administration's representative to the United Nations, Adlai Stevenson (with Mrs. Roosevelt sitting right there as part of the US delegation!)—proved to represent something very different from what I believed in, around policies regarding Cuba and Vietnam.

The young revolutionaries who swept into Havana in 1959, amid the jubilation of huge crowds throughout Cuba, initially had an aura of heroism even in Clearfield. Although the mass media quickly turned hostile as the Cuban Revolution radicalized, I had more information that prevented such an easy turnaround in my own consciousness. There were the glowing accounts, of course, in the *National Guardian* and *Monthly Review*, and debates revealing complexities in *New Politics*.

I. F. Stone's Weekly and *The Progressive* also provided important information that challenged the common notion that the island had fallen into the grip of a Communist tyranny. And C. Wright Mills's essay entitled "Listen, Yankee!" had a powerful impact on me. It had appeared in *Harper's Magazine* and would soon to come out in expanded form as a cheap, popular paperback. I could not see Fidel Castro and Che Guevara as villains, and it seemed obvious to me that the Cuban people themselves should be allowed to determine the direction of their revolution and the fate of their country.

The Kennedy administration's 1961 decision to invade Cuba, foiled at the Bay of Pigs, seemed to reveal a fatal flaw in the liberalism that had once seemed so attractive to me. And then there was the decision by Kennedy and so many other shining liberals to help keep Vietnam divided in violation of the 1956 Geneva Peace Accords, and to support a vicious and unpopular anti-Communist dictatorship in South Vietnam.

Thanks to reading material available in my home, I knew all about this in the early 1960s, well before the big escalation of 1965, and it seemed clear to me that there remained a crying need to go beyond mainstream liberalism— and beyond the failure of most of the Old Left to do just that.

Students for a Democratic Society

I think it was in 1963 that I first became aware of Students for a Democratic Society (SDS). My sister Patty had married a very nice guy named Earl Brecher, with whom she went to Liberia as one of the first Peace Corps volunteers, in a program launched by the Kennedy administration that sent idealistic college graduates to "help" downtrodden areas in Asia, Africa, and Latin America.

Earl's youngest brother, Jeremy, was a couple of years older than me and was involved in this new group, SDS. I read a mimeographed document called the "Port Huron Statement" and many other materials he sent me. During a visit to the wonderful home of Patty's in-laws, in a woodsy Connecticut paradise called Yelping Hill, Jeremy and I talked about folk music, politics, and more.

Jeremy explained to me that, in his opinion, the Communists of the 1930s had been an incredibly impressive force, had accomplished great things, but had also engaged in irresponsible, stupid, self-destructive behavior and policies. They were now incapable of providing a pathway to the future, especially in the new times in which we were living. The rest of the traditional Left was also caught in old ideological ruts and political dead ends that would prevent it from doing the things that needed to be done.

There was a need for a fresh start, for something new—and something new was now coming into being, through movements for peace, for civil rights, et cetera. SDS was part of that. I should think about joining.

The truth in what Jeremy was suggesting is reflected in this summary (from my recent book *Marx, Lenin, and the Revolutionary Experience*) of what happened in the 1960s spilling over into the 1970s:

> There was an explosion of mass action and creative smaller-group efforts, an inspiring, exhilarating commitment to transforming society—a massive upsurge of youthful idealism and action for civil rights of oppressed races and nationalities, against the threat of nuclear war, for civil liberties, against poverty, for campus reform and academic freedom, against the Vietnam war, for women's liberation, against anti-gay prejudice, for cultural freedom and revitalization, against the destruction of the earth's ecology, for the elementary and revolutionary democratic demand to "let the people decide."
>
> Increasing numbers of people decided to speak truth to power, question authority, move from protest to resistance, finally to be realistic by demanding the "impossible" (since those things that were commonly seen as "realistic" and "possible" meant accepting the injustice, oppression, and irrationality of the status quo). The radicalization process helped to show that through collective action people can more effectively deal with their common problems, that if enough people commit themselves to struggles that make sense, it is possible to transform the political climate, change minorities into majorities, and win meaningful victories. Some also learned that electoralism and reformist politics are traps, that ultra-leftism is a dead end, and that society will not be fundamentally transformed unless the working class (society's majority) becomes conscious of the need for this to be so. In 1968 many became especially aware of the power of workers, thanks to the May–June events in France. That year also illustrated that the struggle for liberation is global, with the Tet offensive in Vietnam, the resistance to bureaucratic rule and Soviet invasion of Czechoslovakia, the worker-student upsurge throughout Western and Southern Europe, the brutally repressed student demonstrations in Mexico, the intensified battles for peace and justice in our own land.[2]

In the 1964 presidential election, in the face of the right-wing Republican threat represented by Barry Goldwater, who seemed likely to do things like escalate the Vietnam conflict into a full-scale war, SDS adopted a policy of critical support for the reelection of liberal Texan Lyndon Baines Johnson, advancing a slogan I liked—"Part of the Way with LBJ" (though I openly campaigned "all the way" for him in Clearfield). Of course, after Johnson won by a landslide, he himself began the escalation of the Vietnam War, and in April 1965 SDS organized the first of the mass marches against the war.

By the time I was a senior in high school, I was identifying with SDS enough to decide to send a filled-out membership application form, a long letter explaining who I was and what I thought, and dues money. I received a heartening response from someone named Carolyn Craven welcoming me. But in addition to wolfing down large quantities of SDS literature, I was connecting with much more.

One of the most important influences on me, by this time, was the stimulating radical-pacifist magazine *Liberation*, which contained a proliferation of thoughtful reports, opinion pieces, discussions, and debates about civil rights and peace movements by such experienced activists and theorists as A. J. Muste, Dave Dellinger, Bayard Rustin, David McReynolds, Brad Lyttle, Staughton Lynd, Paul Goodman, and others. Also important for me was a weighty and initially more academic *Studies on the Left*, in which a variety of left-wing scholars and intellectuals (William Appleman Williams, James Weinstein, Stanley Aronowitz, Eugene Genovese, and others) self-consciously sought to map out new pathways of radical thought.

All this seemed particularly vibrant because it was connected with a rising tide of youthful radical activism definitely not dominated by any of the Old Left tendencies. A valuable 1962 survey of how such activism had, since the late 1950s, become manifest at the University of California–Berkeley was offered in another inexpensive popular paperback that I was able to purchase in Clearfield, titled *Student*, by a young David Horowitz (two decades before he swerved so severely and destructively to the right).

In the pages of the liberal weekly *New Republic*, available in my high school library, I could read updated, hip, incredibly exciting reports by Andrew Kopkind on SNCC, Freedom Summer, the New Left, and the momentous Berkeley Free Speech Movement. I was able to supplement this with important articles and essays in *New Politics*—especially thanks to contributions by Hal Draper.

Draper's 1966 essay "The Two Souls of Socialism" (counterposing revolutionary-democratic socialism "from the bottom up" to the top-down elitism of Social Democratic "moderate socialist" reformers and Stalinist authoritarians) was to influence me for years to come. But his on-the-spot coverage of the Berkeley struggles gave some issues of *New Politics* a "must read" quality and culminated in his 1966 classic, yet another cheap paperback, *Berkeley: The New Student Revolt*.

Old Left/New Left Interplay

Of course, the sharp and pugnacious Draper, like other *New Politics* editors, was very much a product of the Old Left, and they were not the only ones reaching out to connect with, and to influence, those of us who were crystallizing into this vibrant New Left. After all, the parent group of SDS was itself a preeminently Old Left formation going back to 1905, the "moderate socialist" League for Industrial Democracy (LID). More or less a front group for the Socialist Party, the LID could boast of two leading personalities, both energetic thinkers and doers, Michael Harrington (then in his late 30s) and Tom Kahn (then in his late 20s).

Harrington, author of the best-selling (inexpensive paperback) classic on poverty in the United States, *The Other America* (1962), was the LID's charismatic chairman. Kahn, LID executive secretary, was a close associate of the brilliant civil rights strategist Bayard Rustin (himself an aide to famous Black trade-union Socialist A. Philip Randolph, and at times to Martin Luther King). Kahn had substantial civil rights experience and had authored an LID pamphlet that offered an incisive radical analysis of what it would take to end racial oppression, *The Economics of Equality*.

Much later I would learn that Harrington and Kahn were protégés of Max Shachtman, who started off in the Communist movement of the early 1920s, then along with James P. Cannon had led the US Trotskyist movement. But there was a sharp break with Trotsky and Cannon in 1940, after which Shachtman led a revolutionary socialist group that by the mid-1950s was evolving in the direction of "moderate socialism" (in the process losing the allegiance of some comrades, like Hal Draper), merging into what was left of the old Socialist Party led by "the grand old man of Socialism," Norman Thomas.

Harrington and Kahn seemed to have absorbed all of what Shachtman represented, and seemed incredibly coherent, capable, razor-sharp—intellectually, organizationally, polemically, factionally. Despite their relative youth, here was the Old Left par excellence!

Listening to Shachtman explain himself (as I did a couple of years later), one heard passionately revolutionary syllables forming stolidly reformist words. Uncompromising notions of class struggle became inseparable from a commitment to the far-from-radical officialdom of the AFL-CIO and its place in the Democratic Party, and the defense of socialism from Stalinist betrayal added up to an alignment with the US government in the cause of Cold War anti-Communism—all with a Marxist flourish. On the other hand, as Kahn later reminisced, Shachtman had driven home, over and over again, this essential idea: "Democracy was not merely the icing on the socialist cake.

It was the cake—or there was no socialism worth fighting for." Of course, this key insight, so alien to ideologies infected by Stalinism, was not unique to Shachtman but can be found, expressed with strikingly similar words, in Rosa Luxemburg and others, including Cannon, Trotsky, and Lenin.

There were other spinoffs from Trotskyism (but with no "moderate socialist" admixture) that sought to have an impact within the New Left milieu—I saw one sign of this in the easy availability, through SDS literature lists, of booklets by C. L. R. James and his co-thinkers, such as *Facing Reality* (of which I couldn't make sense at the time). More accessible was a "Marxist-Humanist" pamphlet by Raya Dunayevskaya, of the small News and Letters group, which seemed incredibly innovative in connecting the civil rights struggle, the Berkeley Free Speech Movement, and the growing movement against the Vietnam War with ideas of Karl Marx, especially his youthful 1844 *Economic and Philosophical Manuscripts*.

There was also the interminably factional and fault-finding Spartacist League, and what struck me as the shrill, super-leftist stridency of the Workers World Party and its affiliate Youth against War and Fascism. Somewhat more interesting to me, but seemingly two or three steps removed from the New Left milieu (and dismissed by many within that milieu), was the more "orthodox" Trotskyism offered by the Socialist Workers Party and the Young Socialist Alliance.

Old Left influences were hardly confined to elements that had associated with defending or breaking away from the perspectives of Leon Trotsky! As already emphasized, the weight and influence of the Communist Party could by no means be discounted—there were still a few thousand CP members (more than all the Trotskyist and ex-Trotskyist groups combined), many with significant political experience and skills developed in earlier decades in the labor, antiracist, and other struggles, drawing on still-significant resources, and backed by the greatly tarnished yet still considerable prestige of "actually existing socialism" in the Soviet Union and Eastern Europe.

In order to reach out to radicalizing youth, the CP established the W. E. B. Du Bois Clubs, which had some appeal in certain areas. Its ideological influences continued to be felt in more independent publications such as the *National Guardian* and *Monthly Review*—although the "leftist" challenge of Maoism (as the Chinese Communist Party increasingly challenged the policies of the Soviet Communist Party in world affairs) soon found influential reflection in their pages. The primary organizational form that Maoism took at that time, however, was in a recent split-off from the Communist Party—the vibrant and active Progressive Labor Movement, which soon renamed itself the Progressive Labor Party and not long after would intervene heavily into SDS itself.

All this helps us to see important aspects of the context within which the New Left grew. But the New Left of the early to mid-1960s does not come into focus until we shift our view to its actual organizations. The perception of that time was that SNCC and SDS together constituted the heart and soul of the vibrant new movement. SNCC had been playing a central role in the civil rights struggle, and SDS—rapidly growing from a couple hundred in 1962 to about five thousand in 1966—had been playing a visible role in anti-apartheid protests, in pressing for "an interracial movement of the poor," in organizing the first major march against the Vietnam War in the spring of 1965, and in articulating a radical vision of social change.

Heart and Soul

A full-scale history of the organization I joined can be found in Kirkpatrick Sale's unsurpassed book *SDS*. If I were to give an account my own experience with the organization, I would need to give attention to where I tried to help build it on a local level once I left Clearfield and went to the University of Pittsburgh. However, the complex history of SDS in Pittsburgh, inseparable from the richer history of more broadly defined New Left and protest currents, will have to be explored another time. In lieu of a full history, perhaps a few snapshots can give some sense of how its "heart and soul" was perceived by one young member in 1965 and '66.

One of the snapshots is a button and a pamphlet that SDS produced, which many of us embraced as our own. The button proclaimed the simple slogan "Let the people decide," and the Port Huron Statement explained its meaning—the need for "participatory democracy." The statement charged that the much-vaunted US commitments to freedom and peace "rang hollow before the facts of Negro life in the South and the big cities of the North" and were "contradicted by [US] economic and military investments in the Cold War status quo."

Claims that the United States stood for social justice were thrown into doubt because "while two-thirds of mankind suffers undernourishment, our own upper classes revel amidst superfluous abundance." US politics "rests in national stalemate, its goals ambiguous and tradition-bound instead of informed and clear, its democratic system apathetic and manipulated rather than being truly "of, by, and for the people." The statement asserted:

In a participatory democracy, the political life would be based in several root principles:

that decision-making of basic social consequence be carried on by public groupings;

that politics be seen positively, as the art of collectively creating an acceptable pattern of social relations;

that politics has the function of bringing people out of isolation and into community, thus being a necessary, though not sufficient, means of finding meaning in personal life;

that the political order should serve to clarify problems in a way instrumental to their solution; it should provide outlets for the expression of personal grievance and aspiration; opposing views should be organized so as to illuminate choices and facilitate the attainment of goals; channels should be commonly available to relate men [i.e., people] to knowledge and to power so that private problems—from bad recreation facilities to personal alienation—are formulated as general issues.

The economic sphere would have as its basis the principles:

that work should involve incentives worthier than money or survival. It should be educative, not stultifying; creative, not mechanical; self-directed, not manipulated, encouraging independence; a respect for others, a sense of dignity and a willingness to accept social responsibility, since it is this experience that has crucial influence on habits, perceptions and individual ethics;

that the economic experience is so personally decisive that the individual must share in its full determination;

that the economy itself is of such social importance that its major resources and means of production should be open to democratic participation and subject to democratic social regulation.

For some of us in SDS, this added up to a genuine socialism. Not all were willing to embrace that tainted word, but we all felt fine with the word "radical," which literally meant going to the root of things and implied the need for fundamental social change.

Another snapshot involves the march against the Vietnam War organized by SANE, held on November 27, 1965, in Washington, DC. A bearded Carl Oglesby, the eloquent president of SDS, takes the podium and explains the pattern of US foreign policy—numerous foreign interventions led by a government committed to the profits of US businesses overseas.

In that speech, he claimed that he no longer considered himself a liberal but was a radical instead. Oglesby noted that the liberalism then prevailing in US politics had two very different components—a corporate liberalism that dominated the economy and the government, and a humanist liberalism that shared many of the same values with the radicals of the New Left but was entangled with a Democratic Party that was deeply committed to the "bipartisan" foreign policy that he had been describing and that had led us into Vietnam. He concluded:

> We are dealing now with a colossus that does not want to be changed. It will not change itself. It will not cooperate with those who want to change it. Those allies of ours in the Government—are they really our allies? If they are, then they don't need advice, they need constituencies; they don't need study groups, they need a movement. And if they are not, then all the more reason for building that movement with the most relentless conviction.
>
> There are people in this country today who are trying to build that movement, who aim at nothing less than a humanist reformation. And the humanist liberals must understand that it is this movement with which their own best hopes are most in tune. We radicals know the same history that you liberals know, and we can understand your occasional cynicism, exasperation, and even distrust. But we ask you to put these aside and help us risk a leap. Help us find enough time for the enormous work that needs doing here. Help us build. Help us shape the future in the name of plain human hope.

Yet at a national antiwar conference held in Washington that same weekend, as a factional war erupted (the "Trots" of the Socialist Workers Party and Young Socialist Alliance had called for a demand of "bring the troops home now," which was denounced as too radical and divisive by many others there), SDS as a national organization held itself aloof. An SDS position paper by Paul Booth and Lee Webb was circulated explaining that it would not be possible to build an antiwar movement in the United States that could actually stop an ongoing war—history showed that such a thing could not be done. Instead, we must patiently and persistently build grassroots movements that could bring about fundamental social change—to prevent "the seventh war from now."

Another snapshot from two months later: I am at a national SDS conference in Champaign-Urbana, Illinois.

Jeremy had taken me under his wing at one point and explained to me that there are very different political currents in SDS. The "right wing" had closer ties to aspects of the Old Left, and especially to the LID. Led by Steve

Max (whose father had been part of the Gates faction that left the Communist Party in the 1950s), this LID-oriented "right wing" favored forging a broad coalition of the labor movement, the civil rights movement, the churches, the peace movement, and the New Left, building for broad reforms and working within the Democratic Party.

The "left wing," dominated by Tom Hayden, was inclined to reject all that and to insist that the only serious path forward was to do community organizing and to build a powerful network of "community unions" that would create genuine participatory democracy at the local level, forging an "interracial movement of the poor" that would actually be able to challenge the corporate elite and put power in the hands of the people. In between these two camps was a more diverse grouping, whose leading personalities included Paul Booth, Clark Kissinger, and Lee Webb, that wanted SDS to encompass *both* of the other currents (coalitionists and community organizers), but also to engage in a broader range of work—student organizing and campus reform efforts, antiwar activity (including an anti-draft campaign), and more.

Another issue was that the formal tie between SDS and the LID was moving toward termination, but the question remained as to what the relationship would be, or if there would be one at all.

Jeremy and a friend of his, Doug Ireland, who were somewhat inclined toward the coalitionist wing and felt that relations with the LID were important, invited me to an informal "bull session" in a room shared by Tom Kahn and Paul Feldman, editor of the Socialist Party paper *New America*. Also present was a young member of the party's Young People's Socialist League but more importantly a seasoned activist from SNCC, Ivanhoe Donaldson. I simply sat, watched, listened. In fact, Kahn and Donaldson did most of the talking, with Feldman chiming in occasionally to agree with one or another thing Kahn said.

It was a fascinating verbal dance. Donaldson and Kahn obviously knew each other well, comparing notes and sharing thoughts, as old friends, on recent and current specifics of the civil rights movement in the South. But the pattern of discussion shifted, with Kahn questioning, then needling, then pulling into a positive mode to explain what he meant. After some positive give-and-take, his considerable humor and sharp criticism would merge into a harder jab, from which he then backed off with a friendly word, which was only to prepare for another, even harder push to drive his point home. Much of the time, it began to seem, he "listened" to Donaldson only for the purpose of advancing his own agenda, to locate the points on which to concentrate his argument.

Kahn was challenging what did seem like a nebulous idealism of what he termed "mystical militants" whom he saw as all too prevalent in SNCC and

SDS. ("We need to deal with the real world, real world!" he would admonish.) Against a naively emotional militancy, he emphasized the necessity of analysis, program, strategy, tactics. One must, he emphasized (employing what was clearly a Marxist perspective, well argued), understand the necessary interplay between the struggles for racial and economic justice and the fact that it is the working class (with all of its diversity and contradictions) that is central to this combined struggle. This made essential the development of closer and broader ties between the civil rights movement and the labor movement. This, in turn, meant that SNCC and others working for civil rights in the South needed to be connecting seriously with AFL-CIO unions there. (This sounded right to me.)

Yeah, Donaldson responded, but those unions are all-white and racist, if they're established at all. Where are these representatives of "progressive" unionism you're talking about? Kahn ticked off the names of AFL-CIO officials in one or another Southern city. Donaldson pointed out the limitations of each—but Kahn would not concede the point.

The discussion then took a more disturbing turn—Kahn's angry, sneering attack on "Stalinist influence" and "Stalinoid" operatives in the civil rights movement. (Inwardly I bristled—it reminded me of J. Edgar Hoover's hateful book that had attacked my own roots.) "What are you talking about?" Donaldson challenged. Kahn named names—this and that "movement lawyer," this and that advisor and financial donor, this and that staff member, and when he refused to consider the SNCC activist's responses and kept on the attack, Donaldson finally walked out.

Then Kahn turned his attention to my SDS comrades. "Was I too hard?" he mused—but this turned out to be the prelude to a similar dance, repeated with substantially the same themes adapted to SDS specifics, and ultimately building up to the same end result.

When we three SDSers were once more by ourselves, Doug furiously uttered curses I had never heard before, Jeremy voiced a despairing commentary about how rigid and destructive Kahn could be, and I passionately concluded that I much preferred the openness of the New Left to the smug and dogmatic certainties of the Old.

Summer of '66

The summer of 1966 was the twilight year of the "old SDS" to which I had been recruited—a little moment in history in which it seemed to me the coherence of the New Left began to unravel, almost as if in fulfillment of Tom Kahn's unpleasant prophecies.

I have had the honor of making a very brief appearance in Kirkpatrick Sale's substantial history and also in *Students for a Democratic Society: A Graphic History*, produced by Harvey Pekar, Paul Buhle, and Gary Dumm, in which I was portrayed as a hardworking young bookkeeper vainly trying to help make sense of the organization's finances.

It is true that for about thirty dollars a week (worth more then than it is now—but still not much), in the summer of 1966, I worked in the SDS national office. I helped go through the mail, helped fill literature requests, and—with substantial tutoring from Clark Kissinger—kept the organization's books and made bank deposits.

While there were certainly financial problems, it seemed to me that SDS's primary problem was that the organization lacked a sufficient infrastructure that could draw together the SDS chapters that were proliferating throughout the country into a cohesive whole. There was no means, organizationally, to carry out a serious political discussion of "what was to be done," to make serious, democratic decisions on that matter, and to carry out those decisions in a meaningful way throughout the United States. Our structure and infrastructure may have been okay for a group of about one thousand— but not for one of five thousand and rising.

It was a summer of intense experiences and discussions with many others in and around the SDS national office. I remember outgoing national secretary Paul Booth, whose apartment I moved into, writing a long position paper that attempted to map out a coherent and multifaceted strategic and organizational perspective for SDS ("I showed it to Heather [his future wife], and she thought it was very good," he said proudly), and I especially liked how it attempted to show that we were part of a mass radical tradition in line with the Populist movement of the 1890s and the early-1900s Socialist Party of Debs—but all this was pretty much ignored by a rapidly growing and radicalizing membership when it was published in *New Left Notes*.

Booth and I stayed up late one night talking about the relationship of the Old Left and the New—agreeing that it was complex. He understood when I explained how people coming from the Communist Party experience had been so important to the person I was (and to what we as New Leftists were, even as we rejected the dogmas and horrors reaching down from the time of Stalin). He added with conviction that there was something similar regarding the background with which he identified—that some of the "social dems" (moderate Socialist Party members whose standard-bearer had been Norman Thomas) had not "sold out" en masse to the US State Department, that their tradition also represented something of value for the New Left. But such things were not seen or accepted, we felt, by many of our SDS comrades.

There were many conversations going on as activists such as us tried to sort out "where we go from here." Well-known Berkeley radical Jerry Rubin came through town for a few days, staying at Booth's and my apartment, to check out SDS and engage in searching discussions—though not long after he would join with Abbie Hoffman to create the Yippies. During his visit, he certainly seemed to have nothing to do with the "turn on, tune in, drop out" ethos of the growing hippie-influenced alternative culture into which he would soon infuse radical politics with outrageous and often hilarious antics.

But drugs were not completely foreign to our own slightly more staid political scene. I remember the outgoing SDS vice president, a young Texan named Jeff Shero, who asked me if it would be okay to store his marijuana in the huge, heavy safe in the SDS national office. (Shocked, I told him no.) "Grass" was proliferating through the youth culture by that time, but it was by no means a staple of the average SDSer, at least in 1966, when it was common for the police to "bust" activists for possession of this illegal substance.

Thus, when fellow organizer Judy Kissinger and I drove the famous protest singer/songwriter Phil Ochs through Chicago one night after he did a big fund-raising concert for SDS, and from the back seat of the car he offered each of us a joint (in my case, the first time anyone ever did that), both Judy and I (again) "just said no."

There were many remarkable people I recall from that summer. I vividly remember a wild yet down-to-earth Bob Speck (another Texan), bushy-haired and bespectacled, who worked very hard in the national office. He was highly opinionated and often disagreed with what I thought (though he liked Howard Fast novels), and he believed in socialism but was inclined to call himself an anarchist because he felt that it would always be necessary to fight against those in authority, no matter what. I remember Art Goldberg, a strange, very tall and thin, simple, warm-hearted, very capable printer who had been saved as a child from the Holocaust and had grown up in a sectarian Christian-communist community, which he left in order to apply the teachings of Jesus in the real world (which he judged with a harsh fundamentalist moralism).

I remember working with a number of young staffers and volunteers who were helping to prepare a mailing of *New Left Notes*, and listening with fascination to an extended and passionate debate between the warm, earnest, and eloquent radical-pacifist Paul Lauter and the no-less warm, though funnier and almost cuddly, left-wing socialist Tom Condit about the importance and possibilities, for revolutionaries, of such things as "trust"—with Lauter insisting on its necessity among revolutionaries, and Condit insisting that this is too fragile a reed on which to build serious politics.

I remember the nascent feminism (though we were not using that word) of dark-haired Arlen Weissman, speaking quietly with thoughtful blue eyes peering from behind wire-rimmed spectacles, and especially that of Judy Kissinger, a sandy-haired, sturdy young mom and diligent organizer. She organized my favorite fund-raiser—a screening of the wonderful Old Left black-and-white film that had been blacklisted in the 1950s, *Salt of the Earth*, which beautifully interwove issues of class, race, and gender into the story of a heroic strike in New Mexico. Judy thought it was about time that women started becoming national officers of SDS, and she was thinking about running for one of those positions.

I drank plenty of beer while talking with other SDS friends working in the national office about the nature of US society, the realities of US radicalism, the possibilities of the future, and the problems of SDS. Eric Chester and I agreed that there was no coherence in SDS—organizationally, politically, or otherwise—and that no actual or potential leaders seemed geared toward confronting this problem.

"Success" would—given the weaknesses—make matters even worse. If the organization grew far more dramatically than it was already growing at the time (and in fact that is precisely what happened as the youth radicalization swept the country), the lack of strong organizational structures, of clear program, of political coherence would overwhelm SDS. This meant that the organizational mess SDS was becoming would not be in a position to win a majority of the American people to the perspectives of "participatory democracy" that we believed in, or to pose a serious challenge to the oppressive power of the corporate capitalist system.

At Clear Lake, Iowa, that summer, there were more SDSers gathered at a national convention than ever before. I listened with rapt attention to the keynote talk of outgoing president Carl Oglesby in which he stated that there was, indeed, a sense of growing crisis in SDS despite the fact, and in some sense because of the fact, that it was on the verge of runaway growth. I was relieved that this insightful spokesman understood the vital importance of coming up with a solution to the crisis, but I wondered what he meant when he prefaced his explanation of what the solution would be by stressing the need for us to "return to basics."

He stated there were two fundamental elements of New Left wisdom that must guide us in the days ahead. (Good, I thought. We need New Left wisdom—but what could it be?) What must guide us, Oglesby explained, are these principles: "Experience teaches," and "Let the people decide."

That was it? "We're screwed!" I thought to myself.

The discussions at the convention were all over the lot. Some people were putting forward some ideas that made sense to me, but these were mixed in and on an equal par with (and therefore canceled out by) all kinds of other notions that were going in a variety of different directions. In the elections for new officers, all of the more experienced members of SDS were shunted aside. Swept into the leadership was a new and less experienced layer, one expressing "openness" and a heightened but ill-defined radicalism.

Jane Adams, whom I knew as a sincere, hardworking organizer but with no clear perspectives of which I was aware, became president (our first female national officer); elected as vice president was the tall, mustachioed Carl Davidson, who appealed to the old traditions of the Industrial Workers of the World but said that instead of workers, we should focus on students as the agent for social change—a movement philosophy he called "student syndicalism." The new national secretary was Greg Calvert, a slight, clean-shaven, curly-headed radical teacher influenced by the theories of someone named Herbert Marcuse, whose soon-to-be influential book *One-Dimensional Man* had recently appeared.

In discussions back in the national office in Chicago, I was astonished when Calvert explained (in line with Marcuse) that the working class could no longer be a revolutionary force. We New Leftists, he argued, must recognize ourselves as the primary force that must challenge the US power structure. We must move "from protest to resistance," directly and with increasing militancy challenging our death-dealing social system with our own lives and bodies—even if we were destroyed in the process.

I was beside myself with anger. All the union people with whom I had grown up in Clearfield were being dismissed. These good people had joined together to fight the good fight for a more decent life. Even though most of them weren't socialists, it seemed to me that socialism or "participatory democracy" or any worthwhile radical change could not be possible unless it made sense to such people as these and unless they became part of the struggle to bring it about.

I was further enraged by what struck me as a blasé, supposedly radical elitism in regard to a majority of the people in our country. It seemed to me, as I thought about how I saw things and how Calvert and other new SDS leaders saw things, that there were two ways of viewing radical politics. One involved a politics of communication: clearly communicating radical ideas to more and more people, and on the basis of those ideas winning them to the struggles against war, against racism, against poverty, for social justice, for "participatory democracy." That is what I identified with. It drew from the best of the radical traditions that had inspired me, and it pointed the way to the creation of a positive future.

The other way to go—and it appeared to be the trajectory into which much of SDS was now being drawn—involved a politics of self-expression. There seemed to be little respect for the struggles and radical traditions of the past, and certainly no respect for most people in the present who were seen as merely corrupted by the affluence of consumer-capitalism and going along with the present-day power structures. To me, this added up to no practical hope for the future. Instead there was the "now" of one's own radical beliefs, resulting in an activism approached simply as an expression of one's own rejection of the status quo. If what you did seemed bizarre or threatening or destructive to the working class, the majority of the people, that was not a problem. The whole point was simply to express yourself as someone who rejected the status quo—even if this was done in a manner that was suicidal.

Words, gestures, postures, and actions that struck me as dramatic stupidities, however, made good theater. They certainly attracted the entrepreneurial empires associated with the news media and popular culture, which projected such stuff throughout the nation in ways that helped to influence swelling numbers of radicalizing youth, many of whom came to identify precisely with such words, gestures, postures, and actions. For many, the styles and fashions of New Leftism became far more important than the political substance—which fatally undercut our hopes for creating a society permeated by "participatory democracy."

While Greg Calvert was absolutely sincere in his passionate call for us to escalate our actions "from protest to resistance," it would prove to be a resistance that was not able to dislodge "the system." In a sense, however, I was wrong and Calvert was right. This particular trajectory did not isolate the New Left. Instead it captured imaginations, turning an aging leftist philosopher like Marcuse, for example, into a cultural icon, and therefore into a highly valued commodity.

The *new* New Left postures and rhetoric blended far more easily with the burgeoning counterculture associated with bohemian "hippies" and the more political, if often outrageous, "Yippies" led by Jerry Rubin and Abbie Hoffman. In some ways this opened up marvelous opportunities for capitalist enterprise. Indeed, there was a lucrative proliferation of cultural commodities made available to the exploding market of radicalizing young people (even as many others—including the bulk of the working-class majority—turned away with incomprehension, disgust, or hostility). High profits and new high-powered careers were made.

On the more radical side of the ledger, there were also immense and liberatory shifts in perceptions, attitudes, values, and lifestyles that have permeated US culture, setting the stage for the later "culture wars," but also expanding a potential base on which future radicals could build. Yet "the system" has adapted and, so far, remains very much in place.

In the course of the summer of '66, "my number came up" within the Selective Service System. I was about to be drafted—but not into the military that was being thrown into the horror of Vietnam. I had earlier filed for status as a conscientious objector, which had been granted by my draft board back in Clearfield. I now arranged for my alternative service to be carried out through employment with the American Friends Service Committee, which opened up a new phase of my life and drew me out of Chicago.

Working in the SDS national office, I had been in a position to see, up close and personal, the utter inadequacy of SDS's national organizational structure—fragmented and all too amateur—and its lack of political cohesion. These two flaws, given the tidal wave of new members, would govern the transition of a small but promising organization into an utterly chaotic national disorganization incapable of doing much more than spinning out of control while being swept along by turbulent events.

SDS ballooned into perhaps one hundred thousand people claiming to be members, with a succession of national leaderships incapable of maintaining much meaningful connection with all those numbers. It finally exploded into a mess of warring factions, most of them infected by a more or less superficial Maoism, and it fell apart after a disastrous 1969 national convention. The Progressive Labor Party vainly attempted to maintain its own SDS for a short while, and most of the other fragments formed, respectively, the Weather Underground, the October League, and the Revolutionary Communist Party. Many of us didn't identify with any of them.

I continued to identify with the New Left for three years after that (ending up briefly in an entity called the New American Movement), before shifting in a decidedly Old Left direction—but all of that adds up to stories taking us beyond this one. I have never regretted these experiences or my engagement with the many people of that time whose lives impacted mine. I learned so much, and there remains much to be learned—positive lessons as well as negative—from the things that happened so many decades back.

In that wonderful study by Van Gosse, *Rethinking the New Left*, the historian correctly insists that the New Left must be seen as something more than SDS and the white student radicals, that it includes the civil rights movement of Martin Luther King and SNCC and others, the movements of other racially and nationally oppressed groups, and the antiwar struggle, the women's liberation movement, struggles for gay and lesbian rights, and so on.

"Taken together, these movements represent the essence of those years we call, somewhat inaccurately, 'the 1960s,'" Gosse comments. "And collectively, they built a new democratic order, based on the legally enforceable civil equality of all people, which has survived and extended itself since the sixties—even as the New Right born during those same years mounted its own massive 'movement of movements' that surged to power in the 1980s and 1990s."[3]

It seems to me that Gosse overstates one aspect of his argument. The "movement of movements" that was the New Left certainly helped to push the United States, in many positive ways, into being a more democratic order—but the persisting elitism, authoritarianism, and oppression inherent in corporate capitalism remain, as does the task of replacing this with a truly "new democratic order."

10

The Triumphant Arc
of US Conservatism

With her book *Invisible Hands: The Making of the Conservative Movement from the New Deal to Reagan* (W. W. Norton, 2009), Kim Phillips-Fein has provided us with a very fine account of how we got where we are—in a stranglehold of big-business conservatism that has by no means been broken by the liberal electoral victory of 2008. She has not only absorbed a considerable amount of secondary literature but has also combed through the archives, combining her impressive research and insights with a well-paced narrative populated with a variety of interesting personalities—all quite well-to-do, all white, almost all male, and yet a very diverse and interesting lot.

This is hardly the only good book on the creation and triumph of the conservative movement in the United States. George Nash's informative and utterly sympathetic *The Conservative Intellectual Movement in America since 1945*; Godfrey Hodgson's coolly analytical *The World Turned Right Side Up: A History of the Conservative Ascendancy in America*; and Alan Lichtman's bristling, massive, seemingly exhaustive *White Protestant Nation: The Rise of the American Conservative Movement* are among other valuable sources for those wanting to understand what has happened in our country since the Second World War. Each tells the story of marginalized intellectual and political elements crystallizing over a thirty-year period into a powerful political presence that shifted the nation's center of gravity far to the right, creating a massive popular base and taking control of the state, with profound impacts on our cultural and economic life.[1]

Invisible Hands does not pretend to be a comprehensive account of the intricacies of right-wing politics in the United States. Instead, it focuses sharply on the interplay of ideology, organization, and economic interest that drove the process forward to ultimate, devastating (though perhaps temporary) triumph. In a sense, the author is guided by the adage "Follow the money." An essential aspect of the story involves the intellectual and political mobilization of the business community, particularly such huge corporations as AT&T, Chrysler, Coca-Cola, DuPont, Exxon, Ford, General Electric, General Motors, B. F. Goodrich, Greyhound, Gulf, IBM, Lockheed Martin, Mobil, Pepsi, Sears, Roebuck, Sun Oil, and U.S. Steel. As the author shows us, they bankrolled small conservative publications, right-wing institutes, foundations, think tanks, educational campaigns, cultural offensives, political mobilizations, and massive electoral efforts. But, in addition to what must ultimately add up to billions of dollars in contributions from 1935 to 2000, these scions, executives, and well-paid representatives of big business intervened in increasing numbers with hearts and minds and hands in the struggle to win their power back, with a vengeance.

Not that big capital had ever completely lost its power in the United States. But as Phillips-Fein shows, the mass mobilizations from the left end of the political spectrum during the Great Depression and again in the wake of the Second World War resulted in a momentous power shift—with radical implications for the working class and other oppressed layers in our society. The militant insurgencies encompassed by, but sometimes bursting beyond, an organized labor movement, which ultimately represented more than a third of the labor force, found reflection in the political arena, particularly in the far-reaching social programs, economic regulations, and Keynesian perspectives represented by Franklin D. Roosevelt's New Deal. All of this horrified and enraged a class whose immense wealth and power, while hardly destroyed, were curtailed and "trespassed" upon by what they saw as unruly and insolent employees, union bosses, red- and pink-hued "do-gooders," and a swelling legion of government bureaucrats. They denounced these government reforms and regulations, over and over and over again, as "socialistic."

Of course, while a militant minority among the insurgencies of the 1930s and mid-1940s had set its sights on replacing capitalism with some variety of cooperative commonwealth, the intention of the Roosevelt administration and its successors—whether Democratic or Republican—up to 1980 was to mitigate mass discontent for the very purpose of preserving the capitalist system. After 1946 this was done within a Cold War context in which anti-Communism served to clip the wings of those with radical aspirations.[2]

But the new orthodoxy predominating in both the Republican and Democratic parties, among mainstream social scientists, and within the population at large, was that government, in the words of pro-business Republican president Dwight D. Eisenhower, should "prevent or correct abuses springing from the unregulated practice of the private economy." Eisenhower articulated that common, "middle of the road" wisdom when he proclaimed: "Should any political party attempt to abolish social security, unemployment insurance, and eliminate labor laws and farm programs, you would not hear from that party again in our political history."

Going against this dominant outlook, the goal of business conservatives was to uproot all manifestations of "collectivism," no matter how mild. As economist Ludwig von Mises, advocate of unrestrained free market forces, emphasized to Leonard Read (chamber of commerce executive and founder of the Foundation for Economic Education), "The only thing that really matters is the outcome of the intellectual combat between the supporters of socialism and those of capitalism." For Mises and his followers, there was no middle way.

Phillips-Fein introduces us to a small, initially beleaguered corps of "free market conservatives" (those who want to conserve traditional power relations benefiting big business) who organized the utterly unsuccessful Liberty League, the more durable but often thwarted National Association of Manufacturers, and the marginal Foundation for Economic Education, which published the small, *Monthly Review*–type journal (with quite different politics, to be sure) called *The Freeman*. Throughout this study, we see that even modest efforts at cultivating right-wing publications and public forums—while sometimes demoralizing—had the effect of building up networks and providing experience that would come into play in later efforts, ultimately contributing to victories in the future. And, as Phillips-Fein points out, "at a time when leading liberal intellectuals like Daniel Bell and Arthur M. Schlesinger, Jr. argued that the rise of fascism and Soviet communism had shattered the capacity for faith in ideology in the West, insisting that most conservatives and liberals alike agreed on the welfare state and the limits of government power, these free market activists understood, in a way that the liberal thinkers did not, the importance of ideas and the need to shape the terms of debate."

By 1955 *National Review* appeared on the right as an increasingly influential rival to the mainstream liberal *New Republic* and the left-liberal *Nation*. Edited by brash, aristocratic William F. Buckley (whose widely read books accused his alma mater, Yale University, of being too liberal and secular, and defended Senator Joseph McCarthy as an anti-Communist hero), this weekly journal fused the conservative traditionalism of academics such as Russell Kirk, who glorified the likes of Edmund Burke and John C. Calhoun, with the acid anti-Communism of such ex-leftist Cold Warriors as James Burnham, and with the free market libertarianism of such economists as Mises. Buckley's magazine held immense appeal, Phillips-Fein notes, for the rising business conservatives, denouncing "labor union monopolies" and "the Big Brother state." She adds: "In addition to articles on the 'atomic disarmament trap,' essays on the South that extolled white southerners as the 'advanced race,' and cultural critiques of such institutions as *The New Yorker*, the magazine in its early years published articles on the labor movement, detailing scandals and malfeasance in the worlds of organized labor as well as the politically dangerous plans of the unions."

DuPont executive Jasper Crane, in the forefront of pioneering business conservatives, emphasized the necessity of the "intellectual foundation" that would guide the "leadership of perhaps the relatively few men who know the truth and won't compromise with evil," to "follow that up with an emotional presentation of the blessings and advantages of our system." A 1944 polemic in defense of "free market" capitalism, *The Road to Serfdom* by Friedrich von Hayek, a disciple of Mises, saw Nazism, communism, socialism, and welfare-state liberalism all as part of an anticapitalist continuum that would destroy freedom. (Hayek regarded freedom as distinct from the notion of *rule by the people*—he and Mises fretted over "the fashionable concentration on democracy.") Hayek's book was embraced as a holy text by people such as Crane, who helped to make it a best seller, with an abridged version in *Reader's Digest* attracting a million readers. They also bankrolled Hayek's Mont Pelerin Society, an international gathering of pro-capitalist academics and intellectuals, who met in secret beginning in 1947, to forge a global cadre and pool of ideas whose influence would gradually permeate the larger culture.

As *Invisible Hands* documents, the array of business corporations cited above made it their business to educate their managerial staffs, their employees, and the larger public (including politicians) in the free market gospel. Not all efforts were successful—some were clumsy and crude—but neither were they wasted and without impact. In addition to the tried and true Foundation for Economic Education, the American Enterprise Association (which later morphed into the influential American Enterprise Institute, soon followed by other conservative think tanks, such as the even more right-wing Heritage Foundation) helped provide increasingly sophisticated materials and perspectives.

But developing theory and disseminating ideological perspectives were, by themselves, not enough. It was essential to engage in the class struggle. Leading the way in smashing strikes, undermining, and, where possible, destroying or preventing the establishment of unions, were such people as Lemuel Boulware of General Electric, who conducted a victorious struggle against the International Union of Electrical Workers; Herbert Kohler, who carried out a protracted war against the United Auto Workers; and Roger Milliken, who closed down his textile mills in South Carolina to prevent them from being unionized. Such men have become icons of the business conservatives as well as active and generous supporters of right-wing causes.

Phillips-Fein also addresses the crucial right-wing effort to build up broad membership organizations. The John Birch Society (named after a US missionary killed by Communists during the Chinese civil war) was formed by candy manufacturer Robert Welch and eleven like-minded industrialists "to start a disciplined, secretive organization committed to protecting American institutions against the Communist threat," with "Communist" defined to include even the "collectivist" impulses of Republican moderates such as Eisenhower. The Birch Society published much material, sent twenty full-time staffers door to door in a successful effort to recruit tens of thousands of members, and focused on working outside the arena of electoral politics—urging its members instead to "join your local PTA [Parent Teacher Association] at the beginning of the school year, and go to work and take it over!" Despite some successes, its extreme positions ("It is realistic to be fantastic," Welch explained) caused some business conservatives to give it wide berth and more "respectable" elements such as *National Review* to criticize it publicly.

Phillips-Fein generally does not give more than fleeting mention to such groups as the college-based conservative outfit Young Americans for Freedom.[3] During the tumultuous 1960s, when the civil rights, antiwar, student, feminist, and other upsurges swept the nation, the Young Americans for Freedom sought, rather ineffectually, to pose a right-wing alternative to the more vibrant New Left, which at that time was swamping the hopes of the "new right." The radicalization of the 1960s and early 1970s, with its anticapitalist orientation, shocked the business conservatives and generated a well-orchestrated backlash. In this tumultuous context, Phillips-Fein zeroes in on Richard Viguerie, the one-time executive secretary of Young Americans for Freedom, whose fund-raising efforts for the rightist youth organization led to his becoming "the self-made man of conservatism. Viguerie was a direct-mail innovator who made a fortune selling his famous list of names of conservative donors to activists eager to dip into the money well." Phillips-Fein continues: "He exercised so much control over the funding base that some critics dubbed him the 'godfather of the right.'"

No less important was the movement-building vision that he helped to propagate in the early 1970s, which she summarizes in this way:

> Viguerie believed that the real base for the conservative movement needed to be blue-collar white people, the descendants of Irish or Italian or Eastern European immigrants, with "traditional" social values. Such voters could, he thought, be wooed away from their support for social and economic programs and labor unions through an appeal to them as individuals concerned about protecting their families, their neighborhoods, and their homes from the dangers posed by radicals.

A popular (if simplistic) notion from the 1930s to the 1970s was that the Democratic Party was the party of labor, while the Republican Party was the party of business. Both have always been, in fact, pro-capitalist organizations with shifting differences regarding the appropriate directions for, and policies of, our capitalist society. In the late nineteenth century both had presented themselves as the party for working people—but Roosevelt's New Deal had forged a more durable working-class base. Right-wing strategists of the 1960s such as Pat Buchanan proposed a future that would make the Republican Party "the party of the working class, not the party of the welfare class." The playing of the race card, often making the necessary points with code words (such as with the party's opposition to "forced busing" designed to create racially integrated schools), was interlarded with tough and angry rhetoric against "tax-and-spend liberals," whom the business conservatives had been fighting since the 1930s. M. Stanton Evans of the American Conservative Union explained: "The important thing . . . is not that some . . . reach their political positions by reading Adam Smith while others do so by attending an anti-busing rally, but that all of them belong to a large and growing class of American citizens: those who perceive themselves as victims of the federal welfare state and its attendant costs."

As *Invisible Hands* demonstrates, business conservatives of the 1970s "sought to create a movement that would be capable of bringing together employees and executives, blue-collar workers and the men who employed them." And "abortion, busing, pornography, gun rights, and crime were exactly the kinds of morally charged and dramatic issues that were capable of galvanizing public support." In the words of Richard Viguerie, "The New Right is looking for issues that people care about, and social issues, at least for the present, fit the bill." This led inexorably to an alliance with the rising current of evangelical Protestant fundamentalism.

Broadening the conservative base by reaching out to Christians had, Phillips-Fein notes, been a goal of business conservatives for many years. In the 1950s the head of the National Association of Manufacturers stressed that "the Christian faith itself offers a tremendous incentive to its followers—the profit which they can hope to attain—the eternal salvation in the world to come." One pro-capitalist minister in the same period undoubtedly spoke for others in concurring, "The blessings of capitalism come from God."[4]

Yet, as one of the key organizers in this effort to wed free enterprise with Jesus later confessed, "Fighting the forces that wanted to abolish the free enterprise system was my mission, not promoting Christ." The influence of the Social Gospel (and, some might argue, of the Jesus who preached the Sermon on the Mount)—eloquently articulated by Walter Rauschenbusch in the early 1900s and by Martin Luther King Jr. in the 1950s and 1960s—was an obstacle partially worn away by the 1970s, through the hard work of well-financed right-wing pastors such as Pat Robertson and Jerry Falwell, who played on a religious revival sweeping through much of the United States. "The evangelical leaders of the 1970s," Phillips-Fein notes, "sought to connect the idea of the market and opposition to the power of government to the war over American culture." Richard Viguerie—who helped to facilitate the connections and finances to make this happen (even though he was not even a Protestant)—exulted: "The next real major area of growth for the conservative ideology and philosophy is among evangelical people."

Another important dimension in the political transformation involved the "whites only" Democrats who had dominated the South since the late 1870s, but who, under the impact of the civil rights legislation passed by the modern-day Democratic Party, had migrated to the Republican Party. Phillips-Fein focuses on North Carolina senator Jesse Helms, "who became known as a strident political leader for the cultural right," but whose political career "had really begun in the world of business conservatism." Helms showed "how the language of the free market could be used in the fight against racial integration." Enormous quantities of money poured into Helms's campaign coffers—not only from Southern textile magnate Roger Milliken, but also from Los Angeles businessman Henry Salvatori, Colorado's Joseph Coors, Pittsburgh's Richard Mellon Scaife, and others. "With the support of such businessmen, Helms used the ideas of individualism, free choice, and property rights to attack any policies that promised greater racial equality and integration." The result was to "create a new kind of southern conservatism—one that could speak to conservatives not only in the South but across the country."

When the political right captured the 1964 Republican Party convention and nominated business conservative Arizona senator Barry Goldwater for president, all of these pieces were far from being securely in place, and Goldwater went down in a devastating defeat. The mainstream media, liberal Democrats, and moderate Republicans all agreed: Goldwater was a nut, the conservative movement had ruined itself, and the far right was forever discredited. Yet the forces drawn together by the business conservatives continued to organize. And by the presidential election of 1980, a right-wing "perfect storm" swept Ronald Reagan into the presidency. As Reagan wrote to Lemuel Boulware, his mentor and General Electric's most prominent class warrior early in his long march to the Oval Office, "I promise you I'll be trying to stir up the business world, including the exhortation to fight back against government's increasing lust for power over free enterprise."[5]

The so-called Reagan Revolution was continued not only by George H. W. Bush, but also—as Phillips-Fein observes—by Democratic president Bill Clinton, who "accomplished much of what Reagan could not: the dismantling of welfare, the deregulation of Wall Street, the expansion of free trade." Organized labor, ravaged during the Reagan years, continued to decline, and economic inequality continued to grow. "He's a Democrat, but I do admire him," Barry Goldwater wrote of Clinton. "I think he's doing a good job."

The once-marginal perspectives of the late 1940s and 1950s belonging to business conservatives had, by the final decades of the twentieth century, become the new political and economic orthodoxy of the United States. The demolition of the assumptions and programmatic vestiges of the New Deal, and of the once-powerful labor movement, seemed to have been largely a "mission accomplished," even before George W. Bush took office. The extent to which President Barack Obama will end up doing the same kind of "good job" as the previous Democratic president remains to be seen. But the story told in *Invisible Hands* suggests that the electoral arena is not, in and of itself, the place to look for major political changes.

If the Phillips-Fein account is accurate, genuine socialists need to avoid pragmatic adaptations to the status quo. Instead, a strong intellectual foundation must be developed, and there must be persistent education, agitation, and organizing. Over a period of decades it is possible for marginalized intellectual and political elements, if they do their job right, to crystallize into a powerful political presence that shifts the nation's center of gravity far to the left, creating a massive popular base and taking control of the state, with profound impact on our cultural and economic life.

11

The New Left and Beyond

This was initially a review of three books, including the first volume of Barry Shep-pard's memoir of his life in the US Trotskyist movement, The Party. *Since I later wrote a substantial review of the two volumes of his memoir—included in this vol-ume—I have removed my comments on what he provides in that book, along with making a few other minor changes.*—P.L.

I remember keenly the mixed feelings that many of my comrades and I had—when we were young radical activists of the New Left in the 1960s—toward the left-wing activists who had gone before.

The Old Left had lost—spectacularly, it appeared—since their organi-zations and influence seemed to have faded away into almost nothing. There were some fine old traditions, perhaps, but these were tainted by defeat and seemed ill-suited to attract the new wave of activists. Many of our generation were prepared to "put our bodies on the line" to advance the civil rights strug-gle against racial segregation, with little patience for what sounded to us like abstract theorizing. In reaction to the horrors of Vietnam, many of us were inclined to say "Make love, not war"—which was hardly consistent with the left-wing rhetoric of the 1930s. While some of the old-timers were delighted that we younger ones were in motion in large numbers, some were also impa-tient with our lack of experience and were inclined to lecture us about the need to accept the wisdom they wished to impart. And we were not always inclined to listen to such stuff.

Our youthful activism proved capable of cracking the stultifying cultural conformism of the 1950s and of tilting politics leftward, but more and more of us concluded that what we were doing was not adequate. We discovered limits to what we could accomplish as racism persisted in multiple domains, as the war in Vietnam continued and appeared to be rooted in much larger patterns of foreign policy and global power struggles, and as we became increasingly aware of other injustices and of interconnections between the various wrongs that we were seeking to set aright.

Some of us turned hungrily, then, to the experience of the Old Left—the amazing triumphs of Eugene V. Debs and the Socialist Party, coupled with the Industrial Workers of the World, during the first two decades of the twentieth century; the mighty upsurge of the 1930s that was apparently spearheaded by the Communist Party, led by the likes of Earl Browder and William Z. Foster, but during which others on the left (various kinds of socialists—some followers of Norman Thomas, some followers of Leon Trotsky, but many others as well) also helped to change the course of history, at least for a while, until the mighty red tide was pushed back by an even mightier combination of post–World War II prosperity and Cold War anti-Communism. It was in this 1950s reality of quiescence, conservatism, and conformity that we had grown up—and it was this reality that we had successfully disrupted. But we now wanted to learn from those who had gone before, in order to absorb insights from their successes and from their mistakes, in the hope that we might ultimately do better than they had.

We accomplished much from the 1960s into the 1980s. Despite conservative backlash and neo-conservative onslaught, the culture and consciousness of masses of people in our society have never flowed back to where they were in the 1950s. Yet, it could be argued, we, too, lost spectacularly—certainly when our accomplishments are measured by our aspirations. And certainly this seems the case when we survey the innumerable injustices, dangers, and atrocities that are so much a part of the twenty-first century. But thanks to relentless capitalist realities, new waves of discontent, protest, and radicalism have been generated and will be generated. And as young activists born in the aftermath of the Vietnam era accumulate experiences of their own and become more serious about their politics, some of them will want to know what happened in the earlier decades that were so central to the lives of those born in the aftermath of World War II. My own experience eventually drew me into the Trotskyist movement—a vitally important part of the scene examined here, but one to be discussed in the next two essays. Many larger numbers were drawn (as I was, initially) to the New Left, and some then moved on to the Maoist movement, and both of these entities will be the focus of this essay.

The volumes examined here—*"Takin' It to the Streets": A Sixties Reader*, second edition, edited by Alexander Blooms and Wini Breines (Oxford University Press, 2003); and Max Elbaum's *Revolution in the Air: Sixties Radicals Turn to Lenin, Mao and Che* (Verso, 2002)—are useful sources on the radicalism of the 1960s and 1970s for thoughtful young activists of today and tomorrow. At the same time, they are quite different from each other. The volume by Bloom and Breines is a massive compilation of documents (designed for college courses) seeking to embrace a multifaceted reality. In some ways, the more analytically satisfying volume is the historical account offered by Elbaum, a thoughtful participant in the developments he describes.

The New Left and Beyond

"Images of the 1950s are distinct: white middle-class families, suburban homes, backyard barbecues, big American cars with tail fins, Little League and Girl Scouts, peace, prosperity, and harmony," write Bloom and Breines at the beginning of their anthology. "So, too, the images of the 1960s: civil rights sit-ins, urban violence, antiwar demonstrations, Black Power salutes, hippie love-ins, draft card burnings, death and destruction in Vietnam, police riots in Chicago, obscenities, killings at Kent State and Jackson State universities."

Describing a social reality in the United States largely characterized, in the decade following World War II, by a stifling cultural and political conformism—rooted in Cold War anti-Communism, an increasingly out-of-control consumerism, and a variety of racial and sexual taboos—Bloom and Breines explain:

> By the early 1960s the postwar consensus had run its course. National and world events, from college campuses to Vietnam, brought many of the basic tenets of American life into sharp consideration. "We are people of this generation," began the Port Huron Statement, the 1962 founding statement of the New Left Students for a Democratic Society [SDS], "bred in at least modest comfort, housed now in universities, looking uncomfortably to the world we inherit."
>
> This handful of students and countless others—women, blacks, Latinos, Native Americans, gays—found little in 1950s mainstream culture and politics to explain the inequalities, restrictions, and discontent, or to enable them to analyze the new world. The underground critiques of the 1950s [provided by the so-called "beatniks" as well as other maverick cultural figures and social critics], as well as movements such as civil rights, offered the first hints of new perspectives and new possibilities. The young and some of the old—critics of the 1950s consensus or apostates from it—would join to confront the new realities of the era. And "the sixties" began.

What follows the editors' thoughtful introduction is an incredibly rich collection of materials. The first section, quite appropriately, focuses on the civil rights movement: Martin Luther King Jr. explaining the power of nonviolent protest, James Farmer of the Congress of Racial Equality describing the Freedom Rides, various young activists of the Student Nonviolent Coordinating Committee (SNCC) giving voice to their experience in struggle. The next section on the student movement includes excerpts from the SDS's Port Huron Statement, radical sociologist C. Wright Mills's "Letter to the New Left," materials on early community organizing efforts and the 1964 Berkeley Free Speech Movement, and more. The next section on Black nationalism and ethnic consciousness explores the trajectory from Malcolm X to proliferating ghetto uprisings to the Black Panther Party, also indicating the rise of liberation struggles among Latinos, Asian Americans, and Native American "Indians." This is followed by a section on the Vietnam War and the antiwar movement.

The next two sections broaden the anthology in two very different directions. On the one hand, we see manifestations of a very diverse, complex "counterculture"—involving not only "sex, drugs, rock and roll," but also new paths in religion and experimental communes, not to mention the emergence of hippies and the more political Yippies. On the other hand, we see various manifestations of the conservative backlash—the Young Americans for Freedom, the John Birch Society, the Christian Crusade, and such political figures as Barry Goldwater, Richard Nixon and Spiro Agnew, George Wallace, Ronald Reagan, and the ominous COINTELPRO—a secret, coordinated government program to spy on and disrupt a variety of organizations associated with dissent, protest, and radical activity.

An entire section is devoted to the amazing and explosive year 1968, and another to the emergence of the multifaceted women's liberation movement. A final section looks at various aspects of the end of the decade—the People's Park struggle, the 1970 protests and killings at Kent State and Jackson State, the rise of the gay liberation movement, the very different countercultural events at Woodstock and Altamont, and the beginnings of the environmental movement. The volume ends with the open-ended retrospective by Julius Lester, in which he writes: "Things happened in the Sixties. We didn't make them happen as much as one action produced ten other actions (but the progression was geometric) and we were swept along by it."

This indicates, on the one hand, the tremendous vitality and the phenomenal shifts in the cultural and political climate represented by the 1960s radicalization. But it also suggests political chaos, a complete inability to develop any effective programmatic and strategic orientation capable of replacing the existing power structure with structures that would truly give "power to the people," the stated goal of the radical activists.

As Elbaum notes in his invaluable study, "By the fall of 1968, public opinion polls indicated that one million students saw themselves as part of the left, and 368,000 'strongly agreed' on the need for a 'mass revolutionary party.'" He also notes that in the same period a growing number of radical activists with several years of experience, recognizing the inadequacy of the New Left, as demonstrated by its organizational amorphousness and programmatic confusion (which caused the virtual collapse of SDS and SNCC), faced "that classic question: 'What is to be done?' In grappling with this problem the young revolutionaries of the late 1960s displayed confusion, naiveté, and sometimes downright foolishness. But the more remarkable thing is how doggedly they worked to overcome their own prejudices and limitations; and how many of the issues they identified remain at the top of the progressive agenda today."

One possibility for the young activists seeking greater political and organizational seriousness was to take a closer look at the so-called Old Left. But its most prevalent currents, the Socialist Party and the Communist Party, while seeming to have much greater political savvy and organizational ability than much of the New Left, nonetheless repelled many of the young activists for more than one reason.

The Communist Party suffered from the Stalinist legacy, with a tainted reputation compounded by a tendency to be uncritical of the USSR as well as sectarian and dismissive toward New Left activists. Many of the Socialists, on the other hand, were so committed to the fight against "Communist totalitarianism" that it seemed difficult to distinguish between them and employees of the US State Department (particularly since some of them actually were), nor were they above red-baiting those to their left. And both Socialists and Communists of the 1960s were supportive, to a large degree, of the Democratic Party—which many of the young activists saw as not being qualitatively different from the Republican Party.

There was another Old Left current that—for a small but significant number of New Left activists—seemed better than the Communist and Socialist parties: the dissident Communists associated with the revolutionary perspectives of Leon Trotsky. These perspectives included Trotsky's theory of permanent revolution, which saw worker-led democratic revolution spilling over into socialist revolution; an unyielding revolutionary internationalism; and a rejection of the bureaucratic dictatorship represented by the Stalin regime in the USSR. The largest grouping of Trotskyists had gathered in the Socialist Workers Party. (As already indicated, I will discuss this elsewhere in this volume.)

Many more New Left activists, searching for greater coherence and effectiveness than could be provided by a group like SDS, were drawn to the example of the Chinese Revolution. Internationally, the Chinese Communist Party under Mao Zedong seemed to represent a more revolutionary element in struggles against imperialism in the 1960s, and throughout the world idealistic militants were drawn to its ideas and example. Mao also initiated the

Great Proletarian Cultural Revolution within his own country, mobilizing young activists in a struggle against bureaucratic elements in his own party and government—and young activists in other countries interpreted this in a very positive manner (which, it later turned out, did not correspond to the destructive and grim realities of that "revolution"). In the United States, Maoism attracted major sections of the New Left.

Elbaum tells us the story of the rise and fall of the "New Communist Movement," associated with the widespread commitment of a very large layer of New Left veterans to "Marxism-Leninism–Mao Tse-tung Thought" and a popular (but divergently interpreted) conception of "party-building."

"Party-Building"

Elbaum identifies certain elements in Leninism that attracted a growing number of activists to either its Trotskyist or Maoist variant—"a worldview unmatched in scope, depth and revolutionary lineage" that "revealed the structural roots of (and connections between) war, discrimination, violence and the blocked channels of the country's formally democratic political system. It foregrounded precisely the issues—imperialist war and domestic racism— which topped the 1960s protest agenda." Elbaum believes this worldview is still relevant. In his view, there are "three crucial issues that . . . remain pivotal to any future attempt at left renewal: commitment to internationalism and anti-imperialism; the centrality of the fight against racism; and the urgency of developing cadre and creating organizations capable of mobilizing working people and the oppressed."

It may be worth taking a moment to define this key word—"cadre"— since it is essential to Elbaum's account. A term often associated with Leninist politics, it refers to *experienced activists, educated in political theory, analytically oriented, with practical organizational skills, who are able attract, motivate, and train new recruits and contribute to expanding efforts in broader movements and larger struggles.* Activists such as Elbaum had concluded that it is impossible to build and sustain a durable organization, movement, or struggle without those who have had the training and experience to function in such a manner, as cadres making use of Marxist perspectives.

To connect with the actual ideas of Marx and Lenin is not to connect with abstract dogmas developed by divine philosophers—their perspectives are grounded in the experience, the insights, the lessons learned by generations of revolutionary and working-class activists, brave and visionary men and women of the nineteenth and early twentieth centuries, from Germany, France, Britain, Russia, and beyond. Committing themselves to these perspectives in the 1960s and '70s, many activists sought to become part of a rich tradition that would draw on past wisdom that could help shape a better future. Those who reached out to the "Third World Marxism" that Elbaum stresses so heavily sought to draw into their thinking and actions the experience of freedom fighters in Asia, Africa, and Latin America.

The Leninist perspective "spoke to the widespread feeling that broad mass movements could only consolidate their gains if they were reinforced by a body of cadre who had the theoretical understanding, political commitment and practical skills to navigate the twists and turns of complex political battles." The New Left activists drawn to the New Communist Movement viewed this as constituting a tremendous advance:

> In melding cadre together into a unified organization, Lenin's requirement that every member participate in advancing an agreed-upon program allowed groups to coordinate multisector, nationwide campaigns and fostered genuine camaraderie. The Leninist stricture that every revolutionary must be responsible to a party unit initially served as a positive corrective to the problems many had experienced in looser New Left groups, whose work was badly hurt by the unaccountable actions of media-created leaders or by the refusal of a numerical minority to abide by the will of the majority.

Yet there was "a dark side" to such an approach. Elbaum notes that the groups in the New Communist Movement succumbed to "a miniaturized Leninism" in which "sixty-year-old polemics written as guidelines for a party of thousands to interact with a movement of millions were interpreted through the prism of how organizations of hundreds (or even dozens) should interact with movements of thousands (or less)." The result—"mechanical formulas and organizational narrow-mindedness," and the New Communist Movement's "vision of a vanguard party was reduced to the model of a sect."

He concludes that "the most damage was done by Maoism," and he cites three particular problems that he associates with distinctive aspects of "Mao Tse-tung Thought": 1) an "underestimation of the importance of democracy, both within the revolutionary movement and—if and when a revolution succeeds—within the new society"; 2) belief in "a single and true Marxist-Leninist doctrine with an unbroken revolutionary pedigree from 1848 to the present," adding up to "one pure tradition that has defeated a series of deviations since Lenin's time"; and 3) a "disastrous . . . tendency to confer vanguard status on a party because it espoused a sanctioned version of Marxism-Leninism rather than because it actually has won the allegiance of workers and the oppressed."

Time and again, the flawed methodology helped to cut across what the activists sought to achieve. "Just when a dose of fresh thinking was needed to transcend the limits of the Stalin-Mao model and expand on the invaluable insights in Lenin's thought, the movement's strongest groups headed in the exact opposite direction." Elbaum walks us through the consequent developments, mergers, splits, fusions, and confusions of a maddening variety of currents and counter-currents: the Revolutionary Union becoming the Revolutionary Communist Party, with a split-off called the Revolutionary Workers Headquarters evolving into the more reasonable-sounding Freedom Road Socialist Organization; the October League becoming the Communist Party (Marxist-Leninist); the League of Revolutionary Black Workers coalescing with others into the short-lived Black Workers Congress; the League of Revolutionary Struggle; the Revolutionary Workers League; the Communist Labor Party; the Communist Workers Party; the Democratic Workers Party; Line of March—all this and much, much more.

Yet it is a worthwhile journey that he takes us on. Elbaum helps us see what some of these activists did right. There were some serious union organizing and community organizing efforts, crucially important antiracist work (peppered with some big mistakes), a serious fumbling on the question of women's liberation in some cases admirably corrected (although—for the most part—the same cannot be said regarding gay liberation). One of the most impressive accomplishments of the New Communist Movement was that it "pointed a way toward building a multiracial movement out of a badly segregated U.S. left." What Elbaum calls "Third World Marxism" enhanced the movement's ability to draw in and empower people of color—some of the groups were predominantly nonwhite, and others were able to break down racial barriers at all organizational levels.

It was by no means the case that its accomplishments and activists simply evaporated with the collapse of the movement. Veterans of this movement—and the ideas, the training, and the lessons they absorbed—have found their way into a number of trade unions, social movements, and progressive organizations that have an impact within the political and cultural life of the United States.

The Future

Elbaum projects a positive vision of what the future movement should look like (based on a brief, almost inadvertent, *pluralist* accomplishment of the New Communist Movement). This involves an openness to and interaction with diverse forces among an evolving array of left-wing forces. The way he puts it is sufficiently striking to justify substantial quotation:

By and large, in the movement's healthiest periods several organizations—both tight-knit cadre groups and other forms—coexisted and interacted while considering themselves part of a common political trend. In such periods the movement was able to field (and train) disciplined bodies of cadre in coordinated campaigns but also to retain flexibility; it also had constant incentive for lively internal debate. Diversity of organizational forms (publishing collectives, research centers, cultural collectives, and broad organizing networks, in addition to local and national cadre formations) along with a dynamic interaction between them supplied (at least to a degree) some of the pressures for democracy and realism that in other situations flowed from a socialist-oriented working class. It freed the movement from pressures to adopt a uniform approach in all sectors during a period where tremendous disparities in consciousness and activity meant that uniformity would be inherently self-defeating.

Elbaum is sufficiently optimistic to add that "for a left confronted by new realities (and willing to face up to the decidedly mixed balance sheet of its own past), fresh analyses, new strategies and new models are required. Developing effective ones will involve drawing on the best of many Marxist and non-Marxist radical traditions, but above all will require a hard-headed look at today's realities, willingness to explore new theoretical terrain, and a good deal of flexibility and experimentation in practical campaigns." It may be that a certain political pluralism—and with it the interplay of ideas and diverse perspectives that such pluralism makes possible—will be a vital element in all of this.

Serious activists seeking to move in such directions in order to change would do well to spend some time absorbing what Bloom/Breines and Elbaum have to offer. Hopefully, the young and maturing comrades of today and tomorrow will absorb the best of what we were, will learn from our sad mistakes, and will draw as well from those who came before us—and this can help them to be better than we were: better in building durable and successful organizations, movements, and struggles; better in interweaving theory and practice in a manner that is creative, open, and principled; better in advancing us to a society of the free and the equal, which has been the goal of so many generations of activists.

12

Making Sense of Trotskyism in the United States

The Socialist Workers Party (SWP) of the United States was for a number of years the largest and strongest section of the Fourth International—both of which were formally established in 1938, both representing the revolutionary socialist perspectives associated with Leon Trotsky. Rooted in opposition to Stalinism in the early Communist movement, the US Trotskyists worked closely with Trotsky in building the Fourth International, the global network of small revolutionary groups adhering to the original "Bolshevik-Leninist" perspectives. They also played a heroic role in US class struggles of the 1930s, and their reputation among many was as unyielding partisans of workers' democracy and Trotsky's revolutionary Marxist orientation. Yet in the nonrevolutionary aridity of 1950s America, their ranks dwindled down to handfuls of stalwarts, perhaps four hundred aging members, in a handful of cities.

The memoirs of Peter Camejo (*North Star: A Memoir*) and Leslie Evans (*Outsider's Reverie: A Memoir*) were produced by two of the most talented of the "1960s generation" rebels who flowed into and revitalized the SWP.[1] Camejo (joining in 1959) was perhaps the best-known activist leader of the party in the 1960s and 1970s, and Evans (who joined in 1961) was perhaps its most capable writer, editor, and educator of that same "youth" layer. Both basically turned away from Trotskyism, quite consciously, during the 1980s. What is strange is that the SWP as a whole absolutely did the same thing—expelling or driving out all those not inclined to go along with the transition to its own esoteric variety of Castroism. Yet to their credit, neither Camejo nor Evans was able to remain inside the newly revised version of the SWP, and their stories each in its own way reveals much about the "how" and the "why" of this development. What each has to say, however, goes beyond the specifics of that experience. Larger questions emerge regarding the nature of activism and social change, the validity of Marxism, and the possibility and/or need of socialism.

Camejo was writing his autobiography in a race with terminal cancer—which he almost won. Evans helped edit Camejo's book and prepare it for publication, and he was consequently inspired to write his own autobiography. But the two books are dramatically different in more than one way. Camejo focuses much more on social movements and struggles, all motivated by a never-ending opposition to the injustices of capitalism. Evans focuses much, much more on political ideas as well as internal life and conflicts within the SWP—and far more than Camejo he has made his peace with the status quo, settling into a niche very much to the right of his fellow memoirist. Camejo rejects the old Trotskyism because he sees it as an obstacle to revolution—Evans rejects it in large measure because he has decided that revolution itself is a bad thing, although this break was neither simple nor easy for him:

> In 1983 I may have begun to have doubts about Lenin and Marxism, but a lifetime of personal and political loyalties didn't die easily or quickly. Part of it was habit, part loyalty to my fellow expellees. Then there were the dead to whom you had to answer. Trotskyism, like most religions, had its many martyrs, who inspired belief and dedication by their example. There was Trotsky himself, assassinated by Stalin's agent in Mexico in 1940. His son, Leon Sedov, was murdered in a . . . hospital in 1938 by Russian doctors secretly working for the KGB. There were the Old Bolsheviks, most of Lenin's Central Committee, shot in the back of the head in the basements of Moscow's Lubyanka Prison, where the cells were conveniently supplied with floor drains. And the countless anonymous victims I had become familiar with from the movement's literature: The Trotskyist prisoners in the Vorkuta labor camp in Siberia, marched in groups to the firing squads in 1937 singing the *Internationale*, and the hundreds of Chinese Trotskyists shot by the Maoists in 1952, it was said after having their tongues cut out so they couldn't shout any last protests. A few of them were jailed instead and remained there until after Mao's death.[2]

In his own fashion, Evans seeks to remain true to this tradition—by writing as honest an account as he can, and certainly respectful of the finest in the old traditions that he has turned away from. As such, his memoir is a treasure trove for those seeking to understand at least some of the dynamics of the SWP in its years of growth and decline while Evans was a member. Yet it is hardly the kind of book one would hand to a young activist to help her or him carry on the revolutionary struggle for a better world, a struggle Evans now rejects.

Camejo also seeks to remain true to his earlier commitments—in his own fashion. But the book's thrust and spirit make it an ideal volume for young activists. He tells us:

The battles in which small groups of Trotskyists fought against Stalinism will go down in history as heroic. Trotskyists were murdered in tremendous numbers in Russia and were persecuted in other countries as well. They faced enormous hostility from the huge mass base of the Communist parties, but also endured attacks from pro-capitalist forces.

As an instrument to revive the mass world movement for social justice, however, I think that Trotskyism had historical, internal, sectarian limits that blocked it from being able to become a critical force for social change. But during the early 1970s I can see in my diary that I still thought it was possible that the Trotskyist movement would gradually, and with occasional opportunities for explosive growth, come to replace the influence of the Stalinists and social democrats.[3]

Both books give a vibrant sense of the perceptions and realities that made believers of Evans, Camejo, and many other activists of that time.

The Good Old Days

An almost glowing chapter in Evans's memoir deals with the amazing year that was 1968. His focus is global, involving a blend of triumph and tragedy: the dramatic surge in the Vietnamese liberation struggle; the decision of President Johnson not to seek reelection due to antiwar pressure; the quest for "socialism with a human face" in Czechoslovakia associated with the "Prague Spring," and the repressive Soviet invasion a few months later; the assassination of Martin Luther King Jr. as he was coming to the aid of striking sanitation workers, followed by enraged urban uprisings in Black communities throughout the nation; militant student strikes throughout the United States; the May–June student and workers' upsurge in France that almost toppled the de Gaulle regime; the mass student struggles in Mexico, violently repressed by the regime; and the militant protests in Chicago during the Democratic Party convention. All of this gave life to what had often been abstract assertions of revolutionary internationalism. "The afterglow of 1968," he writes, "radiated for several years, raising spirits and hopes."[4]

Camejo's account puts us in the thick of the battle. He tells us about tactics and strategy of the late 1960s and early '70s—the remarkable "Battle for Telegraph Avenue" in the radicalizing Berkeley of 1968, the People's Park confrontation, defense campaigns and electoral campaigns. This is presented in the context of a sustained analysis of capitalism, state repression, imperialism, et cetera, that he held as much at the time of writing as at the earlier time of doing. A richly detailed chapter is devoted to the movement to end the Vietnam War, in which Camejo describes and defends the basic SWP strategy. Although less detailed, Evans's account is also positive. He describes the National Peace Action Coalition (NPAC), in which the SWP was a leading force, in competition with the seemingly more radical People's Coalition for Peace and Justice (PCPJ), backed by diverse elements that included the Communist Party, an increasingly ultra-left SDS, and some radical pacifists. He notes that what "NPAC had going for it [was] a clear focus on the war, based on mass peaceful legal demonstrations, and the SWP cadres, who were generally tough dedicated people embedded in the leadership of real antiwar groups in a dozen major cities." When NPAC "called for national demonstrations in Washington and San Francisco for April 24, 1971, PCPJ backed a week of civil disobedience and disruptions in Washington beginning May 1."[5] The two competing actions provided an important test of the counterposed orientations for the anti-war movement.

Reaching a buzz far greater than the planning of the May Day actions, the preparation for April 24 was building all over the country and then came under attack from conservative newspaper columnists Rowland Evans and Robert Novak, who published an attack warning of "Trotskyite Communists . . . [who] were running NPAC" and lamenting that "what makes all this significant is that the Trotskyists are not the few bedraggled malcontents of a generation ago but the most dynamic, most effective organization on the American far left." Leslie Evans comments: "I cite this to show how the government and much of the mainstream press viewed us in those years, and how we viewed ourselves. We had come from the few hundred 'bedraggled malcontents' I had joined in 1961 to become generals of the antiwar army." Indeed, 800,000 in Washington and at least 250,000 in San Francisco mobilized—in contrast to the 16,000 drawn to PCPJ's more "radical" but disparate action on May 1.[6]

That both Evans and Camejo are quite prepared to critically examine and reject much of what they and the SWP did indicates their impartiality and thus gives weight to each of their very positive accounts of the US Trotskyists' role in helping build the mass movement that contributed to ending the US war in Vietnam—a movement of peaceful, legal, broad-based mass actions focused on a central demand: *bring the troops home now*. Their great respect for certain figures in the older generation is also tempered by the fact that they now disagree with much of what these figures stood for.

Among the electoral campaigns run by the SWP—which were always educational campaigns to get out socialist ideas and help build social movements and struggles—the most dynamic by far was the presidential candidacy of Peter Camejo and his running mate, Willie Mae Reid. More than most other candidates, Camejo was able to generate energy and enthusiasm, sometimes break into the mass media, and get out the socialist message. The SWP membership, he suggests, "sensed that, unlike the other party speakers, there was something unique in my presentations that attracted new people to the SWP. However, most people did not realize that it was the nonsectarian manner of my approach—they just thought it was because I was a good speaker, a sort of political stand-up comic who used a lot of humor to illustrate points and keep the audience entertained."[7]

The combined size of the SWP and its youth group, the Young Socialist Alliance, exceeded two thousand people by 1976. Members were mostly in their twenties and thirties, with tremendous energy and commitment. There was a substantial weekly newspaper, *The Militant*; a monthly theoretical/political magazine, the *International Socialist Review* (which Evans edited in its most successful phase); plus the international weekly *Intercontinental Press*, edited by Trotsky's former secretary, Joe Hansen. There was also Pathfinder Press, publisher of a remarkable array of books and popular pamphlets, largely overseen by George Breitman, another veteran of the movement, whose *Malcolm X Speaks* made the speeches of Malcolm X available to millions, and who made excellent editions of Trotsky's writings available throughout the English-speaking world. The SWP also boasted a substantial three-story national headquarters and a chain of combined offices/book stores/forum halls (with weekly forums) in a growing number of cities, maintained by an impressive corps of paid staff and many, many more hardworking volunteer activists.

What Happened?

How could something so good go so wrong? Looming large in both accounts is the figure of Jack Barnes. The rise of Barnes cannot be understood without reviewing some history about, and tracing some tensions within, the US Trotskyist "old guard." Evans gives considerable attention to such matters.

Back in 1953, the semi-retired founder of American Trotskyism, James P. Cannon—now living on the West Coast, surrounded by like-minded comrades there, and in touch with veteran comrades around the country—pressured the new national leadership of union veterans Farrell Dobbs and Tom Kerry into a brutal factional dispute with a significant layer of comrades, led by Bert Cochran. The Cochran group, favoring a dramatic curtailment of open SWP activities in the McCarthyite anti-Communist atmosphere generated by the Cold War, had aligned itself with the leadership of the Fourth International headed by Michel Pablo, who was calling for Trotskyists around the world to fold their banners in order to carry out a "deep entry" into Communist and social democratic movements and organizations. Cannon would have none of this, pressuring a reluctant Dobbs and Kerry onto a course of struggle and split. Working closely with Cannon in this effort were a dynamic husband and wife team, Murry Weiss and Myra Tanner Weiss. Once the integrity of the SWP was preserved, and particularly with Stalinism's crisis generated by the Khrushchev revelations of Stalin's crimes, the couple pushed forward (with apparent support from Cannon) in outward-reaching regroupment efforts among the Left. In the process, they developed a substantial influence among recently recruited younger comrades who were involved in forming a new youth group in the late 1950s, the Young Socialist Alliance (YSA).

Believing that they were the rightful leaders of the SWP, Dobbs and Kerry deeply resented Cannon's interventions and had a profound antipathy toward the "Weissites" (Murry, Myra, and anyone associated with them). But the Weissites were not the only forces involved in building up the YSA. Clusters of young comrades around Tim Wohlforth and James Robertson and new recruits Peter Camejo and Barry Sheppard were also helping lead the newly formed youth group. Dobbs and Kerry, seeking to "tighten up" the party regime, increasingly worked to sideline and marginalize the "Weissites"—and when Wohlforth and Robertson moved into increasingly vociferous opposition (around issues of the Cuban Revolution and the reunification of the Fourth International), they found themselves marginalized and finally expelled (with Wohlforth and Robertson going on to form, respectively, the Workers League, associated with Gerry Healy's Socialist Labor League in Britain, and the Spartacist League). This left Camejo and Sheppard (supporters of the SWP's Dobbs-Kerry leadership) to lead the YSA, but in the radical stirrings of the early 1960s new forces were increasingly drawn in. "The real standout was Jack Barnes, a Carleton College graduate who joined the YSA and SWP in Minneapolis," according to Camejo. "Jack helped recruit a group of very capable leaders into the YSA, including Carleton classmates Larry Seigle, Dan Styron, and Mary-Alice Waters; while at graduate school at Northwestern, Jack brought in brothers Joel and Jon Britton, Lew Jones, and several more from the Chicago area."[8]

Evans adds nuance and detail. Initially, Barnes was not an impressive speaker. "When I first heard him in 1963 he was halting and difficult to follow. Oscar Coover [an older party veteran], who had heard him give a talk in Los Angeles after I had moved to San Francisco, said to me afterwards, 'How can the national office send us somebody like that? He has no idea how to speak, and the way he waves that stump of his around would put anybody off.' Jack did have the habit when speaking of slapping his left elbow where the arm ended [due to a birth defect] with his right hand for emphasis." While he never lost that mannerism, Barnes soon matured as a speaker. By the 1965 YSA convention,

"Barnes emerged as the central leader of the YSA, the most authoritative and assured speaker on the major resolutions on the floor. When it was over, a brief plenum of the newly elected National Committee was called before we all left for home. It was held in a small unheated room. Outside, snow was falling and the temperature inside was near freezing. We were all standing, wearing our overcoats and breathing out white clouds of chill vapor. It made me think of the Bolshevik high command at the Smolny Institute in St. Petersburg during the October Revolution." It was in this setting that Barnes—nominating himself— was overwhelmingly selected as national chairman of the YSA.[9]

By this time, Evans notes, "Jack's standing had risen enormously, from a branch leader in Chicago to the effective head of the party. Farrell Dobbs didn't hand over the post of national secretary until 1972 but it was already clear that Jack and his inner circle were the heirs of the generation of the 1930s. The handful of middle-generation recruits from the late forties and the 1950s, such as Fred Halstead, Dick Garza, Ed Shaw, and Bob Himmel, were subordinate." Yet there were disturbing early signs. An angry dissident from the Bloomington, Indiana, YSA told Evans and his then-wife Kipp Dawson about Barnes's heavy-handedness toward those differing with him, adding: "Jack Barnes is the Stalin of the SWP. . . . The older comrades are desperate for successors so they blind themselves to it but Barnes is building a machine just like Stalin did. He undermines anyone who isn't part of his clique and gets them out of the way. He doesn't want recruits who know anything, nobody who was ever in any other socialist organization. All he wants is empty vessels he can fill up with his picture of himself as another Lenin." Evans and Dawson decided to reserve judgment. By the late 1960s, Evans observed, "Barnes himself adapted publicly to the standards of conduct of the older generation of party leaders, tough but fair. Still, there were differences and warning signs in private. Unlike any of the older group, Jack routinely said vicious things about people to anyone who happened to be around, which I took as a technique to keep people in line as you knew he would pillory you out of your hearing if you displeased him."[10]

The national party leadership—in the minds of some of the new comrades—tended to be ranked in a particular way: "Joseph Hansen and George Breitman were theoreticians, the highest superlative, while Tom Kerry and Farrell Dobbs were at best politicians, able to carry out policy but not to formulate it. George Novack ranked lower still, an educator." All were in their sixties, more or less. There was the need for . . . a Barnes. Even the way he wielded his half-arm "was something of a defiant pose, saying to the world that he was unyielding and wouldn't concede an inch to a physical obstacle. He was the same in politics, hard, ruthless, and unyielding. That was what attracted us to him. The SWP as it existed at the 1963 convention seemed an impossibly weak instrument to rouse and mobilize the millions it would take to turn out the men of property who owned the country. Barnes meant to build a different kind of organization, as hard and mean as himself." Moreover, writes Evans:

> There was a clear strong intelligence that rarely sounded like sloganeering or the tendency in many of the older comrades to approach every new situation with a set of fixed dead categories into which everything had to be shoveled. He looked always at the places where a small group could intervene in a situation to shape it. He was hard, which is what attracted us to him, but he seemed to also be fair. I was surprised at his patience in waiting five more years to assume the title of national secretary when he already carried its authority. He would wait seven years after that, until most of the older generation were dead, before making a decisive move to impose his own vision on the party.

It was clear to those who were watching that there was a Barnes machine, "a group within the younger leadership, most importantly the Carleton people and a few he had picked up in Chicago, who were his base and who were almost always favored in the distribution of important assignments."[11]

The new leadership layer worked hand in glove with the old, in the 1969–74 transition period, around a fierce dispute within the Fourth International that began over whether Trotskyists in Latin America should support a continental strategy of guerrilla warfare or adhere to the traditional Leninist strategy of party-building rooted in the struggles of the working class—but soon encompassing a multiplicity of related issues. By the mid-1970s, SWPers felt, with some justification, that they had more or less won this dispute—but the taste of victory, and the certainty that theirs was the correct understanding of global reality, soured by 1979–80 as the Iranian Revolution that they had supported took an unexpected turn to reactionary Islamic fundamentalism, and as the Sandinista struggle in Nicaragua, which they insisted was about to collapse because it followed the wrong strategy, was swept to victory.

Disorientation and Disaster

The SWP actually began to flounder after the end of the Vietnam War. The question of questions was how to integrate the work of the party with the realities of the US working class. With Barnes and his machine firmly in place, and the old guard moving (or being moved) increasingly to the sidelines, there was a decision to break up large SWP branches and create smaller community branches—which flopped. The decision to shift to working-class struggles was hardly unreasonable, however, though neither Camejo nor Evans give attention to dramatic stirrings in the United Mine Workers (the struggles and triumph of Miners for Democracy), the United Steel Workers (the militant campaign of dissident Ed Sadlowski), the International Brotherhood of Teamsters (where Teamsters for Democracy was making headway), the Oil, Chemical and Atomic Workers (where a militant Tony Mazzocchi was becoming a force in the national leadership and beginning to agitate for a labor party), or the dramatic upsurge in organizing and struggle among service workers and government employees. What they are alert to, however, is how the "turn to industry" was increasingly bungled. Camejo puts it this way:

> The SWP gradually separated itself from all political activity, rendering the membership passive. Finding union jobs in auto, steel, or another industry allowed some members to maintain the illusion they were doing something political. But the SWP leadership went so far as to dictate that members should not be teachers, work for a library, or take any sort of "middle class" job, and there was not to be any more student movement work. This disconnect from reality led to internal conflict, factionalism, and expulsions, until the SWP was reduced to a sect, a cult around Barnes.[12]

While comrades were deployed in industrial jobs, the new party leadership seemed to have little understanding about how the SWP could relate to the actual problems and struggles of workers in the industrial workplaces. Evans along with some other comrades took a job as an iron ore miner on the desolate Minnesota Iron Range—which was hit badly in the 1980s by layoffs brought on by an economic restructuring that led to what some economists called the "de-industrialization of America." A party branch meeting was set to discuss what the comrades' response should be to the layoffs. The branch organizer—in touch with the national office—"proposed that the party members at the next meeting of Local 1938 . . . call for having a Nicaragua slide show." A loyal comrade named Anne Teasdale, "still disbelieving that this could really be the whole of the party's anti-layoff strategy, spoke up. 'Don't we have something to say about what is happening here on the Range, the unemployment, what people are supposed to do about it?' She was met with rage." One leading member accused her of "lowering our international banner" and failing to support revolutions in Central America and the Caribbean. "Others chimed in."[13]

This relates to another key factor that Evans emphasizes, coming into play beginning in 1978. "Jack had had a revelation about Fidel Castro hardly less searing than Saint Paul's on the road to Damascus. . . . Barnes said he was electrified by suddenly understanding that the Cubans had a strategy to intervene to promote revolutions." Struggles in Nicaragua, El Salvador, Grenada, and elsewhere provided proof that Cuba was becoming the fount of world revolution. He adds: "It was clear that Jack was determined to make a turn toward Havana and that Joe Hansen was on the outs with the party's younger inner circle." Hansen died in at the beginning of 1979—but Michael Baumann, who had been working closely with Hansen on *Intercontinental Press*, told Evans that "Joe didn't agree with Jack on anything by the time he died." Camejo reported to Evans shortly before his own death in 2008 that Hansen had approached him in the late 1970s with a proposal to form a bloc against Barnes. "Barnes is completely unacceptable. You can't treat people like that," Evans quoted Camejo as saying. "Peter added that he was frightened and quickly ended the discussion."[14]

Evans was disturbed by the "whispering campaign without a vote or documents," utilized by the Barnes machine to "overturn forty or fifty years and turn the orthodox into outcasts," recognizing: "This was going to be bad." His next comments are revealing: "It was clear that Jack's basic motivation in his whole current political shift was to seek the approval of Havana, which had close ties with Moscow, where Trotsky was a demonic figure. But I was still reluctant to break with the party's favorable assessment of the Cuban government on its home turf." Aside from hoping that Barnes might be right, there was another reason for not challenging the reorientation. "There were two small opposition groups in the party that had done that, and become very isolated as a result. One was composed of Tom Kerry's supporters, led by Nat Weinstein in San Francisco and Lynn Henderson in Minneapolis. The other was based in New York, led by George Breitman, trade unionist Frank Lovell, and Steve Bloom. I thought Weinstein was hopelessly dogmatic and sterile. I was friends with Breitman and held him in high esteem, but didn't agree with him that the Cuban state was an undemocratic dictatorship though with an anti-imperialist and anticapitalist character."[15]

A new party leadership school was established, with the students handpicked and the classes taught by Barnes and trusted lieutenants. "The first graduates began giving classes and internal speeches saying Trotsky's theory of Permanent Revolution was an ultra-left mistake and that his claim to have reached agreement with Lenin in April 1917 on the aims of the Russian Revolution was not true," according to Evans. At the 1981 SWP convention, 42 percent of the National Committee, mostly seasoned and somewhat critical-minded comrades in their thirties and forties, were replaced by little-known younger "hards." He comments: "The purge list included Dick Roberts, the party's only economist; Jeff Mackler, a leader of the teachers union; Ray Markey, president of the New York librarians union; Kipp

Dawson, Syd Stapleton and Lew Jones, all important leaders in the antiwar work; and myself. . . . Most of us concluded that the change of line being hinted at in the corridors was going public soon and the New York leadership wanted to strip potential critics of the status as National Committee members before any discussion began. We still thought there would be a discussion." In fact, the regularly scheduled national convention that was to occur in 1983 was canceled in order to block the discussion, with expulsions already in full swing.[16]

Over the next several years, Barnes's SWP engineered splits in other sections of the Fourth International, creating small groups of co-thinkers who would sell *The Militant* in their respective countries, uncritically praising Fidel, Cuba, and (for a time) the Nicaraguan Sandinistas. By 1990 they formally announced what had been true for several years—their abandonment of the Fourth International, in preparation for a new "communist international" that would be created (they were sure) by Cuban and Central American revolutionaries. Camejo, who had little problem with supporting Fidelistas and Sandinistas, was too opposed to sectarianism, and too popular among activists, to be trusted by the Barnes machine—and special, quite successful efforts were made in 1982 to put him outside of the SWP. He comments:

> The Barnes cult added a distinctive twist. They decided to refer to themselves publicly as "communist," which they do to this day. In the world of political sects this is a conscious effort to remain isolated. It assures their few followers that they stand alone, that they will prove right and everyone else wrong. The cult leader has mystical inherent knowledge that no one else is able to attain except by becoming a follower.[17]

In the course of the 1980s and '90s, the SWP devolved into a small and isolated entity—with little connection to the social struggles of its time. Its international collaborators fared no better. But the sad tale cries out for explanations. How could this have happened? What explains the degeneration? It cannot be laid simply at the feet of Jack Barnes. For Marxists, the "evil genius" theory just won't do.

Original Sin?

For Camejo, the methodology of Barnes was rooted in a sectarian quality inherent in Trotskyism itself—which then caused him to carry out the quest for relevance in a hopelessly sectarian manner—changing one rigid "orthodoxy" (a Trotskyism distinct from the revolutionary Trotsky) for another (a

Castroism distinct from the revolutionary Fidel). The crisis arose in the organization as early as 1970, in Camejo's opinion, with the choice facing the
SWP being either to go "forward, evolving into an organization connected
with the realities of the national and international living struggles of real
people; or inward, self-isolating from realities because those realities did not
correspond to a preconceived idea ordained as the unchangeable truth."[18]

Camejo was transformed by the international work he did in Latin
America in the late 1970s. Sent by the SWP to Nicaragua in 1979, he was
able to see a mass popular revolution up close and personal. He describes a
young militant of the newly victorious FSLN (Sandinista National Liberation Front) addressing the laboring poor in a Managua barrio:

> As he spoke it dawned on me. The way he communicated, the message
> he gave, was what I had always tried to say; but he used only clear, under-
> standable words about his message built on the living history of Nicaragua
> and the consciousness of the workers and their families who were listening.
>
> He explained how Nicaragua belongs to its own people. How rich
> foreigners had come and taken their country from them but that they
> were the people who worked and created the wealth of their nation. They
> had the right to run it and to decide what should be done. He spoke
> about the homeless children in the streets and how under the US-backed
> dictatorship nothing was done for them. He described in detail how the
> FSLN was trying to solve each problem. That it would take time. That
> Nicaragua was still in danger of foreign intervention. To never forget
> those who gave their lives so that Nicaragua could be a free nation. At
> each mention of the departed, the crowd shouted, "*Presente*," to affirm
> that the missing ones were still with them, here. At every meeting of the
> Sandinistas, regardless where it was held, someone would read off the
> names of people from that block, school, or union who had given their
> lives for freedom. Everyone at the meeting would shout "*Presente*."
>
> My mind began to race. Of course this young man was not going
> to use terms that would lead to confusion; he would place these issues in
> the culture, history, and language of his people. It dawned on me—that
> is why this movement had won. They didn't name their newspaper after
> some term from European history; they didn't speak of "socialism" or
> "Marxism." While the rest of the left of the 1960s and '70s was in decline
> throughout Latin America, caught up in the rhetoric of European Marx-
> ism and the influence of Stalinism, the FSLN had delivered a great vic-
> tory for freedom.[19]

Camejo describes this experience as a "tipping point" for him, and while
the SWP leadership was willing to place Fidelista and Sandinista certainties

into its "program" (chucking the erstwhile Trotskyist certainties), it seemed incapable of emulating the example of being connected with living struggle. In one of his book's few glaring errors, however, Camejo incorrectly characterizes the position of the Fourth International majority, led by Ernest Mandel, as being hypercritical and even hostile to the Sandinistas—which might strengthen his point, if true, but whose inaccuracy throws the overarching point into question. In fact, Mandel hailed the Sandinista revolution and suggested that a variant of the "dictatorship of the proletariat," political rule by the toiling masses, had been established in revolutionary Nicaragua. (There are some who would criticize the pro-Sandinista attitude of both the Fourth International majority and of Camejo as a betrayal of the Trotskyist program—which might cause Peter to say: "See, *that's* what I'm talking about.")

The approach that Camejo criticizes is reflected in a comment Farrell Dobbs made to him: "The program has been developed. Our job is to implement it." Evans reports a similar comment from Barnes (before his Fidelista revelation): "One day Jack and I were talking in the headquarters and he told me his opinion that all serious theoretical work had been completed by Marx, Engels, Lenin, and Trotsky and there was nothing for future generations to do but apply the existing theory to specific political situations." Camejo appropriately notes that this is "contrary to the essence of Marx' writings about the materialist basis of science and how it applies to economic and social relations. Science is a process, not a discovery or revelation by a genius. Not only is a political program an evolving concept, but it also requires continuous discussion and debate in order for it to be effective. And it must, most important of all, be tested against reality."[20]

Such an open and critical-minded approach can also be found—explicitly stated—in the writings of George Breitman and Joe Hansen, regardless of whether one agrees with some of their conclusions. But Evans reports on some similar stirrings from US Trotskyist patriarch James P. Cannon in 1964–65. "The party is too ingrown," he said. "It has become intolerant of differences of opinion. It doesn't work with real people in the world. All of its activities are self-generated—*Militant* sales drives, election campaigns for our own candidates, forums in our own hall of ourselves talking to ourselves. This isn't a way to build a live organization. If this goes on much longer the party will cease to exist." He went on: "I haven't said anything publicly in the party because I haven't seen an issue where these sectarian tendencies could be corrected and I didn't want to undermine Farrell and Tom. But now there is one."[21]

Evans continues: "Here Jim produced a pamphlet called *The Triple Revolution* written by the futurist Robert Theobald and published by the Center for the Study of Democratic Institutions in Santa Barbara. The three revolutions supposed to be taking place in the world were in the growth of atomic weaponry, in struggles for human rights, but mainly in automation, leading, Theobald argued, to massive structural unemployment in the near term." Cannon asked Evans to take up these issues and to write about them in the party on his behalf.[22]

When it became known to Barnes that Evans was moving in this direction, he let it be known that such a thing would not be welcome—but also Evans concluded, after some investigation, that Theobald and Cannon were wrong, and he dropped the matter. Cannon himself—satisfied that the SWP's energetic engagement with building the antiwar movement was shifting the party in an outward-moving direction—set the Triple Revolution discussion aside, without repudiating its importance.

What is clear is that the "original sin" that Camejo perceives—while identifying a genuine problem—is overstated and by itself inadequate in explaining the SWP disaster. There were substantial elements within the Trotskyist tradition and among some of its adherents that strongly pushed against the sectarian, dogmatic, ingrown "orthodoxy" that he criticizes.

Evans reaches for a different variant of "original sin" to help explain the SWP disaster—Leninism. To make this case, he offers a set of authoritarian quotations in Lenin's *Collected Works* from the civil war period of 1918–20 and concludes: "Lenin, as his published works showed, was committed to an extreme Jacobin dictatorship over the whole of society to remold it to his vision."[23] He goes on to assert:

> The general pattern internationally was that most of the [Fourth International] sections that had sided with Cannon and the SWP in the 1953 split were of the hard party type, while those led by the Europeans were looser, as a legacy of having been committed to deep entry in larger left parties in the 1950s. The hard parties with their super centralist structures more often than not ended up with a mad captain at the helm, sailing ahead with seeming unanimity among the ranks until they hit the iceberg. Witness Healy in England, Moreno in Argentina, or the still long surviving cult around Pierre Lambert in France. This centralist and ideologically intolerant structure seemed to produce the same result not only for little parties but for national states both great and small, as witness Stalinist Russia, Enver Hoxha's Albania, Mao's China, and Ceausescu's Romania to name a few. In the case of the state rulers the Trotskyists attributed everything to the virus of Stalinism, which in turn they explained by the economic privileges of the party bureaucracy in an economy of scarcity. This neatly exempted them from any charge of similarity. Yet the same totalitarian virus decimated the various Trotskyist

parties in the 1970s and 1980s, at least those of the hard Leninist sort. Draw your own conclusion.[24]

There is much scholarship that would need to be confronted and refuted (or reinterpreted) to make this interpretation of Lenin stick. The desperate and often disastrous "emergency measures" of the Bolsheviks during the civil war period and its immediate aftermath do not provide a fair characterization of Leninist organizational principles as they actually developed from 1902 to 1917. What passed for good "Leninism" under Stalin and his disciples (or under Barnes and other sectarian cultists) is another matter. The fact remains, what Evans tells us about the organizational perspectives of Cannon, and of the SWP during the period of Cannon's leadership, does not harmonize well with his generalization—or with any notion of Leninism à la Cannon leading to the Barnes disaster.

In a conversation in Cannon's home in the early 1960s, Evans commented on a dissident in the YSA, suggesting "we would be better off if we could get him out." Cannon asked: "Does he do anything for the movement?" Evans conceded that, yes, he "read French and had presented a talk on Ernest Mandel's *Marxist Economic Theory*, which was not yet available in an English translation." Cannon responded sternly, "Well, that is something. The party is a voluntary organization. You can't hire and fire in the party. If you lose an experienced person you can't go out on the street and hire a replacement. You have to conserve what you have."[25] Or consider Evans's description of the 1963 national convention of the SWP:

> I now had my first chance to observe how party discussions and inter-nal democracy worked. Mimeographed internal bulletins began to arrive from New York. All party members were permitted to write their views, to be printed in the bulletin during the preconvention period and, if it involved a resolution, to be put up for a vote at the coming conven-tion. This was an internal discussion, however; all party members were expected to present the majority line when speaking to nonmembers.
>
> There were some factions that were spread as minorities within sev-eral branches, and two that controlled their branches outright. The first type included a group around Jim Robertson and Tim Wohlforth, who dismissed the Cuban Revolution as an authoritarian nationalist event and who were opposed to the reunification with the International Secretariat. Another faction supported Arne Swabeck, one of the original founders of the movement, who lived in Los Angeles and had become convinced that Mao Zedong represented a true socialist tendency.
>
> There was a small group in Detroit who thought the Soviet Union

was some kind of new capitalist state as contrasted with the party majority position that it was defined by the nationalized property and only the
bureaucratic government needed to be removed. The two factions that
had their whole branch behind them were in Seattle, led by Dick Fraser
and Clara Kaye, who championed "revolutionary integration" for the black
movement and opposed any support of black nationalism, and in Mil-
waukee, led by James Bolton, who had a pro-Maoist position similar to
that of Swabeck. Articles defending and opposing these variegated viewpoints filled many thick mimeographed bulletins. Also there were a few
very long, almost incomprehensible, articles larded with abstruse organic
and early computer analogies signed by a single individual, Lynn Marcus.
When I asked about him I was told his real name was Lyndon LaRouche
and his party name was an immodest contraction based on Lenin and
Marx. . . . I had spoken before the branch that spring to propose that the
militant black nationalism of the Muslims was a progressive force that
should be supported despite their strident antiwhite rhetoric. This was
met with general skepticism. I felt vindicated when the main party resolution, titled "Freedom Now," written by George Breitman in Detroit, called
for support to black nationalism and the Nation of Islam.[26]

At the same time, Evans was struck by "the heat of the majority supporters' hostility to all the minority tendencies," and this would culminate—
finally—in an organizational tightening under the Dobbs/Kerry regime as
part of the leadership transition to the Barnes regime. Yet he notes that Cannon had disagreements with "the tightening up process that Jack Barnes had
been shepherding through the national structure."[27] After Cannon's death,
Evans was assigned to go through his papers in order to help compose and
edit new volumes of his writings. His comments, again, give the sense of a
different Leninism than is described in the sweeping generalization:

Reading over fifty years of Cannon's letters several things struck me. In
the early sixties in Los Angeles I had seen that he held meetings of the
local National Committee members and outraged New York by sending in policy proposals in the name of the Los Angeles NC group, like
a dual Political Committee. I always assumed that dated only from his
somewhat early retirement to Los Angeles in 1950. Not so. In 1936 the
Trotskyists had dissolved their organization to join the Socialist Party
with the aim of connecting with a developing left wing. During most of
1937 Cannon lived in California, and from there he repeatedly upstaged
the elected leadership of his group in New York, mailing out counter-
proposals to theirs to the faction national committee. This wouldn't have
been tolerated for a minute in the Barnes-led SWP. Sharp exchanges

took place openly between leaders of the Cannon faction without hiding them from other tendencies in the Trotskyist group. Another thing that struck me was Cannon's attitude toward former factional opponents. A surprising number of his close associates and even friends had earlier been bitter enemies: Sylvia Bleeker and Morris Lewitt, Joseph Hansen, and Art Sharon were all members of the Shachtman faction or, worse yet, part of the clique around Martin Abern, one of the three original Trotskyist leaders, infamous for his onionskin copies of leadership documents that went out regularly to his select list.

Cannon's two closest friends seemed to be Ray Dunne in Minneapolis, who had always been a Cannonite, but the other was Joseph Vanzler, party name John G. Wright, who was described in a May 1933 letter to Cannon from George Clarke as "the vanguard of the freaks" and a supporter of the B. J. Field minority. . . . All of these people became part of the party's central leadership without prejudice over their former alignments. No such thing ever happened under Barnes. Anyone who opposed him was forever marked and generally quickly expelled.[28]

At one point, a Barnes loyalist threatened Evans around pursuing the Triple Revolution thesis with the comment: "The Political Committee has had a meeting about that and has ruled that it is prohibited to discuss it. Cannon is completely out of line to try to raise it and if he pursues it any further he will be expelled. You had better shut up about it." While Evans learned from a more seasoned comrade that "no one was going to expel Jim Cannon from the SWP," he concluded that this meant "Barnes didn't have the power to do everything he might want to do."[29] More, it suggests a qualitative difference between the Leninism of Cannon's party and that of the Barnes regime.

Digging Deeper

If "the inherent sectarianism of the Trotskyist program" and "the inherent authoritarianism of Leninist organizational principles" do not provide the answer to the question of the qualitative change in the SWP, where can we look?

For any Marxist group that wishes to bring about revolutionary change, one obvious question—if one is a Marxist—is "what is its relationship with the organized working class?" Camejo comments:

Unions, which at one point had organized 33 percent of American labor, had shrunk to just 12 percent. No major political opposition appeared. Yes, there were many defensive struggles as the industrial unions were weakened by corporate and governmental attacks, which had stepped

up under Reagan. But labor had no labor party or any kind of effective
defense strategy. By the early 1980s the industrial working class and its
unions had been in a sharp decline for two obvious, interconnected reasons. First was the growth of globalization; second was the union capitu-
lation to the Democratic Party. At every level the unions, pushed by the
Democratic Party, were capitulating, supposedly a necessary step for U.S.
corporations to be competitive in the global economy.[30]

The world had changed in important ways, and the SWP leadership—
with few and marginal exceptions—didn't see it coming. Indeed, it might
have made sense if the SWP *had* actually looked more carefully and thoughtfully at the dynamics of Triple Revolution that Jim Cannon vainly pointed
to. The automation and computerization discussed in that document did not
bring mass unemployment in the immediate term, but they did contribute
to the steady erosion of the industrial working-class base that had been the
source of traditional union power—and these developing technologies were
very much related to what came to be tagged "globalization." (The so-called
"revolutions" in human rights and in weaponry also moved in slower and
more complex—but no less transformative—ways.)

One must also give attention to the "great divide" represented by the Second
World War, which brought into being a very different world than the one framing
the perspectives of Lenin, Trotsky, and their comrades. Young SWP and YSA
members—reading the "classic" texts that had been written in qualitatively different contexts, and themselves having come into adulthood and consciousness
in profoundly altered sociocultural contexts—could not easily grasp the actual
meaning of what Lenin or Trotsky might be saying. But they did not know that.
This naturally contributed to a stilted understanding of the texts, contributing to
flattened and simplistic applications, and to growing disorientation.

Related to this, the vanguard layers of the working class—at least in
the United States—had been nurtured by a labor-radical subculture from the
post–Civil War era of the 1860s down to the 1940s. The cadres of the early
SWP had been shaped by and were an integral part of that labor-radical subculture. But the class-conscious working-class layers were fragmented and
eroded by the profound economic, political, cultural, social, and economic
changes of the post–World War II period—whose components included a
fierce and stultifying Cold War anti-Communism, an unprecedented relative
prosperity, working-class suburbanization, transformations in an increasingly
conformist mass popular culture, and more. The subculture of the radicalized
sections of the labor movement, and those radicalized sections of the labor
movement themselves, were no longer the vibrant reality they once had been

as young members flowed into the SWP and YSA in the 1960s and early '70s.

In *"Left-Wing" Communism, an Infantile Disorder*, Lenin emphasizes that when would-be revolutionaries feel they must maintain "iron discipline," if their Marxism and their organization are not actually rooted in vanguard layers of the working class and intimately connected with mass struggles, their efforts will "inevitably fall flat and end up in phrase-mongering and clowning."[31] One might say that this is precisely the essence of the "Barnesism" emerging from the accounts of Camejo and Evans.

Some left critics may be inclined to see Barnes's adaptation to the Cuban and Nicaraguan revolutionaries as the opposite of "ultra-leftism" (instead reflecting a submission to "the conservative elements of those national programs"). This gets into analyses of the Cuban and Nicaraguan revolutions that are beyond the scope of this review. But Lenin's decisive point—that no "Leninism" is possible if there is a disconnect between would-be revolutionaries and the actualities of working-class life and struggle—points up the fatal problem that faced and finally overwhelmed the SWP. The lack of possibility for democratic correction, due to the deepening authoritarianism and cultism represented by the Barnes regime, sealed its fate. Perhaps all this was not inevitable—but that is the way it happened.[32]

Aftermath

In reaction to their experiences in the Trotskyist movement, the two authors went down different pathways.

Evans participated in two efforts to pick up some of the political pieces after the mass expulsions from the SWP—helping to found, in turn, Socialist Action and then Solidarity, both of which still exist as fairly small groups. Before the end of the 1980s, he had given up on socialist activism and—essentially—on socialism and Marxism altogether. Acquiring additional skills and knowledge upon returning to university life, he went on to play an impressive role as a web journalist for the International Institute, associated with University of California, Los Angeles, as well as a staff member of the World Health Organization and the World Bank (of all things). Also, he and his wife have been quite active in their local neighborhood committee's highly focused efforts to protect their own community in South Los Angeles, contending with "gang crime, illegal dumping, graffiti vandals, drug houses, and abandoned buildings." Evans, appearing defensive about his new course, goes on the offensive to justify it: "For Trotskyists all politics is global. If it doesn't involve a foreign war for which imperialism can be excoriated, or a union-busting multinational corporation, it is hardly worth talking about."[33]

There is an element of truth to this—but it is not totally true, in my opinion.

Camejo was unable to give up on the radical activism that animated most of his life. He joined together in the mid-1980s with a short-lived "nonsectarian" left-wing group called the North Star Network, made up of former SWPers and other radicals. The group ended up getting involved in Jesse Jackson's Rainbow Coalition—which he considers "a major political mistake" since it became "just another name for keeping progressives in the Democratic Party."³⁴ (One of the appendices of his book contains an analytical critique entitled "The Origins of the Two-Party System.") He also established ties with a breakaway from the Communist Party, Committees of Correspondence, and with a Maoist-influenced group called Line of March—but concluded that intertwined vestiges of Stalinism and reformism hindered both from becoming effective left-wing forces.

For a time, thanks to considerable expertise on the capitalist economy, he worked very successfully for the investment firm of Merrill Lynch. From there he branched out into helping left-leaning people make "socially responsible" investments, and also with raising substantial amounts of money—through his business and financial contacts—for such things as fighting AIDS, job creation, immigrant rights, unionization, and protection of the environment. He became perhaps the most dynamic—and one of the most radical—figures in the Green Party of California, running for governor and then becoming Ralph Nader's vice-presidential running mate in 2004. While raising questions about using the word "socialism," and insisting that Marx should not be treated uncritically as a deity, he continued to embrace the socialist goal (preferring the term "economic democracy") and a broadly Marxist analytical framework.

Both Camejo and Evans appear to have ended up with wives whom they have loved and who love them, children, grandchildren, and interesting personal experiences, some of which are discussed or alluded to in their books. And both felt a need to share their reflections about US Trotskyism with readers whom they knew would be mostly on the Left—which is our good fortune.

13

Revolutionary Redemption

To many who were paying attention, the US Socialist Workers Party of the 1960s and 1970s seemed an incredibly vibrant organization: between one and two thousand activists animated by high ideals and dynamic Marxism, with a conception of socialism both democratic and revolutionary, and a proven capacity to organize—in impressive united front efforts—effective social movements and struggles capable of bringing about positive change.

Barry Sheppard has performed a great service to activists and historians of the US Left by providing a coherent account of the SWP as it became revitalized in the 1960s, as it reached its zenith in the 1970s, and then as it self-destructed in the 1980s. *The Party: The Socialist Workers Party 1960–1988* aims to tell, through one person's political memoir, the story of an organization that had a generally unacknowledged yet not insignificant impact on the politics and culture of the United States. The first volume took the story up to 1973, tracing the upward trajectory of that party's fortunes and impact. The second volume covers the continued upward trajectory, then the disorientation and awful crash of the 1980s.[1]

Sheppard's role in all of that—revitalization, glory days, and destructive crescendo—has been remembered, sometimes bitterly, by many who went through the experience. In the second volume of his memoir, he himself has acknowledged some of the incredibly negative things that he did in this terrible third phase. Indeed, some saw his glowing first volume as self-serving and predicted that he would be unable to write the second darker volume. It would force him to deal with the tragic failure of the party to which he devoted himself, and to face what he himself did to bring that failure about. He would not be able to do that, I was assured. It seems to me they were wrong about the first volume, and—obviously, in light of its appearance—they were wrong about the second.

These two volumes will continue to be "must reads" for all young activists who wish to challenge the power of the corrupt and profiteering 1% in order

to create a society of "life, liberty and the pursuit of happiness" for the 99%—
what some of us still would call a transition from capitalist tyranny to socialist
democracy, which can only be brought about by the working-class majority.
Such activists will be looking for explanations of what went on before, in
struggles of the past, from which lessons can be learned of what to do (and
what not to do) in the future.

As with volume one, the second volume of *The Party* provides an
extremely valuable and important contextualization of the story—providing
extensive background especially on international developments: the 1973 coup
in Chile, the Arab-Israeli War, the revolutions in Portugal, Iran, Nicaragua,
Grenada, the Soviet invasion of Afghanistan, the rise and repression and persistence of the workers' Solidarity movement in Poland. The volume also gives
attention to domestic social struggles (an especially good chapter is provided
on busing and antiracist struggles in Boston). But what makes these volumes
unique is their focus on the effort to build, and the ultimate disastrous failure
in building, a genuinely revolutionary socialist party in the United States in
the twentieth century.

Prelude

The SWP was formed in 1938, but its origins were in the heroic years of the early
Communist movement. The pioneers of US Communism were inspired by the
1917 workers' and peasants' revolution in Russia, led by Lenin, Trotsky, and
other outstanding revolutionary Marxists who went on to establish a Communist International in 1919. But many of them were also rooted in deep traditions
of American radicalism and labor activism associated, for example, with the
Socialist Party of Eugene V. Debs and the Industrial Workers of the World.

After Lenin's death, however, the Russian Revolution's goal of soviet
democracy and the commitment to a liberating revolution worldwide gave
way to a bureaucratic dictatorship under Joseph Stalin, preaching "socialism
in one country" and advancing cynical policies to enhance its own power and
privileges. This change did not triumph without a struggle, and Leon Trotsky
was one of the leaders who heroically yet unsuccessfully opposed this bureaucratic degeneration both within the Soviet Union and in the member parties
of the Soviet-dominated Communist International.

American Trotskyists formed the Communist League of America in
1928, standing as a beacon of early revolutionary-democratic ideals of early
Communism against the corruptions, cynicism, and murderous authoritarianism of Stalinism. While far smaller than the Communist Party and the
largely reformist Socialist Party, the US ranks of the Trotskyists grew amid

the labor radicalization generated by the Great Depression. By 1935—after playing an outstanding role in various labor struggles, especially in the Minneapolis general strike—they were able to merge with other radical labor forces to form the Workers Party of the United States. This was soon followed by a decision to enter the Socialist Party in order to link up with that organization's growing left wing, although they were soon driven out (along with much of the broader left wing) by the reformist leadership.

The subsequent formation of the Socialist Workers Party, with significant influence in sectors of the labor movement (partly traced in Art Preis's classic *Labor's Giant Step*) and among prominent intellectuals and cultural figures (explored in Alan Wald's *The New York Intellectuals*), seemed to its members and supporters to be the beginning of an important new phase of revolutionary struggle in the United States. This was taking place as part of a coming-together of like-minded groups around the world to establish, with Trotsky, what was called the World Party of Socialist Revolution—the Fourth International.

The earlier US Trotskyists, such as James P. Cannon, had blazed the trail of applying all of this to US realities, connecting revolutionary Marxism to American radical traditions, also helping to develop a model of seriously democratic and cohesive organizational functioning. In the 1950s and 1960s, central party leaders Farrell Dobbs and Tom Kerry (and, for a time, Murry Weiss and Myra Tanner Weiss) each in their own way sought to extend and refine this model under new circumstances, developing the conception of an experienced leadership team that would integrate into itself younger comrades who would be capable of assuming leadership of the party.

There were important contributions from others as well. In the period after the Second World War, Joe Hansen developed a notion of "deformed workers' states" to help explain the nature of the Communist regimes established in Eastern Europe. Related to this was his conception of "workers and farmers government" that sought to make sense, initially, of revolutions (and different possibilities of development) in so-called third world countries. Another innovation was his penetrating analysis of the Cuban Revolution that, although hardly uncritical, identified its revolutionary essence and possibilities.

Sharing this approach to Marxism was George Breitman, who was able to utilize the insights and methodology of Lenin and Trotsky to shed light on issues of racism and nationalism—developing a pioneering analysis of Black nationalism and the significance of Malcolm X. Breitman also developed a challenging analysis of the 1960s radicalization in comparison to the radicalizations of the early 1900s and of the 1930s, indicating that in some ways it was deeper than the others, if one considers how multifaceted the 1960s radicalization was, and especially if one understands the essentially work-ing-class composition of the new social movements.

Glory Days

The glory days of the 1960s radicalization forms the backdrop to the first vol-ume of Sheppard's account. He also gives considerable attention to develop-ments and major struggles inside the global network of Trotskyist groups, the Fourth International. Nor does he shy away from discussing factional disputes inside the SWP. Some of these gave rise to splits and competing groups—such as the Spartacist League and the Workers League (the latter gradually evolv-ing into the Socialist Equality Party), while others (such as the Proletarian Orientation Tendency and the Internationalist Tendency) did not. But the thrust of the first volume is a straightforward narrative of the on-the-ground development of "the Party" as an impressive force on the US Left.

The dramatic influx of young activists from the mid-1960s to the early 1970s had a profoundly transformative impact on the SWP. Yet the new recruits were themselves transformed as they became integrated into the Trotskyist movement, finding their understanding and self-confidence greatly enhanced by the program and political method of revolutionary Marxism (presented in a variety of publications, educational activities, one-on-one discussions, et cetera) and their political effectiveness and impact greatly enhanced by the party's organizational structures and norms.

In part, this was accomplished by creating a youth group, the Young Socialist Alliance (YSA), rooted on the campuses and acting as a magnet for some of the brightest children of the white-collar and blue-collar working class. There was, as there has been for quite some time, some confusion over the class nature of this layer—the fuzzy and often contradictory term "middle class" was often applied to them. This was a prelude to categorizing the entire working class as "the middle class" in the United States. It is an important point to which we will need to return later.

Among the new recruits were important clusters of African American and Latino activists, and also a significant percentage of women, some of whom assumed a significant leadership role in the efforts of the SWP and YSA. The party's earlier work on issues of race and nationalism contributed to the ability of some comrades to play a role not only in African American but also in Chicano and Puerto Rican struggles.

The fact that the SWP had seriously engaged—in the 1950s and early '60s—with such works as Friedrich Engels's *Origin of the Family, Private Property and the State* and Simone de Beauvoir's *The Second Sex*) made it more sensitive and responsive to early feminist stirrings coming out of the new radicalization and enabled it to connect very positively to the rising women's liberation movement. In addition, the recruitment of a growing number of gay and lesbian comrades—combined with influences and insights that were part of the new radicalization—enabled the SWP finally to scrap a narrow and destructive policy that had banned homosexuals from membership.

Perhaps the SWP's most profound accomplishment involved its central role in the creation of the massive and powerful antiwar movement, through persistent united front efforts, that proved capable of helping to end the US war in Vietnam. The details of that story were told in Fred Halstead's classic *Out Now! A Participant's Account of the Movement against the Vietnam War*— but Sheppard adds additional details and insights of his own about this heroic achievement.

A sense of the realities, and of how the realities were perceived by the party leadership, can be summed up in the final three paragraphs of this memoir's first volume:

> The radicalization had a massive impact on the SWP. Coming out of the witch-hunt years [of the 1950s], the SWP had become smaller in numbers, and older. Of course, it had recruited young people throughout those years, but not many and, usually, not for long. The process that led to the foundation of the Young Socialist Alliance in 1960—even with only about 130 members—situated the SWP to participate effectively in the youth radicalization which was just beginning.
>
> The recruitment and training of young people saved the SWP as a revolutionary organization at that point. Revolutionary socialist organizations generally do not last long in unfavorable times, and the SWP had been running out of time. The new layer of young people, and the opportunities provided to intervene in real struggles, gave the organization another lease on life. The older generation, that came out of the labor radicalization of the 1930s which was renewed for a time after World War II, was able to pass the torch on to the new generation.
>
> The older leaders—especially Farrell Dobbs—understood that this process, in order to succeed, had to go all the way to replacing the older central leadership with a new one from the new generation. He sought to accomplish this in a phased way, while the older leaders were still around to train the new leadership. The transition in leadership was essentially completed by the end of the 1960s. Thus the SWP was in good shape to face the challenges of the next decades—or so we thought.[2]

Something Terrible Happened

Barry Sheppard was a central leader who helped bring this about—and who
then helped to transform the organization into what seemed a very bad dream:
an authoritarian sect, dominated by a cult figure, wracked by internal trials
and expulsions, increasingly an ingrown and dogmatic little universe having
little relationship to the people and the struggles of the larger society.

A new leadership had been nurtured by Dobbs and other old-timers who
led the party. Sheppard was part of that younger layer. But it was headed by
a tough, smart, capable person (whom Sheppard and others admired very
much) named Jack Barnes. The new leadership initiated a "turn to industry" that seemed consistent with the old traditions of the Marxist left, and it
sought to apply Marxism in new and creative ways to the realities of the 1970s
and 1980s, being open to learning from the revolutionary upsurges in Central
America and the Caribbean as the one decade gave way to the other.

Yet the revolutionary expectations that the leadership had for the US
working class didn't "work out"—particularly as a phenomenon that came
to be known as "globalization" had a devastating impact on the industrial
centers into which the SWP was sending its young cadres. The new leadership intensified pressure on comrades to go into industry, where cadres were
expected to "talk socialism to workers" instead of listening to and learning
from other workers, and instead of participating in a clear-eyed manner in the
life of the workplace and actual union struggles. The impact of this ill-con-
ceived orientation was a gut-level erosion of confidence in the US working
class, covered over by "class struggle" posturing and persistent declarations
that the workers were moving "to center stage of U.S. politics."

The lure of successful revolutions in Nicaragua and Grenada—naturally
inspired by the example of the Cuban Revolution personified by Fidel Castro—seemed to suggest a different kind of breakthrough than what had been
promised by the "proletarian" Trotskyism of the older comrades. Barnes and
those around him underwent a profound conversion, seeing the Trotskyism
represented by the Fourth International as irrelevant to the promising revolutionary wave represented by Fidel and those influenced by him.

The Barnes leadership—Barry Sheppard very much included—made
a decision to transform the SWP into a "sister organization" of the Cuban
Communist Party, with all of the deep-going theoretical shifts that this
involved. Trotsky's theory of permanent revolution, the centrality of workers' democracy to socialism, support for the democratic struggles in the
bureaucratically ruled "workers' states," the Leninist-Trotskyist norms of
internal party democracy, any critical-minded questioning of the party

leadership, and even inclinations to push against sectarian arrogance toward those outside the party—all were seen as impediments to the kind of organization that the SWP needed to be, in the view of the Barnes leadership. Increasingly, the party became an insulated universe separate from the lives and struggles of the workers and the oppressed, with organizational norms tightened in the name of a bogus "Leninism" and a systematic repression and expulsion of those adhering to the traditional perspectives and norms of the SWP.

Hundreds of actual and potential dissidents were expelled in trumped-up trials. This included most of the veterans of the 1930s and 1940s, and also experienced younger activists in the mass movements and trade unions. According to Sheppard (who played a central role in the carnage), the expulsion of dissident factions, one associated with George Breitman and Frank Lovell and the other with Nat Weinstein and Lynn Henderson, "marked the death-knell of the SWP. No tendencies or factions have ever again appeared in the party in the decades since. Internal life became monolithic, and top-down commandism became the norm."[3] As this was happening, hundreds more comrades drifted out "for personal reasons," some concluding that perhaps they were not real revolutionaries after all. Those who remained tended to define and shield themselves with militant adherence to a "correct" politics as defined by Jack Barnes.

Sheppard sees the development of a cult around Barnes (beginning in the late 1970s) as the most debilitating development leading to the SWP's decline:

> The formation of a cult in the party leadership blocked correction of political errors in the turn to industry, the assessment of the change in the objective situation in the Caribbean, the question of permanent revolution, and other theoretical and political errors. The cult prevented correction of the degeneration of the party's organizational practice.[4]

As Sheppard notes, the term "cult" can have different meanings. His usage involves political cults, the best known being the personality cults of Stalin and Mao Zedong, who oversaw bureaucratic institutions of immense power and material resources, each of whom became "a supreme arbiter, in whom all final authority in all matters rested." But there are also "cults in small socialist groups . . . not based on such material interests." In the case of Barnes, his early talents included an ability to help draw comrades of different generations and with different perspectives together in a collective leadership process. As his authority in the SWP grew, however, he evolved into a "star" with special status. "He became the sole initiator of policy, and the supreme arbiter in any discussion. The obvious result was a growing fear among other leaders of freely expressing their views, else they be deemed 'wrong.'"[5]

Over time, "the 'star' system of leadership became more and more exacerbated and entrenched, including special treatment and perquisites for the top leader, special standards that applied to Jack Barnes and some around him, and not to the ordinary members."[6] Near the conclusion of the volume, Sheppard provides details on the pure and simple material corruption of Barnes and his few intimate associates—the use of SWP resources to provide a very free and comfortable lifestyle, divorced from the day-to-day lives and far above the material conditions of regular party members.

Redemption

How could something that seemed so good turn so bad? How could someone like Barry Sheppard, who helped bring about such a terrible transformation, ever redeem himself?

The first step of redemption was to run afoul of Barnes, who dominated the nightmare regime that Sheppard had helped create; then, to be broken and marginalized, and leave the SWP. The second step was to rebuild his life, critically reflecting on his experience, while attempting to remain true to the best of what he had believed in. The third step was to do more than beat himself up or apologize (although apologize he does, devoting an entire chapter in the second volume to "My Culpability")—but rather to try to explain how it was that something so good had turned so bad. The destructive mistakes he made cannot be undone, but they can be explained in ways that can help others learn both from the positive and negative aspects of the SWP experience.

Regardless of whether one agrees with Barry Sheppard's interpretations and assessments of what happened, he has had the courage and the stamina to draw together a unified narrative, providing a considerable amount of recollection and documentation, which can be extremely useful in trying to understand this political experience that thousands of us shared. What is particularly impressive is that, unlike all too many who went through this experience, he remains true to the idealism and revolutionary Marxist convictions that drew him, and others of us, into the SWP. For those who have "moved on," this is bound to be exasperating—but this is what has made it possible for him to take on (and to want to take on) the difficult task of writing these two volumes.

Recent memoirs by erstwhile comrades of Sheppard's—Peter Camejo and Leslie Evans—provide interpretations and valuable details not found in these two volumes. There are also well-documented accounts of the struggle against the SWP's degeneration (in a three-volume digitized work titled *In*

Defense of American Trotskyism, published by the Marxist Internet Archive). All are worth considering as one seeks to piece together the full story. There will probably be other contributions as well. But *The Party: The Socialist Workers Party 1960–1988* will stand as an essential account.

Those of us "who were there" and who can identify aspects of his account that strike us as wrong should certainly do so. In this spirit, I want to offer two corrections.

One mistake in Sheppard's account has to do with one of the essential positions of the oppositional current that I was part of. In deciding to orient to a presumed Castroist "new international" that was expected to arise out of the Cuban, Nicaraguan, and Grenadian revolutions—hailed as the "three giants of the Caribbean"—the Barnes leadership had, as already noted, decided to break from traditional Trotskyist perspectives. Sheppard writes:

> The Weinstein tendency rejected this orientation, mocking the whole concept of the "three giants." The Breitman group was closer to our view, but didn't see the potential for the advance of the Nicaraguan and Grenadian revolutions to positively affect Cuba. Both tendencies were not enthusiastic about the opportunities these developments opened for the SWP and the Fourth International.[7]

This mischaracterizes the position of the Breitman caucus, of which I was a member. Under Breitman's tutelage, I composed a substantial study entitled "Permanent Revolution in Nicaragua," which would have been a submission on behalf of the caucus to the preconvention discussion bulletins for the regular party convention had Barnes not undemocratically canceled it. The point of this contribution was to argue and document that Barnes and Weinstein were wrong to counterpose Trotsky's theory of permanent revolution with the actualities of the Nicaraguan revolution (with Weinstein adhering to the former, Barnes embracing the latter, and both seeing the one incompatible with the other). Rather, we in the Breitman caucus saw the dynamics of permanent revolution being reflected in the actualities of the Nicaraguan revolution.

We were, in fact, quite "enthusiastic about the opportunities these developments opened for the SWP and the Fourth International." After the expulsions, this study was published by the Fourth Internationalist Tendency, of which Breitman was a central leader, which included a laudatory introduction by Breitman himself.

A second correction has to do with Sheppard's account of how he, Tom Leonard, and Wendy Lyons went to Breitman's apartment (appropriately in 1984) in order to expel him from the Socialist Workers Party. It is not that his account is completely wrong—but I think it leaves readers with the wrong impression. He writes: "Breitman had been in poor health for some time. I can still see him wilting in front of us, holding his head, barely able to speak, never thinking he could be expelled from the SWP, the party he had been a founding member and central leader of for decades."[8] Of course, Sheppard was there, was able to observe how ill Breitman was, and was also able to observe Breitman's personal hurt over this shameful act. It is simply not true, however, that Breitman never thought he could be expelled. By that time, people all around him were being expelled, and it was clear to any knowledgeable person that the Barnes leadership had people like Breitman on a short list for expulsion from the SWP. George Breitman was a tough-minded revolutionary veteran who had been centrally involved in this factional struggle since 1981. He knew what Barnes had become and had been actively anticipating the possibility of the expulsion for some time. What Sheppard observed as "wilting" was more likely akin to nausea than surprise. Indeed, after this expulsion (and another aimed at George Weissman, who told them to go to hell and slammed the door in their faces), the three Barnesites "went to a bar and drank a number of martinis, ostensibly to celebrate but in reality to numb ourselves to the disgraceful thing we had done."[9]

Regardless of any errors and analytical or interpretive limitations, it seems to me that these two volumes are written by a person who is, to the best of his abilities, trying to be honest, trying to tell the truth, trying to get it right. Central to the meaning of his life is his ability to contribute to the building of a consciousness and a social movement that will ultimately be capable of helping a working-class majority to replace capitalism with socialism. This redemptive act—trying to explain what actually happened, so that the positive and negative lessons can be learned by future revolutionaries—is what gives *The Party* a value transcending any legitimate criticism that may be warranted.

The first volume provides a clear, vivid, accurate description of how many of us who joined the SWP actually perceived the organization we were joining. Despite our undoubtedly idealized notions of what that organization was, many of the positive qualities we perceived were actually there. And the glowing promise of what the SWP might become was not completely at odds with future possibilities.

Considering its organizational and political strengths, the intergenerational accumulation of political experience going back for decades, and the admirable qualities of many who were part of the SWP, it is conceivable that this organization of two thousand dedicated activists—if it had remained true to the best of what it was—might have doubled or tripled in size, and continued to play an outstanding role in the struggles for a better society down to the present time. SWPers played key roles in social movements and struggles, and in developing radical consciousness, that helped change the history of our time. Over the years, many former SWPers have continued to do so. It has not been demonstrated that some "iron law" existed to prevent such an organization from continuing to play such a role in the last two decades of the twentieth and into the twenty-first centuries.

This is what made the actual corruption and terrible crash of the party so devastating for so many of those who lived through the trauma. The reactions of different comrades varied. Some refused to believe the painful truths of what happened, and they remained members or uncritical sympathizers even as the organization shattered and dwindled. Among those who broke with the SWP, some sought an explanation for the debacle in some variety of "original sin"—presumably inherent in some deep flaw in the ideas of SWP founder James P. Cannon or Leon Trotsky or Vladimir Ilyich Lenin. Some concluded that they had, in fact, been profoundly mistaken in adhering to Marxism and believing that socialism is necessary or possible.

Trying to Understand

One of the interesting features of Sheppard's account is his return to, and straightforward defense of, those revolutionary orientations of Lenin, Trotsky, and Cannon that he had embraced in the late 1950s and early '60s, but which, as a Barnes lieutenant in the early 1980s, he had been inclined to bend and break. As already suggested, this helps give his account an elemental political coherence that may also have been essential to his ability (or inclination) to produce this account in the first place.

In a way related to this, for the most part Sheppard is not inclined to see seeds of future problems in the way oppositional groups were dealt with in the 1960s and 1970s. It is quite significant, however, that he acknowledges three errors in the way the SWP leadership handled these oppositions. One error involves a failure (contrary to genuine Leninist organizational practice) to include representatives of minority tendencies in the political leadership of the SWP, and a second involves a tendency to harden and exacerbate political differences with the dissidents—both of which did much to polarize attitudes and relationships. A third error—made in relation to the expulsion of the Internationalist Tendency—involves a blurring of the party's Control Commission with the party leadership when it was engaged in a fierce factional struggle. The function of the Control Commission was to handle questions having to do with internal functioning, discipline, and so on. Its authority depends on scrupulous fair-mindedness and neutrality, enabling it to defend organizational principles and membership rights, which is why Sheppard naturally gives the matter considerable weight.

Still, there is much in the earlier party leadership's handling of oppositionists that he defends. In regard to the 1974 "re-registration" expulsion of the Internationalist Tendency, advanced by the Control Commission, Sheppard gives a lengthy and detailed explanation of how and why it made sense. But the dialectics of reality means the same thing can have both positive and negative qualities. The negative flip side of the "re-registration" expulsion weakened the party. It helped make comrades with critical ideas less inclined to raise and press them, because to do so would "prove" that "they were on their way out" of the SWP, words that I heard more than once within the party's rank and file.

Actually, Sheppard himself had absorbed the same politically corrupting lesson, as he recounts in the second volume. He had instinctively understood, when he discovered some of his privately expressed criticisms had aroused Barnes's ire, that a failure to back off would have terrible consequences for him:

> I had devoted my life to building and leading the SWP. The prospect of being out of it was terrifying and almost inconceivable. I knew I would be shunned by my former comrades and closest friends, as well as by the membership at large that had looked up to me as a central leader and teacher for decades. Under this pressure, I now see, I did everything I could to please Jack in the (vain) hope I would be spared the axe.[10]

If a central leader such as Sheppard felt this, think of how the membership as a whole must have instinctively felt (covered over with plenty of rationalization, to be sure). This situation did not drop from the sky. The pre-existing internal culture of the SWP had to make possible this kind of development.

Sheppard also defends the Dobbs and Kerry leadership's tightening of party discipline through a 1965 document on organizational principles—though he gives a vague nod to the retired James P. Cannon's "Don't strangle the party" admonition from the same period.

One concept stressed in the 1965 document is "party loyalty"—and much of what Sheppard says in its defense is quite reasonable. "Loyalty to the party is the bedrock of democratic centralism," he writes, "which is democracy in decision-making and unity in action in carrying out decisions." In the very next breath, he emphasizes the very same point: "Loyalty to the party is the concept that the SWP is the party you build and defend no matter what your criticisms. It is the bedrock of party organization. Without loyalty to the party there can be no common ground for either democratic discussion or unity in action."[11]

The question can be raised, however, as to the specific criteria for determining such party loyalty. Is it disloyal to believe that a particular convention decision undermines the party's program and is contrary to its principles? Should someone who believes that the party program is in need of revision, in the light of new realities, be considered "disloyal" to that program? Who decides whether a member is disloyal? According to Sheppard, by the late 1970s Barnes believed (and others accepted) "that the leadership must be loyal to him personally and centered on him personally."[12] Those who didn't see things that way, and who disagreed with one or another perspective to which Barnes adhered, were viewed as politically incorrect, as possibly disloyal, and as probably "on their way out."

Another aspect of the internal culture of the SWP that may have contributed to the triumph of "Barnesism" is a certain narrowness in the way Marxism came to be engaged with. There was a tendency to be ingrown, to be dismissive of all Marxists whose Leninist-Trotskyist credentials were not clear and in order, and—with a self-assured arrogance—to be rigid and polemical in ways that Marxism was to be understood and applied.

The Marx who said "doubt everything" (and who freely made use of the ideas of "non-Marxist" and even bourgeois thinkers) was not held up as a model. There was a veering away from considering even such Marxists as Georg Lukács, Antonio Gramsci, E. P. Thompson, Paul Sweezy, C. L. R. James, Hal Draper, Harry Braverman, Sheila Rowbotham, and others. There were outstanding countertendencies, to be sure, that could be found in the thinking and writings of some figures—Joe Hansen, George Breitman, George Weissman, at times Cannon himself. But many members felt restraints on critical thinking, a concern to "get it right" (as defined by certain party authorities), a fear of going too far in thinking for one's self.

In Barry Sheppard's account, however, none of these factors—previous mishandling of oppositionists in the SWP, problematical organizational conceptions propagated by the Dobbs-Kerry leadership, limitations on critical thinking and on the way Marxism was understood and utilized by many in the party—explains what happened. And I would agree that, by themselves, they do not provide an adequate explanation.

The problem is, however, that the "deeper" explanation Sheppard provides is incredibly thin. There is an obligatory Marxist genuflection to the larger "objective" political conditions—failure of world revolution, failure of the radicalization process to sweep through the US working class as expected—and then Jack Barnes, an impressive person who lost his way, somehow assumes great psychological and organizational power over his comrades, becoming a cult figure and leads the party astray. Sheppard reflects:

> It would be naïve to think that the membership itself could resist this juggernaut. It could only have been stopped in the Political Committee itself. Jack couldn't do it—he didn't understand what he was fashioning. It was up to the rest of us on the Political Committee, but we failed. The responsibility is primarily mine, since I was the first to understand it, and next to Jack I had the greatest leadership authority.[13]

This remarkable passage raises more questions than it answers. For Sheppard to imply that only he could have saved the world revolution (or at least the revolutionary party) from Big Bad Barnes, but that he screwed up, places far too much blame on him, and it seems implausible, given his earlier explanation of his own vulnerability. Why did the entire Political Committee fail? Why was the membership itself incapable of facing and resolving the problem? If the answer to all of this was that there was a powerful and destructive cult of Jack Barnes, the question remains: why was there such a cult, how could it have arisen in the excellent party that Sheppard tells us about in volume one of *The Party*, with all the excellent traditions associated with Dobbs, Cannon, Trotsky, Lenin, and the Bolsheviks?

The Past and the Future

What strikes me as the missing piece in Sheppard's analysis has been put forward more than once (for example, in my review of the memoirs by Camejo and Evans).

For Marxists, there is a need to trace the answers to such riddles to a historical materialist exploration of broader and deeper cultural, social, and economic developments than can be provided by a focus on ideas and personalities. It is obvious that the ideas of Karl Marx, Rosa Luxemburg, Vladimir Ilyich Lenin, Leon Trotsky, James P. Cannon, and others who influenced revolutionary socialists in the United States cannot be understood without reference to this larger context that they were part of. This larger context involved a global mass workers' movement that evolved at least from the 1860s down to the Second World War, and that movement was shaped by larger social, economic, cultural, and political realities.

The impact of the Second World War, and the immense changes that followed in its wake, profoundly altered the social, economic, and cultural realities that had given rise to the workers' movement and its left wing, within which the ideas of the revolutionary Marxists had developed and made sense. Even though the words of the revolutionaries continued to be read and studied, the nature of the labor movement (which gave the words their distinctive meaning) qualitatively changed, fragmenting and eroding.

In the United States, capitalism generated a recomposition of the working class in a manner that increasingly de-radicalized the rank-and-file layers that had been the base of labor insurgencies from the time of the Knights of Labor down to the heroic struggles in the Congress of Industrial Organizations. It was within that broad working-class activist milieu that Socialist, Communist, and Trotskyist organizations had flourished, and within that context the earlier cadres of US Trotskyism had been formed and the political perspectives of American Trotskyism had practical meaning.

After the Second World War, the broader economic, social, and cultural context was changed, and in the 1950s and early 1960s, the shrinking number of US Trotskyists—despite their strength of character and ideas—had become relatively threadbare and brittle as a political force.

When new recruits began to flood into the ranks of the SWP in the 1960s and 1970s, they mostly came from the campuses, not the factories. They engaged with the writings of Lenin, Trotsky, and Cannon, but they did not automatically consider the disconnect between the revolutionary texts and the changed contexts. They came from a different experience and with a different consciousness. Important political work was done—especially in struggles against war, racism, and sexism—but the revolutionary working-class orientation that had been at the heart of American Trotskyism was understood and practiced in a different, more abstract, less vibrant manner than had been the case earlier.

This was inevitable, if one accepts the Marxist precept that being determines consciousness—how we live, what we actually experience, determines how we think. People from different realities will understand and apply the same ideas differently. In fact, some serious efforts to remain true to the old perspectives necessarily generated sectarian results. In my opinion, this is not because the old perspectives were inherently sectarian (on the whole, they were not), but because the context in which they had made sense no longer existed.

A majority of the youthful layer of US Trotskyists—although students and ex-students—were predominantly children of the blue-collar and white-collar working class. But they tended to see themselves, and to be seen, as "middle class" (especially since traditionally, before World War II, it was typically the children of "the upper and middle classes" who went to colleges and universities). Nor was there the broader labor-radical subculture that had existed from the 1860s to the 1940s. The actual working class and its consciousness had been evolving, since the 1950s, mostly without the benefit of such a subculture.

Nonetheless, there existed the conceptualization among SWPers that the Socialist Workers Party alone was the nucleus of what would become the mass revolutionary party of the working class. This had made sense in the 1930s and 1940s when (1) a mass workers' movement existed as a powerful force within the working class, (2) within that mass workers' movement there was a substantial left wing, and (3) in that left wing of the mass workers' movement there were three major currents—reformist-oriented Social Democrats, authoritarian-opportunist Stalinists, and revolutionary socialists influenced by Trotsky. Obviously, only the Trotskyists in that context had the capacity to provide *revolutionary* leadership to the working class, and in that context they also had a realistic possibility of doing so.

Just as obviously, however, the realities of the 1960s and 1970s were qualitatively different. The SWP's reasonable self-conceptualization in 1938 could not make the same kind of sense in 1978. It was disconnected from the real world.

If one was oblivious to how the realities of the past were qualitatively different from those of the present, as so many SWP members were, attempts to apply the old perspectives could be relevant only to the internal universe of a political sect, not to the actual lives of working people living and struggling in the larger society. It is within this framework that the decline of the Socialist Workers Party (as a Trotskyist organization) can best be understood. Within this context the previously discussed factors could assume decisive importance: rigidity in organizational and theoretical conceptions, limitations on critical thinking, growing intolerance toward oppositionists, the nurturing of an ingrown organizational subculture, the susceptibility of comrades to the development of cultism.

Our present-day reality in 2012 is as different from the 1960s as that decade was from the 1930s. Capitalist globalization has been generating economic and cultural crises and radicalizing discontent, revolutionary ferment, occupations, insurgencies. The decomposed working classes have been recomposing in ways that give new relevance to revolutionary Marxism. A labor-radical subculture has also been in the process of recomposing. New possibilities are emerging. This reality provides the vital context that gives Barry Sheppard's contribution particular resonance. He himself explains it quite well:

> I believe the worldwide crisis of the capitalist system that began in 2007 represents a massive attack on the working class. The drive by the government and the corporations to make the working people bear the burden of this crisis will impel new forms of struggle and organizations

to emerge. The rebuilding of a revolutionary socialist party is an urgent necessity to help lead this process as it unfolds. A new radicalization will develop, and we must coalesce a conscious Marxist party out of it and to lead it to victory.

I hope this political memoir will help in this process, both by preserving positive lessons and pointing to some things to avoid in the experience of the SWP. People from other traditions, new and old ones, will also contribute to this necessary rebirth.[14]

The rebirth that Sheppard anticipates is, in fact, being prepared by struggles in workplaces and communities throughout the United States. In a special appendix to the second volume of *The Party*, Sheppard provides "An Example of Work in the Unions," a fine account of the courageous and creative work of Caroline Lund, his beloved companion, a working-class militant in an auto plant and a dissident trade unionist in the United Auto Workers. Lund's work was cut short when she succumbed to ALS—amyotrophic lateral sclerosis (commonly known as Lou Gehrig's disease)—but her example will have value for activists prepared to continue and multiply such efforts to advance the consciousness and the struggles of the working class.

14

Ancestors and Descendants
of the Occupy Movement

The Occupy Wall Street Movement that blossomed in the autumn of 2011 spread far beyond New York City—to six hundred communities within the United States and in more than three hundred additional cities in eighty-two different countries. The focal point of protest was against the domination of the global economy, and its corresponding political structures, by a very small but very wealthy and powerful minority—it was commonly posed as a struggle against oppression by the 1% of the other 99% of the population, in the United States and globally. This remarkable movement involved many hundreds of thousands and had the support of millions.

In my native Pittsburgh, roughly four thousand marched in support of these issues, and then several hundred stalwarts occupied Mellon Park. The Pittsburgh occupation continued until early February 2012, when the park was peacefully vacated. For a few months more, the Occupy movement continued to function. Afterward, the politically diverse layer of activists involved in Occupy Pittsburgh continued to be involved in a variety of efforts, including a broad range of economic justice, human rights, antiracist, and antiwar activities.

There are already a number of books providing information on such developments in the United States as a whole, and beyond. And, of course, there is still a considerable amount of information on the Internet.[1] The occupation sites in Pittsburgh and various other cities became centers for innumerable political meetings and assemblies, the organization of many protest activities, and a variety of teach-ins, forums, and other educational activities, and seemingly never-ending and animated discussions among many thousands of individuals.

The first item below was an educational talk for Occupy Boston's ongoing Howard Zinn Lecture Series; I gave it again, slightly modified, at an Occupy Pittsburgh teach-in held at the United Steel Workers international headquarters.

The second item attempts to sketch a Marxist take on the Occupy movement. The various organizations of the US Left—all of which were quite small compared to the huge numbers involved in Occupy—sought to relate to these amazing developments, and there were differences regarding how to do this most intelligently and

235

effectively. Some argued that all the socialist groups should set aside their differences, fuse into a single unified party, and help to provide revolutionary leadership for the Occupy movement. In my article—which first appeared in the February 16, 2012, issue of Links: International Journal for Socialist Renewal, *a widely read online publication—I also explained why I disagreed with that course of action, and what I thought was a more reasonable approach—*P.L.

I. THE ANCESTORS (2011)

As someone who has been substantially involved in Occupy Pittsburgh, and who has recently returned from London, where I was able to rally with sisters and brothers from the London Occupation (in the face of an enormous police confrontation), it is a genuine pleasure and honor for me to have an opportunity to speak with activists who are part of Occupy Boston.

In London, I heard the working-class singer Billy Bragg being joined by many others in the crowd to sing a wonderful song about the Diggers, an extremely radical movement that was part of the English Revolution of the 1640s. I think it is a great source of strength to be able to draw from one's own revolutionary traditions, from our own history, as we engage in present-day struggles for radical social change.

"We are the 99%" is the wonderful slogan of our movement—which recognizes that the wealthy 1% that controls the economy and, for all practical purposes, that controls the government of our country, has interests that are fundamentally different from ours. Our struggle is to replace the tyranny of the 1% with a deep and genuine democracy—rule by the people—in which the free development of each person will be the condition for the free development of everyone. We seek a community, animated by liberty and justice for all, and animated by what some would call a spirit of brotherly and sisterly love.

This goal will not be achieved quickly or easily but only by a sustained, massive, multifaceted, powerful social movement. I believe that in order to make our movement as strong and effective as it needs to be, we need to explore and learn from experiences of the past—from struggles and social movements that have actually brought about changes for the better in our country.

It is altogether appropriate to start our exploration with the words of Howard Zinn. "Democracy does not come from the top, it comes from the bottom," Zinn tells us at the beginning of his wonderful film *The People Speak.* "The mutinous soldiers, the angry women, the rebellious Native Americans, the working people, the agitators, the antiwar protesters, the socialists and anarchists and dissenters of all kinds—the troublemakers, yes, the people who have given us what liberty and democracy we have."

These splendid troublemakers that Zinn tells us about were not the entire 99% of their time—they were a militant minority who fought for the interests of the 99%, and who did that by reaching out to persuade their sisters and brothers to join them in the struggle for a better world, and to include more and more and more of them in the struggle, a struggle taking place under the shadow of what some refer to as "globalization," dominated by multinational corporations that seek to amass huge profits for the 1% at the expense of the rest of us.

Radical Social Movements of the Past

Back in the 1880s, when labor activists were founding the American Federation of Labor (AFL), they explained in the preamble of their constitution: "A struggle is going on in the nations of the civilized world between the oppressors and the oppressed of all countries, a struggle between capital and labor, which must grow in intensity from year to year and work disastrous results to the toiling millions of all nations if [they are] not combined for mutual protection and benefit."

This is more true now than it was 125 years ago. We must join together—the many millions—to resist and overcome our oppression and exploitation.

The occupation movement that has swept through our country—that millions of us are part of and identify with—consists, of course, of more than those of us who have been able to sleep and eat and live at the various occupation sites. We are many, and our ideas and aspirations are shared by many, many more in our country. According to the polls recently published in the *New York Times*, about 25 percent of the people in the United States oppose what we stand for, and about 45 percent agree with our ideas, with the other 30 percent not yet knowing enough to decide. It seems to me a worthy goal for our movement is to make that 45 percent solid, add to that as much of the 30 percent as possible, and even win over some of the critical 25 percent.

I think we can learn something of value in the history of earlier social movements. In what follows, I will offer the words from some past leaders of the labor movement and the civil rights movement.

But right off the bat, we need to be careful about what we mean by "leaders." As the great socialist and union organizer Eugene Victor Debs put it:

> I am not a labor leader; I do not want you to follow me or anyone else; if you are looking for a Moses to lead you out of this capitalist wilderness, you will stay right where you are. I would not lead you into the promised land if

I could, because if I led you in, some one else would lead you out. You must use your heads as well as your hands, and get yourself out of your present condition; as it is now the capitalists use your heads and your hands.

Many years later, Ella Baker—who worked with the NAACP, the Southern Christian Leadership Conference, and the Student Nonviolent Coordinating Committee—explained her own leadership role in a way that Debs would have liked:

You didn't see me on television, you didn't see news stories about me. The kind of role that I tried to play was to pick up pieces or put together pieces out of which I hoped organization might come. My theory is, strong people don't need strong leaders.

Genuine leaders are those who help more and more people among the 99% to think critically and organize themselves effectively. That is a very radical, revolutionary notion. And Ella Baker was a revolutionary. She emphasized that racial integration by itself was not an adequate goal. "In order for us as poor and oppressed people to become part of a society that is meaningful," she explained, "the system under which we now exist has to be radically changed . . . It means facing a system that does not lend itself to your needs and devising means by which you change that system." What Baker is describing is a power struggle in which the 99% are freed, in increasing measure and eventually completely, from the oppressive power of the 1%.

Related to these insights are the additional comments of A. Philip Randolph, who played a central role in both the labor and the civil rights movements. "Power and pressure are at the foundation of the march of social justice and reform. . . . Power and pressure do not reside in the few, an intelligentsia, [but instead] they lie in and flow from the masses," he stressed, adding: "Power is the active principle of . . . the organized masses, the masses united for a definite purpose."

This idea was developed with special eloquence by Martin Luther King Jr., and it is worth giving attention to how he put it. Here are his words:

The plantation and ghetto were created by those who had power, both to confine those who had no power and to perpetuate their powerlessness. The problem of transforming the ghetto, therefore, is a problem of power—confrontation of the forces of power demanding change and the forces of power dedicated to the preserving of the status quo. Now power properly understood is nothing but the ability to achieve purpose. It is the strength required to bring about social, political and economic change.

Explicitly drawing from the experience of the labor movement, King emphasized:

> Power is the ability to make the most powerful ... say 'Yes' when they want to say 'No.' That's power. . . . Power at its best is love implementing the demands of justice, and justice at its best is power correcting everything that stands against love. . . . Let us be dissatisfied until the tragic walls that separate the outer city of wealth and comfort and the inner city of poverty and despair shall be crushed by the battering rams of the forces of justice.

One aspect of these comments from King involved a belief in the need for a radical, even revolutionary, change in the system—what we saw Ella Baker also calling for. And like Baker, like A. Philip Randolph, like Gene Debs and others we are looking at, King was convinced that the capitalist system, controlled by the top 1%, needed to be replaced with political and economic rule by the 99%.

His wife, Coretta Scott King, later recalled that "within the first month or so of our meeting," in 1952, King was talking to her "about working within the framework of democracy to move us toward a kind of socialism," arguing that "a kind of socialism has to be adopted by our society because the way it is, it's simply unjust." As she elaborated: "Democracy means equal justice, equity in every aspect of our society," and she noted that her husband "knew that the basic problem in our society had to do with economic justice, or . . . the contrast of wealth between the haves and the have-nots."

Reform and Revolution

A significant difference between the radicalism of the labor and civil rights movements and the radicalism of our own occupation movement is that ours—unlike theirs—does not at present have a practical, immediately winnable demand or set of demands. The civil rights movement demanded (and eventually won) an end to Jim Crow segregation laws and the right of African Americans to vote in the Southern states. The trade union movement demanded employer recognition of the unions, plus higher wages, a shorter workday, and improved working conditions.

I want to return to that question of our occupation movement not having practical demands, but first I want to point out a problem with narrowing down the struggle solely to so-called "practical demands."

In fact, the leadership of the old American Federation of Labor tended to narrow the whole struggle down to such "pure and simple" practicality.

Pennsylvania Federation of Labor president James Maurer (himself a dedicated socialist) left us this excerpt of one of AFL president Samuel Gompers's speeches:

> If a workingman gets a dollar and a half for 10 hours' work, he lives up to that standard of a dollar and a half, and he knows that a dollar seventy-five would improve his standard of living, and he naturally strives to get that dollar and seventy-five. After that he wants two dollars and more time for leisure, and he struggles to get it. Not satisfied with two dollars he wants more; not only two and a quarter, but a nine-hour workday. And so he will keep on getting more and more until he gets it all or the full value of all he produces.

Despite rhetoric that retained something of the ardor and implications associated with the old revolutionary orientation in the AFL preamble, a growing number of AFL leaders—including Gompers himself—began to pull in a different direction that enabled them to adapt to the prejudices of some skilled workers (against the unskilled, against new immigrants, against Blacks and Asians and other people of color, against female wage-workers) and also to make far-reaching compromises with some of the more astute representatives of the capitalist system. Much of the labor movement became moderate, conservative, undemocratic, and corrupt.

Such things—rooted in the disconnect between the original sweeping ideals and radical-democratic commitments on one end and the narrower day-to-day practical struggles on the other—contributed to the decline of the spirit and the power of unions in this country.

In stark contrast to this was the uncompromising radicalism of the Industrial Workers of the World (IWW), which in 1905 declared:

> The working class and the employing class have nothing in common. There can be no peace so long as hunger and want are found among millions of the working people and the few, who make up the employing class, have all the good things of life. Between these two classes a struggle must go on until the workers of the world organize as a class, take possession of the means of production, abolish the wage system, and live in harmony with the Earth.

IWW organizer Elizabeth Gurley Flynn explained what she and other radical labor organizers saw as the necessary link between practical struggles and revolutionary spirit:

What is a labor victory? I maintain that it is a twofold thing. Workers must gain economic advantage, but they must also gain revolutionary spirit, in order to achieve a complete victory. For workers to gain a few cents more a day, a few minutes less a day, and go back to work with the same psychology, the same attitude toward society is to achieve a temporary gain and not a lasting victory. For workers to go back with a class-conscious spirit, with an organized and determined attitude toward society means that even if they have made no economic gain, they have the possibility of gaining in the future. In other words, a labor victory must be economic, and it must be revolutionizing.

Vision and Organization

This outlook animated many of the organizers and activists in the three big general strikes of 1934—in Toledo, Minneapolis, and San Francisco—that during the Great Depression helped pave the way for the Congress of Industrial Organizations. These three victories rocked the labor movement, particularly due to the revolutionary orientation of the strikes' leadership.

"Our policy was to organize and build strong unions so workers could have something to say about their own lives and assist in changing the present order into a socialist society," Minneapolis strike leader Vincent Raymond Dunne matter-of-factly commented. On the West Coast, Harry Bridges, heading up the great longshoremen's strike, offered the view that "the capitalistic form of society . . . means the exploitation of a lot of people for a profit and a complete disregard of their interests for that profit, [and] I haven't much use for that." Coming out of the Toledo struggle, A. J. Muste commented:

[I]n every strike situation, the policy of drawing in the broadest forces—all the unions, unemployed organizations, political parties and groups—must be carried out in order to break down trade union provincialism; to politicalize the struggle; develop class consciousness; face the workers with the problems of conflict with capitalist governmental agencies, etc.

Each of these strikes—and many others during the 1930s—was successful because it benefited from significant backup (a rich pool of experience, skills, analyses, and other resources) from a variety of organizations and institutions.

The same holds true for the later civil rights movement. Aldon D. Morris, in his fine study *The Origins of the Civil Rights Movement*, has emphasized the role of what he calls "movement halfway houses." He describes these as having "a relative isolation from the larger society" and not having a mass membership, but as "developing a battery of social change resources such as skilled activists, tactical knowledge, media contacts, workshops, knowledge of past movements and a vision of a future society."

Among those institutions that he identifies in this manner, and as playing a vital role in the origins of the civil rights movement, are the religious-pacifist Fellowship of Reconciliation, the radical educational center known as the Highlander Folk School (which also played a role in labor efforts of the 1930s), and the Southern Conference Educational Fund. Organizations and parties of the left (particularly those of the Socialists and Communists) also played a significant role.

This was also very much the case in the union struggles of the 1930s. A veteran of the Women's Emergency Brigade, which emerged during the great Flint sit-down strike of 1937 and helped to build the United Auto Workers, once commented: "I know that there was a Socialist Party and Communist Party helping to organize. Although I never belonged to a Party, I feel that had it not been for the education and the know-how that they gave us, we wouldn't have been able to do it."

The Meaning of Occupy

Before summing up some of what emerges from these explorations, I want to come back to the point raised a few minutes ago in these remarks—the lack of specific, practical demands in today's occupation movement. This has been a focal point for some critics of our movement.

But it is not clear to me that this is a fatal flaw. It seems to me that we can, in fact, find precedents in the struggles of the past. I want to give one example.

In 1877, there was a massive labor uprising of railroad workers and working-class sympathizers and communities spanning a number of cities including Chicago, Baltimore, Pittsburgh (where there was a big explosion), St. Louis, New York, and Martinsburg, West Virginia. As the experienced labor activist J. P. McDonnell explained: "The strike is a result of desperation. There was no concerted action at the start. It spread because the workmen of Pittsburgh felt the same oppression that was felt by the workmen of West Virginia." Local police, state militia, and federal troops were used to violently put down the rebellion.

Even though it did not have focused practical demands, the uprising gave vibrant expression to the rage and indignation of the working class over the assaults on their living standards, their dignity, and their communities by the railroad corporations and other industrial robber barons who ruled the US economy. The uprising was defeated, but the working class was not demoralized, but energized. According to Samuel Gompers, "The railroad strike of 1877 was the tocsin [the alarm bell] that sounded a ringing message of hope to us all."

Coming out of that amazing and transformative experience was a new mood, a new consciousness, a new politics, and new layers of organizers and activists who went on to build powerful movements, organizations, and struggles on behalf of the working-class majority over the coming decades. And that is true of our own rebellion, this amazing uprising represented by the Occupy movement. Dozens and hundreds and thousands and more people involved in our movement all across the United States are helping change the consciousness and politics of our country and will be playing an essential role in the struggles and the victories of the future.

In those future struggles, we can learn much from the past movements that we have been focusing on here. Those who were most effective and were able, first of all, to remain true to the struggle for liberation had a clear understanding of the existing power structure and a vision of an alternative that would give political and economic power to the people.

There was an understanding that the conscious, militant minority must not set itself up as self-proclaimed leaders or condescending saviors. Nor is the job of the radical minority to develop ingrown "perfect" communities that will be a present-day alternative to the corrupt order of the wealthy and powerful 1%—there is a crying need for such an alternative, and that is what the radical minority must struggle for, but the goal cannot be achieved if the minority focuses on cultivating its own perfection. Nor can we afford to become disunited so that some fragments of the 99% seek to realize their individual desires or improve their material conditions, while forgetting about the needs and the dignity and the rights of all.

Instead, we must be reaching out to help spread consciousness and skills among more and more people—to help build mass struggles in which ever-larger segments of the oppressed majority will develop the ability to push back various aspects of their own oppression, ultimately liberating themselves and all of society from the power of the wealthy, profiteering 1%. To help sustain such efforts, we must build institutions and organizations that can make available social change resources such as skilled activists, tactical knowledge, media contacts, workshops, knowledge of past movements, and a vision of a future society.

There is a need for practical struggles and demands that can win relatively modest, but often life-enhancing, improvements in the here and now. But no less important is the need to strengthen the spirit of those who must continue the struggle—giving people more than short-term improvements, giving them a clear understanding of what's wrong with the status quo, giving them skills and inspiration and motivation to do something about that.

In explaining that "power concedes nothing without a demand," the great antislavery leader Frederick Douglass added an incredibly important insight. "Find out just what a people will submit to," he pointed out, "and you have found out the exact amount of injustice and wrong which will be imposed upon them." He concluded: "The limits of tyrants are prescribed by the endurance of those whom they oppress."

Flowing out of our occupation movement must be ongoing efforts to build the consciousness, the understanding, the organizational skills, and the capacity for unified and uncompromising struggle that will put an end to such submission and tyranny, giving greater and greater understanding and strength to the majority of our people. That must be the goal of our movement.

II. Revolutionary Organization and the "Occupy Movement" (2012)

The Occupy movement has been having a profound impact on the socialist left in the United States. I want to share some information on this, focusing on my own experience, and relate it to broader issues of Marxism and organization that I have been engaged with for some time.

In my native Pittsburgh, members of the International Socialist Organization, the Party for Socialism and Liberation, the Workers International League, and Committees of Correspondence, plus a number of independent socialists have been active (some more active, some less) in the Occupy movement. I know similar things can be said of the Occupy movement in a number of other cities. One can easily find substantial reports, animated discussions, and analyses about the Occupy movement in publications and on websites associated with the International Socialist Organization (ISO), Solidarity, Socialist Action, Committees of Correspondence, Freedom Road Socialist Organization, Socialist Party, Socialist Alternative, Workers International League, Workers World Party, the Party for Socialism and Liberation—and I am confident that the list is not complete. All of this is easily accessible online. And all of these organizations, I think, are wrestling with the question of what new tasks are raised for us by the Occupy movement in which many of us are actively involved.

There are some socialist activists who have called for us all to merge together in a single revolutionary organization, implying that this would make us more effective at this key moment. Based on my own experience, it seems obvious to me that this would be a serious mistake. Here I will argue that there is a better approach, consistent both with my experience and with a party-building perspective that I have been writing about for some time.

A Unified Revolutionary Party?

In Pittsburgh, members of the Party for Socialism and Liberation, the Workers International League, and my own ISO are not in the same organization. This has not prevented us from working quite well together in antiwar, pro–public transit, and Occupy-related struggles. If instead—in an effort to create a single socialist group—we were enmeshed in struggles with each other over what should be our common political program, how we should define the very conception of socialism, et cetera, I think our ability to work effectively would be undermined. Now we can agree to disagree on certain principled questions (to be discussed and debated in appropriate contexts) while forming a positive working relationship around questions where we stand on common ground.

Ultimately, people from these groups may come together in the same revolutionary socialist organization—just as many Bolsheviks, for example, found themselves together in the Russian Communist Party with comrades who had been Mensheviks, Left-Socialist Revolutionaries, Bundists, anarchists, and others. There was a similar coming-together process in the formation of the early Communist movement in the United States and other countries. Momentous experiences and historical forces have a way of bringing revolutionaries from different backgrounds together. Such forces are at work, and such experiences are shaping up, that can bring such an outcome to the United States in the future.

Many of us on the US socialist left agree on the need for such an organization. A working-class revolution and socialist transformation in the United States will not come about spontaneously. It will come about only if knowledgeable activists and skilled organizers, dedicated to such goals, work very hard to bring them about. This would add up to a US equivalent to what Bolshevism was in Russia. Such a thing cannot be forced through cobbling together different socialist groups. Nor will it be a replica of Russian Bolshevism. But the effort to bring such a thing into existence can be strengthened, as we are intimately involved in the struggles of our time, by critically engaging with the ideas and experiences of Lenin, Trotsky, Rosa Luxemburg, Antonio Gramsci, and other revolutionary Marxists from the twentieth century's early communist movement, as well as by the history of US class struggles and revolutionary traditions.

As we engage in the struggles of today and tomorrow, the theory and history of those who went before should be pondered and shared as widely and deeply as possible. Those who are growing into effective activists and organizers in the mass struggles unfolding in our time can benefit from this. Such activists, and the growing number of workers and oppressed people who increasingly share in their vision, also absorbing their knowledge and political skills, can grow into a powerful force to bring about the political, social, and economic transformation that we need. As a mass phenomenon, this becomes part of a broad labor-radical subculture, nourishing a revolutionary class consciousness that will animate a substantial and increasingly influential layer of the working class—which constitutes a working-class "vanguard" that is the only serious basis for the US equivalent of Bolshevism.

As Lenin explained in "*Left-Wing" Communism, an Infantile Disorder*, any effort to create a cohesive, disciplined revolutionary party in the absence of such a development will result in phrase-mongering and pretentious clowning destined to fall flat on its face. (Many of us have certainly seen examples of that!) Yet as Lenin, Trotsky, Luxemburg, and others have also emphasized, it also takes the dynamic and creative interplay of genuine mass struggles and a serious party of the socialist vanguard to bring about the revolutionary power shift, the radical democracy, and the socialist reconstruction of society that are so badly needed. That is the goal, and its realization transcends the current goals of all the organizations on the US socialist left.

Today there is no Leninist party in the United States. There is no "embryo" or "nucleus" of such a party in our country (although some would-be Leninist groups would not agree with this claim, because they think they are that). The responsibility of all is to help create the preconditions for the crystallization of a labor-radical subculture, a revolutionary class consciousness, a mass vanguard layer of the working class, an accumulation of experience and understanding, and cadres that will bring into being an organization, a genuine party, that can help usher in what Eugene V. Debs once called "the third American revolution."[2] The coming-together of a revolutionary workers' party is not possible now—the effort to force that into being, whether through self-appointment of one or another small group or through some hothouse mergers of small groups, will be counterproductive.

For now, we must immerse ourselves in the struggles of our time, create united fronts of socialists and others, carry out serious education on what actually happened in struggles of the past, and engage in the serious-minded discussion and debate necessary for continuing political clarification. Debate and united struggle can go together. In 1905, Lenin called for "a fighting unity" of socialist and revolutionary groups against the tsarist regime while urging Russian activists "not to spoil things by vainly trying to lump together heterogeneous elements. We shall inevitably have to . . . march separately, but we can . . . strike together more than once and particularly now." Insisting that "in the interests of the revolution our ideal should by no means be that all parties, all trends and shades of opinion fuse in a revolutionary chaos," Lenin emphasized that "only full clarity and definiteness in their mutual relations and in their attitude toward the revolutionary proletariat can ensure maximum success for the revolutionary movement."[3]

The Challenge of Occupy

As one who has been immersed in Occupy Pittsburgh from its inception, I am seeking to apply this orientation to the realities around me. Along with many others in this remarkable movement, I have been engaged in an intensive thinking and rethinking process, finding the new experiences challenging and changing me in multiple ways. There is much that I still must process before drawing all of the conclusions that are inherent in the unfolding reality of Occupy. But there are several things I am certainly able to state for purposes of this discussion.

The statement of principles adopted by Occupy Pittsburgh in November 2011 (consistent with those adopted by Occupy Wall Street in New York) gives a sense of the nature of our struggle:

We, the individuals of Occupy Pittsburgh, have assembled to resist and abolish the political, social, and economic injustices that confront us and our communities.

We recognize that the current system encourages large corporations and the wealthy 1% to wield excessive influence over our political and legal systems, economy and culture.

We recognize that this prevents genuine democracy and deprives us of our liberties, sacrifices our health, safety and well-being, threatens our relationship with the rest of the world, has destroyed and continues to destroy cultures and peoples throughout the world, and critically compromises the ecological systems that sustain life itself.

We are a nonviolent, decentralized movement working to create a just society.

We are claiming a space for public dialogue and the practice of direct democracy for the purpose of generating and implementing solutions accessible to everyone.

To this end, we are exercising our rights to assemble peacefully and to speak freely, thus demonstrating our commitment to the long work of transforming the structures that produce and sustain these injustices.

Also to that end, we are working against all forms of inequality and discrimination including those based on age, ability, diagnosis, size, religion or lack thereof, class, culture, immigration status, nationality, history of incarceration, housing status, race, color, ethnicity, indigenous status, sex, gender identity and sexual orientation.

We stand in solidarity with those who have come before us, in Pittsburgh and elsewhere, who have fought for political, social and economic justice.

We are united, in strength and courage with the Occupations around the world. We are your next-door neighbors. We are your friends. We are your relatives. We are the 99%.

The Occupy movement, in its opposition of the 99% to the 1%, creates, in highly popularized form, a class analysis that is consistent with Marxism. The modern-day system of corporate rule and exploitation overseen by the wealthy 1% (and their servants in the upper fringe of the 99%) is what we mean by "capitalism." The heart and soul, and great majority, of the 99% are the "working class" (blue-collar, white-collar, unemployed, et cetera). The goal of establishing the democratic control of the 99% over our economic and political life is what we understand as "socialism." This actually reflects radical traditions that run deep in the history of the United States.

It was, for example, Martin Luther King Jr. who emphasized that the triple evils of racism, exploitation, and war are interrelated and deeply rooted in the very nature of the US socioeconomic system, insisting that the "whole structure must be changed . . . American must be born again!"[4] What the Occupy movement has done, and the way it has defined itself, has resonated powerfully among millions of people in the United States. We in the Occupy movement have a responsibility to be true to that, and to sustain and expand it to the best of our abilities. What we are about, as defined in the Occupy Pittsburgh statement, involves winning the overwhelming majority of the 99% in support of and struggle for the commitments and goals of replacing the power of the 1% with the power of the 99%.

Socialists involved in Occupy have a responsibility to explain how we see things—that this movement of and for the 99% is basically a *working-class movement*, and that its stated goal of waging a struggle for universal human rights, a central aspect of which is economic justice (the possibility of a decent life for each and every person), is—along with the notion of rule by the people over our economic and political life—what socialism is all about. Moreover, our Occupy movement represents a life-giving revitalization of the labor movement as a whole.

In the United States, the trade union movement has often been mistakenly identified as "the labor movement," but it is only a defensive fragment of the labor movement. Once upon a time, the trade unions were built by radicals and revolutionaries—varieties of socialists and communists and anarchists and other labor radicals (some of whose voices can be found, for example, in the anthology *Work and Struggle*).[5] They provided militancy, broad social vision, and tough-minded democracy that gave life to the unions. They also built mass movements for social reforms (universal suffrage, an eight-hour workday, an end to child labor, universal public education, women's rights, opposition to racism, and more), and some of them labored to build working-class political parties, although this had much less success in the United States than in other countries. A full-fledged labor movement consists of all these elements.

Since the 1930s and 1940s, there has been a narrowing of the labor movement to the trade unions alone, accompanied by a marginalization of the radicals and revolutionaries, and an accommodation with the corporations and the pro-capitalist state (and entanglement with the pro-capitalist Democratic Party). Over the years, the spirit has increasingly gone out of this fragmented labor movement, with hierarchy and bureaucracy crowding out rank-and-file democracy, and with workers feeling increasingly alienated from this fragment of a movement that claims to speak for them. Much of the current union leadership recognizes that it is caught in a dead end. Because unions are facing an extended onslaught from the big-business corporations of capitalism, combined with the recent economic downturn, it seems unlikely that they will be able to survive unless there is a change in the nature and orientation of the labor movement. More than anything that the union leadership has been able to generate in recent decades, the Occupy movement has powerfully placed issues of economic justice in the national consciousness and mainstream political dialogue. It has tilted political reality in a way that opens up new possibilities and new, life-giving spirit for organized labor.

This helps to explain the unprecedented support by organized labor for the radicalism of the Occupy movement, and a strong trend within Occupy toward working together with unions and certain reform struggles (for health care, public transport, education, et cetera), which helps generate a larger, more diverse, multifaceted working-class movement. One of the strengths of Occupy Pittsburgh has been its commitment to a close working relationship with the unions and other elements of the broadly defined working class of the Pittsburgh area. This defines the primary responsibility of socialists in the Occupy movement: helping to build a sense of class consciousness and class struggle, helping to nurture an undercurrent of socialist consciousness, helping to advance the possibility of a mass socialist consciousness and mass socialist movement in the foreseeable future, connected with real struggles for economic justice through direct confrontation with the wealthy 1% of corporate capitalism.

We have been subjected to evictions of our Occupy encampments from the public spaces (Pittsburgh, one of the last, being finally dislodged several days before this writing), where we directly and vibrantly confronted the authority of the capitalist power structure. There are important challenges we face while seeking to reorient to the new situation.

One challenge is represented by two factions among some of our anarchist brothers and sisters, some of whom want to build more or less utopian "communities" and activist "families" as alternatives to the status quo (apart from both the 1% and from the 99%), others inclined to break with the unions and mount masked minority confrontations against the 1%, independently of the 99%. In either case, the resulting isolation of Occupy activists, it seems clear, would be bound to marginalize our movement.[6]

A very different challenge comes from powerful forces—particularly among our trade union allies—that will be pushing in this presidential election year to draw all activism into the camp of the pro-capitalist Democratic Party. "There is one common feature in the development, or more correctly the degeneration, of modern trade union organizations in the entire world," Trotsky noted as World War II was beginning to unfold. "It is their drawing closely to and growing together with the state power."

His analysis is worth lingering over: "They have to confront a centralized capitalist adversary, intimately bound up with state power. . . . In the eyes of the bureaucracy of the trade union movement the chief task lies in 'freeing' the state from the embrace of capitalism, in weakening its dependence on trusts [the big-business corporations], in pulling it over to their side."[7] But the state in capitalist society is essentially an instrument for preserving the exploitative system of capitalism. Likewise, the presumed means for winning this capitalist instrument to "our side"—the Democratic Party—is absolutely committed to preserving the capitalist system. Given these realities, subordinating our struggle to a hoped-for Democratic Party victory is a highly dubious pathway for Occupy and the working class as a whole.

Such challenges are hardly new. Rosa Luxemburg noted the two dangers many years ago: "One is the loss of mass character; the other, the abandonment of its goal. One is the danger of sinking back to the condition of a sect; the other, the danger of becoming a movement of bourgeois [capitalist] social reform."[8]

This challenging moment is exactly the wrong time for socialists to channel their attention and energies into the project of merging into a multi-tendency socialist organization. If all the members of all the socialist organizations in the United States were prepared to adhere to some ideal program and orientation free of "non-essentials" and sectarianism, and were able to do that quickly and efficiently, then such a notion could be considered reasonable. But to state the matter like that is to highlight its impossibility. On the other hand, I know from my experience that the kind of "fighting unity" Lenin spoke of—involving cooperation among members of different socialist groups, and united front–type efforts—is something that is definitely possible and fruitful.

What we need to build with others, in this context, is an increasingly influential, dynamic, explicitly working-class current in the Occupy movement, a community-labor Occupy, which is both inclusive and politically independent. "The Occupy moment" may pass before the end of 2012. But for now socialists must remain committed to Occupy, and to helping draw its energies and activists into mass struggles of and for the working class, around issues of transit, health care, education, housing, jobs, economic justice, environmental preservation, opposition to war, and so on, at the same time doing what we can to build class consciousness and socialist consciousness.

In this context, and in the future struggles, socialists and their various organizations will have an opportunity to help create the preconditions for a unified revolutionary party. This will involve the development of struggles and a subculture that will help bring into being a class-conscious layer of the working class. It will also involve the accumulation and education and development of cadres, the organizing experience and testing of political perspectives, the united front efforts and more that will create the possibilities for the creation of a mass revolutionary party of the working class. Many of us, currently in one or another organization or in no organization at the present, will be part of that.

Lenin, Luxemburg, Trotsky

In the face of new and challenging realities, it seems to me that it makes sense to share and make use of the ideas of Lenin, Luxemburg, Trotsky, and others associated with their revolutionary Marxist orientation. Their theorizations are based on a considerable amount of political experience accumulated by the global labor movement, buttressed by analyses coming from some of the finest minds associated with the revolutionary tradition. Given the persisting dynamics of global capitalism, the Marxism of Lenin, Luxemburg, Trotsky, and others from the early Communist movement continue to have considerable resonance for our own time. The Occupy movement, and the larger revitalized working-class movement that is struggling to come into being, can be helped enormously if revolutionary socialists engage in critically and creatively applying our perspectives to the realities around us, now and within the next phase of Occupy and working-class struggles.

Acknowledgments

I am pleased to have the opportunity to draw together this set of historical writings. It presents much of what I have done, and have been doing, over the years as a historian, teacher, writer, and activist. I especially appreciate the commitment of friends at Haymarket Books (particularly Anthony Arnove and Ahmed Shawki) to the publication of this collection. Thanks are also due to Brian Baughan, Nisha Bolsey, Rachel Cohen, Julie Fain, Dao X. Tran, and others at Haymarket who worked with me to turn the manuscript into a book.

I must also thank my patient and loving and incredibly supportive friend Nancy Ferrari for being all of those things and more.

My family has been an integral part of my immersion in "Left Americana": my parents, Gaston Le Blanc and Shirley Harris Le Blanc, were part of the leftwing of the labor movement and inspired me, and my sisters, Patty Le Blanc and Nora Le Blanc, shared the experience. My father's brother, Adrian Le Blanc, was also part of the scene, as have been my Aunt Eve and my cousins Judy, Daniel, and Adrian Nicole. And then there are my amazing sons, my good comrade Jonah McAllister-Erickson (and his wonderful companion Jessica Benner) and my beloved Gabriel Le Blanc who died as this book was being prepared for publication, and who with Rima Le Blanc brought into being the truly spectacular Sophia Noelle and Zachary. I must also acknowledge a long-departed Russian-Jewish immigrant garment worker who gave me my first labor history book, *Labor's Untold Story* (by Richard O. Boyer and Herbert M. Morais), with the inscription: "From your great-grandpa, Harry Brodsky." Harry's artistic son George, and the pioneering social worker George married, Rose Margolis Brodsky, were also important to me

Among my many comrades in the Trotskyist movement of long ago, those who mentored me in ways that have had special impact include Frank Lovell, Sarah Lovell, George Breitman, Evelyn Sell, and Ruth Querio. Also—earlier—there was Jeremy Brecher, who introduced me, and more or less recruited me, to Students for a Democratic Society, and some people whom I got to know only much later but who were doing things that powerfully inspired me when I was a teenager: Joel Geier, Rachelle Horowitz, Norman Hill, Velma Hill, David McReynolds. Another mentor under whom I worked in the American Friends Service Committee was the truly admirable Allan Brick, a disciple of A. J. Muste. Also central to my development was my connection with Paul Sweezy and Harry Magdoff.

Among those who were especially important in actually teaching me about the history of the United States, at the University of Pittsburgh, were David Montgomery, Larry Glasco, Van Beck Hall, Richard N. Hunt, Peter Karsten, and Dick Oestreicher. Important for me as well was my association with the contradictory and inspiring Philip S. Foner (who used some of my stuff—but also gave me so much). A battalion of pals and associates with whom I have journeyed, at one point or another, in more or less academic and/ or literary but often also activist explorations in the history of "Left Americana" include these individuals: Joe Auciello, Tom Bias, Steve Bloom, Paul Buhle, Sheila Cohen, Tim Davenport, Kipp Dawson, the late David Demarest, Angela Dillard, Dianne Feeley, David Finkel, Dan Georgakas, the late Russ Gibbons, Michael Goldfield, Al Hart, John Hinshaw, Peter Hudis, Brian Jones, Dan La Botz, Bruce Levine, Stephanie Luce, Charlie McCollester, Mark McColloch, Scott McLemee, Kim Moody, the late Bruce C. Nelson, Manny Ness, Bill Onasch, Bryan Palmer, Bill Pelz, Andy Pollack, Russell Pryor, Peter Rachleff, Carl Redwood, Dave Riehle, Alan Ruff, the late Steve Sapolsky, George Shriver, Jane Slaughter, Sharon Smith, the late Jean Tussey, Tom Twiss, Alan Wald, and Michael Yates.

Taken together, all those mentioned are among the people I imagined I was writing to when I composed various essays in this book. (All these people and more. Boggles the mind.)

Sources

With a single exception, the materials gathered in this volume have been published or disseminated previously, in some version or another.

"Introduction: Engaging with History"—although it contains and alludes to much that I have shared in the classroom, particularly at La Roche College, where I have taught since 2000—was written especially for this volume.

"Socialism in the United States: Absent and Latent" is a revised version of "The Absence of Socialism in the United States: Contextualizing Kautsky's 'American Worker,'" *Historical Materialism* 11, no. 4 (2003): 125–70.

"Haymarket Revolutionaries: Albert Parsons and His Comrades" is a revised and expanded version of "Working-Class Revolutionaries of 1886: Albert Parsons and His Comrades," *Bulletin in Defense of Marxism*, no. 29 (April 1986) and no. 30 (May 1986).

"Brookwood Labor College" is a revised version of an article which first appeared in Immanuel Ness, *Encyclopedia of American Social Movements*, 4 vols. (Armonk, NY: M. E. Sharpe, 2004).

"U.S. Labor Vanguards in the 1930s" has taken the form of various versions, including in greatly expanded form in John Hinshaw and Paul Le Blanc, eds., *U.S. Labor in the Twentieth Century: Studies in Working-Class Struggles and Insurgency* (Amherst, NY: Humanity Books, 2000), 129–61. The version in this volume approximates a presentation I gave at the Dissenting Traditions conference, which honored Bryan Palmer and was held at Trent University, October 23–25, 2015, in Peterborough, Ontario, Canada.

"Remembering Ruth Querio" is a revised version of an essay that first appeared under the title "Snapshots of American Trotskyism" and is an appendix to my long introductory essay in Paul Le Blanc, ed., *In Defense of American Trotskyism: Revolutionary Principles and Working-Class Democracy* (New York: Fourth Internationalist Tendency, 1992).

"The Marxism of C. L. R. James" is a significantly revised version of an article published under that title in *Against the Current*, no. 60 (January/February 1996).

"Martin Luther King: Christian Core, Socialist Bedrock" is a slightly revised version of an article that first appeared in *Against the Current*, no. 96

(January/February 2002).

"Revolutionary Road, Partial Victory: The March on Washington for Jobs and Freedom" first appeared in *Monthly Review* 65, no. 4 (September 2013); it was drawn from the book I co-authored with Michael Yates, *A Freedom Budget for All Americans: Recapturing the Promise of the Civil Rights Movement in the Struggle for Economic Justice Today* (New York: Monthly Review Press, 2013) and slightly revised for this volume.

"A Reluctant Memoir of the 1950s and 1960s" first appeared in two parts in *Against the Current*, nos. 134 and 135 (May–June 2008) and (July–August 2008).

"Triumphant Arc of US Conservatism" first appeared under the title "Know Thine Enemy" in *Monthly Review* 62, no. 1 (May 2010); I have added several footnotes that provide additional informative sources.

"The New Left and Beyond" is a revised version of "Books about Yesterday's Activism for Activists of Today," which first appeared in *Monthly Review*'s MRzine, December 1, 2006 (http://mrzine.monthlyreview.org/2006/leblanc120106.html). It originally included a review of the first volume of Barry Sheppard's political memoir on the US Socialist Workers Party, but I have cut that so as not to duplicate material in "Revolutionary Redemption," my full review of both volumes, included in this volume.

"Making Sense of Trotskyism in the United States" first appeared online in the journals *Labor Standard*, September 2010 (www.laborstandard.org/New_Postings/Camejo_Evans_Review.htm), and *Links: International Journal of Socialist Renewal*, October 1, 2010 (http://links.org.au/node/1923).

"Revolutionary Redemption" appeared earlier, as "Revolutionary Redemption, Lessons for Activists," in *Labor Standard*, April 2012 (www.laborstandard.org/Sheppard_Memoirs_Review_by_Le_Blanc.html) and *Links: International Journal of Socialist Renewal*, April 11, 2012 (http://links.org.au/node/2817).

"Ancestors and Descendants of the Occupy Movement" consists of two parts: the first was disseminated as an online talk posted in 2011 by Occupy Boston activists (https://www.youtube.com/watch?v=QsUGt3e8Hl4), and as a printed speech, "Ancestors of Occupy," in the online edition of *Socialist Worker*, December 12, 2011 (http://socialistworker.org/2011/12/12/the-ancestors-of-occupy); the second part appeared as "Revolutionary Organization and the 'Occupy Moment'" in *Links: International Journal of Socialist Renewal*, February 16, 2012 (http://links.org.au/node/2749).

Notes

Note on the Epigraph

Hilda Worthington Smith (1888–1984), known to friends as Jane, was a lifelong partisan of women's rights, racial equality, peace, economic justice, and workers' education. A founding leader of the Bryn Mawr School for Women Workers, she served as director for its first thirteen years (the school was established in 1921 and closed down in 1938 for being too radical). This poem is recited at the conclusion of the documentary *The Women of Summer* (1986), produced by Suzanne Bauman and Rita Heller.

Preface

1. These essays relate to other things I have written about the Left in the United States. The shortest and the sweetest, in my opinion, is *A Short History of the U.S. Working Class* (1999), while the grimmest—sorting through the good, the bad, and the ugly—is *Marx, Lenin, and the Revolutionary Experience* (2006). One that allows many of those on the left who made the history to speak for themselves—from Tom Paine and Frances Wright and Frederick Douglass to A. Philip Randolph and Genora Dollinger and Cesar Chavez—is *Work and Struggle: Voices from U.S. Labor Radicalism* (2011). One of the most important, which won a Choice Award for Outstanding Academic Title, was coauthored with Michael Yates, *A Freedom Budget for All Americans: Recapturing the Promise of the Civil Rights Movement in the Struggle for Economic Justice Today* (2013). Paul Le Blanc, *A Short History of the U.S. Working Class* (Chicago: Haymarket Books, 2016); Paul Le Blanc, *Marx, Lenin, and the Revolutionary Experience: Studies of Communism and Radicalism in an Age of Globalization* (New York: Routledge, 2006); Paul Le Blanc, *Work and Struggle: Voices from U.S. Labor Radicalism* (New York: Routledge, 2011); Paul Le Blanc and Michael Yates, *A Freedom Budget for All Americans: Recapturing the Promise of the Civil Rights Movement in the Struggle for Economic Justice Today* (New York: Monthly Review Press, 2013).
2. John W. Baer, *The Pledge of Allegiance, A Revised History and Analysis, 1892–2007* (Annapolis, MD: Free State Press, 2007); Peter Dreier, "Bob Greene Ignores the Socialist Origins of the Pledge of Allegiance," *Huffington Post*, December 24, 2013 (http://www.huffingtonpost.com/peter-dreier/pledge-of-allegiance-origins_b_4497369.html); Thomas Barthel, *Abner Doubleday: A Civil War Biography* (Jefferson, NC: McFarland, 2010), 216; "Abner Doubleday," Wikipedia, https://en.wikipedia.org/wiki/Abner_Doubleday. Also see Edward Bellamy, *Looking Backward, 2000–1887* (Oxford, UK: Oxford University Press, 2007), with a valuable introduction by Matthew Beaumont, plus Csaba Toth, "Utopianism as Americanism," *American Quarterly* 45, no. 4 (December, 1993): 649–58.
3. Diane Ravitch, ed., *The American Reader* (New York: HarperCollins, 2000), xvii, 605; Alan Singer, "Review," *OAH Magazine of History* 6, no. 1 (Summer 1991): 55; on Ravitch's subsequent evolution, in the early twenty-first century, see Kevin

Carey, "The Dissenter," *New Republic*, November 23, 2011, and Kristina Rizga, "The Education of Diane Ravitch," *Mother Jones*, March 10, 2011.

4. Richard Rorty, *Achieving Our Country: Leftist Thought in Twentieth-Century America* (Cambridge, MA: Harvard University Press, 1998); John Nichols, *The "S" Word: A Short History of an American Tradition . . . Socialism* (London: Verso Books, 2011); Michael Kazin, *American Dreamers: How the Left Changed a Nation* (New York: Vintage, 2011).

5. An outstanding example in print can be found in Thomas E. Woods, Jr., *The Politically Incorrect Guide to American History* (Washington, DC: Regnery, 2004), designed, according to the publisher's blurb, to "give you all the information you need to battle and confound left-wing professors, neighbors, and friends."

6. For examples of more serious conservatism, see Russell Kirk, *The Conservative Mind, from Burke to Eliot* (Washington, DC: Regnery, 2001); James Burnham, *The Machiavellians: Defenders of Freedom* (Washington, DC: Regnery, 1987); George H. Nash, *The Conservative Intellectual Movement in America since 1945* (Wilmington, DE: Intercollegiate Studies Institute Books, 1996); George W. Carey, ed., *Freedom and Virtue: The Conservative/Libertarian Debate* (Wilmington, DE: Intercollegiate Studies Institute Books, 1998).

7. Although himself a centrist Democrat, Huntington authored two influential studies helping push US politics rightward: *The Crisis of Democracy* (New York: New York University Press, 1975), which argued that an "excess of democracy" threatened to make a majority of the people in the United States feel entitled to rights and benefits—so-called "entitlements"—that would undermine the governing system, and *The Clash of Civilizations* (New York: Simon and Schuster, 1996), which argued that the threat of Islam posed the biggest threat to Western world domination).

8. Crane Brinton, *Ideas and Men: The Story of Western Thought* (Englewood Cliffs, NJ: Prentice-Hall, 1950), 453. For additional details on origins of the left–right conceptualization in the French Revolution, see David Caute, *The Left in Europe since 1789* (New York: McGraw-Hill, 1966), 26–32.

9. Classic statements of the pro-capitalist case, presented in the early 1960s, can be found in Milton Friedman, *Capitalism and Freedom* (Chicago: University of Chicago Press, 1962) and John Chamberlin, *The Enterprising Americans: A Business History of the United States* (New York: Harper and Row, 1963), although later social and economic developments lend plausibility to such critiques as Paul A. Baran and Paul M. Sweezy, *Monopoly Capital: An Essay on the American Economic and Social Order* (New York: Monthly Review Press, 1966); Michael Yates, *Naming the System: Inequality and Work in the Global Economy* (New York: Monthly Review Press, 2003); and Naomi Klein, *The Shock Doctrine: The Rise of Disaster Capitalism* (New York: Picador, 2007). Inequality is actually greater today than that indicated by the 1990s figures cited in those three works. For more updated information, see G. William Domhoff, *Who Rules America? The Triumph of the Corporate Rich* (New York: McGraw-Hill, 2013).

10. Norberto Bobbio, *Left and Right: The Significance of a Political Distinction* (Chicago: University of Chicago Press, 1996), 60.

11. Ibid., 62.

12. Ibid., 60.

13. Chris Harman, *A People's History of the World: From the Stone Age to the New Millennium* (London: Verso, 2008); Eric Wolf, *Europe and the People without History* (Berkeley: University of California Press, 2010); Leo Huberman, *Man's Worldly Goods: The Story of the Wealth of Nations* (New York: Monthly Review Press, 2009; original publication, 1936). For a fairly comprehensive survey of professional historiography, see Patrick Manning, *Navigating World History: Historians Create a Global Past* (New York: Palgrave Macmillan, 2003), but also see Samir Amin, *Global History: A View from the South* (Capetown: Pambazuka Press, 2011).

14. Gary Nash, *Red, White, and Black: The Peoples of Early North America* (New York: Pearson, 2014); Louis M. Hacker, *The Triumph of American Capitalism* (New York: Columbia University Press, 1940); Ronald Takaki, *A Different Mirror: A History of Multicultural America* (New York: Little, Brown, 2008).

15. V. L. Parrington, *Main Currents in American Thought* (three volumes in one) (New York: Harcourt Brace, 1930); Merle Curti, *The Growth of American Thought* (New Brunswick, NJ: Transaction Books, 1981); F. O. Matthiessen, *American Renaissance: Art and Expression in the Age of Emerson and Whitman* (New York: Oxford University Press, 1968); Richard Hofstadter, *The American Political Tradition, and the Men Who Made It* (New York: Vintage Books, 1973); Daniel Aaron, *Men of Good Hope* (New York: Oxford University Press, 1961); C. L. R. James, *American Civilization*, Anna Grimshaw and Keith Hart, eds. (Cambridge, MA: Blackwell, 1993); Pauline Maier, *American Scripture, Making the Declaration of Independence* (New York: Vintage Books, 1998); Eric Foner, *The Story of American Freedom* (New York: W. W. Norton, 1999); Christopher Lasch, *The Agony of the American Left* (New York: Vintage Books, 1968); Alan Wald, *The New York Intellectuals* (Durham: University of North Carolina Press, 1987); Michael Denning, *The Cultural Front: The Laboring of American Culture in the Twentieth Century*, 2nd rev. ed. (London: Verso, 2011); Paul Buhle, ed., *Popular Culture in America* (Minneapolis: University of Minnesota Press, 1987).

16. Ravitch, *The American Reader*; Bernard Smith, ed., *The Democratic Spirit* (New York: Alfred A. Knopf, 1941); Howard Zinn and Anthony Arnove, eds., *Voices of a People's History of the United States*, 3rd ed. (New York: Seven Stories Press, 2014); Paul Le Blanc, ed., *Work and Struggle: Voices from U.S. Labor Radicalism* (New York: Routledge, 2011); Richard Hofstadter (with Clarence L. Ver Steeg and Beatrice K. Hofstadter), ed., *Great Issues in American History*, 3 vols. (New York: Vintage Books, 1969–82); Herbert Aptheker, ed., *A Documentary History of the Negro People of the United States*, 7 vols. (New York: Citadel Press, 1962–94).

17. Among the explorations of the discipline of history that have influenced me are E. H. Carr, *What Is History?* (New York: Vintage Books, 1967); Eric Hobsbawm, *On History* (London: Abacus, 1998); Richard J. Evans, *In Defense of History* (New York: W. W. Norton, 2000); Peter Novick, *That Noble Dream: The "Objectivity Question" and the American Historical Profession* (Cambridge, UK: Cambridge University Press, 1988); Eric Foner, *Who Owns History? Rethinking the Past in a Changing World* (New York: Hill and Wang, 2003).

18. Jesse Lemisch, "The American Revolution Seen from the Bottom Up," in Barton J. Bernstein, ed., *Towards a New Past: Dissenting Essays in American History* (New York: Vintage Books, 1967), 29.

19. Marcus Rediker, "Jesse Lemisch and History from the Bottom Up" (http://marcusrediker.com/writings/jesse-lemisch.php#place4).

20. Stephen Tonsor, "The Conservative as Historian: Francis Parkman," *Modern Age* 27, no. 3 (Summer/Fall 1983): 246.

21. Francis Parkman, "The Failure of Universal Suffrage," *North American Review* 127, no. 263, July–August 1878, 2, 4.

22. Francis Jennings, "Francis Parkman: A Brahman among Untouchables," *William and Mary Quarterly* 42, no. 3 (July 1985): 305–28; Mark Peterson, "How (and Why) to Read Francis Parkman," *Common-Place* 3, no. 1 (October 2002) www.common-place.org.

23. Howard K. Beale, *Theodore Roosevelt and the Rise of America to World Power* (New York: Collier Books, 1962), 41–47; Theodore Roosevelt, *How the West Was Won*, excerpted in Edward H. Spicer, *A Short History of the Indians in the United States* (New York: D. Van Nostrand, 1969), 237; Gabriel Kolko, *The Triumph of Conservatism: A Reinterpretation of American History, 1900–1916* (New York: Free Press, 1977), 57–138.

24. Alvin M. Josephy, Jr., *The Patriot Chiefs: A Chronicle of American Indian Resistance*, rev. ed. (New York: Penguin Books, 1993); Dee Brown, *Bury My Heart at Wounded Knee: An Indian History of the American West* (New York: Henry Holt, 2007); Francis Jennings, *The Founders of America: How Indians Discovered the Land, Pioneered in It, and Created Great Classical Civilizations; How They Were Plunged Into a Dark Age by Invasion and Conquest; and How They Are Reviving* (New York: W. W. Norton, 1994); Roxanne Dunbar-Ortiz, *An Indigenous Peoples' History of the United States* (New York: Beacon, 2014).

25. Hofstadter, *The American Political Tradition*; Eric Foner, "The Education of Richard Hofstadter," in Foner, *Who Owns History?*, 25–46; William Appleman Williams, *The Tragedy of American Diplomacy*, 50th anniversary ed. (New York: W. W. Norton, 2009); Paul Buhle and Edward Rice-Maximin, *William Appleman Williams: The Tragedy of Empire* (New York: Routledge, 1995).

26. A. M. Simons, *Social Forces in American History* (New York: Macmillan, 1911), 317, 318; Richard Hofstadter, *The Progressive Historians: Turner, Beard, Parrington* (New York: Vintage, 1970), 196–97.

27. Leo Huberman, *We the People: The Drama of America*, rev. ed. (New York: Harper & Brothers, 1947), xi–xii.

28. Staughton Lynd, *Doing History from the Bottom Up* (Chicago: Haymarket Books, 2014), xi, xiv, xv.

29. Howard Zinn, *The Politics of History*, 2nd ed. (Urbana: University of Illinois Press, 1990), xi, 54–55.

30. Howard Zinn, *A People's History of the United States* (New York: HarperCollins, 2005).

31. Gordon S. Wood, *The Radicalism of the American Revolution* (New York: Vintage Books, 1993), 5, 234.

32. Terry Boulton, *Taming Democracy: "The People," the Founders, and the Troubled Ending of the American Revolution* (New York: Oxford University Press, 2009), 4; Alfred F. Young, *Liberty Tree: Ordinary People in the American Revolution* (New York: New York University Press, 2006), 5–6.

33. James M. McPherson, *Abraham Lincoln and the Second American Revolution* (New

York: Oxford University Press, 1992), 62, 63, 64. More detailed exploration
of the Civil War's meaning can be found in James M. McPherson, *Battle Cry
of Freedom: The Civil War Era* (New York: Oxford University Press, 1988),
and Bruce Levine, *The Fall of the House of Dixie: The Civil War and the Social
Revolution That Transformed the South* (New York: Random House, 2013).

34. Edmund S. Morgan, *The Birth of the Republic, 1763–1789* (Chicago: University of
     Chicago Press, 1956); Edmund S. Morgan, *American Slavery, American Freedom:
     The Ordeal of Colonial Virginia* (New York: W. W. Norton, 1975); Gerald Horne,
     *The Counter-Revolution of 1776: Slave Resistance and the Origins of the United
     States of America* (New York: New York University Press, 2014).

35. C. L. R. James, "Revolution and the Negro," *New International* 5, no. 12
     (December 1939): 339–43; Benjamin Quarles, *The Negro in the American
     Revolution* (Chapel Hill, NC: University of North Carolina Press, 1961);
     Alfred F. Young, ed., *The American Revolution: Explorations in the History of
     American Radicalism* (DeKalb: Northern Illinois University Press, 1976); Edward
     Countryman, *The American Revolution*, rev. ed. (New York: Hill and Wang,
     2003); Gary B. Nash, *The Unknown American Revolution: The Unruly Birth of
     Democracy and the Struggle to Create America* (New York: Penguin Books, 2006);
     Ray Raphael, *A People's History of the American Revolution: How Common People
     Shaped the Fight for Independence* (New York: HarperCollins, 2002).

36. Eric Foner, *Give Me Liberty! An American History* (New York: W. W. Norton,
     2006); Paul S. Boyer, *American History: A Very Short Introduction* (New York:
     Oxford University Press, 2012).

37. Paul Le Blanc and Tim Davenport, eds., *The "American Exceptionalism" of Jay
     Lovestone and His Comrades, 1929–1940* (Chicago: Haymarket Books, 2016);
     Diego Rivera and Bertram D. Wolfe, *A Portrait of America* (New York: Covici-
     Friede, 1934).

38. Bertram D. Wolfe, *Diego Rivera: His Life and Times* (New York: Alfred A. Knopf,
     1939), 373–74. I have taken the liberty of breaking one very long paragraph into
     four shorter ones.

Chapter One

1. This initial paragraph was written in 2015. The original version of my essay
    appeared under the title "The Absence of Socialism in the United States:
    Contextualizing Kautsky's 'American Worker'" in *Historical Materialism* 11, no. 4
    (2003), along with Kautsky's essay and several new articles. Kautsky's essay can
    also be found in Richard B. Day and Daniel Gaido, eds., *Witnesses to Permanent
    Revolution: The Documentary Record* (Chicago: Haymarket Books, 2011), 609–61.
    A key aspect of the perspective on Kautsky advanced here was later argued even
    more strongly by Lars Lih—for example, in *Lenin Rediscovered: What Is to Be
    Done? in Context* (Leiden: Brill, 2005), and "Kautsky When He Was a Marxist"
    (2011), Historical Materialism: http://www.historicalmaterialism.org/journal/
    online-articles/kautsky-as-marxist-data-base. Also relevant to the question
    of Kautsky's Marxism is Paul Blackledge, "Historical Materialism, from the
    Second to the Third International," in *Reflections on the Marxist Theory of History*
    (Manchester, UK: Manchester University Press, 2006).

2.   See the introduction and conclusion of Louis M. Hacker's classic *The Triumph of American Capitalism* (New York: Columbia University Press, 1941), and Paul Sweezy's perceptive review "The Heyday of the Investment Banker," in Paul M. Sweezy, *The Present as History: Essays and Reviews on Capitalism and Socialism* (New York: Monthly Review Press, 1953), 153–55, for striking examples of a disillusioned ex-socialist and a persistently optimistic socialist.
3.   A tip of the hat to the 1956 dissident-Communist mimeographed satire *Lifeitselfmanship: Or How to Become a Precisely-Because Man*, reproduced by its author in Jessica Mitford, *A Fine Old Conflict* (New York: New York: Alfred A. Knopf, 1977), 323–33.
4.   Scholarly contributions to this view of Kautsky include Massimo Salvadori, *Karl Kautsky and the Socialist Revolution 1880–1938* (London: New Left Books, 1979); Gary P. Steenson, *Karl Kautsky, 1854–1938: Marxism in the Classical Years* (Pittsburgh: University of Pittsburgh Press, 1978); Dick Geary, *Karl Kautsky* (Manchester, UK: Manchester University Press, 1987); and Moira Donald, *Marxism and Revolution: Karl Kautsky and the Russian Marxists, 1900–1924* (New Haven, CT: Yale University Press, 1993).
5.   See Carl Schorske, *German Social Democracy 1905–1917* (Cambridge, MA: Harvard University Press, 1955); Paul Frölich, *Rosa Luxemburg: Her Life and Work* (New York: Monthly Review Press, 1972); Vladimir Ilyich Lenin, *The Proletarian Revolution and the Renegade Kautsky*, vol. 3, *Selected Works* (New York: International Publishers, 1967); Karl Korsch, *Marxism and Philosophy* (New York: Monthly Review Press, 1971). Also see Paul Le Blanc, *From Marx to Gramsci: A Reader in Revolutionary Marxist Politics* (Atlantic Highlands, NJ: Humanities Press, 1996).
6.   John Rees, *The Algebra of Revolution: The Dialectic and the Classic Marxist Tradition* (London: Routledge, 1998), 83.
7.   Werner Sombart, *Why Is There No Socialism in the United States?* (White Plains, NY: M. E. Sharpe, 1976).
8.   Selig Perlman, *A Theory of the Labor Movement* (New York: Macmillan, 1928). This perspective shapes much of what can be found in the first substantial history of US labor of which Perlman was a central author—John R. Commons et al., *History of Labor in the United States*, 4 vols. (New York: Macmillan, 1918–35).
9.   Daniel Bell, *Marxian Socialism in the United States* (Princeton: Princeton University Press, 1967), vii, viii, 5, 193.
10. See Chaim Waxman, ed., *The End of Ideology Debate* (New York: Funk and Wagnalls, 1968).
11. Herbert Marcuse, *One Dimensional Man* (London: Sphere Books, 1968), 13, 21, 25, 28.
12. James Boggs, "The American Revolution, Pages from A Negro Worker's Notebook," *Monthly Review* (July–August 1963): 15, 16.
13. Paul Sweezy, "Marx and the Proletariat," in *Modern Capitalism and Other Essays* (New York: Monthly Review Press, 1972), 160, 161, 165. Later, resurgent struggles among sectors of the working classes of various industrialized countries caused Sweezy and others to shift back to a more positive view of their revolutionary potential.
14. Donald, *Marxism and Revolution*, 91–93, 111–13; Daniel Gaido, "'The American

Worker' and the Theory of Permanent Revolution: Karl Kautsky on Werner Sombart's *Why Is There No Socialism in the United States?*," *Historical Materialism* 11, no. 4 (2003): 79–124.

15. Karl Kautsky, *The Road to Power: Political Reflections on Growing into the Revolution*, John H. Kautsky, ed. (Atlantic Highlands, NJ: Humanities Press, 1996), 90–91.

16. Karl Kautsky, *Selected Political Writings*, Patrick Goode, ed. (London: Macmillan, 1983), 72–73.

17. Donald, *Marxism and Revolution*, 169, 249–56; Paul Le Blanc, "Luxemburg and Lenin on Organization," in *Rosa Luxemburg: Reflections and Writings*, Paul Le Blanc, ed. (Amherst: Humanity Books, 1999), 99.

18. Karl Kautsky, *The Materialist Conception of History*, abridged by John H. Kautsky (New Haven: Yale University Press, 1988), 410, 412–13, 522.

19. Geary, 105, 109. Geary stretches things considerably in attributing Kautsky's qualities to Friedrich Engels, who can hardly be accused of making Marxism "a recipe for inaction."

20. Carl Marzani, ed., *The Open Marxism of Antonio Gramsci* (New York: Cameron Associates, 1957), 33, 42. See Georg Lukács, *A Defence of History and Class Consciousness: Tailism and the Dialectic* (London: Verso, 2000).

21. This convergence of factors in the 1820s through 1840s is capably identified in Lewis S. Feuer, "The Alienated Americans and Their Influence on Marx and Engels," in *Marx and the Intellectuals: A Set of Post-Ideological Essays* (Garden City, NY: Anchor Books, 1969), 164–215. For valuable reflections on the radicalism of the transcendentalists, see Octavius Brooks Frothingham, *Transcendentalism in New England: A History* (New York: Harper and Brothers, 1959; originally published 1876); F. O. Matthiessen, *American Renaissance: Art and Expression in the Age of Emerson and Whitman* (New York: Oxford University Press, 1941), 3–175; and David Herreshoff, *The Origins of American Marxism, From the Transcendentalists to De Leon* (New York: Monad Press, 1973), 11–30. A useful survey of utopian socialist communities is offered by Morris Hillquit, *History of Socialism in the United States*, rev. ed. (New York: Funk and Wagnalls, 1910), 23–131; and a later study by Loyd D. Easton, "Economic Democracy in Ohio's Owenite and Fourierist Communities," *Essays on Socialism*, Louis Patsouras and Jack Ray Thomas, eds. (San Francisco, CA: Mellen Research University Press, 1992), 9–23, which argues persuasively that some of them were more substantial and successful than is often assumed. Rich details on the early workingmen's parties and other forms of labor radicalism in the United States of this time are to be found in Edward Pessen, *Most Uncommon Jacksonians: The Radical Leaders of the Early Labor Movement* (Albany: State University of New York Press, 1967), and Sean Wilentz, *Chants Democratic: New York City and the Rise of the American Working Class, 1788–1850* (New York: Oxford University Press, 1986).

22. Feuer, "The Alienated Americans," 198–209, 215; Maximilien Rubel, "Notes on Marx's Conception of Democracy," *New Politics* 1, no. 2 (Winter 1962): 78–90; Richard N. Hunt, *The Political Ideas of Marx and Engels*, vol. 1, *Marxism and Totalitarian Democracy, 1818–1850* (Pittsburgh: University of Pittsburgh Press, 1974), 52, 67; Hal Draper, *Karl Marx's Theory of Revolution*, vol. 1, *State and Bureaucracy* (New York: Monthly Review Press, 1977), 135.

23. In addition to sources already cited, see: Nelly Rumyantseva, ed., *Marx and
    Engels on the United States* (Moscow: Progress Publishers, 1979); C. L. R. James,
    "In the American Tradition: The Working-Class Movement in Perspective," in
    *C. L. R. James and Revolutionary Marxism: Selected Writings of C. L. R. James,
    1939–1949*, Scott McLemee and Paul Le Blanc, eds. (Amherst, NY: Humanity
    Books, 1994), 144–53; Raya Dunayevskaya, *Marxism and Freedom from 1776
    until Today* (Atlantic Highlands, NJ: Humanities Press, 1982), chapter 5; Terry
    Moon and Ron Brockmeyer, *Then and Now: On the 100th Anniversary of the First
    General Strike in the U.S.* (Detroit: News and Letters, 1977); Bruce Levine, *The
    Spirit of 1848: German Immigrants, Labor Conflict, and the Coming of the Civil
    War* (Urbana: University of Illinois Press, 1992); David Montgomery, *Beyond
    Equality: Labor and the Radical Republicans 1862–1872* (New York: Alfred A.
    Knopf, 1967). The classic non-Marxist elaboration of the importance of the
    frontier is to be found in Frederick Jackson Turner, *The Frontier in American
    History* (New York: Macmillan, 1921).
24. Eleanor Marx and Edward Aveling, *The Working-Class Movement in America*,
    Paul Le Blanc, ed. (Amherst, NY: Humanity Books, 2000; originally published
    1888). Some passages in this essay are drawn from my introduction to that work.
25. Marx and Engels, "Manifesto of the Communist Party," in Paul Le Blanc, *From
    Marx to Gramsci: A Reader in Revolutionary Marxist Politics* (Amherst, NY:
    Humanity Books, 1996), 130; Melvyn Dubofsky, *Industrialism and the American
    Worker, 1865–1920* (Arlington Heights, IL: AHM Publishing, 1975), 3.
26. Rumyantseva, ed., *Marx and Engels on the United States*, 284, 333–34. Engels was
    among the first to stress the importance of ethnic diversity in fragmenting class
    consciousness—an essential point that would be elaborated brilliantly in Herbert
    Gutman, *Work, Culture, and Society in Industrializing America* (New York: Alfred
    A. Knopf, 1976). Other useful historical surveys include: Howard Zinn, *A
    People's History of the United States* (New York: Harper and Row, 1980); Alan
    Dawley, *Struggles for Justice, Social Responsibility and the Liberal State* (Cambridge:
    Harvard University Press, 1991); Ronald Takaki, *A Different Mirror*; and Paul
    Le Blanc, *A Short History of the U.S. Working Class: From Colonial Times to the
    Twenty-First Century* (Amherst, NY: Humanity Books, 1999).
27. Rumyantseva, *Marx and Engels on the United States*, 272.
28. In *The Yankee International: Marxism and the American Reform Tradition, 1848–
    1876* (Chapel Hill: University of North Carolina Press, 1998), Timothy Messer-
    Kruse suggests that there were, in fact, certain dogmatic, sectarian, "workerist"
    elements in the early Marxist orientation in the United States that blocked its
    connection with indigenous radical traditions that might have helped generate a
    multifaceted mass socialist movement.
29. In addition to works cited in note 26 above, valuable information on US
    capitalism and anticapitalist movements can be found in the substantial account
    by participant-observer Friedrich A. Sorge in his classic *Labor Movement in the
    United States: A History of the American Working Class from Colonial Times to 1890*,
    Philip S. Foner and Brewster Chamberlin, eds. (Westport, CT: Greenwood Press,
    1977), as well as in Louis M. Hacker, *The Triumph of American Capitalism* (New
    York: Columbia University Press, 1941); Leo Huberman, *America, Incorporated:
    Recent Economic History of the United States* (New York: Viking Press, 1940); and

Mari Jo Buhle, Paul Buhle, and Dan Georgakas, eds., *Encyclopedia of the American Left* (Urbana: University of Illinois Press, 1992). Philip S. Foner's ten-volume *History of the Labor Movement in the United States* (New York: International Publishers, 1947–94) remains an invaluable resource.

30. Indeed, this question becomes the organizing (and distorting) theme of R. Laurence Moore's informative but somewhat stilted study *European Socialists and the American Promised Land* (New York: Oxford University Press, 1970).

31. Sombart, *Why Is There No Socialism in the United States?*, 21–22, 119.

32. Karl Kautsky, "The American Worker," *Historical Materialism* 11, no. 4 (2003): 32.

33. Ibid., 30.

34. See especially C. Vann Woodward, *The Origins of the New South, 1877–1913* (Baton Rouge: Louisiana State University Press, 1951), but also Hacker, *The Triumph of American Capitalism*, and Dawley, *Struggles for Justice: Social Responsibility and the Liberal State.*

35. Kautsky, "The American Worker," 16.

36. Ibid, 23, 28, 38.

37. Ibid., 38. Kautsky does not deal with the fact that the actual history of class struggle in the United States involves much greater violence than is the case in Europe. See Louis Adamic, *Dynamite: The Story of Class Violence in America* (New York: Viking Press, 1931), which documents this reality while suggesting how it interlinks with the relative conservatism indicated by Sombart and Kautsky.

38. Kautsky, "The American Worker," 41.

39. Ibid., 21–22. A suggestive case study illustrating such a transition from bourgeois narrowness ("stingy in … personal consumption … puritanical and full of contempt, not only for senseless luxury and pomp, but also for serious art and science") to bourgeois cultural hegemony (with the resulting "army of unproductive workers, lackeys of all sorts, learned and unlearned, aesthetic and unaesthetic, ethical and cynical") can be found in Francis G. Couvares, *The Remaking of Pittsburgh: Class and Culture in an Industrializing City, 1877–1919* (Albany: New York University Press, 1984).

40. Kautsky, "The American Worker," 41. The seduction of creative intellectuals by capitalism is suggested by comments of the once-leftist filmmaker Elia Kazan—in his memoir Elia Kazan, *A Life* (New York: Anchor/Doubleday, 1989), 459—describing his thinking in the early 1950s: "Was I really a leftist? Had I ever been? Did I really want to change the social system I was living under? Apparently that was what I'd stood for at one time. But what shit! Everything I had of value I'd gained under that system."

41. Kautsky, "The American Worker," 41. See Loren Baritz, *The Servants of Power: A History of the Use of Social Science in American Industry* (New York: John Wiley and Sons, 1965), and Elizabeth A. Fones-Wolf, *Selling Enterprise: The Business Assault on Labor and Liberalism, 1945–1960* (Urbana: University of Illinois Press, 1994). But see Daniel Bell's complaint over countervailing tendencies regarding some intellectuals and artists becoming ideologically subversive "protagonists of the adversary culture" in *The Cultural Contradictions of Capitalism* (New York: Basic Books, 1976), 221.

42. See Paul M. Sweezy, *The Theory of Capitalist Development* (New York: Monthly

Review Press, 1968; originally published 1942), 254–69; Paul A. Baran and Paul
M. Sweezy, *Monopoly Capital: An Essay on the American Economic and Social Order*
(New York: Monthly Review Press, 1966), 14–51; and John Bellamy Foster, *The
Theory of Monopoly Capitalism: An Elaboration of Marxian Political Economy* (New
York: Monthly Review Press, 1986).

43. Kautsky, "The American Worker," 58; Sweezy, *The Theory of Capitalist
Development*, 262, 269.
44. Kautsky, *The Road to Power*, 82–83.
45. Kautsky, "The American Worker," 72.
46. Kautsky was unambiguously opposed to racism as he understood it—for
example, see Kautsky, *The Materialist Conception of History*, 116–46. Yet it must
be noted that, as with so many white leftists, he failed to deal with white racism
even when—as with any adequate analysis of the US working class—it was a
central element in what he was analyzing. On limitations of white socialists in
the United States regarding race, see Robert Allen (with Pamela Parker Allen),
Reluctant Reformers: The Impact of Racism in American Social Reform Movements,
rev. ed. (Washington, DC: Howard University Press, 1983), 208–16; Sally M.
Miller, ed., *Race, Ethnicity and Gender in Early Twentieth Century American
Socialism* (New York: Garland Press, 1996), 33–44, 153–98; Philip S. Foner,
Socialism and Black Americans: From the Age of Jackson to World War II (Westport,
CT: Greenwood Press, 1977).
47. Kautsky, "The American Worker," 72.
48. Ibid.
49. Ibid., 55, 74.
50. A .M. Simons, *Social Forces in American History* (New York: Macmillan, 1911);
Morris Hillquit, *History of Socialism in the United States*, rev. ed. (New York: Funk
and Wagnalls, 1910); Austin Lewis, *The Militant Proletariat* (Chicago: Charles
H. Kerr, 1911). For a capable survey of US socialist thought in this period, see
Jessie Wallace Hughan, *American Socialism of the Present Day* (New York: John
Lane, 1911). On Walling, see John Boylan, *Revolutionary Lives: Anna Strunsky
and William English Walling* (Amherst: University of Massachusetts Press,
1998)—with points indicated above in *Socialism As It Is* (New York: Macmillan,
1912), 331; *The Larger Aspects of Socialism* (New York: Macmillan, 1913), xii; and
Progressivism—and After (New York: Macmillan, 1914), 207–19.
51. Leon Trotsky, "Presenting Karl Marx," *Living Thoughts of Karl Marx* (New York:
Longmans, Green and Co., 1939), 34.
52. Ibid., 35.
53. Lewis Corey, "The American Revolution," *Modern Quarterly* 6, no. 3 (Autumn
1932): 28. Various "exceptionalist" explanations are critically examined in the
detailed and valuable but hardly conclusive study by Seymour Martin Lipset
and Gary Marks, *It Didn't Happen Here: Why Socialism Failed in the United States*
(New York: W. W. Norton, 2000). In some ways more satisfactory (and far
more lively) is the information-packed study by Patricia Cayo Sexton, *The War
on Labor and the Left: Understanding America's Unique Conservatism* (Boulder,
CO: Westview Press, 1991). Also see Jerome Karabel's fine essay "The Failure of
American Socialism Reconsidered," *Socialist Register* 16, no. 16 (1979): 204–27.
54. Lewis Corey, *The Decline of American Capitalism* (New York: Covici Friede,

1934); Alex Bittelman and V. J. Jerome, *Leninism the Only Marxism Today* (New York: Workers Library Publishers, 1934), 6. Also see William Z. Foster, *History of the Communist Party of the United States* (New York: International Publishers, 1952), 271–73; Theodore Draper, *American Communism and Soviet Russia: The Formative Period* (New York: Viking Press, 1960), 268–81, 405–41; and Robert J. Alexander, *The Right Opposition: The Lovestoneites and the International Communist Opposition of the 1930s* (Westport, CT: Greenwood Press, 1981), 113–15.

55. Bertram D. Wolfe, *What Is the Communist Opposition?*, 2nd enlarged ed. (New York: Communist Party, USA [Opposition], 1933), 15.

56. Bertram D. Wolfe, "Marx and America," *Modern Monthly* (August 1933): 432, 433. A more specific aspect of the Lovestone faction's "American exceptionalism" perspective was that (in the words of critic James P. Cannon) "they foresaw [in 1928–29] no economic crisis on the American horizon and consequently no prospects for a radicalization of the American working class" (James P. Cannon, *The First Ten Years of American Communism: Report of a Participant* [New York: Lyle Stuart, 1962], 183). The Lovestoneites shifted away from this specific view when the Great Depression hit, though years later Wolfe commented: "That the American economy was still destined to ascend and take greater precedence in world power for some time to come can now with hindsight be declared to be clear, as the next three or four decades were to show, despite the Great Depression." Bertram D. Wolfe, *A Life in Two Centuries* (New York: Stein and Day, 1981), 461.

57. See Robert Hessen, ed., *Breaking with Communism: The Intellectual Odyssey of Bertram D. Wolfe* (Stanford, CA: Hoover Institution Press, 1990), and Paul Buhle, *A Dreamer's Paradise Lost: Louis C. Fraina/Lewis Corey (1892–1953) and the Decline of Radicalism in the United States* (Atlantic Highlands, NJ: Humanities Press, 1995).

58. Corey, *Decline of American Capitalism*, 24; George Novack, "Historians and the Belated Rise of American Imperialism" (first published 1935), in *America's Revolutionary Heritage: Marxist Essays*, George Novack, ed. (New York: Pathfinder Press, 1976), 292, 293–94, 295.

59. Novack, "Historians and the Belated Rise of American Imperialism," 296.

60. Trotsky, "Presenting Karl Marx," 40. Trotsky's points are elaborated in rich detail in Harry Magdoff, *Imperialism: From the Colonial Age to the Present* (New York: Monthly Review Press, 1978).

61. Eric Foner, "Why Is There No Socialism in the United States?," *The Future of Socialism*, William K. Tabb, ed. (New York: Monthly Review Press, 1989), 275–76.

62. Georg Lukács, *Tactics and Ethics: Political Essays, 1919–1929*, Rodney Livingston, ed. (New York: Harper and Row, 1972), 243–44.

63. Antonio Gramsci, "Americanism and Fordism," *Selections from the Prison Notebooks*, Quintin Hoare and Geoffrey Nowell Smith, eds. (New York: International Publishers, 1970), 280–81, 285, 303, 317. Also see Melvyn Dubofsky, "A New Look at the Original Case: To What Extent Was the United States Fordist?," in *Hard Work: The Making of Labor History* (Urbana: University of Illinois Press, 2000), 201–19.

64. C. L. R. James, *American Civilization* (Cambridge, MA: Blackwell, 1993), 122,

123.

65. Harry Braverman, "The New America," *American Socialist* 3, no. 7 (July 1956): 11. This can be linked to important left-wing cultural influences discussed in Michael Denning's valuable study *The Cultural Front: The Laboring of American Culture in the Twentieth Century* (London: Verso, 1998), although Denning's overly broad conceptualization of the "popular front" distorts his material—as demonstrated in Frank A. Warren, "A Flawed History of the Popular Front," *New Politics* 7 (Winter 1999): 112–25. Also relevant to Braverman's comments is George Lipsitz's *Rainbow at Midnight: Labor and Culture in the 1940s* (Urbana: University of Illinois Press, 1994).

66. Braverman, "The New America," 10. Also see Harvey Swados's classic 1957 essay, "The Myth of the Happy Worker," reprinted in Harvey Swados, *A Radical's America* (Boston: Little, Brown, 1962), 111–20.

67. Braverman, "The New America," 11.

68. Leon Samson presents these ideas in *Toward a United Front* (New York: Farrar and Rinehart, 1935), and they are analyzed in John H. M. Laslett and Seymour Martin Lipset, eds., *Failure of a Dream? Essays in the History of American Socialism* (Garden City, NY: 1974), 70–72, 443–62. Also see John P. Diggins, *The Rise and Fall of the American Left* (New York: W. W. Norton, 1992), 187–217; Richard H. Pells, *The Liberal Mind in a Conservative Age: American Intellectuals in the 1940s and 1950s* (New York: Harper and Row, 1985), 130–62; and Kent Worcester, *C. L. R. James: A Political Biography* (Albany: State University of New York Press, 1996), 103–15.

69. Peter Drucker, *Max Shachtman and His Left: A Socialist's Odyssey through the "American Century"* (Atlantic Highlands, NJ: Humanities Press, 1994), 263, 292.

70. Michael Harrington, *Socialism* (New York: Bantam Books, 1972), 305–29; William Bohn, *I Remember America* (New York: Macmillan, 1962), 244–45. For a look at the dark side of this orientation, see Paul Buhle, *Taking Care of Business: Samuel Gompers, George Meany, Lane Kirkland, and the Tragedy of American Labor* (New York: Monthly Review Press, 1999), and Eric Thomas Chester, *Covert Network: Progressives, the International Rescue Committee and the CIA* (Armonk, NY: M. E. Sharpe, 1995). Perceptive critiques of such "socialism" were advanced by other comrades of Max Shachtman who didn't follow his rightward trajectory—Hal Draper, *Socialism from Below*, E. Haberkern, ed. (Atlantic Highlands, NJ: Humanities Press, 1992), 2–30, 58–105, 108–31, and Julius Jacobson, "Coalitionism: From Protest to Politicking," in *Autocracy and Insurgency in Organized Labor*, Burton Hall, ed. (New Brunswick, NJ: Transaction, 1972), 324–45.

71. See Paul Buhle, *C. L. R. James: The Artist as Revolutionary* (London: Verso, 1988), and Scott McLemee, "American Civilization and World Revolution: C. L. R. James in the United States, 1938–1953 and Beyond," in *C. L. R. James and Revolutionary Marxism*, 209–38.

72. C. L. R. James, "The Revolutionary Answer," in *C. L. R. James and Revolutionary Marxism*, 180. Also see Scott McLemee, ed., *C. L. R. James on the "Negro Question"* (Jackson: University of Mississippi Press, 1996); Alexander Saxton, *The Rise and Fall of the White Republic: Class Politics and Mass Culture in Nineteenth Century America* (London: Verso, 1990); David Roediger, *The Wages*

of Whiteness: Race and the Making of the American Working Class (London: Verso, 1991); Noel Ignatiev, *How the Irish Became White* (New York: Routledge, 1995); Karen Brodkin Sacks, "Toward a Unified Theory of Class, Race, and Gender," *American Ethnologist* 16, no. 3 (1989): 534–50; and Karen Brodkin, *How the Jews Became White Folks and What That Says about Race in America* (New Brunswick, NJ: Rutgers University Press, 1999). Also see pathbreaking works by George Breitman—*Marxism and the Negro Struggle* (New York: Merit Publishers, 1965); *How a Minority Can Change Society: The Real Potential of the Afro-American Struggle* (New York: Merit Publishers, 1965); and *The Last Year of Malcolm X: Evolution of a Revolutionary* (New York: Schocken, 1968). Meriting attention as well are pioneering contributions reflected in Herbert Aptheker, *Afro-American History: The Modern Era* (Seacaucus, NJ: Citadel Press, 1973), and evaluated in Herbert Shapiro, ed., *African American History and Radical Historiography* (Minneapolis, MN: MEP Publications, 1998).

73. Michael Goldfield, *The Color of Politics: Race and the Mainsprings of American Politics* (New York: The New Press, 1997), 30–31.

74. C. L. R. James, "Perspectives and Proposals," in *Marxism for Our Times: C. L. R. James on Revolutionary Organization*, Martin Glaberman, ed. (Jackson: University of Mississippi Press, 1999), 160.

75. James, *American Civilization*, 166–98.

76. Martin Glaberman, "Theory and Practice," in *Marxism for Our Times*, 199; Martin Glaberman and Seymour Faber, *Working for Wages: The Roots of Insurgency* (Dix Hills, NY: General Hall, 1998), 31. Relevant to these points is Jeremy Brecher, *Strike!*, rev. ed. (Boston: South End Press, 1997). Considerable attention to the interplay of economic, cultural, political and labor-organizational factors can be found in the contributions—by various radical scholars and thoughtful labor activists—in John Hinshaw and Paul Le Blanc, eds., *U.S. Labor in the Twentieth Century: Studies in Working-Class Struggles and Insurgency* (Amherst, NY: Humanity Books, 2000).

77. Harry Braverman, *Labor and Monopoly Capital: The Degradation of Work in the Twentieth Century* (New York: Monthly Review Press, 1974), 409. Relevant to this point is Couvares, *The Remaking of Pittsburgh*. Also see David M. Gordon, Richard Edwards, and Michael Reich, *Segmented Work, Divided Workers: The Historical Transformation of Labor in the United States* (Cambridge: Cambridge University Press, 1982).

Chapter Two

1. See the editors' preface and the section entitled "The Heritage" in *Haymarket Scrapbook*, David Roediger and Franklin Rosemont, eds. (Chicago: Charles H. Kerr, 1986), 7, 175–251.

2. William Z. Foster, introduction to Vito Marcantonio, *Labor's Martyrs: Haymarket 1887, Sacco and Vanzetti 1927* (New York: Workers Library, 1937).

3. Diego Rivera and Bertram D. Wolfe, *Portrait of America* (New York: Covici-Friede, 1934), 151.

4. James P. Cannon, *Letters from Prison* (New York: Merit Publishers, 1968), 278, 324.

5. Harry Barnard, *The Eagle Forgotten: The Life of John Peter Altgeld* (New York: Duell, Sloan and Pearce, 1938), 76, 77.
6. George Schilling, "History of the Labor Movement in Chicago," in *The Life of Albert R. Parsons* (Chicago: Lucy R. Parsons, 1889), xxii–xxiii.
7. Nathan Fine, *Labor and Farmer Parties in the United States, 1828–1928* (New York: Russell & Russell, 1961), 90.
8. Richard Schneirov, "Albert Parsons and the American Origins of May Day," *In These Times*, May 2–8, 1979.
9. *Labor Standard*, August 19, 1877, 1. The entire speech is reproduced in Paul Le Blanc, *Work and Struggle: Voices from U.S. Labor Radicalism* (New York: Routledge, 2011), 141–45.
10. A variation of Harrison's comments can be found in Franklin, "A Few Words," *The Alarm*, September 19, 1885, p. 1, which reports that in addressing a Trades and Labor Assembly demonstration, Harrison claimed to have "got many good ideas from the socialists," though "my socialism respects the stars and stripes." For a biography of this fascinating politician, see Claudius O. Johnson, *Carter Henry Harrison I: Political Leader* (Chicago: Chicago University Press, 1928).
11. See chapter titled "The Preacher: Johann Most, Terrorist of the Word," in Max Nomad, *Apostles of Revolution* (New York: Collier Books, 1961), 257–99, and Frederic Trautmann, *The Voice of Terror: The Biography of Johann Most* (New York: Praeger, 1980).
12. Friedrich Sorge, *Labor Movement in the United States: A History of the American Working Class from Colonial Times to 1890* (Westport, CT: Greenwood Press, 1977), 211. A chapter is devoted to the Pittsburgh conference and the role of Johann Most in Tom Goyens, *Beer and Revolution: The German Anarchist Movement in New York City, 1880–1914* (Urbana: University of Illinois Press, 2007), 86–109.
13. Carolyn Ashbaugh, *Lucy Parsons: American Revolutionary* (Charles H. Kerr, 1976), 58. The version of the *Communist Manifesto* available in English was the 1850 translation by the remarkable but little-known British Chartist intellectual Helen Macfarlane. For her translation, plus other writings, and the scant biographical information we have on her, see David Black, ed., *Helen Macfarlane: Red Republican* (London: Unkant Publishers, 2014).
14. Henry David, *The History of the Haymarket Affair* (New York: Collier Books, 1963), 129; Philip S. Foner, ed., *The Autobiographies of the Haymarket Martyrs* (New York: Monad Press, 1977), 43.
15. Sorge, *Labor Movement*, 204.
16. Paul Avrich, *The Haymarket Tragedy* (Princeton: Princeton University Press, 1984), 73–74; James Green, *Death in the Haymarket* (New York: Anchor Books, 2006), 129–30.
17. Albert R. Parsons, *Anarchism: Its Philosophy and Scientific Basis* (Chicago: Mrs. A. R. Parsons, 1887), 173.
18. Foner, ed., *Autobiographies*, 88.
19. Bessie Louise Pierce, *A History of Chicago*, vol. 3 (New York: Alfred A. Knopf, 1957), 266–67.
20. Sorge, *Labor Movement*, 210.
21. Le Blanc, *Work and Struggle*, 11–14. A rich source on the left wing of the

German American workers' subculture in Chicago is Hartmut Keil and John B. Jentz, eds., *German Workers in Chicago: A Documentary History of Working-Class Culture from 1850 to World War I* (Urbana: University of Illinois Press, 1988). Also relevant to issues discussed here are scholarly essays in Hartmut Keil and John B. Jentz, eds., *German Workers in Industrial Chicago, 1850–1910: A Comparative Perspective* (Urbana: University of Illinois Press, 1983).

22. Avrich, *Haymarket Tragedy*, 131; Bruce C. Nelson, *Beyond the Martyrs: A Social History of Chicago's Anarchists*, 1870–1900 (New Brunswick, NJ: Rutgers University Press, 1988), 128.

23. Nelson, *Beyond the Martyrs*, 127–148; Avrich, *Haymarket Tragedy*, 132–36.

24. Avrich, *Haymarket Tragedy*, 136, 140–46; Nelson, *Beyond the Martyrs*, 139–40, 141, 146, 148–49.

25. "The Workers' Marseillaise," *Songs of the Workers: On the Roads, in the Jungles, in the Shops* (Chicago: Industrial Workers of the World, 1919), 10.

26. Avrich, *Haymarket Tragedy*, 149

27. E. H. Carr, *Michael Bakunin* (New York: Vintage Books, 1961), 390–409; George Woodcock, *Anarchism: A History of Libertarian Ideas and Movements* (Cleveland, OH: Meridian Books/World Publishing, 1962), 171–79; Most quoted in Avrich, *Haymarket Tragedy*, 164.

28. On Kropotkin, see Woodcock, *Anarchism*, 184–221, and Roger N. Baldwin, ed., *Kropotkin's Revolutionary Pamphlets: A Collection of Writings by Peter Kropotkin* (New York: Vanguard Press, 1927). An outstanding collection contextualizing Kropotkin and other left-wing libertarians can be found in Daniel Guerin, ed., *No Gods, No Masters: An Anthology of Anarchism* (Oakland, CA: AK Press, 2005). On Tucker, whose anti-statist perspectives evolved into a right-wing libertarianism (that is, an anti-statism dedicated to conserving capitalism), see James J. Martin, *Men against the State: The Expositors of Individualist Anarchism in America, 1827–1908* (Colorado Springs: Ralph Myles, 1970), 202–78; Benjamin R. Tucker, *State Socialism and Anarchism and Other Essays* (Colorado Springs: Ralph Myles, 1985); and Michael E. Coughlin, Charles H. Hamilton, and Mark A, Sullivan, eds., *Benjamin R. Tucker and the Champions of Liberty: A Centenary Anthology* (St. Paul, MN: Coughlin and Sullivan, 1985)—online at http://www.uncletaz.com/liberty/. For documentary reflection of continuities and discontinuities of left-wing and right-wing libertarianism in the United States, see Henry J. Silverman, ed., *American Radical Thought: The Libertarian Tradition* (Lexington, MA: D. C. Heath, 1970). Writings of Marx and Lassalle, among others, can be found in Albert Fried and Ronald Sanders, eds., *Socialist Thought: A Documentary History*, rev. ed. (New York: Columbia University Press, 1993).

29. Avrich, *Haymarket Tragedy*, 170.

30. Green, *Death in the Haymarket*, 141.

31. See Christine Heiss, "German Radicals in Industrial America: The Lehr-und-Wehr Verein in Golden Age Chicago," in Keil and Jentz, eds., *German Workers in Industrial Chicago*, 206–23.

32. Avrich, *Haymarket Tragedy*, 150–51.

33. Ibid., 175, 185–86, 195.

34. Alan Calmer, *Labor Agitator: The Story of Albert R. Parsons* (New York: International Publishers, 1937), 83–84; David, *History of the Haymarket Affair*,

168–69; Avrich, *Haymarket Tragedy*, 192–94; Michael J. Schaack, *Anarchy and Anarchists* (Chicago: J. J. Schulte, 1889), 175.

35. Philip S. Foner, *History of the Labor Movement in the United States*, vol. 2 (New York: International Publishers, 1955), 98.

36. David, *History of the Haymarket Affair*, 156.

37. David, *History of the Haymarket Affair*, 150; Sorge, *Labor Movement*, 204

38. *Alarm*, April 3, 1886, 4.

39. David, *History of the Haymarket Affair*, 161.

40. Ibid., 161–62.

41. Ibid., 161.

42. Schaack, *Anarchy and Anarchists* 190–91.

43. Quoted in Foner, *History of the Labor Movement*, vol. 2, 107.

44. Samuel Yellen, *American Labor Struggles* (New York: Monad Press, 1974), 58–59; David, *History of the Haymarket Affair*, 182.

45. David, *History of the Haymarket Affair*, 192.

46. Schaack, *Anarchy and Anarchists*, 206.

47. Avrich, *Haymarket Tragedy*, 234.

48. David, *History of the Haymarket Affair*, 344–46; Bernard Mandel, *Samuel Gompers* (Yellow Springs, OH: Antioch Press, 1963), 56.

49. Timothy Messer-Kruse, *The Trial of the Haymarket Anarchists: Terrorism and Justice in the Gilded Age* (New York: Palgrave Macmillan, 2011), 8. Also see the same author's *The Haymarket Conspiracy: Transatlantic Anarchist Networks* (Urbana: University of Chicago Press, 2012). These informative contributions are well worth engaging with, despite problematical aspects touched on here, but engaging with other works is necessary to secure a more rounded understanding.

50. Green, *Death in the Haymarket*, 124.

51. Avrich, *Haymarket Tragedy*, 73.

52. Ibid., 393.

53. William D. Haywood, *The Autobiography of Big Bill Haywood* (New York: International Publishers, 1966), 31.

54. Eugene V. Debs, *Writings and Speeches of Eugene V. Debs*, Joseph Bernstein, ed. (New York: Hermitage Press, 1948), 22.

55. *The Founding Convention of the IWW: Proceedings* (New York: Merit Publishers, 1969), 172.

56. Relevant to this are Roediger and Rosemont, eds., *Haymarket Scrapbook*, and Paul Buhle, "German Socialists and the Roots of American Working-Class Radicalism," in *German Workers in Industrial Chicago*, Keil and Jentz, eds., 224–35.

Chapter Four

1. Irving Bernstein, *Turbulent Years: A History of the American Worker, 1933–1941* (Chicago: Haymarket Books, 2010), and Art Preis, *Labor's Giant Step: Twenty Years of the CIO* (New York: Pathfinder Press, 1972).

2. James R. Green, *The World of the Worker: Labor in Twentieth-Century America* (New York: Hill and Wang, 1980), 172–73; Bernstein, *Turbulent Years*, 775.

3. Melvyn Dubofsky, "Not So 'Turbulent Years': A New Look at the 1930s," in

American Working-Class History, Charles Stephenson and Robert Asher, eds. (Albany: State University of New York Press, 1986).

4.   Preis, *Labor's Giant Step*, 19–33; Bernstein, *Turbulent Years*, 217–317.

5.   Dubofsky, "Not So 'Turbulent Years,'" 209.

6.   Ibid., 213–15.

7.   Louis Adamic, *My America, 1928–1938* (New York: Harper and Brothers, 1938), 446–47.

8.   John Bodnar, *Workers' World: Kinship, Community and Protest in Industrial Society, 1900–1940* (Baltimore: Johns Hopkins University Press, 1982), 166, 180, 182, 183; John Bodnar, "Immigration, Kinship, and the Rise of Working-Class Realism in Industrial America," *Journal of Social History* 14, no. 1 (Fall 1980): 47, 48, 50, 53, 55.

9.   Alice and Staughton Lynd, eds., *Rank and File: Personal Histories by Working-Class Organizers* (Boston: Beacon Press, 1973), 4–5.

10. Dubofsky, "Not So 'Turbulent Years,'" 218, 219.

11. Sol Dollinger, interviewed by Nelson Blackstock, late 1990s, from "Louis Proyect: Unrepentant Marxist" (http://louisproyect.org/2015/01/04/sol-dollinger-interview).

12. George Breitman, Paul Le Blanc, and Alan Wald, *Trotskyism in the United States: Historical Essays and Reconsiderations* (Amherst, NY: Humanity Books, 1996), 72; Robert J. Alexander, *The Right Opposition: The Lovestoneites and the International Communist Opposition of the 1930s* (Westport, CT: Greenwood Press, 1981), 29–30; Harvey Klehr, *The Heyday of American Communism: The Depression Decade* (New York: Basic Books, 1984), 153, 225.

13. Three books documenting Communist strength (and limitations) in the CIO, and the destruction of that strength in the late 1940s and early 1950s, are Bert Cochran, *Labor and Communism: The Conflict that Shaped American Unions* (Princeton: Princeton University Press, 1977); Robert H. Zieger, *The CIO, 1935–1955* (Chapel Hill: University of North Carolina Press, 1995); and Judith Stepan-Norris and Maurice Zeitlin, *Left Out: Reds and America's Industrial Unions* (Cambridge, UK: Cambridge University Press, 2003). Also see Ronald L. Filippelli and Mark D. McColloch, *Cold War in the Working Class: The Rise and Decline of the United Electrical Workers* (Albany: State University of New York Press, 1995).

14. Len De Caux, *Labor Radical: From the Wobblies to CIO, a Personal History* (Boston: Beacon Press, 1970), 242–43.

15. This and much else in this essay is elaborated at length, with further documentation, in Paul Le Blanc, "Revolutionary Vanguards in the United States During the 1930s," in *U.S. Labor in the Twentieth Century: Studies in Working-Class Struggles and Insurgencies*, John Hinshaw and Paul Le Blanc, eds. (Amherst, NY: Humanity Books, 2000), 129–61.

Chapter Five

1.   Additional background on "the Allentown situation" can be found in James P. Cannon, *The History of American Trotskyism* (New York: Pathfinder Press, 1972), 228–31.

2.   J. P. Cannon to Ruth Querio, January 17, 1936.

Chapter Six

1.   Among the important studies of his life and ideas are Paul Buhle, *C. L. R. James: The Artist as Revolutionary*; Kent Worcester, *C. L. R. James: A Political Biography*; Aldon Lynne Nielsen, *C. L. R. James: A Critical Introduction* (Jackson: University Press of Mississippi, 1997); Frank Rosengarten, *Urbane Revolutionary: C. L. R. James and the Struggle for a New Society* (Jackson: University Press of Mississippi, 2008). Collections of essays on him worth consulting include Page Henry and Paul Buhle, eds., *C. L. R. James's Caribbean* (Durham, NC: Duke University Press, 1992); Selwyn R. Cudjoe and William E. Cain, eds., *C. L. R. James: His Intellectual Legacies* (Amherst: University of Massachusetts Press, 1995); Grant Farred, eds., *Rethinking C. L. R. James* (Oxford, UK: Blackwell, 1996). Special mention should be made of an incredibly rich account—Constance Webb, *Not without Love: Memoirs* (Lebanon, NH: University Press of New England, 2003). Among the important collections of James's writings are Anna Grimshaw, ed., *The C. L. R. James Reader* (Oxford, UK: Blackwell, 1992); Scott McLemee and Paul Le Blanc, eds., *C. L. R. James and Revolutionary Marxism*; Scott McLemee, ed., *C. L. R. James on "The Negro Question"*; Martin Glaberman, ed., *Marxism for Our Times*; David Austin, ed., *You Don't Play with Revolution: The Montreal Lectures of C. L. R. James* (Oakland, CA: AK Press, 2009); Noel Ignatiev, ed., *A New Notion: Two Works by C. L. R. James* (Oakland, CA: PM Press, 2010). James's major books include: *Black Jacobins: Toussaint L'Ouverture and the San Domingo Revolution* (New York: Vintage, 1989); *World Revolution 1917–1936: The Rise and Fall of the Communist International* (Atlantic Highlands, NJ: Humanities Press, 1993); Anna Grimshaw and Keith Hart, ed., *American Civilization*; *Mariners, Renegades and Castaways: The Story of Herman Melville and the World We Live In* (Hanover, NH: University Press of New England, 2001); *Modern Politics* (Oakland, CA: PM Press, 2013); *Nkrumah and the Ghana Revolution* (London: Allison Busby, 1982). There is additional information and analysis offered in my essay contained in the volume that I co-edited with Scott McLemee, referred to above. That essay has the same title as this one, and is consistent with what I present here, but it has significantly different content. (Also, an error in that essay asserts that one of my informants, Evelyn Sell, became a member of the Johnson-Forest tendency while in the Detroit branch of the SWP—but while she was positively impressed with some of James's ideas, and for a time agreed with its "state capitalist" analysis, she was not affiliated with that tendency.)
2.   Martin Glaberman, introduction to *Marxism for Our Times*, xxv.
3.   Scott McLemee, "American Civilization and World Revolution," in McLemee and Le Blanc, eds., *C. L. R. James and Revolutionary Marxism*, 209.
4.   John Bracey, "Nello," in *C. L. R. James and Revolutionary Marxism*, McLemee and Le Blanc, eds., 54.
5.   Buhle, *C. L. R. James*, 127.
6.   C. L. R. James, *A History of Negro Revolt* (London: Race Today Publications, 1985).
7.   Frank Lovell in *James P. Cannon As We Knew Him*, Leslie Evans, ed. (New York:

Pathfinder Press, 1976), 138–39.

8. Kent Worcester, "Third Camp Politics: An Interview with Phyllis and Julius
    Jacobson," *New Politics*, June 16, 2016, http://newpol.org/content/third-camp-
    politics-interview-phyllis-and-julius-jacobson. My thanks to Scott McLemee for
    sharing the photocopy of an earlier transcript of this interview.

9. Rosengarten, *Urbane Revolutionary*, 62–84; Worcester, *C. L. R. James*, 126–28,
    142, *C. L. R. James*; Buhle, *C. L. R. James*, 119–23; J. R. Johnson [C. L. R. James],
    Marxism and the Intellectuals (Detroit: Facing Reality Publishing Committee,
    1962); James, "Letters on Organization," in *Marxism for Our Times*, 67–68,
    75–77, 78, 81–84, 98; Webb, *Not without Love*, 288.

10. Walton Look Lai, "C. L. R. James and Trinidadian Nationalism," in Henry
    and Buhle, *C. L. R. James's Caribbean*, 188–204; James, *Nkrumah and the Ghana*   ·
    Revolution, 176–86.

11. James Boggs, Grace Lee Boggs, Freddy Paine, and Lyman Paine, *Conversations
    in Maine: Exploring Our Nation's Future* (Boston: South End Press, 1978), 287;
    Rosengarten, *Urbane Revolutionary*, 76.

12. Ethel Mannin, *Comrade O Comrade* (London: Jarrolds, 1945), 133–35;
    Rosengarten, *Urbane Revolutionary*, 94.

13. Worcester, *C. L. R. James*, 122, 123; a similar, and similarly critical, description is
    offered in Webb, *Not without Love*, 211–12.

14. Rosengarten, *Urbane Revolutionary*, 77, 78.

15. Webb, *Not without Love*, 237, 290.

16. Anna Grimshaw, introduction, to C. L. R. James, *Special Delivery: The Letters of
    C. L. R. James to Constance Webb, 1939–1948*, Anna Grimshaw, ed. (Oxford, UK:
    Blackwell, 1996), 3, 4, 17; Martin Glaberman, introduction, *Marxism for Our
    Times*, xxiii.

17. Rosengarten, *Urbane Revolutionary*, 66, 68, 71–72; Raya Dunayevskaya, *The
    Philosophic Moment of Marxist-Humanism* (Chicago: News and Letters, 1989).

18. Cynthia Cochran, interviewed by Nelson Blackstock from "Louis Proyect:
    Unrepentant Marxist" (http://louisproyect.org/2014/08/17/the-cochranite-
    interviews-cynthia-cochran).

19. Rosengarten, *Urbane Revolutionary*, 80, 94.

20. C. L. R. James, "Letters on Organization," *Marxism for Our Times*, 74

21. Rosengarten, *Urbane Revolutionary*, 85.

22. Farrukh Dhondy, *C. L. R. James: A Life* (New York: Pantheon Books, 2001), xiv–
    xv.

23. Webb, *Not without Love*, 204–5, 245.

24. James, "Letters on Organization" in *Marxism for Our Times*, 76–77, 82–83.

25. Boggs and Paine, *Conversations in Maine*, 282, 285.

26. James, "Letters on Organization" in *Marxism for Our Times*, 82–83.

27. Ibid., 83-84; Webb, *Not without Love*, 249–50, 252, 266.

28. "Revolution and the Negro," in *C. L. R. James and Revolutionary Marxism*,
    McLemee and Le Blanc, eds., 77–87.

29. See George Breitman, ed., *Leon Trotsky on Black Nationalism and Self-
    Determination*, 2nd ed. (New York: Pathfinder Press, 1978). Also see Robert
    Allen, *Reluctant Reformers: The Impact of Racism on American Social Reform
    Movements* (Washington, DC: Howard University Press, 1974), 226–31.

30. "The SWP and Negro Work," SWP New York Convention Resolutions, 11 July 1939, in *Leon Trotsky on Black Nationalism*, 71, 72.

31. "The Right of Self-Determination and the Negro in the United States of North America," SWP New York Convention Resolutions, 11 July 1939, in *Leon Trotsky on Black Nationalism*, 76, 77.

32. Ibid., 77.

33. Ibid., 78.

34. "The SWP and Negro Work," SWP New York Convention Resolutions, 11 July 1939, in *Leon Trotsky on Black Nationalism*, 73.

35. Anthony Marcus, ed., *Malcolm X and the Third American Revolution: The Writings of George Breitman* (Amherst, NY: Humanity Books, 2005).

36. *The Invading Socialist Society*, in Noel Ignatiev, ed., *C. L. R. James: A New Notion*, 28.

37. James, "Marxism for Our Times," in *Marxism for Our Times*, 55–57, 59–61. "Basically, he accepted the idea that the modern proletariat was organized by the process of production itself and the vanguard party had become a brake on revolutionary developments," Glaberman explained succinctly in a summary of this line of thought (in a letter to the author, January 14, 1991).

38. A. B. B. (C. L. R. James), "Philosophy of History and Necessity," *New International*, October 1943, 275, 276.

39. C. L. R. James, "Lenin and the Vanguard Party," *The C. L. R. James Reader*, Anna Grimshaw, ed. (Oxford, UK: Blackwell, 1992), 327. Scholars whose understanding of Lenin has coincided with what James presented in the 1940s include E. H. Carr, Stephen Cohen, Isaac Deutscher, Tamás Krausz, Paul Le Blanc, Moshe Lewin, Lars Lih, Ernest Mandel, Antonio Negri, August Nimtz, John Riddell, and Alan Shandro, among others (despite some interpretive differences among them).

40. There has been some confusion regarding the initial appearance of this document. The following explanation that James wrote in 1945 helps clarify: "My ideas are expressed tentatively and in a restricted sphere in the document 'Education, Propaganda, Agitation,' presented to the October 1944 Plenum [of the Workers Party national committee]. After the Plenum it was handed into the National Office for distribution to the membership with whom I hoped to discuss it. The long delay in its publication has prevented this." J. R. Johnson, "The Bolshevik Party," *Internal Bulletin*, July 1945 (https://www.marxists.org/history/etol/document/workersparty/wp-ib/0759-may-1945-Int-bul.pdf). The document appears to have been reproduced, finally, in May 1945 (https://www.marxists.org/history/etol/document/workersparty/misc/0480-1945-Edu-Prop-Agit-johnson.pdf).

41. Works providing the historical context for all of this include Art Preis, *Labor's Giant Step*; George Lipsitz, *Rainbow at Midnight*; Michael Denning, *The Cultural Front*; Alice and Staughton Lynd, eds., *Rank and File*; Eric Foner, *Give Me Liberty!*, 600–807.

42. James, "Education, Propaganda, Agitation," in *Marxism for Our Times*, 3.

43. Ibid., 6.

44. Ibid., 4, 6.

45. Ibid., 7, 9.

46. Ibid., 15.
47. Ibid., 7, 9, 10.
48. Ibid., 9–10.
49. Ibid., 11.
50. Kent Worcester, "C. L. R. James and the American Century," in Cudjoe and Cain, *C. L. R. James*, 182; Glaberman, introduction, *Marxism for Our Times*, xxvi.
51. James, "Education, Propaganda, Agitation," 16–17, 19.
52. Ibid., 19–20, 21.
53. Ibid., 23.
54. Ibid., 38.
55. Ibid., 23–24.
56. James, "Marxism for Our Times" in *Marxism for Our Times*, 57. For a different (positive but not uncritical) appraisal of Trotsky, see Paul Le Blanc, *Leon Trotsky* (London: Reaktion Books, 2015).
57. Leon Trotsky, *The History of the Russian Revolution*, vol. 3 (New York: Simon and Schuster, 1936), 168–69.
58. James, "Marxism for Our Times," 58–59.
59. Trotsky, *The History of the Russian Revolution*, 169–75.
60. Karl Marx, "Inaugural Address of the Workingmen's International Association," in Karl Marx and Friedrich Engels, *Selected Works*, vol. 2 (Moscow: Progress Publishers, 1973), 17.
61. Leon Trotsky, "The United Front for Defense" (February 23, 1933), in Leon Trotsky, *The Struggle Against Fascism in Germany*, George Breitman and Merry Maisel, eds. (New York: Pathfinder Press, 1971), 367.
62. C. L. R. James, *Notes on Dialectics: Hegel, Marx, Lenin* (Westport, CT: Lawrence Hill, 1980), 117, 118, 119.
63. Ibid., 226.
64. C. L. R. James, Raya Dunayevskaya, and Grace Lee, *State Capitalism and World Revolution* (Chicago: Charles H. Kerr, 1986); C. L. R. James, Grace C. Lee, and Pierre Chaulieu (Cornelius Castoriadis), *Facing Reality* (Detroit: Bewick, 1974).

Chapter Seven

1. Martin Luther King Jr., "How Should a Christian View Communism?," in *The Strength to Love* (New York: Pocket Books, 1964), 115; Keith D. Miller, *Voice of Deliverance: The Language of Martin Luther King, Jr., and Its Sources* (Athens: University of Georgia Press, 1998), 105.
2. Coretta Scott King, "Thoughts and Reflections," in *We Shall Overcome: Martin Luther King, Jr., and the Black Freedom Struggle*, Peter J. Albert and Ronald Hoffman, eds. (New York: Pantheon Books/United State Capitol Historical Society, 1990), 253, 254, 255.
3. Coretta Scott King, *My Life with Martin Luther King, Jr.* (New York: Holt, Rinehart and Winston, 1969), 29.
4. Ibid., 25–40, 43–45; photograph of "Coretta Scott at Progressive Party convention, Philadelphia, July 1948" (holding "Wallace/Taylor '48" pennant and wearing convention participant's badge) in Clayborne Carson, ed., *The Papers of Martin Luther King, Jr.*, vol. 2, *Rediscovering Precious Values, July 1951–November*

1955 (Berkeley: University of California Press, 1994), photographs following page 37 (fourth photo).

5. Letter to Coretta reproduced in *The Autobiography of Martin Luther King, Jr.*, Clayborne Carson, ed. (New York: Time Warner, 1998), 36. On Robeson and the Progressive Party see Martin Bauml Duberman, *Paul Robeson: A Biography* (New York: Ballantine Books, 1989), and Curtis D. MacDougall, *Gideon's Army*, 3 vols. (New York: Marzani and Munsell, 1965).

6. Richard Lischer, *The Preacher King: Martin Luther King, Jr. and the Word That Moved America* (New York: Oxford University Press, 1997), 67; David J. Garrow, *Bearing the Cross: Martin Luther King, Jr., and the Southern Christian Leadership Conference* (New York: Vintage Books, 1988), 43.

7. Walter Rauschenbusch, *Christianity and the Social Crisis* (New York: Macmillan, 1907), 327, 408.

8. Ibid., 409, 413.

9. Reinhold Niebuhr, *Moral Man and Immoral Society* (New York: Charles Scribner's Sons, 1932), 149, 194.

10. Ibid., xv, 180.

11. Miller, *Voice of Deliverance*, 5, 41–44.

12. Howard Thurman, *A Strange Freedom: The Best of Howard Thurman on Religious Experience and Public Life*, Walter Earl Fluker and Catherine Tumber, eds. (Boston: Beacon Press, 1998), 138, 143, 146; Rauschenbusch, *Christianity and the Social Crisis*, 84, 91.

13. *The Autobiography of Martin Luther King, Jr.*, Clayborne Carson, ed. (New York: Time Warner, 1998), 351.

14. Ibid., 1–2, 10–11.

15. Aldon D. Morris, *The Origins of the Civil Rights Movement: Black Communities Organizing for Change* (New York: Free Press, 1984), 139, 140.

16. Ibid., 157–66. Also see Jo Ann Ooiman Robinson, *And Abraham Went Out: A Biography of A. J. Muste* (Philadelphia: Temple University Press, 1981), and Nat Hentoff, ed., *The Essays of A. J. Muste* (New York: Simon and Schuster, 1970).

17. Morris, *The Origins of the Civil Rights Movement*, 141–57; John M. Glen, *Highlander: No Ordinary School, 1932–1962*, 2nd ed. (Knoxville: University of Tennessee Press, 1996), 25, 27, 28; Myles Horton, with Judith Kohl and Hebert Kohl, *The Long Haul: An Autobiography* (New York: Doubleday, 1990), 43–44. Also see Eliot Wigginton, ed. *Refuse to Stand Silently By: An Oral History of Grass Roots Activism in America, 1921–1964* (New York: Anchor Books, 1992).

18. Glen, *Highlander*, 155–206.

19. Morris, 166–73; Irwin Klibaner, "Southern Conference Educational Fund," *Encyclopedia of the American Left*, Buhle, Buhle, and Georgakas, eds., 736–37; Frank T. Adams, *James A. Dombrowski: An American Heretic, 1897–1983* (Knoxville: University of Tennessee Press, 1992); Garrow, *Bearing the Cross*, 98. An informative and insightful insider's account of the early civil rights movement by Anne Braden, *The Southern Freedom Movement in Perspective*, was published as a special issue of the socialist magazine *Monthly Review*, July–August 1965. The basic story it tells is essentially corroborated in elaborate detail by later scholarship: John Egerton, *Speak Now against the Day: The Generation before the Civil Rights Movement in the South* (Chapel Hill: University of North

Carolina Press, 1995); Taylor Branch, *Parting the Waters, America in the King Years 1954–63* (New York: Simon and Schuster, 1989); and Taylor Branch, *Pillar of Fire, America in the King Years 1963–65* (New York: Simon and Schuster, 1999). Also relevant is Gerald Horne, *Black and Red: W. E. B. Du Bois and the Afro-American Response to the Cold War, 1944–1963* (Albany: State University of New York Press, 1986), especially 223–75.

20. Jervis Anderson, *A. Philip Randolph: A Biographical Portrait* (New York: Harcourt Brace Jovanovich, 1973), 63; Paula F. Pfeffer, *A. Philip Randolph, Pioneer of the Civil Rights Movement* (Baton Rouge: Louisiana State University Press, 1990), 10; Kenneth O'Reilly, *Black Americans: The FBI Files*, David Gallen, ed. (New York: Carroll and Graff, 1994), 312.

21. Bayard Rustin, "In Memory of A. Philip Randolph," reprint from *AFL-CIO American Federationist*, June 1979, 2.

22. Anderson, *A. Philip Randolph*, 248.

23. David J. Garrow, *The FBI and Martin Luther King, Jr.* (Harmondsworth, England: Penguin Books, 1983), 21–77; Branch, *Parting the Waters*, 208–12; Ben Kamin, *Dangerous Friendship: Stanley Levison, Martin Luther King, Jr., and the Kennedy Brothers* (East Lansing: Michigan State University Press, 2014).

24. Joanne Grant, *Ella Baker: Freedom Bound* (New York: John Wiley and Sons, 1998), 100, 102–3, 111, 218; Barbara Ransby, *Ella Baker and the Black Freedom Movement: A Radical Democratic Vision* (Chapel Hill: University of North Carolina Press, 2003), 73–74, 94–98. Also see Paul Le Blanc and Tim Davenport, eds., *The "American Exceptionalism" of Jay Lovestone and His Comrades, 1929–1940* (Chicago: Haymarket Books, 2016), 52–56, 408–44.

25. Jervis Anderson, *Bayard Rustin: Troubles I've Seen, A Biography* (New York: HarperCollins, 1997), 238; O'Reilly, *Black American*, 382–423; Dan Georgakas, "Bayard Rustin," in *Encyclopedia of the American Left*, Buhle, Buhle, and Georgakas, eds., 663–65. A 1967 telephone interview with Shirley Harris Le Blanc (my mother)—at that time a student in the University of Pittsburgh's Graduate School of Social Work—elicited Rustin's comment about the *Communist Manifesto*.

26. Ossie Davis and Ruby Dee, *With Ossie and Ruby: In This Life Together* (New York: William Morrow, 1998), 249–51; Conrad Lynn, *There Is a Fountain: The Autobiography of a Civil Rights Lawyer* (Westport, CT: Lawrence Hill, 1979), 184; Garrow, *Bearing the Cross*, 717; Michael Eric Dyson, *I May Not Get There with You: The True Martin Luther King, Jr.* (New York: Free Press, 2001), 88.

27. Garrow, *Bearing the Cross*, 310, 323.

28. I. F. Stone, "The March on Washington," in *In a Time of Torment* (New York: Vintage Books, 1968), 123–24.

29. A. Philip Randolph, introduction to *A "Freedom Budget" for All Americans* (New York: A. Philip Randolph Institute, 1966), vi; King, *A Testament of Hope: The Essential Writings and Speeches of Martin Luther King, Jr.*, James M. Washington, ed. (San Francisco: Harper Collins, 1986), 578.

30. Randolph, introduction, *A "Freedom Budget" for All Americans*, iii.

31. Ibid., iv, vi. Generous excerpts from the Freedom Budget can be found in Philip S. Foner and Ronald L. Lewis, eds., *Black Workers: A Documentary History from Colonial Times to the Present* (Philadelphia: Temple University Press, 1989), 571–80.

Also see Anderson, *A. Philip Randolph*, 330, 344; Pfeffer, *A. Philip Randolph*, 286–91.

32. David L. Lewis, *King: A Biography*, rev. ed. (Urbana: University of Illinois Press, 1978), 385.

33. King, *Testament of Hope*, 650, 674–75.

34. Gerald D. Knight, *The Last Crusade: Martin Luther King, Jr., the FBI, and the Poor People's Campaign* (Boulder, CO: Westview Press, 1998), 52; Lewis, *King*, 380.

35. Raymond S. Franklin and Solomon Resnik, *The Political Economy of Racism* (New York: Holt, Rinehart and Winston, 1973), 203–33; Adolph Reed Jr., *Stirrings in the Jug: Black Politics in the Post-Segregation Era* (Minneapolis: University of Minnesota Press, 1999), 55–78; Mary L. Dudziak, *Cold War Civil Rights: Race and the Image of American Democracy* (Princeton, NJ: Princeton University Press, 2000).

36. Anderson, *Bayard Rustin*, 289; Anderson, *A. Philip Randolph*, 345; Robert L. Allen, *Black Awakening in Capitalist America: An Analytic History* (Garden City, NY: Anchor Books, 1970), 110–14.

Chapter Eight

1. "The March Should Be Stopped," *New York Herald Tribune*, June 25, 1963; cited in Jervis Anderson, *Bayard Rustin*, 250.

2. Charles Euchner, *Nobody Turn Me Around: A People's History of the 1963 March on Washington* (Boston: Beacon Press, 2010), xv, 57–58; Branch, *Parting the Waters*, 182, 256–57, 836, 861–62; Garrow, *FBI and Martin Luther King, Jr.*, 153–56.

3. Russell Baker, *Looking Back* (New York: New York Review of Books, 2002), 80; John D'Emilio, *Lost Prophet: The Life and Times of Bayard Rustin* (Chicago: University of Chicago Press, 2003), 345, 369.

4. D'Emilio, *Lost Prophet*, 344, 346–50.

5. Branch, *Parting the Waters*, 836–38, 861–62, 902–3; Euchner, *Nobody Turn Me Around*, 58.

6. Jervis Anderson, *A. Philip Randolph*, 110–19.

7. Clayborne Carson, "Rethinking African American Political Thought in the Post-Revolutionary Era," in Brian Ward and Tony Badger, eds., *The Making of Martin Luther King and the Civil Rights Movement* (New York: New York University Press, 1996), 117. Also see Paul Le Blanc, "Martin Luther King, Jr.: Christian Core, Socialist Bedrock," *Against the Current*, January/February 2002, http://solidarity-us.org/node/1030.

8. Anderson, *Bayard Rustin*, 238.

9. Maurice Isserman, *If I Had a Hammer: The Death of the Old Left and the Birth of the New Left* (New York: Basic Books, 1987), 189, 190; Michael Harrington, *Fragments of the Century: A Social Autobiography* (New York: E. P. Dutton, 1973), 117. Also see Peter Drucker, *Max Shachtman and His Left: A Socialist's Odyssey through the "American Century"* (Atlantic Highlands, NJ: Humanities Press, 1993). Shachtman became a Cold War anti-Communist, supporting US foreign policy in regard to Cuba, Vietnam, and elsewhere, which caused splits among his followers. Despite Shachtman's conviction that the United States could afford both "guns and butter," it is widely felt that the Vietnam War fatally undermined

struggles for economic justice that Rustin, Randolph, and King sought to advance.

10. Tom Kahn, "Radical in America," *Social Democrat* (Spring 1980): 3, 4; Levison quoted in D'Emilio, *Lost Prophet*, 327; Stokely Carmichael, with Ekwueme Michael Thelwell, *Ready for Revolution: The Life and Struggles of Stokely Carmichael (Kwame Ture)* (New York: Scribner, 2003), 158.

11. Tom Kahn, *Unfinished Revolution* (New York: Socialist Party–Social Democratic Federation, 1960), 45, 59.

12. Ibid., 6.

13. Michael Harrington, *The Other America: Poverty in the United States* (New York: Scribner, 1997; originally published 1962), 1–2.

14. Anderson, *A. Philip Randolph*, 299; Daniel Levine, *Bayard Rustin and the Civil Rights Movement* (New Brunswick, NJ: Rutgers University Press, 2000), 272n17; Garrow, *Bearing the Cross*, 280.

15. Anne Braden, "The Southern Freedom Movement in Perspective," *Monthly Review* 17, no. 3 (July–August 1965): 46, 47.

16. Ibid., 47–48.

17. Branch, *Parting the Waters*, 816.

18. Bayard Rustin, preface to Tom Kahn, *Civil Rights: The True Frontier* (New York: Donald Press, 1963), 3.

19. Kahn, *Civil Rights*, 4, 9, 13, 14.

20. Cleveland Sellers, with Robert Terrell, *The River of No Return: The Autobiography of a Black Militant and the Life and Death of SNCC* (Jackson: University of Mississippi Press, 1990), 62.

21. Euchner, *Nobody Turn Me Around*, 77; Anderson, *Bayard Rustin*, 241; D'Emilio, *Lost Prophet*, 344.

22. Branch, *Parting the Waters*, 846–48; Anderson, *Bayard Rustin*, 247–48; D'Emilio, *Lost Prophet*, 338–39, 347.

23. "Socialist Party Testifies Before Congress: Rights Bill Needs to Be Expanded and Strengthened," *New America*, August 10, 1963, special supplement, 2–4.

24. Anderson, *Bayard Rustin*, 242; Euchner, *Nobody Turn Me Around*, 77.

25. Euchner, *Nobody Turn Me Around*, 78.

26. Malcolm X, "Message to the Grassroots," in *Malcolm X Speaks*, George Breitman, ed. (New York: Grove Press, 1990), 16.

27. Anderson, *Bayard Rustin*, 242.

28. Carmichael, *Ready for Revolution*, 330–31.

29. Sellers, *River of No Return*, 65, 66.

30. Quoted in Anderson, *Bayard Rustin*, 262.

31. "Socialist Party Conference on Civil Rights Revolution," *New America*, September 24, 1963, 5.

32. I. F. Stone, "The March on Washington," in *The Best of I. F. Stone*, Karl Weber, ed. (Washington, DC: Public Affairs, 2006), 189–90.

33. A. Philip Randolph, introduction to *A "Freedom Budget" for All Americans: Budgeting Our Resources, 1966–1975 to Achieve "Freedom from Want"* (New York: A. Philip Randolph Institute, October 1966), iii.

34. Ibid., vi.

35. Martin Luther King, Jr., foreword to *A "Freedom Budget" for All Americans: A*

Summary (New York: A. Philip Randolph Institute, 1967), 1.

36. Bayard Rustin to A. H. Raskin, 8 May 1986, *I Must Resist: Bayard Rustin's Life in Letters*, Michael G. Long, ed. (San Francisco: City Lights Books, 2012), 465.

Chapter Nine

1. Van Gosse, *Rethinking the New Left: An Interpretative History* (New York: Palgrave Macmillan, 2005).

2. Paul Le Blanc, *Marx, Lenin, and the Revolutionary Experience: Studies in Communism and Radicalism in the Age of Globalization* (New York: Routledge, 2006), 244.

3. Gosse, *Rethinking the New Left*, 4.

Chapter Ten

1. George Nash, *The Conservative Intellectual Movement in America since 1945* (Wilmington, DE: Intercollegiate Studies Institute, 1996); Godfrey Hodgson, *The World Turned Right Side Up: A History of the Conservative Ascendancy in America* (New York: Houghton Mifflin, 1996); Alan Lichtman, *White Protestant Nation: The Rise of the American Conservative Movement* (New York: Atlantic Monthly Press, 2008).

2. Among sources on the wing-clipping are Ellen Schrecker, *Many Are the Crimes: McCarthyism in America* (Princeton, NJ: Princeton University Press, 1999); Robert W. Cherny, William Issel, and Kieran Walsh Taylor, eds., *American Labor and the Cold War: Grassroots Politics and Postwar Culture* (New Brunswick, NJ: Rutgers University Press, 2004); and Griffin Fariello, *Red Scare: Memories of the American Inquisition* (New York: W. W. Norton, 2008).

3. A scholarly exploration of its early years can be found in John A. Andrew III, *The Other Side of the Sixties: Young Americans for Freedom and the Rise of Conservative Politics* (New Brunswick, NJ: Rutgers University Press, 1997); a participant's attempt at a comprehensive history is Wayne J. Thorburn, *A Generation Awakes: Young Americans for Freedom and the Creation of the Conservative Movement* (Ottawa, IL: Jameson Books, 2010).

4. Two useful works that delve more deeply into this matter are Frank Schaeffer, *Crazy for God: How I Grew Up as One of the Elect, Helped Found the Religious Right, and Lived to Take All (or Almost All) of It Back* (New York: De Capo Press, 2007) and Kevin M. Kruse, *One Nation under God: How Corporate America Invented Christian America* (New York: Basic Books, 2015).

5. One of the most incisive and informative surveys of the practical impacts of this class war against labor and the Left can be found in the work of late sociologist Patricia Cayo Sexton, *The War on Labor and the Left: Understanding America's Unique Conservatism* (Boulder, CO: Westview Press, 1992).

Chapter Twelve

1. Peter Camejo, *North Star: A Memoir* (Chicago: Haymarket Books, 2010); Leslie

Evans, *Outsider's Reverie: A Memoir* (Los Angeles: Boryana Books, 2010).
2. Evans, *Outsider's Reverie*, 312.
3. Camejo, *North Star*, 115–16.
4. Evans, *Outsider's Reverie*, 194.
5. Camejo, *North Star*, 55–69; Evans, *Outsider's Reverie*, 211.
6. Evans, *Outsider's Reverie*, 211–12.
7. Camejo, *North Star*, 129–30.
8. Ibid., 37.
9. Evans, *Outsider's Reverie*, 158, 178.
10. Ibid., 151, 178, 227.
11. Ibid., 143, 158, 178–79.
12. Camejo, *North Star*, 176.
13. Evans, *Outsider's Reverie*, 289.
14. Ibid., 253–54, 256.
15. Ibid., 279.
16. Ibid., 277–78, 303. For details and documentation on the struggle in the SWP and the expulsion campaign, and an analysis of its background, context, and meaning, see *In Defense of American Trotskyism: The Struggle inside the Socialist Workers Party, 1979–1983*, edited by Sarah Lovell (with an essay by Frank Lovell) in 1991, Marxists Internet Archive, http://www.marxists.org/history/etol/document/fit.htm; and *In Defense of American Trotskyism: Revolutionary Principles and Working-Class Democracy*, edited (with a major essay) by the present author in 1992, Marxists Internet Archive, http://www.marxists.org/history/etol/document/fit/revprinindex.htm.
17. Camejo, *North Star*, 176.
18. Ibid., 114, 115.
19. Ibid., 170, 171.
20. Camejo, *North Star*, 115; Evans, *Outsider's Reverie*, 226.
21. Evans, *Outsider's Reverie*, 155.
22. Ibid.
23. Ibid., 285.
24. Ibid., 294.
25. Ibid., 162.
26. Ibid., 130–31.
27. Ibid., 131, 234.
28. Ibid., 233.
29. Ibid., 156.
30. Camejo, *North Star*, 173.
31. This passage from Lenin's *Left-Wing Communism, an Infantile Disorder* can be found in V. I. Lenin, *Revolution, Democracy, Socialism: Selected Writings*, Paul Le Blanc, ed. (London: Pluto Press, 2008), 306.
32. Among other books shedding light on the story of the US SWP explored in Camejo and Evans are the following: Fred Halstead, *Out Now! A Participant's Account of the American Movement against the Vietnam War* (New York: Monad/Pathfinder, 1978); Tim Wohlforth, *The Prophet's Children: Travels on the American Left* (Atlantic Highlands, NJ: Humanities Press, 1994); George Breitman, Paul Le Blanc, and Alan Wald, *Trotskyism in the United States: Historical Essays and*

Reconsiderations (Atlantic Highlands, NJ: Humanities Press, 1996); Paul Le Blanc and Thomas Barrett, eds., *Revolutionary Labor Socialist: The Life, Ideas, and Comrades of Frank Lovell* (Union City, NJ: Smyrna Press, 2000); Anthony Marcus, ed., *Malcolm X and the Third American Revolutions: The Writings of George Breitman* (Amherst, NY: Humanity Books, 2005); Barry Sheppard, *The Party: The Socialist Workers Party 1960–1988*, vol. 1 (Chippendale, Australia: Resistance Books, 2005), and *The Party: The Socialist Workers Party 1960–1988*, vol. 2, *Interregnum, Decline and Collapse, 1973–1988* (London: Resistance Books, 2012).
33. Evans, *Outsider's Reverie*, 399.
34. Camejo, *North Star*, 180–81.

Chapter Thirteen

1. Sheppard, *The Party*, vols. 1 and 2.
2. Sheppard, *The Party*, vol. 1, 336.
3. Sheppard, *The Party*, vol. 2, 288.
4. Ibid., 301.
5. Ibid., 207–10.
6. Ibid., 211.
7. Ibid., 298.
8. Ibid., 299.
9. Ibid.
10. Ibid., 300.
11. Ibid., 50.
12. Ibid., 322–23.
13. Ibid., 323.
14. Ibid., 7–8.

Chapter Fourteen

1. Writers for the 99%, *Occupying Wall Street: The Inside Story of an Action that Changed America* (Chicago: Haymarket, 2012); Carla Blumenkranz, Keith Gessen, Mark Greif, Sarah Leonard, and Sarah Resnick, eds., *Occupy! Scenes from Occupied America* (London: Verso, 2011); Paul Mason, *Why It's Still Kicking Off Everywhere: The New Global Revolutions* (London: Verso, 2013); Marina Sitrin and Dario Azzellini, *They Can't Represent Us! Reinventing Democracy from Greece to Occupy* (London: Verso, 2014).
2. This matter is discussed at length in Paul Le Blanc, "The Third American Revolution: How Socialism Can Come to the United States," in Frances Goldin, Debby Smith and Michael Steven Smith, eds., *Imagine Living in a Socialist USA* (New York: HarperCollins, 2013), 249–61.
3. Vladimir Ilyich Lenin, "A Militant Agreement for the Uprising," in *Revolution, Democracy, Socialism*, 177, 179–80.
4. Martin Luther King Jr., "Where Do We Go From Here," in *A Testament of Hope*, 250–51.
5. Paul Le Blanc, *Work and Struggle: Voices from US Labor Radicalism* (New York:

Routledge, 2011).
6. In contrast, there are excellent anarcho-syndicalist comrades, close to
    the traditions of the old IWW, whose perspectives overlap with those of
    revolutionary socialism.
7. Leon Trotsky, "Trade Unions in the Epoch of Imperialist Decay," in *Writings
    in Exile*, Kunal Chattopadhyay and Paul Le Blanc, eds. (London: Pluto Press,
    2012), 211.
8. Rosa Luxemburg, "Organizational Questions of Russian Social Democracy," in
    Socialism or Barbarism: Selected Writings, Paul Le Blanc and Helen C. Scott, eds.
    (London: Pluto Press, 2010), 101.

Index

A. Philip Randolph Institute, 125

Aaron, Daniel, xxi

Abolitionists (against slavery), 100

Achieving Our Country (Rorty), xiv

Adamic, Louis, 74

Adams, Jane, 174

AFL-CIO, 28, 68, 136, 144, 164, 170

Afghanistan, Soviet invasion and war in, 218

African Americans, as workers, 7, 13, 65; centrality to US history, xxx, 25, 28, 79, 93, 101; civil rights movement, 158, 159, 166; James on, 90, 94, 100–3, 110; Johnson-Forest tendency on, 93; King on, 117–46, 239; nationalism, 160; Parsons on, 35–36; social inequality, 19, 29, 149; SWP and, 220; under slavery, xxvii; white workers, 14, 31

Agnew, Spiro, 190

The Agony of the American Left (Lasch), xxii

Altgeld, John Peter, 54, 55

The Almanac Singers, 149

Amalgamated Clothing Workers of America, 60

Amalgamated Meatcutters and Butcher Workmen, 148

Amalgamated Textile Workers of America, 60

The American (Fast), 149

American Civil Liberties Union (ACLU), 65

American Communist Party: A Critical History (Howe and Coser), 153

American Conservative Union, 184

American Dreamers (Kazin), xv

American Enterprise Institute, 182

American Exceptionalism, 21–23

American Federation of Labor (AFL), 6, 11, 16, 28, 43, 49, 53, 57, 61, 65–67, 73, 147, 237, 239, 240

American Federation of Teachers, 60, 69

American Friends Service Committee (AFSC), xi, 176

American History: A Very Short Introduction (Boyer), xxx

American Indians. *See*: Native Americans

The American Political Tradition (Hofstadter), xxi, xxv

American Railway Union, 13

The American Reader (Ravitch), xiv, xxii

American Renaissance (Matthiessen), xxi

American Revolution (1775–83), xxi, xxiii, xvii, xxviii–xxix, xxx, 110

American Scripture (Maier), xxii

American Slavery, American Freedom (Morgan), xxx

"The American Worker" (Kautsky), 10, 15–21

The American Worker (Romano and Lee), 100

American Workers Party, 68, 74, 77, 83, 121

Americana, definition of, xi

"Americanism," as radical-democratic ideology, 27; as reactionary ideology, 21

"Americanism and Fordism" (Gramsci), 24–25

Ameringer, Oscar, 65

Anarchism, xvi, xxxii, 33, 38–55; defined, xvi, 40

Anarchism: Its Philosophy and Scientific Basis (Parsons), 40

Anatomy of Revolution (Brinton), xvi

Animal Farm (Orwell), 153

Another Country (Baldwin), 160

anti-Communism, 66, 78, 132, 151, 153,

287

Brookwood and, 66, 121; Cannon
and, 164; Communist League of
America, 68, 74; critique by C. L. R.
James, 111–15; Evans on, 98;
Fourth International, 219; Kautsky
and, 4, 8, 9, 17; on US working class
5, 8; opposition to Stalinism, 104,
109, 154, 191, 199; Shachtman, 134,
165; Sheppard, 227, 230; SWP, xxxi,
34, 214, 218, 231, 232; theories of, 9,
21–22, 24, 90, 91, 99, 101, 113, 191,
197, 206, 218, 222, 225, 250
Trotskyism, 1930s, 77; Braverman, 26;
Breitman, 102; Camejo, 197–216;
Cannon, 155, 164; Communist
League of America, 69, 121; James,
89, 91–94, 98, 102, 104; Johnson-
Forest Tendency, 111; New Left, 165,
187, 192; Querio, 81–87; Shachtman,
27; Sheppard, 187–88, 197–216
Truman, Harry S., 144
Tucker, Benjamin, 46
The Turbulent Years (Bernstein), 73
"The Two Souls of Socialism" (Draper), 163

The Unfinished Revolution (Kahn), 134
"Union Maid," 148
Union of Soviet Socialist Republics
(USSR). *See*: Soviet Union
Union Theological Seminary, 123
United Auto Workers (UAW), 68, 74,
136, 182, 233, 242
united front, 79, 217, 221, 246, 251
United Electrical, Radio and Machine
Workers of America (UE), 148
United Federation of Teachers (New
York City), 159
United Mine Workers of America
(UMW), 60, 205
United Steelworkers of America (USW),
74, 205, 235
United Stone and Allied Products
Workers of America, 147–48, 149
University Association for Labor
Education, 69
Urban League, 136, 138, 139, 140

van Gogh, Vincent, 148
Van Ronk, Dave, 157
vanguard organizations, xxxi, 33, 67–68,
73–79, 97, 98, 105–8, 112, 114, 190,
193–94, 230, 232, 245–47
Vanzetti, Bartolomeo, 64
Vanzler, Joseph, 213
Ver Steeg, Clarence, xx
Vietnam War, 62, 81, 125, 128–29, 144,
160–63, 168, 176, 187–90, 199, 204,
221. *See also* anti-war in Vietnam
movement
Viguerie, Richard, 183, 184, 185
*Voices of a People's History of the United
States* (Zinn and Arnove), xx

Wald, Alan, 219
Wallace, George, 190
Wallace, Henry, 118, 156
Waller, Gottfried, 48, 53
Walling, William English, 20, 21
War and Peace (Tolstoy), 150
War Resisters League, 125, 133
Ward, Harry F., 123
Ward, Matthew. *See*: Denby, Charles
Ware, Norman, 65
Washington, Booker T., 110
Waters, Mary-Alice, 202
We the People (Huberman), xxiv
"We Shall Overcome," 123
Weather Underground, 176
The Weavers (singing group), 149, 157
W. E. B. Du Bois Clubs, 165
Webb, Constance, 93, 95, 96, 99, 100
Webb, Lee, 168, 169
Weber, Max, 5, 6
Weinstein, James, 163
Weinstein, Nat, 206, 223, 225
Weiss, Murry, 202, 219
Weiss, Myra Tanner, 202, 219
Weissman, Arlen, 173
Weissman, George, 226, 229
Welch, Robert, 183
West, Don, 122
West Side Philosophic Society of
Chicago, 35
What Is To Be Done? (Lenin), 109